4540

D1362623

The Anglo-Saxon Chronicle

Translated and edited by
G. N. GARMONSWAY
Professor of English,
Kings College, University of London,
1956–65

J. M. Dent & Sons Ltd, London

No. 624   ISBN (if a Hardback) 0 460 00624 x

No. 1624   ISBN (if a Paperback) 0 460 01624 5

TO
PATRICIA

ACKNOWLEDGMENTS

In the preparation of this book I am deeply indebted to two Cambridge scholars. To the late Professor H. M. Chadwick who in tutorials delighted to use the *Chronicle* as a base for deep raids into the disputed territory of Anglo-Saxon institutions. To his successor, Professor Bruce Dickins, whose learning is equalled only by his unselfishness in giving others the benefit of it: he has read the typescript and proofs, given me salutary advice at all stages of the work, and put me even more in his debt by writing a Prefatory Note.

The arrangement of the texts in this volume follows that in Earle and Plummer's *Two of the Saxon Chronicles Parallel* (Oxford University Press) by kind permission of the publishers.

G. N. GARMONSWAY.

King's College,
London.
29 January 1953.

NOTE TO THE SECOND EDITION

An early call for the reprinting of this book has enabled me to make several improvements in the translation. I am particularly indebted to Dr Florence Harmer for many acute criticisms and suggestions, and also to Dr Dorothy Whitelock who very kindly put at my disposal renderings of various passages from her forthcoming volume of *English Historical Documents*. I am also grateful to Mr Peter Clemoes and to Professor Norman Davis for other helpful criticisms.

G. N. G.

24 November 1954.

PREFATORY NOTE

WHEN Sir Frank Stenton was an undergraduate at Keble he attended A. S. Napier's professorial lectures on Anglo-Saxon. No one, he told me, could understand why he went, though, even then, he had made up his mind to work in the field he has so richly adorned. There is no compulsion to write on the Anglo-Saxon or the Norman period. Anyone moved to write on either period ought to be curious enough to acquire some first-hand knowledge of the vernacular sources,[1] or, if that be too difficult, to seek informed advice. For lack of these obvious precautions more than one academic historian of the last fifty years has followed grotesquely antiquated translations and given a fresh lease of life to extraordinary misrenderings, particularly of the Peterborough Annal for 1137, which, like *Hamlet*, is full of quotations. Lest one seem to hawk at gnats the examples cited are from historians whose distinction in scholarship was recognized by their election to the British Academy. H. W. C. Davis, in *England under the Normans and Angevins* (first published in 1905 and now in its thirteenth edition of 1949), renders *þa diden hi alle wunder* as 'Then did they all wonder' [*recte* 'Then they committed every atrocity'] and *hengen bryniges on her fet* as 'hung burning things [*recte* coats of mail] on their feet'; these go back through Anna Gurney of 1819 to Edmund Gibson's Latin of 1692. Again, Sir Charles Oman, *On the Writing of History* (London 1939), translated *War sæ me tilede. þe erthe bar nan corn. for þe land was al for don. mid suilce dædes* as 'The Earth bears no corn: you might as well have tilled the sea: the land is all ruined by evil deeds' [*recte* 'Wherever there was tillage the earth bore no corn, for the land was ruined by such deeds']. The second clause goes back ultimately to Gibson's 'Litus arabant, *i.e.* Frustra arabant,' and in other respects the translation is definitely worse than either Anna Gurney's of 1819 or James Ingram's of 1823.

With these examples in mind it can scarcely be argued that a new translation of the *Anglo-Saxon Chronicle* was a needless luxury. For a moment in 1909 it seemed as though E. E. C. Gomme's would fill the need, though some of the finer points escaped him; he failed, for example, to bring out the precise meaning of *can*, *sceal*, and *wille*. Unhappily it was held to have infringed the copyright of Charles Plummer's edition and had to be withdrawn. I was lucky enough to get a copy. For the next generation the only versions in print were Ingram's of 1823 and Giles's of 1847. Elfred Gomme was killed in action in 1917 while serving as a captain in the Suffolk Regiment, but his publishers, to their credit, never regarded their reissue of Giles as more than a makeshift. The copyright difficulty was apparently

[1] Conversely it is just as important that a historian of Anglo-Saxon or of Middle English literature should be familiar with the political, constitutional, economic, and artistic background of his period.

surmounted, and in the nineteen-twenties I was asked to look into Gomme's version and advise if the necessary corrections could be made in the sheets before they were photographed for reproduction. Regretfully—for Gomme was the brother of an old friend—I concluded that a satisfactory revision would involve a complete resetting, which the publishers were not prepared to undertake. So the matter stood for many years till Messrs J. M. Dent decided to replace Ingram which, with some additions from Giles, had been issued as No. 624 of Everyman's Library. Now at last, for the first time, we have in Mr Garmonsway's book an accurate and idiomatic rendering of all the annals in Plummer's edition. This corresponds page for page with the Anglo-Saxon, and to it are added an excellent introduction and up-to-date identifications of the place-names recorded. I do not forget *The Peterborough Chronicle translated with an Introduction* by Harry A. Rositzke (New York 1951), which came out when Mr Garmonsway's translation was practically complete. I need do no more than point out that Mr Garmonsway has run a longer course and that, over Dr Rositzke's distance, I should give him the verdict by several lengths.

BRUCE DICKINS.

Corpus Christi College,
Cambridge.

CONTENTS

ABBREVIATIONS

A. Versions of the Anglo-Saxon Chronicle

Ā   The Parker Chronicle: Corpus Christi College, Cambridge, MS. 173

A   A Cottonian Fragment: British Museum, Cotton MS. Otho B xi, 2.

B
C   The Abingdon Chronicles   British Museum, Cotton MS. Tiberius A vi.
British Museum, Cotton MS. Tiberius B i.

D   The Worcester Chronicle: British Museum, Cotton MS. Tiberius B iv.

E   The Laud (Peterborough) Chronicle: Bodleian MS. Laud 636.

F   The Bilingual Canterbury Epitome: British Museum, Cotton MS. Domitian A viii.
     Entries in English (F) and in Latin (F Lat).

H   A Cottonian Fragment: British Museum, Cotton MS. Domitian A ix.

I   An Easter Table Chronicle: British Museum, Cotton MS. Caligula A xv.

(See pages xxiv–xxv for facsimile of folios 132*b* and 133*a*.)

B. Other Abbreviations

BT and BT Suppl.	J. Bosworth and T. N. Toller, *An Anglo-Saxon Dictionary*, 1882–98 (*Supplement* 1908–21).
DEPN	Eilert Ekwall, *The Concise Oxford Dictionary of English Place-names* (3rd ed.), 1947.
EETS	Early English Text Society.
EH	Bede's *Ecclesiastical History* (in *Venerabilis Baedae Opera Historica* ed. Charles Plummer, 1896.)
EHR	*English Historical Review*.
EPN	English Place-Name Society publications. (Abbreviations for counties, where they occur following a place-name, are those used in the Society's publications.)
LSE	*Leeds Studies in English*.
MLN	*Modern Language Notes*.

MLR	*Modern Language Review.*
OE	Old English.
ON	Old Norse.
Plummer	Charles Plummer, *Two of the Saxon Chronicles Parallel*, 1892–9.
RES	*Review of English Studies.*

For the most part the spelling of Anglo-Saxon names in the translation is that of Sir Frank Stenton, *Anglo-Saxon England*, 2nd ed., 1950 (Oxford).

> Note: In references to periodicals, the numeral which precedes gives the volume, that which follows the page. Roman numerals are prefixed to the volume number if the periodical has more than one series.

INTRODUCTION

§ 1

'Philosophically considered, this ancient record is the second *great pheno-menon in the history of mankind'* (James Ingram, Rawlinson Professor of Anglo-Saxon in the University of Oxford, 1803–8, President of Trinity College, Oxford, 1824, in the Preface to his translation of the *Saxon Chronicle*, 1823).

A DISTINGUISHED American critic[1] in writing of the *Anglo-Saxon Chronicle* has said: 'From almost any significant point of view it may indeed be regarded as the most important work written in English before the Norman Conquest.' The average Englishman, frequently ignorant of and often complacent about the rich and varied panorama of his medieval heritage, may regard this judgment as surprising, but it is indisputable that this critic from his distant vantage ground has recognized the uniqueness of the *Chronicle* and understood its compelling interest both for the historian and the student of literary history. The former declares[2] that 'none among all the materials for English history possesses authority for a longer period than the series of annals which it is convenient to call the Old English Chronicle. From the age of the Saxon migration to the anarchy of Stephen's reign, they continue to offer information which may be rejected but cannot be ignored. The criticism of the *Chronicle* is the basis of Early English historiography.' The literary critic[3] finds in these same annals the beginnings of English prose, the unmannered simplicity of which found continuous expression in devotional books and vernacular sermons down to Tudor times when it became the language of More and Tyndale, and the instrument in the following century of the translators of the Authorized Version of the Bible.

This is high and justifiable[4] praise, but what may astonish most is that the *Chronicle* was written in English at all, in an age when historical, legal, and diplomatic documents were almost always written in Latin. In this it is unique, and it is a remarkable fact that its scribes chose English rather than Latin as their medium, particularly since there is good reason to suppose that none of the early documents from which the earliest annals were derived were written in English. It has been frequently pointed out that English was the only vernacular language,

[1] F. P. Magoun, Jr, 18 *Harvard Studies and Notes in Philology and Literature* (1935), 69–70.

[2] F. M. Stenton, 'The South-Western Element in the Old English Chronicle' (*Essays in Medieval History presented to Thomas Frederick Tout* 15, Manchester 1925).

[3] R. W. Chambers, *On the Continuity of English Prose from Alfred to More and his School* (EETS, Oxford 1932).

[4] In contrast to the 'grandiloquent terms' (as Earle called them) of Ingram, quoted at the head of this chapter.

except Irish, to be used for historical purpose in North-West Europe in the Dark Ages. Indeed the Irish annals and an early Russian chronicle (which goes by the name of Nestor's) were the only other histories to use their native tongue in the whole of Europe before 1200. This fact is of far-reaching importance; for if the *Chronicle* is essential to the historian as 'the fundamental authority for Old English History' it is also 'the first national continuous history of a western nation in its own language,' and 'the first great book in English prose.' In its pages can be traced the continuous development of early English prose style [1] throughout the centuries of the Saxon period to the middle of the twelfth century. 'The historians insist that English literature was dead at the time of the Conquest,' remarks R. W. Chambers, 'yet, so long as there is any *Chronicle* at all, they cannot get on without its telling phrases.'

The first English short story appears in annal 755, and the beginnings of English biography go back to the chronicler's character study of William the Conqueror. If the range of early narrative prose is to be measured, contrast the first halting, laconic entries with the vigour and clarity of the writing in the tenth century on the one hand, and the individual, often impassioned phrasing of Æthelred and Stephen's days on the other. If the language seldom 'proliferates into an extra surprise of simile or metaphor or revealing detail,' [2] and lacks all artifice and embellishment, yet it is all the more successful as a chronicler's instrument.

Why was English used? Perhaps, it must be confessed, by default, because of the decay of Latin studies, and the almost complete disappearance of spoken Latin in this country in the ninth century when the first compilation of the *Chronicle* was made. Although English scholars had been pre-eminent in Western Europe in Bede's day and during the remainder of the eighth century, learning in England had, as Alfred testified, 'so utterly fallen away that there were very few on this side of the Humber who could understand their mass-books in English, or translate even a letter from Latin into English; and I believe there were not many beyond Humber. So few of them were there that I cannot remember even a single one south of the Thames when I succeeded to the kingdom.' On the Continent, the vernacular does not appear in original prose works, but only in translation from the Latin; in this country, in contrast, the laws, wills, and many charters appear in English, and the *Chronicle* can claim to be by far the oldest historical prose in any Germanic language, which by the time of the Conquest had developed for itself an easy, commanding utterance, surpassing the immediate requirements of the mere unambitious annalist. Neither was the record of passing events perfunctory or haphazard, nor under-

[1] See G. C. Donald, *Zur Entwicklung des Prosastils in der Sachsenchronik* (Marburg 1914).

[2] The phrase is from an article on Charles Dickens (who, of course, excels at this) by T. C. Worsley. Notice the isolated attempts to give colour in *unarimedlico herereaf* and *swa fyr* (473 A̅), *yð hengestas* (1003 E), *swa drane doð on hiue* (1127 E), *nu him behofed pæt he crape in his mycele codde in ælc hyrne* . . . (1131 E). See W. H. Stevenson, 14 *EHR* 38, note 29. For some judicious remarks on the style of the *Chronicle*, see Margaret Ashdown, *English and Norse Historical Documents* (Cambridge 1930), 14–18.

taken merely when their importance could not fail to arrest the annalist's attention, nor made 'by men in a monkish solitude, familiar with the lettuces of the convent garden, but hearing only faint dim murmurs of the great transactions which they slowly jot down in the barren chronicle.'[1] On the contrary few events which we now recognize as significant fail to receive a notice or to leave an imprint, faint though it may be. The devotion of the scribes generation after generation commands our admiration. In centres of learning throughout the kingdom the work went on without a serious break, despite the vicissitudes of the nation twice compelled to submit to a foreign invader and continuously subjected to piratical raids along her shores and deep into the heart of the country. In the Parker manuscript of the *Chronicle* the record was kept up for 200 years in the same book, while at Peterborough the writing went on almost a century after the last Saxon king was slain at Hastings, and in days when English was no longer the language of the court or of the schools. Something of the spirit of Martin, abbot of Peterborough during the anarchy of Stephen's reign, must have informed these pious men. 'During all these evil days' writes the chronicler in annal 1137, 'he governed his abbacy under great difficulties for twenty and a half years and eight days. He provided everything necessary for the monks and the visitors, and was liberal in alms-giving: he was careful to see that the monks got their commons, and punctilious in holding commemoration feasts.' For the majority of years there is a careful record, and if the writer's attitude rarely proclaims itself from behind his anonymity, there is an occasional glimpse of 'how it strikes a contemporary.' It is at such a moment we meet the lively, rounded 'profile' of William the Conqueror seen 'plain' by one 'who had looked on him, and at one time had dwelt in his court.' On another page the massacre of the monks at Glastonbury in 1083 reads like an eye-witness account, as if the chronicler was for once driven from his camera obscura by the violence of events to photograph on the spot. Occasionally too the laconic dryness of the annalist is lost, as when he is moved by the miracle of Divine intervention in bringing about the dispersal of the Danes in 896 to voice his relief and to take stock of the national position.

However it is not for the annalist to generalize about the course of history, or to indicate the relation between one event and another. Whether the historian approach his subject with the methods of the scientist, or believe 'that the uniqueness of the events studied by him excludes the possibility of their being classified or generalized about in any way,' he would almost certainly agree that what separates him from the annalist and chronicler is that the latter never attempts to explain events or to 'subsume them under a general rule, or to assimilate them to other events of a similar kind.'[2] Such, in essence, was the distinction

[1] Walter Bagehot, *Literary Studies: Edward Gibbon* (Everyman ed.) II. 30.
[2] The phrases are from Patrick Gardiner, *The Nature of Historical Explanation* (Oxford 1952), 41. Mr Gardiner, in his attractive essay, argues that history no more than science can do without generalization. The difference between the annalist and the historian in this respect was drawn, not by Mr Gardiner, but by his reviewer in *The Times Literary Supplement* (5 September 1952).

drawn by Gervase, a monk of Christ Church, Canterbury, in the preface to his English History written in Latin in 1163:

'The historian and the chronicler have one and the same intention and use the same materials, but their modes of treatment are different and so is the style of their writing. Both have the same object in view because both eagerly pursue truth. The style of treatment is different because the historian marches along with a copious and eloquent diction, while the chronicler steps simply and briefly. The historian "pours forth swelling phrases and words half a yard long"; the chronicler "practises a woodland muse on a humble oaten pipe." The historian sits "among men who are impressive talkers and string together grand words"; the chronicler stays beneath the cottage of poor Amyclae so that he shall not have to fight for his poor dwelling. It belongs to the historian to strive after truth, to charm his hearers or readers by his sweet and elegant language, to inform them of the true facts about the actions, character, and life of the hero whom he is describing, and to include nothing else but what seems in reason to be appropriate to history. The chronicler reckons up the years of the Incarnation of Our Lord and the months and kalends that compose the years, briefly sets forth the actions of kings and princes and what takes place in those same years and months, and mentions also events, portents, miracles. But there are very many who, while writing chronicles or annals, go beyond their proper limits, for they delight to make broad their phylacteries[1] and enlarge the borders of their garments. Setting out to compile a chronicle, they march along in the manner of a historian, and try to weight with swelling words what they ought to have said shortly and in unpretentious language after the manner of ordinary writing.'

No one, however, has looked with greater imaginative insight into the chronicler's mind than Dr Plummer,[2] or been able to convey so eloquently to a modern reader what the chronicles stood for to the men and women of the past. 'A chronicle,' he writes, 'was not a device for arranging a store of events, and for reducing the accumulations of history to literary order. It was not (what it at length became) a method, a system of registration, whereby each event was put into its chronological place. The chronicle form had a more primitive use. This was to *characterize* the receding series of years, each by a mark and sign of its own, so that the years might not be confused in the retrospect of those who had lived and acted in them. . . . To posterity they present merely a name or two, as of a battlefield and a victor, but to the men of the day they suggested a thousand particulars, which they in their comrade-life were in the habit of recollecting and putting together. That which to us seems a lean and barren sentence, was to them the text for a winter evening's entertainment.'

---

[1] Gervase may have in mind something more biting than a reference to Matthew xxiii. 6, since the word *philacterium* was used of mnemonic doggerel of the 'Thirty days hath September, April, June, and November' type, composed by Bede and others to aid their pupils in their computation. The OE word for such was *gerim* (cf. S. J. Crawford, *Byrhtferth's Manual* 41, and Heinrich Henel, *Studien zum altenglischen Computus* (Leipzig 1934), 15, note 49).

[2] Plummer II. xix–xxi.

§ 2

'*I command to depart from me the mermaids, who are called sirens, and also the Castalian nymphs, that is to say the mountain elves, who dwelt on mount Helicon; and I will that Phoebus depart from me, whom Latona, the mother of the sun and Apollo and Diana, bore in Delos, as ancient triflers have declared; and I trust that the glorious cherubin will come to me, and with his golden tongs bring to my tongue from off the heavenly altar a spark of the burning coal and touch the nerves (recte sinews) of my dumb mouth, that I may thereby have the power by sagacious study to translate this Paschal cycle into English in a scholarly fashion*' (Byrhtferth, *fl.* 1000; Crawford's translation).

In its use of an annalistic framework for its history the *Chronicle* shows a rare instinct for chronology. A historian nowadays is usually able to date events with fair precision, but in medieval times 'little scientific inspection of inherited chronology was possible even for the most careful historian,'[1] and for him computation was often difficult or impossible, nor in the forefront of his intention. If he wrote in Latin, he might endeavour by various methods of reckoning then in vogue to time the march of events, but the histories of the Teutonic peoples in the vernacular, with the exception of the *Chronicle*, rarely evince any such concern. And, of course, the very uniqueness of the *Chronicle* invalidates the comparison, for it is the sole example in Western Europe of the history of a Teutonic nation in its own language which has been preserved to us until the beginnings of Norse historical writing in the twelfth century.

The Scandinavian historians, however, fail all too frequently to provide the vertebrae of a chronological system. Ari, the first historian of Iceland, occasionally employs a relative chronology to date some of the events he describes, and most ambitiously in the closing paragraph of his *Íslendingabók*, where he fixes the time of Bishop Gizurr's death:

'In the same year died Pope Paschalis the Second, earlier than Bishop Gizurr, and Baldwin, king of Jerusalem, and Arnold, patriarch in Jerusalem, and Philip, king of the Swedes; and later the same summer Alexis, king of the Greeks. He had been thirty-eight years on the throne in Constantinople. Eysteinn and Sigurðr had then been seventeen years kings in Norway after their father Magnús, son of Óláfr, the son of Harold. It was 120 years after the fall of Óláfr Tryggvasonr, and 250 after the slaughter of Edmund, king of the English, and 516 years after the death of Pope Gregory that brought Christianity to England according to the dating; and he died in the second year of the kingdom of the Emperor Phocas, 604 years after the birth of Christ according to the generally accepted dating; that makes 1,120 years altogether.'

Snorri Sturluson in the next century, however, is rarely concerned to make it clear when the events he describes took place. In the *Prose Edda* he may throw out an antiquarian guess that the Peace of King Fróði happened at the time when the Emperor Augustus made peace

[1] C. W. Jones, *Bedae Opera de Temporibus* (Cambridge, Mass. 1943), 383, para. 1.

over all the world and Christ was born, or preface his *Heimskringla* with a reference to the 'Age of Burning' which was followed by the 'Age of Barrows,' but further than this—except of course the mention of the names of the Scandinavian kings whose reigns he describes—he does not attempt to go.

In this particular, at least, the *Chronicle* is superior to Norse historical writing.[1] Although the latter provides a more colourful and animated procession of events, arranged with an eye for possible irony and dramatic situation, the historian has frequently been exasperated, not so much by its 'errors and fictions'[2] as by its lack of feeling for an absolute chronology. In contrast, it is remarkable to find the *Chronicle* adopting the framework of the annalist, for although annalistic writing had been introduced into medieval Europe from the fourth century by Eusebius, St Jerome, Prosper Tiro, Cassiodorus, Isidore, and others, all of whom wrote in Latin, it is unlikely that it was introduced into England until much later. Nor, of course, when it was adopted was the form rigorously adhered to; even in works like Bede's *Chronica Maiora* or the Annals of St Neot many events are not dated precisely, and a similar looseness can be found in the *Chronicle* itself.

It is well known that the origin of annalistic writing derives from the practice of entering short historical notices on the pages of Easter Tables, which were drawn up to enable the clergy to ascertain the day on which Easter was to be observed in any particular year.[3] When Gervase defines the province of the chronicler as one who should record the appearance of portents, amongst other things, he provides a hint as to the link between the chronicle and the Easter Table. The peculiar interest of the chronicler in portents, eclipses, comets, and other celestial phenomena may of course reflect merely the normal interest in the supernatural, or may arise from the desire to recall to memory a particular year by reference to supramundane events such as would be likely to linger in folks' memories, but it may also derive ultimately from the great prominence given to astronomical entries[4] in the Easter Table, for a knowledge of the movements of the sun and moon was of supreme importance in its calculus. The curious may get some impression of what these calculations involved by looking at note 2 on p. xxi, or at the Introduction to the Book of Common Prayer, or better still in the pages of Poole and Jones.[5] The former

---

[1] The annalistic notices which appear at the end of chapters in *Guðmundarsaga* (of the *Sturlunga* compilation), and which date events by references to Guðmund's age, present a difficult problem. Mr Peter Foote tells me that they appear to have been in the saga from the beginning, but as yet no source for them has been discovered.

[2] Charles Oman, *England before the Norman Conquest* (Methuen, 4th ed. 1919), 575, note 2. It is perhaps significant that the *Heimskringla* is not listed in the index of F. M. Stenton's history.

[3] 'In the poorest ecclesiastical centres books of history were not deemed necessary, but an Easter-table was essential.' C. W. Jones, *op. cit.* 116.

[4] C. W. Jones, *op. cit.* 119. Cf. also *ib.* 140 for an interesting semantic comment on the word 'annal,' where he points out that Bede used *annalis* as an adjective denoting phenomena characterizing the lunar or solar year.

[5] R. L. Poole, *Chronicles and Annals* (Oxford 1926), 19–22. C. W. Jones, *op. cit.* 11 and *passim*.

reproduces [1] an Easter Table which is drawn up in the usual eight columns, which give on each line: the Year of Grace, the Indiction Number, the Epact, the Concurrent, the Lunar Cycle, the Paschal Term, Easter Day, the Age of the Moon on Easter Day.[2] At four-year intervals in the left-hand margin stands the letter B to mark

[1] R. L. Poole, *op. cit.* frontispiece, which is a reproduction of an Easter Table of the tenth century written at the monastery of Einsiedeln in Switzerland. See also D. Talbot Rice, *English Art 871–1100* (Oxford 1952) Plate 67a and F. Wormald, *English Drawings of the Tenth and Eleventh Centuries* (London 1952) Plate 34(a) and (b), and Sir Thomas Kendrick, *Late Saxon and Viking Art* (London 1949) Plate xvii, for simplified Easter Tables of *c.* 1073. S. J. Crawford, *Byrhtferth's Manual* (Oxford 1929), plate facing p. 150, and text and translation pp. 145 ff.

[2] For more accurate descriptions of these eight rubrics, see C. W. Jones, *op. cit.* 53: the following notes will explain the usual procedure for arriving at the date of Easter from the tables.

The Rubrics:
  I. Year of Grace: the year from the Incarnation of Our Lord.
  II. Indiction Number: the number of the year in a 15-year cycle beginning with 1 September 312.
  III. Epact: the age of the Moon in days on the first day of the year, reckoned as beginning 22 March.
  IV. Concurrent: the number of the day of the week on 24 March (i.e. numbering 1–7, Sunday (1) to Saturday (7)).
  V. Lunar Cycle: the number of the year in a lunar cycle of 19 years (usually known as 'the Golden Number').
  VI. Paschal Term: the date of the Jewish Feast of the Passover, the 14th day of the lunar month Nisan, which would be the full moon after the Spring Equinox.
  VII. Easter Day.
  VIII. Age of Moon on Easter Day.

The second line of Poole's reproduction of the Einsiedeln Easter Table is for the year 964, and the rubrics are set out thus:

I	II	III	IV	V	VI	VII	VIII
Year	Ind.	Epact.	Conc.	Lun. Cycle	Pas. Term	Easter Day	Age of Moon
964	7	4	5	12	k̄.ap̄.	III. nõ. ap̄.	16
					[= 1 April]	[= 3 April]	

964 was the twelfth (*recte* 15th) year of the fifty-first 19-year Lunar Cycle with the Epact 4. Hence the 14th moon (the Paschal Term) fell on 1 April [(22 — 4) + 14 — 31 = 1; column 6 corroborates the date]. The concurrent in the table was 5, which meant that 24 March was a Thursday and 1 April therefore a Friday. Easter Day was the Sunday next following, i.e. 3 April. It will be seen that the Indiction Number and the Year in the Lunar Cycle are unnecessary for the calculation. I have avoided making the calculation for the first annal (for 963) on the Einsiedeln reproduction, first, since the epact for that year is greater than 14 and the calculation therefore more complicated (30 — 23 + 14 + 22 — 31 = 12), and also because it is given in error as 24 (for 23); *luna xiv* in 963 was on Sunday, 12 April, therefore Easter Day was celebrated a week later on 19 April.

It will be noticed that the table heads the sequence of years from 969: 'The Twenty-fourth Cycle'; this, of course, is the Dionysiac reckoning from 532. Despite this heading across the page, however, the numbers of the years in the Lunar Cycle have been copied mechanically, and are all 3 lines lower on the page than they should be.

each leap-year (the intercalated day being called *bissextum* or *dies bissextus*). Above the lines of astronomical data is an occasional obit or longer notice, and it is important for our purpose to notice that the space in the left-hand margin, between two successive B's, has been filled by the continuation of one of the entries which runs across the page. No doubt this practice of using the margin between successive leap-years explains the arbitrary runs of annals in fours and eights which we find in the Saxon *Chronicle*; in relating the events of the invasion it has been dependent upon a series of annals written up in this fashion in an Easter Table.[1] However, there was usually room on the wide margins, despite the traditional eight columns, to make a second entry in addition to that which gave the date of the Easter festival. As C. W. Jones points out (p. 117), 'the earliest entries imitate the historical record of Easter Day in brevity, not because there was no more room, for second entries were few, but because the writer conceives of the second entry in terms of the first. *Augustinus obiit* is like *pascha xi kal. mai.*' This is well exemplified by the annals which constitute Chronicle I, the beginning of which is reproduced [2] on the plate in this book (see pp. xxiv–xxv and Appendix A). Although of slight importance in itself, this chronicle is unique amongst its fellows because it has been preserved to us written on an Easter Table, and I have therefore designated it appropriately as 'An Easter Table Chronicle.'

There was, however, a second link between the Easter Tables and the earliest chronicle which was forged by the custom of the early computists to expound the scientific theory which lay behind their tables. Thus Bede in his *De Temporum Ratione* follows his Paschal Table by an extensive exposition which in C. W. Jones's large-paged edition occupies more than one hundred pages of print; this was an expansion of his

---

[1] But see C. W. Jones, *Saints' Lives and Chronicles* (Ithaca, N.Y. 1947), 190.
[2] British Museum, Cotton MS. Caligula A xv, folios 132b–133a. On folios 122b, 123a of this manuscript, which contains much computistical material, appear the two drawings at the head of the Easter Tables referred to on p. xxi note 1, reproduced by Francis Wormald, *loc. cit.* Our plate shows a nine-column Easter Table drawn more accurately and with greater skill than that from Einsiedeln referred to above. It is later—the original hand appears to stop at 1073 (cf. Francis Wormald, *op. cit.* 67), and therefore as is customary adds extra subsidiary columns to the traditional eight. For example, the concurrents are identified by letters as well as by numerals: $1 = F = $ Sunday; $2 = E = $ Monday; $3 = D = $ Tuesday; $4 = C = $ Wednesday; $5 = B = $ Thursday; $6 = A = $ Friday; $7 = G = $ Saturday. The reduction by one day in a leap-year is also shown. March 24 was the day chosen for the concurrent calculation because it was the place of the bissextile or leap-year intercalation. In 988 (the year which begins the 53rd Lunar Cycle) the first letter given in the Concurrent column is $G (= 7) = $ Saturday (i.e. 24 March—Sat.), but since this was a leap-year the concurrent was reduced by one to $A (= 6) = $ Friday; in other words, because it was a leap-year 24 March fell on a Friday, not on a Saturday.
The last two columns (really one, ruled as two) make up a table of nine columns, of which this is the sole example (cf. Heinrich Henel, *Studien zum altenglischen Computus* (Leipzig 1934), 28). These two give the weeks (*ebdomas*) and days (*dies*) from Christmas to Quadragesima (the first Sunday in Lent), and therefore an indication of the number of Sundays after Epiphany.

manual *De Temporibus* written twenty-two years earlier. Part of this kind of commentary would be devoted to an explanation [1] of the particular era which had been adopted in the table, i.e. whether the years were reckoned from the Creation of the World or from the year of Christ's Passion, etc. From this it was a natural step to draw up a brief chronicle in illustration, which would record memorable events within the era. In consequence the linking of chronicle and Easter Table became a tradition. As C. W. Jones says (p. 119):

'As the Hebrew Bible had stimulated chronographic writing and the creation of chronicles, and as the Easter Tables stimulated the creation of annals, so did the union of theory and practice in the computistical works of the fourth century lead to the union of chronicles and annals. Had Bede created *De Temporum Ratione* without a chronicle, his book would have been incomplete, just as it would have been incomplete without an annual calendar with martyrological entries and Easter Tables with annals.'

Perhaps Bede's experience of the limitations of the chronicle-form, gained in his two computistical works *De Temporibus* and *De Temporum Ratione*, led him to choose a less constricted frame for his *Ecclesiastical History*. Here, at all events, the action does not move within the narrow 'sets' of the annalist, but can employ the resources of the entire stage. The chapter division in each of the five books is as theme and subject-matter dictate, and not entirely according to an artificial chronological sequence. As Sir Frank Stenton says, 'in an age when little was attempted beyond the registration of fact, Bede had reached the conception of history.' Nevertheless at the end of the *Ecclesiastical History* (V. 24) he adds a chapter headed 'A Chronological Recapitulation of the Whole Work, also concerning the author himself,' and begins: 'I have thought fit briefly to make a summary in chronological order of those things which have been set out more fully, in order that they may be the better memorized.' [2] In some manuscripts of the *History* there are additions to this epitome which Bede himself made, and in some the epitome was continued to 766, thirty-one years after his death. Such insertions and additions show how readily the epitome might provide the material with which to start or amplify a chronicle, and indeed many medieval plagiarists on the Continent whose chronicles display an insatiable appetite for English news are merely looting the ample storehouses of Bede's *History*, *Epitome*, and the *Chronica Minora* and *Maiora*. It was therefore natural enough for the begetters of the *Chronicle* to copy the convention of annalistic writing for their own purposes, particularly since they made such liberal use of Bede's *Epitome* for the early years of the Christian era. It is very likely too, as we shall see, that some early annals in Anglo-Saxon may also have provided them with a model; even Bede himself, as C. W. Jones suggests (p. 121), was probably relying on Easter Table annals for the mass of fixed dates around which the *History* is so often written.

[1] e.g. Bede, *De Temporum Ratione*, chap. xlvii.

[2] See C. W. Jones, *Saints' Lives and Chronicles*, cap. III, and his opinion, 'the *Recapitulatio* is basically a set of Paschal annals' (p. 32).

ANNI DNI	Indic	Epac	Concurren	Terminus pasch	
cccc	D. Lxxviii	i	Null	A	GB	vii	Non Ap	v
cccc	D. Lxxxix	ii	xi	E	i	viii kł Ap	i
cccc	D. xc	iii	xii	E	ii	idus Ap	vi
cccc	D. xci	iiii	iii	D	iii	iiii N Ap	ii
cccc	D. xcii	v	xiiii	C	B B	v	vi kł Ap	v
cccc	D. xciii	vi	xxv	A	vi	iiii id Ap	iii
cccc	D. xciiii	vii	vi	G	vii	iii kł Ap	vi
cccc	D. xcv	viii	xvii	E	i	xiiii kł mai	iiii
cccc	D. xcvi	ix	xviii	E	DB	iii	vi id Ap	vii
cccc	D. xcvii	x	ix	C	iiii	vi kł Ap	iii
cccc	D. xcviii	xi	xx	B	v	viiii kł mai	i
cccc	D. xcix	xii	i	A	vi	ii N Ap	iiii
	cccc	xiiii	xii	G	EB	i	ix kł Ap	vii
	cc i	xiiii	xxiii	E	ii	ii id Ap	v
	cc ii	xv	iiii	D	iii	kłde Ap	i
	cc iii	i	xv	C	iiii	ix kł Ap	iiii
	cc iiii	ii	xxvi	B	AB	vi	iii id Ap	ii
	cc v	iii	vii	G	vii	iiii kł Ap	vi
	cc vi	iiii	xviii	E	i	xx kł mai	iii

ANNI DNI	Indic	Epac	Concurr	Terminus pasch	
cc vii	v	Null	E	ii	Non Ap	v
cc viii	vi	ix	D	CB	iiii	viii kł Ap	i
cc ix	vii	xx	B	v	idus Ap	vi
cc x	viii	i	A	vi	iiii N Ap	ii
cc xi	viiii	xii	G	vii	xi kł Ap	
cc xii	x	xxiii	E	EB	ii	iiii id Ap	iii
cc xiii	xi	iiii	D	iii	iii kł Ap	vi
cc xiiii	xii	xv	C	iiii	xiiii kł mai	iiii
cc xv	xiii	xxvi	B	v	vi id Ap	vii
cc xvi	xiiii	vii	A	GB	vii	iii kł Ap	iii
cc xvii	i	xviii	E	i	xx kł mai	i
cc xviii	ii	i	D	iii	iiii N Ap	iiii
cc xix	iii	xii	D	iiii	ix kł Ap	vii
cc xx	iiii	xxiii	C	B B	v	iii id Ap	v
cc xxi	iiii	iiii	A	vi	kłde Ap	i

On þison geare forð ferð scē dunstan ge boren. 7 þe

449

Dies pasch	Luna	Ebd	Dies	
vi	ID AP	xiiii	viii	vi	Her forð ferde scē dunstan arceb. 133
ii	kł AP	xx	vii	v	
xi	kł iii	xxi	v	iiii	Her sigric to rome.
NŌN AP		xvii	vi	iii	
vi	kł AP	xix	vii	i	
xvi	kł iii	xx	vii		
kł ðe APR	xxvi	vii	vi		
xi	kł iii	xxvii	v	v	
ii	ID AP	xiiii	iv	iii	Her sigric asc forð ferde.
v	kł AP	xx	vii	ii	Her aelfric b þon to rome
xx	kł iii	xxvi	v		
v	ID AP	xiiii	vii	vi	
ii	kł AP	xxi	vii	v	
IDUS APR		xvii	v	iiii	
NŌN APR	xviii	viii	iii		
v	kł AP	xxi	vii	ii	
xvi	kł iii	xxvii	vii		
kł ðe AP	xxvii	vii	vi	Her forð ferde aelfric b.
ii	kł iii	xiiii			Her Alfeh b for to rome
Dies pasche	Luna	Ebd	Dies	
vii	IDUS AP	xiiii	iv	iiii	
v	kł AP	xxi	vii		
xx	kł iii	xxvii	vii	i	
v	ID AP	xiiii	iv		
vii	kł AP	xviii	v	vi	
IDUS APR		xvii	vii	iiii	Her pær cante papa hir geþuncan.
NŌN APR	xxi	vii	iii	Her pær scē aelfeh ge martyriod.	
vi	kł iii	xxvii	vii	ii	
iii	ID AP	xvii	xvii	i	
kł ðe APR	xiiii	vii	vi	Her forð ferde aðelred kyng.	
xx	kł iii	xxvii	vii	v	Her pær cnut corone to kynge.
vii	ID AP	xxvii	vii	iiii	
iiii	kł AP	xviii	vii	iii	
xx	kł iii	xiiii		i	Her forð ferde lyfing ærceb. 7 ageldus
iiii	ID AP	xxvi	vii		coma feng to þon b gær.

EASTER TABLE WITH ANNALS
Caligula A xv, folios 132b and 133a

§ 3

The saint, the scholar, from a circle freed
Of toil stupendous, in a hallowed seat
Of learning, where thou heard'st the billows beat
On a wild coast, rough monitors to feed
Perpetual industry.

Wordsworth, of the Venerable Bede.

Thanks to the example of Bede, the *Chronicle* is the first history written in English to use his masterly innovation of reckoning years as from the Incarnation of Our Lord—'Years of Grace' as they were called in England. We have become so accustomed to the dating A.D.[1]—*anno Domini*, 'in the year of our Lord'—that it is difficult to realize that other ways of reckoning to fix a date were once in existence. A historian could refer to an event as having happened so many years after the Creation of the World, or so many years after a king or emperor's accession or coronation, or, since theirs was an office held for a single year, to the names of Roman consuls.[2] It was also customary to give the 'Indiction' number, which marked the place[3] of any given year in a series of cycles of fifteen years' duration which began according to Eastern practice, not on 1 January, but on 1 September of the year A.D. 312. It is clear that this last system was of little use in fixing a date if it was not known how many cycles had passed, or if there was doubt when the cycle began: in fact Bede, in the last sentence of chap. xlviii ('De Indictionibus') of *De Temporum Ratione*, for some reason[4] gave the date as 24 September.

Bede's interest in chronological problems was quickened by the contemporary dispute about the correct date for the observance of Easter. It is clear from the almost verbatim way in which he reports Wilfrid's speech at the Synod of Whitby, a decade before his birth, that he appreciated the importance of the Easter Tables of the Syrian monk Dionysius Exiguus,[5] which had calculated Easter to fall on the Sunday on or after the fifteenth day of the moon following the Spring Equinox. It was this reckoning which Wilfrid upheld at the Synod, and it is referred to again by Bede when he quotes (*EH* II. 19) the letter written by Pope John IV to the Irish in 640, admonishing them to observe Easter 'between the fifteenth day of the moon and the twenty-first, as approved[6] by the Council of Nicea.' The *Liber de paschale* of

[1] See C. W. Jones, *op. cit.* for an account of how 'Bede pioneered, this time by accident,' in inventing the reckoning B.C.

[2] See R. L. Poole, *Studies in Chronology and History* (Oxford 1934), chap. I.

[3] Annal 1090 E in the *Chronicle* is introduced by the words INDICTIONE XIII: arrived at thus: 1090 — 312 = 778; 778 ÷ 15 = 51 (cycles of 15 years) + 13 (the Indiction Number).

[4] See C. W. Jones, *op. cit.* 382–4 for a discussion on the reasons for this.

[5] See annal 625 E.

[6] C. W. Jones, *op. cit.* 91 note 5, has shown that the approval must refer to the continuation (627–721), by Felix, abbot of the monastery of Gillitanus in N. Africa, of Dionysius' Easter Table (532–626). Bede himself extended the table still further to 1063 in his *De Temporum Ratione* (see reference in chap. lxv.)

Dionysius, 'who led the Paschal use of Alexandria to victory in the Roman Church'[1] was not only important to Bede for this reason, but also because it introduced a new method of identifying any particular year in the tables by numbering from the Incarnation instead of from A.D. 284, the year of the Emperor Diocletian's accession. Dionysius thought it incongruous to perpetuate 'the memory of the impious persecutor in my cycles, choosing rather to denote the times from the birth of Our Lord Jesus Christ.' So each line of his tables began with the Year of Grace, and was followed, as we have seen the practice was, by astronomical data for the calculation of the date of Easter. As C. W. Jones remarks (p. 117), 'Our Era was born. It has, of course, been truly said that Dionysius did not recognize the eventual uses of his innovation. Few inventors do.'

Indeed it is also true to say that Bede himself did not immediately take advantage of the new method of reckoning—A.D. In his first computistical work, De Temporibus Liber (703), written when he was thirty, he makes no practical use of it, except to speak (chap. xvi) of the fifth age of the world as extending up to the Incarnation. The Chronica Minora which he appends to the work, lists the names of biblical patriarchs and Roman emperors with the length of their lives and reigns, and adds a few references to English history, but does not fix an absolute chronology either by calculating from the beginning of the world or from the Incarnation. In the De Temporum Ratione, which was written in 725 as an amplification of De Temporibus, Bede reviews[2] in chap. xlvii the evidence for arriving at dates for the Incarnation and the Passion. Yet in the more comprehensive chronicle, Chronica Maiora,[3] which occupies the whole of chap. lxvi, there is still no attempt to use the new reckoning, except in a few places (cf. ff. 518, 586). Instead, at the end of reigns or sections of the chronicle, he gives the annus mundi, and makes a new set of calculations based on the Vulgate instead of on the Septuagint. It is remarkable that he refrained, for, as C. W. Jones has said (p. 121),

'he had sufficient stimulation to use another era, for the charge of heresy levelled against him for his era mundi in De Temporibus still rankled. Because of the likeness of De Temporum Ratione and De Temporibus we would expect him there, if anywhere, to avoid challenging his opponents with a reiteration of the suspect doctrine. Moreeover, in De Temporum Ratione the theory of the Dionysiac era was treated in full. But, though the Chronicle in De Temporum Ratione was for these reasons the ideal place to introduce a new method, he did not do so.'

However, six years later in his greatest work, the Ecclesiastical History, he gives the Dionysiac reckoning the full weight of his authority, and by reason of his reputation as a scholar ensured for it wide prominence[4] and popularity, especially on the Continent where

---

[1] W. Levison, 'Bede as Historian' (op. cit.), 114.

[2] See C. W. Jones, op. cit. 70.

[3] The two chronicles can be conveniently compared in Theodor Mommsen's edition, Chronica Minora (Monumenta Germaniae Historica, Auctores Antiquissimi, IX, XI, XIII, Berlin 1892–98) III, 247–327.

[4] See R. L .Poole, Medieval Reckonings of Time (London 1918), 40.

some of the oldest existing manuscripts of the *History* were written. As Levison [1] has pointed out, the dating *anno Domini* was particularly useful in the writing of English history; the Anglo-Saxons reckoned time by the regnal years of their kings, 'but if bishops of several of the little Anglo-Saxon kingdoms came together at a synod and had to date its decrees by the years of each of their kings, this method of reckoning became troublesome and moreover did not correspond with the unity of the English Church.' Thus the compilers of the *Anglo-Saxon Chronicle* inherited the advantages of a computistical system which had been introduced by Bede in the *History* and its *Epitome*, and rejected not only earlier less efficient methods of reckoning, but also the experiments of the *Chronica Minora* and *Maiora*. Nevertheless, despite the advantages, the *Chronicle* inherited one serious disadvantage which was inherent in annalistic writing, namely the absence of any precise indication when the year was supposed to begin. As late as 1200, Gervase in his *History* (I. 88) complains that falsehood creeps into chronicles because there is a difference of opinion, among other things, about the beginning of the year, whether to reckon from the Annunciation, the Nativity, the Circumcision, or the Passion. Nor sometimes are we in any better position to-day to know which *caput anni* a chronicler is using for his *annus domini* in a particular annal; and when in like ignorance one medieval chronicler copies from another, the result is confusion worse confounded.

Writing in 725 Bede says [2] that the English custom of beginning the year on Christmas Day was falling into disuse, but it would appear to have been revived by about 1000, for Ælfric's Catholic *Homilies* [3] open with a sermon on The Beginning of the World, immediately followed by one of 25 December. Since the *Chronicle*, as we have seen, is adopting the era of the Incarnation, it would have been proper to this reckoning to begin the year with the Annunciation (25 March), except that the word 'Incarnation' was subsequently applied to the 'Nativity' and the reckoning thereby deferred for nine months.[4] For secular affairs, the beginning of the Roman civil year on 1 January was also used; the Irish chroniclers reckoned from it, but there is no evidence to show that it was ever employed by the *Chronicle*. Also, in the third century A.D. another date was introduced for taxation purposes. Just as our income-tax year begins on 5 April,[5] so 1 September was chosen as the beginning of a period for tax assessment, made, not every year, but every fifteenth year, and known as the Indiction. Bede in his *De Temporum Ratione* (chap. xlviii) wrote about the use of indictions, and 'by the last sentence of this chapter, imposed upon the Latin Middle Ages a chronological year which has caused both medieval and modern

[1] W. Levison, *England and the Continent in the Eighth Century*, 84.
[2] *De Temporum Ratione* xv (ed. C. W. Jones, *op. cit.* 211–12): 'Antiqui autem anglorum populi . . . incipiebant autem annum ab octavo kalendarum ianuariarum die, ubi nunc natalem domini celebramus.'
[3] P. Clemoes draws my attention to the homily for the Circumcision (Thorpe I. 98–100), where Ælfric discusses when the year should begin.
[4] W. H. Stevenson, 13 *EHR* 75 note 26.
[5] i.e. eleven days after 25 March where the year began before 1752 (as Professor Dickins reminds me).

historians considerable difficulty'[1] for there he stated categorically that the Indiction reckoning began on 24 September, and in fact in his *History* used [2] this *fiscal* date for the beginning of the *religious* year which he adopted from Dionysius, the Year of the Incarnation.

Consequently there is the possibility that the *Chronicle* may have used any of the following dates, set out in chronological order, for the opening of the year:

(*a*) 25 March *preceding* our 1 January: the Annunciation (Stylus Pisanus).

(*b*) 1 September: the Greek or Byzantine Indiction date.

(*c*) 24 September: the Caesarean Indiction date (Mid-Autumn Day).

(*d*) 25 December: Christmas Day (Mid-Winter's Day).

(*e*) 1 January.

(*f*) 25 March *following* our 1 January: the Annunciation (Stylus Florentinus).

In actual fact, so far as can be seen, the dates (*a*), (*b*), and (*e*) above are never used in the *Chronicle* for New Year's Day, nor apparently was an Easter commencement ever in use, as Plummer thought. For most of the *Chronicle* the year begins at Christmas, but evidence has been brought forward in support of beginnings on 24 September preceding our 1 January, and for 25 March following it; in such entries, according to our modern reckoning, some events are likely to be recorded one year too late or one year too early respectively. Thus the solar eclipse of 29 October 878 happened too late for entry under a year which the chronicler closed at 23 September; while the lunar eclipse of 30 January 1078, if it had been recorded in manuscript E as it was in D, would have been put under 1077, for that annal in E before its close goes on to record two February obits, apparently because the chronicler ended his year either at Easter or on 24 March.

M. L. R. Beaven [3] demonstrated that the Indictional reckoning (from 24 September) was used in the Alfredian chronicle 866–78, and that it was still in vogue, at least in the south of England, until the first half of the tenth century. Thus from 866 to 878, annal after annal begins with a reference to movements of the Danes to winter-quarters in the autumn, and several end with descriptions of Alfred's naval cruises which would normally be undertaken in summer weather. R. H. Hodgkin,[4] however, thought the change to a Christmas reckoning took place earlier in 891, and that 890 was the last of a series of annals regularly reckoned as beginning with the September Indiction.[5] Finally,

---

[1] C. W. Jones, *op. cit.* 382 for a discussion of this.

[2] So Poole, F. M. Powicke, Jones, Stenton, and most of the authorities. W. Levison, however, maintains that Bede in his *History* began the year of the Incarnation on Christmas Day (*England and the Continent in the Eighth Century*, Appendix VI), and is supported by P. H. Blair in *Chadwick Memorial Studies* 248 note.

[3] 33 *EHR* 328–42.   [4] 39 *EHR* 497–510.

[5] Cf. 'The Chronology of the Parker Chronicle, 890–970' (69 *EHR* 59–66) where Richard Vaughan, of Corpus Christi College, Cambridge, produces evidence that from 955 onwards the Parker Chronicle (A) begins its year at Mid-winter; up to this date the Indictional beginning (24 September) is used.

R. L. Poole pointed out that some of the entries [1] during the eleventh century appeared from internal evidence to be based on a year beginning with the Annunciation following 1 January (Stylus Florentinus).

The dating of the *Chronicle* has also to be corrected in places for other reasons, chiefly on account of mechanical errors which a scribe is capable of making when copying from one manuscript into another. He may easily misread [2] the Roman numerals of his original, or omit to jump [3] a year or years when blank annals occur, or he may even repeat [4] the number of a year when passing on to the next; or some later scribe may go back and 'correct' [5] numberings under the false impression that as they stand they are wrong. In the translations in this book an attempt has been made to adjust the dating where, for the above reasons, it is necessary to do so; such adjustments are shown in square brackets before the event or events to which they are appropriate. No attempt has been made to reconcile the chronological discrepancies which for various other reasons sometimes arise between one version and another.

§ 4

'The living tradition of Alfred, recorded by chroniclers and poets, is one of the things which kept the English spirit alive in the three centuries after the defeat at Hastings' (R. W. Chambers).

In the popular mind the beginning of the *Chronicle* has always been associated with the name of King Alfred, and with Winchester, the old capital of Wessex. The only written testimony to Alfred's part in its composition, however, is post-Conquest, in Geoffrei Gaimar's *L'Estorie des Engles*, where in lines 3451–2 the Norman poet writes:

Il fist escrivere un livre Engleis
Des aventures e des leis,

'a book of events and laws' which might well describe a manuscript of the *Chronicle* like the Parker, in which the annals are followed by a text of the laws. Lacking other extrinsic evidence, some scholars have claimed that Alfred, who himself translated many Latin books into English and commissioned others from his scholars, may well about 891 have ordered some older recension of the *Chronicle* to be brought up to date and maintained, possibly writing or providing some of the material himself from his own experiences in the Danish war. It is

[1] 16 *EHR* 719–21. The annals are 1009, 1010, 1041 D, 1044 C, 1045 C, 1046 C, 1049 C, 1050 C, 1051 C, 1065 C, 1077 E.

[2] e.g. XIII for III (836).

[3] e.g. 754–845 where the scribe omitted to pass over the two annals 754, 756, for which there should have been no entries.
    The scribe of B deals with this kind of difficulty in his own original way: although he does not always prefix an entry with the date, he usually writes down the numerals for all those years for which there is no entry. Thus almost two whole pages (fols. 2*b*–3*a*) are taken up by the writing out of the roman numerals CXC to CCCLXXX for these missing years. The scribe of D also rules lines for each annal up to A.D. 262 and enters every numeral, even if there is no annal to record.

[4] 1043 E, 1052 D.

[5] 892–928 A, where the scribe added one to the original numberings.

true that his translation of the *History* of Orosius contains many close verbal resemblances to passages in the *Chronicle*, and both translation and original are cast in annalistic form,[1] but the phraseology and vocabulary are such as could hardly have been avoided by any contemporary military or political historian, and, in fact, recur in the *Chronicle* after his time.

Both C. Plummer and R. H. Hodgkin have argued, perhaps more ardently than convincingly, that 'the work was substantially a product of Alfred's reign, inspired by Alfred and at times loosely supervised by him, though like other Alfredian works not actually written at his dictation';[2] and Plummer[3] would 'place in the forefront of the chronicle the inscription which encircles Alfred's jewel +AELFRED M/EC H/EH/T GEWYRCAN, "Alfred ordered me to be made,"' and chose the symbol Æ for Alfred's original chronicle, partly because 'it expresses the fact that this original stock branches out on the one side into our $\overline{A}$, and on the other into our E, the two chronicles which are furthest apart from one another in character, as they are in time, of all our existing chronicles.'

Stenton, however, has reminded us[4] that Alfred may not have been the only patron of letters in the Wessex of his day, and that some noble, probably in the south-west, may have commissioned the work, particularly since these early annals give prominence to events in Dorset and Somerset, rather than to those which took place in Hampshire: thus, details are given of the day to day movements of Alfred before the battle of Edington (878), and obscure villages in the south-west where he sheltered before he struck back at the Danes are mentioned by name. On the other hand, the annalist betrays no special interest in Winchester which, as Stenton says, had not reached in Alfred's time the eminence it enjoyed in the tenth and eleventh centuries as the most important town south of the Thames.

At all events it is clear that in the time of Alfred a chronicle extending to the year 891 was made, and, as with his translation of the *Cura Pastoralis*, copies were circulated[5] to various centres of learning, where they were maintained and kept up to date from official bulletins of national events which were subsequently issued, as well as by the addition of many items of purely provincial and local interest. From these at times other copies were made as requested, and the surviving manuscripts of the *Chronicle* are, for the most part, transcripts of such

[1] i.e. so many years before (or after) the foundation of the city of Rome.

[2] R. H. Hodgkin, *A History of the Anglo-Saxons* (Oxford 1935) II, 624.

[3] Plummer II. civ.

[4] F. M. Stenton, 'The South-Western Element in the Old English Chronicle' (*Essays in Medieval History presented to Thomas Frederick Tout*, 15–24, Manchester 1925).

[5] R. H. Hodgkin 39 *EHR* 507–8 suggested 890 (or the beginning of 891) rather than 892, as Plummer thought, was the date at which the transcripts were sent out, first because of the change in the system of calculating the year which he observed to begin in 891, and secondly because of the confusion in the numbering of the annals which creeps into the different versions of the *Chronicle* at this point.

It should be noticed, however, that copies of the *Cura Pastoralis* were sent out to episcopal sees, and *not* to monasteries.

copies; they have, as Plummer has shown, complex and intricate textual histories.

Whether this primary compilation was inspired by Alfred or some nobleman of his court, it is noteworthy that it was made towards the end of the century the beginning of which had seen the whole of England united under the royal house of Egbert and during the reign of the most distinguished prince of that house, whose energies and genius had successfully preserved the nation in its struggle for survival against the Danes. When A. L. Rowse[1] spoke recently of the similarity of our situation in the last war and that of the Elizabethans facing the might of Spain, he might equally well have drawn the comparison with England of Alfred's day, her king a fugitive from an occupying power. Little wonder that a post-Conquest poet praised Alfred as *Englene hurde, Englene durlyng*, when he recalled the miraculous way in which the king had confounded his enemies before the year was out. 'Such a situation,' wrote Rowse, 'a smaller people facing a great ordeal and coming through unitedly, toned up by it, seems to have been just that which preceded some of the most outstanding outbursts of creative activity in European societies.' The great literary activity of Alfred's reign is witness to the truth of this, and the *Chronicle*, in particular, is the expression of

'pride in the hard fighting of the West Saxons. The chroniclers felt that great things had been done, and that the memory of them should be perpetuated. There was pride also in the blood royal of the House of Egbert and its descent from Cerdic (good propaganda for all Anglo-Saxons); also in its descent from Woden (this probably had some propaganda value in conversation with the heathen Danes). The emphasis on the Bretwaldaship was also as likely as not something more than a piece of antiquarianism.'

This eloquent analysis [2] of the ideas and motives of the compilers of the *Chronicle* finds confirmation in the following century. At the beginning, in striking contrast to the annals at its close which describe the bitterness of defeat under Æthelred the Unready, this same consciousness of the achievements of the House of Wessex becomes triumphantly vocal, and in the Brunanburh panegyric finds exultant expression, not in the sober periods of prose, but in the quickened excitement of verse:

> Ne wearð wæl mare
> on þis eiglande æfre gieta
> folces gefylled beforan þissum
> sweordes ecgum þæs þe us secgað bec,
> ealde uðwitan, siþþan eastan hider
> Engle and Seaxe up becoman,
> ofer brad brimu Brytene sohtan,
> wlance wigsmiþas Wealas ofercoman,
> eorlas arhwate eard begeatan.

[1] *A New Elizabethan Age* (Presidential Address to the English Association, July 1952) 4–5.

[2] R. H. Hodgkin, *op. cit.* II. 627.

§ 5

'*The questions of provenance and interdependence of the various versions* [of the *Chronicle*] *are so complicated that any discussion soon assumes the appearance of an essay in higher mathematics*' (Dom David Knowles).

Any account of the *Anglo-Saxon Chronicle* is necessarily based on Charles Plummer's revision of the edition of John Earle [1] (1865) which was published in two volumes by the Oxford University Press in 1892–9. 'Apart from one or two quite minor details,' wrote R. W. Chambers in 1928, 'the research of the last quarter of a century has left Dr Plummer's conclusions unassailed'—and this is equally true to-day. Plummer's edition (which my translation follows both in text and pagination) gives prominence on opposite pages to manuscripts $\overline{A}$ and E, associated respectively with the names of Archbishop Parker (1504–75) and Archbishop Laud (1573–1645); manuscript A is now in the Library of Corpus Christi College, Cambridge, and manuscript E in the Bodleian at Oxford. The other manuscripts were once in the possession of Sir Robert Cotton (1571–1631), and are to be found in the Cottonian collection of manuscripts in the British Museum.

Seven manuscripts of the *Chronicle* are extant: these Plummer designated $\overline{A}$, A (also styled G and W), B, C, D, E, F. These seven manuscripts can be divided into four groups: A (G, W) is a transcript of $\overline{A}$; B and C are sister texts, for B, as far as it goes, is practically identical with C, both having been copied from the same manuscript; and F is a bilingual epitome of E. Although the term 'Anglo-Saxon Chronicle' is loosely used to describe all these manuscripts, yet $\overline{A}$, C, D, and E, as Plummer said, 'have every right to be considered distinct and individual chronicles; the fact that they grow out of a common stock, that even in their later parts they use common material, does not make them one chronicle.'

Their growth, however, differs in one important particular. In one manuscript, the Parker, we can watch the development as each scribe takes up the pen where his predecessor left off: in each generation, throughout the reigns of Alfred, Athelstan, and Edgar until after the accession of Æthelred, this chronicle was maintained by as many as ten [2] successive scribes in the same monastic house, and the lineaments of its growth can be traced on its pages. In contrast, the other manuscripts, being copies made no earlier than the tenth century from lost originals, display no such 'rings' of early development: they begin as root-stocks upon which scions were subsequently budded. The root-stocks, however, sprang originally from the Alfredian chronicle, and were reared independently in different parts of the country. For most, if not all, of their length the chronicles, other than the Parker, show the

---

[1] It is proper for me to recall the acknowledgment made by John Earle to Archdeacon Charles Hardwick, Fellow of St Catharine's College, Cambridge, a good Anglo-Saxon scholar, who compared Earle's text of $\overline{A}$ with the manuscript at Corpus.

[2] Possibly nine; see A. H. Smith, *The Parker Chronicle* (London 1935), 3 note.

same handwriting, for the first task of each scribe was to copy up the story of the centuries before his time; most of the scribes of the Parker manuscript, on the other hand, had the advantage of seeing history in the making, and their record is almost contemporary.

I. Manuscript Ā (The Parker Chronicle)
Corpus Christi College, Cambridge, MS. 173, folios 1–32:
[60 B.C.–A.D. 1070]

The chronicle is introduced by a Genealogical Preface and followed by the Acts of Lanfranc (in Latin), the Laws of Ine and Alfred (in English), etc. The manuscript formerly belonged to Archbishop Parker, and was part of his bequest to the college. A facsimile of part of the manuscript has been published by Robin Flower and Hugh Smith, *The Parker Chronicle and Laws* (EETS, London 1941). Up to the eleventh century it belonged to the Old Minster, otherwise St Swithin's, Winchester, and it went, possibly after the Conquest, to Christ Church, Canterbury.

The handwriting of thirteen, possibly fourteen, scribes can be traced in the manuscript: the first scribe copied up to the end of the annal for 891 and there stopped, after writing añ dcccxcii in the margin of the next line which was left blank. The second scribe continued the annal for 891 on the top of the next page with a description of the appearance of a comet, but did not delete the year number 892 on the previous page. A later scribe was misled by this into thinking that the year of the comet was 892, he therefore added one to the year correctly given as 892, and made it 893: this same 'correction' was made to each annal up to 929. For more than thirty years after 891, the manuscript gives a full and contemporary account of the wars of Alfred and his son Edward the Elder; although the other manuscripts of the *Chronicle*, except E, have almost identical material up to 918, the six entries 919–24 are peculiar to Ā. Thereafter half a page is left blank; then, at the top of the next page, annal 925 makes the bald announcement of Edward's death and Athelstan's accession.

'From Athelstan to Æthelred the Unready the *Chronicles* become quite barren . . . yet these fifty years were the most successful and glorious in the whole Anglo-Saxon period.'[1] Incidentally, the annal for 1001, the longest of them all, describing Danish naval raids in Hampshire and Devon, was the last to be written at Winchester. This section of the Parker manuscript, however, is remarkable for the introduction of four occasional poems, written in conscious imitation of earlier Old English alliterative verse. The first, a panegyric on Athelstan's victory at *Brunanburh* (937) over the combined forces of the Scots and Vikings from Ireland, is a rousing paean and the first patriotic poem in the English language. The second celebrates the liberation of the Five Boroughs in 942. The third and fourth on the

[1] R. W. Chambers, *England before the Norman Conquest* (London 1928), 232.

other hand have the literary merits of the average academic exercise; the one fails to rise to the occasion of Edgar's coronation in 973, and the other, after a brief obituary at his death in 975, quickly seeks comfort in describing the salutary effects of the appearance of the comet whereby God signalized his disapproval of Mercian apostasy. The first two poems also appear in manuscripts B, C, and D, and the second two also in manuscripts B and C, but not in D; these versions of the poem were no doubt derived from supplements to the original chronicle sent out officially in the tenth century from the court in Wessex, or from some centre of learning in the south.[1]

Before Ā left Winchester, probably after the Conquest, a copy was made: this copy is designated A by Plummer, and W by Thorpe; the manuscript was destroyed except for a few leaves in the Cottonian fire of 1731, and is now British Museum, Cotton Otho B xi, 2. Before the fire, however, it was made the basis of an edition of the Chronicle by Abraham Wheloc (Cambridge 1643); two sixteenth-century transcripts [2] of the manuscript are also in existence, one in the British Museum and the other in the Library of Trinity College, Dublin.

Although the entries from 975 to 1001 in Ā are sparse, they are nevertheless independent of all the other manuscripts. It is difficult to understand why nothing more was added at Winchester after 1001, unless the sight in 1006 of 'an arrogant and confident Danish host passing the gates of Winchester on its way to the coast, bringing provisions and treasure from a distance of more than fifty miles inland,' destroyed further endeavour. It was probably not until after the Conquest that the neglected chronicle came to Canterbury; had it been there in 1011 the martyrdom of Archbishop Ælfheah must surely have compelled the attention of a scribe. Earle [3] thought that the transfer was made as a result of the exertions of the monks of Canterbury to replace some of their losses in books after the great fire of 1067. In any case the annals after 1001, meagre as they are, were added there, as well as many other additions throughout its pages which relate to Canterbury and its see: these additions are shown in Plummer's edition and in the present translation in small roman or in *italic*.

A good French translation of Ā has been made by Marie Hoffmann-Hirtz, *Une chronique anglo-saxonne, traduite d'après le manuscrit 173 de Corpus Christi College, Cambridge* (Strasbourg 1933).

[1] See Alistair Campbell, *The Battle of Brunanburh* (London 1938) for a critical edition of the poem; also the Introduction 1–7, 34–8 for a succinct account of the growth of the various manuscripts of the *Chronicle* in the early stages of their development. See also N. Kershaw, *Anglo-Saxon and Norse Poems* (Cambridge 1922) for another edition of the *Brunanburh* poem, with a spirited prose translation, to which I am indebted.
[2] See Alistair Campbell, *op. cit.*, Appendix I. 133 ff.
[3] John Earle, *Two of the Saxon Chronicles* (Oxford 1865), xxiii.

II. Manuscripts B and C (The Abingdon Chronicles):

Manuscript B: British Museum, Cotton MS. Tiberius A vi, folios 1–34:
[A.D. 1–A.D. 977]

Manuscript C: British Museum, Cotton MS. Tiberius B i, folios 115–64;
[60 B.C.–A.D. 1066]

Manuscript B was probably introduced by a Genealogical Preface similar to that in $\overline{A}$. It has, however, become detached from the manuscript, and folio 178 of British Museum manuscript Cott. Tib. A iii is most likely the missing leaf—designated β by Plummer. If this be so 'Beta comes originally from Abingdon,' as Bruce Dickins says,[1] 'and represents a West Midland, probably Worcester, recension of the Preface which differed in some respects from that found in $\overline{A}$. Moreover it modifies the Alfredian ending and continues the genealogy to Edward the Martyr, omitting the length of his reign though there was plenty of space in the manuscript. It, or its archetype, must therefore have been written in 977, or early in 978, since Edward was brutally murdered on 18 March of the latter year.' Cotton manuscript Tiberius B i is interesting because the first part contains the Old English version of Orosius's *History of the World*; this is followed by a Metrical Calendar and some Gnomic Verses. The chronicle follows without a break, opening with a short undated annal at the foot of folio 115 v.

Both these manuscripts B and C are eleventh-century copies of an exemplar which ultimately derived from another copy of the original Alfredian chronicle to 891, generally supposed to have been sent to Abingdon in north-east Wessex, though of this we cannot be certain. Down to 915 (which corresponds to $\overline{A}$'s annal 918) the continuation in this lost exemplar was based on supplementary material from Wessex; but at this point, possibly due to its proximity to Mercia, the chronicle harked back to the year 902 to copy out a short chronicle now known as the *Mercian Register*,[2] which gave a summary account down to 924 of the resistance of Æthelflæd, Lady of the Mercians, against the Danes. Thereafter the chronicle turned again to West-Saxon continuations for its information, and used much the same material as the Parker Chronicle for the reigns of the kings from Athelstan to Edgar, adding occasional original entries (e.g. 971, 977).

Manuscript B is a copy of this lost chronicle, possibly made about 1000 for St Augustine's, Canterbury, in view of Joscelin's description of it as *Hist. Sax. S. Augustini Cant*. However, no further entries were made there. In contrast, another copy, our manuscript C, continued the record up to 1066. It may be [3] that part of this continuation was added in the original Abingdon chronicle after the copy to 977 had been

[1] *The Genealogical Preface to the Anglo-Saxon Chronicles* (Occasional Papers II, Department of Anglo-Saxon, Cambridge 1952), 6.
[2] In Plummer's edition (and in this translation) the *Mercian Register* appears at the foot of pp. 93–105. See Plummer's note which is reproduced on p. 93.
[3] See Alistair Campbell, *op. cit.* 3 note 1.

made for Canterbury, and that a copy of this (to 1048, say) was made in the eleventh century, to be continued to 1066 by another scribe, whether at Abingdon or elsewhere. C ends abruptly in 1066 in the middle of a description of the Battle of Stamford Bridge. 'This is not,' says R. W. Chambers, 'because the patriotic scribe dropped his pen with horror at the news of Hastings, but because the manuscript has been mutilated at this point.' However, a century later, another scribe finished the annal by adding a few lines of vivid narrative, telling how a gallant Norwegian held the bridge at Stamford against the English advance.

Plummer remarks [1] that 'the annals peculiar to C are of great interest, and often form our most valuable authority for the times to which they refer. Even when D or E are parallel with C, C will generally be found to be more original than either. Another feature of C is its strongly anti-Godwinist tone, in contrast to the attitude of D and E.

There is a scholarly edition, with translation, of the annals in C from 978 to 1017 in Margaret Ashdown, *English and Norse Documents relating to the Reign of Ethelred the Unready* (Cambridge 1930). The whole text was edited by Harry A. Rositzke, *The C-Text of the Old English Chronicles* (Bochum-Langendreer 1940).

III. Manuscript D (The Worcester Chronicle)
British Museum, Cotton MS. Tiberius B iv:
[A.D. 1–A.D. 1079, with the addition
of an annal 1080 (= 1130)]

There is a spacious dignity about the handwriting and lay-out of the page of this manuscript. The tinted washes of red and pale blue of the letters and numerals which introduce some of the annals are particularly pleasing. The manuscript was copied about 1050 from a lost original, and continued at some place in the West Midlands, probably Worcester, up to 1079; from 1033 onwards there are several entries which relate to Worcester, Evesham, and Pershore. 'The manuscript is not now complete. An attempt has been made to replace the matter missing between annal 262 and the middle of the first line of annal 693 by the insertion, in a late sixteenth-century hand, of annals (extending from 262 to 633) from other sources.' [2] A twelfth-century addition, after the annal for 1079, records (*s.a.* 1080) the defeat of Angus, earl of Moray, in 1130.

The lost original,[3] however, was a north-country not a West Midland chronicle, probably compiled at Ripon, where the receipt of a copy of the Alfredian chronicle to 891 provided material for its inception. The northern scribes, in contrast to those of manuscripts $\overline{A}$, B, and C, were not content merely to copy out and continue the Wessex exemplar,

---

[1] Plummer II. xcii: see also note 4 on the same page for detailed references of C's unique additions, both of original annals and phrasing.

[2] E. Classen and F. E. Harmer, *An Anglo-Saxon Chronicle* (Manchester 1926), xiii.

[3] In a catalogue of the Cathedral Library at Durham, drawn up in the early twelfth century, under the heading *Libri Anglici* is a mention of *Cronica duo Anglica*. (See R. M. Wilson, 5 *LSE* 7)

but chose to check its veracity and to add to its range by reference to Bede's *Ecclesiastical History*, whereas the exemplar had usually [1] relied on the *Chronological Summary* to that work and not upon the *History* itself for some of the information required for early annals. In addition a series of annals from a Northumbrian chronicle known as the *Gesta Veterum Northanhymbrorum*, which is now lost, was added over the period 733 to 806. They also substituted a Preface based on Bede for the Genealogical Preface which Æ, and probably B, had used.

For the early tenth century this northern chronicler used the 'first Wessex continuation' which ran from 891 to 924, but again showed his independence in his treatment of the *Mercian Register* and a second group of northern annals which apparently ran from 901 to 966. Instead of copying them both wholesale into his work (as the archetype of B and C did with the *Mercian Register*) he attempts an amalgam of all three. As Plummer has shown (*op. cit.* II. lxxii f.) this results in certain inconsistencies: certain annals are omitted, and several events are entered twice: 'there are two accounts of the battle of Tettenheal, one under 909, the other under 910, both showing points of resemblance with the *Mercian Register* 910; the death of Æthelred of Mercia and the submission of London and Oxford to Edward the Elder are mentioned, both under 910 and under 912; the ravages of the *here* from Brittany are mentioned briefly in 910, and more fully in 915. The explanation seems to be that 912 and 915 come from the main chronicle, 909 from the *Mercian Register*, while the part of 910 here dealt with comes from the northern source.' For the rest of the tenth century, Alistair Campbell has suggested [2] that although this northern monastery received the *first* part (925–55) of the 'second Wessex continuation' in the form in which it was sent to Winchester and Abingdon, the *second* instalment (958–75) differed from the version received in the south, the modification consisting mainly in the supersession of poems written in conventional alliterative measures by others whose rhythms suggest the Anglo-Saxon equivalent of 'free verse.' It has been suggested [3] that two of these poems, *sub* 959 and 975, were composed by Wulfstan, the author of *Sermo Lupi ad Anglos*. The agreement of D and E for the years which follow (978–81) points to their continued dependence on some central source of information. The similarity of D, E with C for the years 983–1018 suggests that, for this section at least, both D and E were indebted to Abingdon for material.

From the accession of Cnut in 1016, D is especially well informed on Anglo-Scandinavian relations and about events in the north of England. However, the presence of west-country notices from 1033, and its resemblance to the twelfth-century chronicle of Florence of Worcester, led Plummer to assume that about 975 the manuscript was sent from the north to some monastery in the Worcester diocese, possibly Evesham, the knowledge of northern events being derived from the close connection of the sees of York and Worcester between 972 and 1016, when

[1] For details supporting these views of Plummer see his edition, II. lxi, xviii ff.

[2] Alistair Campbell, *op. cit.* 6–7.

[3] K. Jost, 'Wulfstan und die angelsächsische Chronik' (47 *Anglia* 105 ff.) 1923.

the two sees were held together. In 1040, too, when Bishop Lyfing was
compelled to resign the bishopric of Worcester it was given to Ælfric
who was already archbishop of York. Yet, consideration must be
given to Stenton's [1] opinion that 'the indications of such an origin are
by no means convincing. The most prominent figure in the later part of
the chronicle is Archbishop Ealdred of York, and it is at least possible
that this section was originally composed by a member of his circle.'
At all events, the close connection of Worcester and York, and the fact
that Ealdred was first appointed bishop of Worcester in 1047 and made
archbishop of York in 1060, where he died in 1068, may well explain
D's competence in speaking of both northern and western events.
Stenton [2] has also pointed out that 'the emphasis, peculiar to this
manuscript, which is laid on the English descent of Queen Margaret of
Scotland (*s.a.* 1067) suggests that its final form may have been destined
for the Scottish court . . . and the late addition which records the defeat
of Angus, earl of Moray, in 1130, strengthens the possibility of a
Scottish destination for the manuscript.'

A scholarly edition of the D text, with an Introduction and an
especially helpful glossary, has been published by E. Classen and F. E.
Harmer, *An Anglo-Saxon Chronicle* (Manchester 1926).

IV. (a) Manuscript E (The Laud (Peterborough) Chronicle), Bodleian
MS. Laud 636:
[A.D. 1–A.D. 1153]

(b) Manuscript F (The Bilingual Canterbury Epitome), British Museum,
Cotton MS. Domitian A viii:
[A.D. 1–A.D. 1058]

(a) The Laud Manuscript was written at Peterborough at various
dates in the twelfth century from 1121 to 1154. The first scribe copied as
far as 1121, and the last wrote the annals from 1132 to 1154, doubtless
not until after the accession of Henry II, when the disturbed days of
Stephen's reign were over. In 1116, much of the monastery at Peterborough had been destroyed by fire, and it was perhaps as a result of
efforts to repair some of the loss that this copy of a chronicle borrowed
from St Augustine's, Canterbury, was made. As he copied, however,
the first scribe took the opportunity to interpolate versions of spurious
charters, some brief notices of local events, and several passages in
Latin which dealt with ecclesiastical or foreign affairs. The Kentish
chronicle which he followed is now lost, but it had apparently drawn
upon much the same material as D from the time of Alfred to the
beginning of the eleventh century, but with certain differences of treatment. Although E [3] had used the same northern adaptation of the
Alfredian chronicle to 891 as D, it differed from it in making no use of
the 'first Wessex continuation' (to 924) or of the *Mercian Register*;
hence the information provided after the entry for 892 is meagre up to
924. Like D, for the years 925–75, it relies upon a modified form of

[1] *Anglo-Saxon England*, 681.   [2] *op. cit.* 680.
[3] For a detailed analysis of the 'complex relations of D and E,' see
Plummer II. lx–xiv.

'second Wessex continuation' but unaccountably omits[1] the *Brunanburh* poem, and dismisses the injustices of Edgar's reign with one brief sentence. From 978–81, as noticed already, it is in accord with D; and from 983–1018 these two chronicles not only run in harmony with each other but also with C, which suggests that all three were benefiting from the same source or sources of information. From 1018 onwards, C, D, and E sometimes derive annals from the same sources, but in general they are independent; after 1023, however, E develops considerably in originality. Henceforth northern events are mentioned only when of national importance, and the scene of interest shifts to the south of the country. Plummer's revelations[2] of E's inside information are too lively to omit:

'He gives by far the best account of the course of affairs on the death of Cnut (1036); he knows the death-place of Harold Harefoot (1039). His entry of Edward the Confessor's accession is shown to be strictly contemporary; he knows the names of the Vikings who ravaged Sandwich (1046a), and of the English abbots who attended the Council of Rheims (1046b); he knows how Harold gave up his ship to his cousin Beorn, and how the 'lithsmen' of London translated Beorn's body after his treacherous murder by Swegen. He knows the exact day on which the foreign archbishop, Robert, returned to Canterbury from Rome (1048); and he tells, with perhaps a spice of malicious glee, how he left his pallium behind him in his hurried flight from England (1052). He knows that Æthelric, bishop of Selsey, had been a monk of Christ Church, Canterbury (1058); and he alone tells of Harold's naval expedition against William in 1066. But the most striking instance of his detailed local knowledge is in the narrative of the outrages of Eustace of Boulogne and his followers at Dover (1048). Whereas D gives the impression that the outrage took place on Eustace's first landing in England, E knows that it really happened when he was on his way home after his interview with the king; he knows too that he and his followers stopped at Canterbury on their way to Dover and refreshed themselves there; he knows exactly how the scuffle arose, and the numbers slain on either side; he has all a neighbour's indignation that an Englishman should be slain 'on his own hearth'; he asserts, with perhaps a touch of excusable bias for his own side, that Eustace's statement of the case to the king was partial and untrue, and tells with evident approval how Godwin refused to carry out Edward's orders against the men of Dover, "because he was loth to mar his own province."'

It was this abundant detail about southern affairs in the Peterborough Chronicle which led Plummer to suppose that although the early affinities of the archetype before 1022 were with the Worcester Chronicle and the north, it had arrived at St Augustine's, Canterbury, about that date; and there it must have remained until sent on loan to Peterborough in 1121 for copying.

The copy made at Peterborough is our manuscript E; the subsequent additions are perhaps the most famous in the entire *Chronicle*. The annal for 1137, which describes the anarchy of Stephen's reign, 'has

[1] See Alistair Campbell, *op. cit.* 36–7.   [2] Plummer II. xlviii–ix.

frequently been quoted, often mistranslated, by historians, and well deserves its fame. A faint undertone of querulousness cannot mar the vividness of the description of the state of the country during the anarchy.'[1]

Harry A. Rositzke, *The Peterborough Chronicle* (New York 1951) is a good translation of the E text, with introduction and commentary.

(b) Manuscript F, British Museum, Cotton MS. Domitian A viii:
[A.D. 1–A.D. 1058]

This chronicle is a bilingual (English and Latin) epitome of this same Canterbury chronicle, and was made at Christ Church, Canterbury, after the Conquest. F. P. Magoun described it as 'something of a stepchild among the versions of the Old English annals,' although he has done much to remove this reproach by his writings [2] about it. It has, however, less value for the historian than the other chronicles despite its original Preface, and is something of a curiosity in that each annal is first written in Old English and then in Latin, thus foreshadowing the time when Englishmen in the later Middle Ages would cease to write the history of their country in their own language. The wheel had come full circle: the vernacular chronicle which had sprung from Latin originals gave birth in its declining years to a chronicle in Latin. Nor during its lifetime or afterwards was its influence upon historians who wrote in Latin entirely negative: Asser, the biographer of Alfred, had embodied the substance of annals 851–87 in his *Life* of the king, and towards the end of the tenth century ealdorman Æthelweard used, as one of the authorities for his *Chronicon*, an early version of the original Ælfredian chronicle, and one which was apparently more authentic than any of those which the chronicle texts have preserved. After the Conquest, Henry of Huntingdon was indebted to E and C, and Florence of Worcester to a West Midland version of the *Chronicle* which resembled D, the Worcester Chronicle,[3] while Hugh Candidus was clearly familiar with E which was in his own monastery at Peterborough.

[1] Bruce Dickins and R. M. Wilson, *Early Middle English Texts* (Cambridge 1951), 4. Professor Dickins has pointed out to me that the account of the disorders in Normandy after William I's death given by Ordericus Vitalis (VIII. 4) is earlier than, and uncommonly close in general outline to, part of this annal.

[2] F. P. Magoun, Jr, 'The Domitian Bilingual of the *Old-English Annals*: Notes on the F-Text' (6 *Modern Language Quarterly* 371–80, Harvard) and *Annales Domitiani Latini*: An Edition (9 *Medieval Studies* 235–95, Toronto); and 'The Domitian Bilingual of the *Old-English Annals*: The Latin Preface' (20 *Speculum* 65–72). See also C. H. Fernquist, 'Study on the O.E. Version of the Anglo-Saxon Chronicle in Cott. Domitian A viii' (13 *Studier i modern Språkvetenskap* 39–103).

[3] See F. M. Stenton, *Anglo-Saxon England*, 681–2, also his contributions to *Essays in Medieval History presented to Thomas Frederick Tout* 19–22, iv/9 *Transactions of the Royal Historical Society* (1926) 163 ff., and 24 *EHR* 79.

To the above versions of the Chronicle are to be added the brief chronicles H and I.

H (British Museum, Cotton MS. Domitian A ix, on the single leaf folio 9) deals with events of 1113 and 1114, and was probably written at Winchester (cf. *he com to Wincestre*, annal 1114), certainly in some monastic house where the Old English literary tradition was preserved in greater purity than at Peterborough.

The folio was discovered by J. Zupitza and published by him in 1 *Anglia* 195–7.

I (British Museum, Cotton MS. Caligula A xv, folios 132*b*–139) was written at Christ Church, Canterbury, on an Easter Table, and has been referred to above (p. xxii). It runs from 988 to 1268. See plate (pp. xxiv–xxv) for a reproduction of folios 132*b* and 133*a*. A translation of the Old English annals, together with the entries in Latin to Stephen's death, is given in the Appendix. It will be noticed that the native language persists until 1109, and after that date is only once used again to record the dedication of the cathedral church at Canterbury in 1130.

The text (to 1202) is printed by Felix Liebermann, *Ungedruckte Anglo-Normannische Geschichtsquellen* (Strasbourg 1879), 1–8.

§ 6

Hit com him on mode, and on his mern þonke,
þet he wolde of Engle þa æðelæn tellen.

The previous section has described the way in which the various manuscripts of the *Chronicle* developed out of copies of an original archetype (designated æ by Plummer) which were circulated to various parts of the country and supplemented from time to time by subsequent news bulletins from Wessex. But how did the authors of the archetype set about their task of drawing up a chronicle, and whence did they draw the information necessary to sketch a history of England from the beginning of the Christian era to Alfred's own day?

It is clear that they were fortunate enough to possess a still older chronicle to build upon, a chronicle which Plummer denotes as Æ. Opinions differ, however, as to how far it went; Plummer himself thought that it ran as far as 891, to the point where the first scribe of the Parker Chronicle left off. This cannot be proved, however, and there is equal reason for believing that it extended no further than the annal for 855, where the magniloquent coda tracing Æthelwulf's ancestors back to Adam surely makes a fitting close for a chronicle which has celebrated the deeds of the House of Egbert. It is perhaps of some significance in support of this view that for the period 840–65 only seven annals appear, whereas before that time the annals are almost consecutive,[1] while that for 855 is in the nature of a summary of the last years of Æthelwulf's life. Alternatively it has been suggested that it closed at the year 887, since Asser, who had used it for his *Life of King Alfred*, ceased to be indebted to it after that date. Later, in the twelfth

[1] H. M. Chadwick, *The Origin of the English Nation* (Cambridge 1907) 25 note 3.

century, the author of the Latin *Annals of St Neot* was also to translate some annals from this older chronicle, but as he relies on Asser, not on the chronicle, for the years 842–87 we cannot pick up any clue from his work which might help. Nevertheless the dating of his annals for the previous hundred years or so does prove that a chronicle older than æ once existed, for whereas he copied dates correctly, the scribe of æ did not, because he omitted to leave the annals 854 and 756 blank, and so came to be two years behind in his dating from 755 to 828, and three years out from 829 to 839, if not 845—mistakes which were to be perpetuated in all the existing versions of the *Chronicle* which copied from him. The *Annals* cannot therefore have been copied from æ, but both must derive from Æ, the first correctly, the second with the chronological dislocation.

As H. M. Chadwick was the first to show succinctly in his *Origin of the English Nation* (pp. 25 ff.) this older chronicle (Æ), whatever its length, was 'a highly composite document,' and at least eight sources of information had gone to its making. The first three of these provided material for writing the early history of Northumbria and Mercia, and another three embodied traditions relating to Wessex and the south:

(i) The chronological summary appended by Bede to his *Ecclesiastical History*.

(ii) A series of annals extending from Bede's death to the time of Ecgberht of Wessex, no doubt intended as a continuation of the summary.

(iii) Lists of Northumbrian and Mercian kings with their genealogies [1] (e.g. 547, 560, 626, etc.).

(iv) A short epitome of ecclesiastical history from the beginning of the Christian era to the year 110.

(v) A list of the bishops of Winchester to 754.

(vi) A series of West Saxon annals in Latin extending from the invasion to the middle of the eighth century, incorporating some based on oral tradition which may originally have been set down in the seventh century. As Chadwick has pointed out (*op. cit.* 27), it is perhaps significant that genealogies are provided for almost every West Saxon king down to and including Ine, whereas none are given after his accession *s.a.* 688: this would suggest that a change of authorship took place at some time before the accession of the next king in 726. The annals for the seventh century certainly give the impression of being a contemporary record of events: the battle *on Posentesburh* 661 is precisely dated as fought 'at Easter,' and it is improbable that 'any annalist of a later generation would have set down that there was a great destruction of birds in 671.' [2] That a chronicler was writing down a history of Wessex in the middle of the seventh century is of course a fact of intrinsic importance, but it also carries implications of much greater value and significance. For if this be true, the picture of the

---

[1] See P. H. Blair, in *Chadwick Memorial Studies* 250 for an account of manuscripts which contain such lists.

[2] F. M. Stenton, iv/9 *Transactions of the Royal Historical Society* (1926), 163–4. Stenton's lively analysis in this paper of the beginnings of Anglo-Saxon historical writing should be read in full. Cf. also G. H. Wheeler, 36 *EHR* 161 ff.

Saxon invasions in the earliest annals comes into sharper focus, and has better definition by being taken at short range: the authenticity of an eighth- or ninth-century record of events around A.D. 500 is likely to be viewed with some suspicion, but the evidence of a chronicler writing about 650 is not so lightly to be dismissed.   In fact 'it would have been possible for an aged annalist writing in the middle of the seventh century to have set down, even at that late date, information received in youth from men who were living in the time of Cerdic himself.' [1] Moreover the antiquity of such information is indicated by the presence [2] of certain linguistic peculiarities, particularly in the case-endings of proper names, such as had become archaic by the ninth century.

(vii) A continuation of (vi), the West Saxon chronicle up to the middle of the eighth century, by the addition of summaries of the reigns of Cynewulf and Beorhtric, which were not much beyond the reach of living memory in the time of Æthelwulf.   It is possible that after 754 to 823 there was no written source about West Saxon history for the chronicler to follow.   As Chadwick [3] pointed out, 'between 754 and 823 we find probably only five West Saxon entries in sixty-eight years.   Moreover they differ entirely in character from the preceding entries.   The entries for 755 [757] and 784 [786] are summaries of reigns which must have been written after the reigns were ended.   In 787 [789] we hear of an event which the writer makes no attempt to date.' The famous annal for 755 [757], which relates the story of Cynewulf and Cyneheard, contains the only piece of Anglo-Saxon saga material [4] which has been handed down to us in the original vernacular; and, with other evidence, 'suggests that Anglo-Saxon prose had an existence throughout the whole of the Anglo-Saxon period, and that it was developed and polished and cultivated in the oral tradition of a well-developed and valuable saga-literature.'

(viii) A series of contemporary continental annals for the years 880–90.

From 823 to 840, as we have already seen, the run of annals is almost consecutive, in contrast to the sparseness from 840 to 865.   It is of course possible that the original archetype (Æ) went no further than 840; and that the following annals, including the genealogy under 855, were written up by Alfred's scribes to fill the gap until 865, the eve of the great Danish invasions.   It is not likely that the memory of that year and those which followed would pass quickly from men's minds.

G. N. GARMONSWAY.

[1] F. M. Stenton, *op. cit.* 166.
[2] W. H. Stevenson, 14 *EHR* 38.
[3] *op. cit.* 26.
[4] C. E. Wright, *The Cultivation of Saga in Anglo-Saxon England* (Edinburgh 1939), 70 and 26. Cf. C. L. Wrenn, 'A Saga of the Anglo-Saxons' (25 *History* 208–15), and G. Turville-Petre, 'The Intellectual History of the Icelanders' (27 *History* 111–23).

SELECT BIBLIOGRAPHY

1. EDITIONS

1643   A. Wheloc, *Chronologia Anglo-Saxonica* (Cambridge).

1692   E. Gibson, *Chronicon Saxonicum* (Oxford).

1823   J. Ingram, *The Saxon Chronicle* (London). (Text and Translation; the translation was reprinted in Everyman's Library, 1912.)

1848   R. Price, *Monumenta Historica Britannica* (London).

1861   B. Thorpe, *The Anglo-Saxon Chronicle according to the Several Original Authorities* (Rolls Series). (Vol. I Texts; vol. II Translation).

1865   J. Earle, *Two of the Saxon Chronicles* (Oxford).

1892   C. Plummer, *Two of the Saxon Chronicles Parallel* (Oxford). (Vol. I Texts; vol. II Preface, Introduction, Notes, etc.). The annals 787–1001 are published separately.

1926   E. Classen and F. E. Harmer, *An Anglo-Saxon Chronicle from British Museum, Cotton MS., Tiberius B. iv* (Manchester).

1935   A. H. Smith, *The Parker Chronicle (832–900)* (London).

1940   H. A. Rositzke, *The C-Text of the Old-English Chronicles* (34 Beiträge zur englischen Philologie (ed. Max Förster). Bochum-Langendreer).

1941   Facsimile by Robin Flower and Hugh Smith, *The Parker Chronicle*.

1954   Facsimile by Dorothy Whitelock, *The Peterborough Chronicle and Laws* (EETS).
(Early English Manuscripts in Facsimile, vol. IV. Rosenkilde and Bagger, Copenhagen; George Allen & Unwin, London; The Johns Hopkins Press, Baltimore).

1958   Cecily Clark, *The Peterborough Chronicle, 1070–1154* (Oxford English Monographs, Oxford, 2nd edition, 1970).

II. STUDIES AND NOTES

(a) General

1896   C. Plummer, *Venerabilis Baedae opera historica* (Oxford).

1898   J. H. Ramsay, *The Foundations of England* (London).

1899   W. H. Stevenson, 'The Beginnings of Wessex' (14 *EHR* 32–46).

1902   C. Plummer, *The Life and Times of Alfred the Great* (Oxford).

1905   H. M. Chadwick, *Studies on Anglo-Saxon Institutions* (Cambridge).

1907   H. M. Chadwick, *The Origin of the English Nation* (Cambridge).

1908   W. G. Collingwood, *Scandinavian Britain* (London). (Introductory chapters by F. York Powell.)

1909   F. M. Stenton, 'Æthelwerd's Account of the Last Years of Alfred's Reign' (24 *EHR* 79–84).

1913   A. Mawer, *The Vikings* (Cambridge).

1914   G. C. Donald, *Zur Entwicklung des Prosastils in der Sachsenchronik* (Marburg).

1919   C. Oman, *England before the Norman Conquest* (London).

1922   F. Viglione, *Studio critico-filologico su l'Anglo-Saxon Chronicle, con saggi di traduzioni* (Pavia).

1923   A. Mawer, 'The Redemption of the Five Boroughs' (38 *EHR* 551–7).

1923   J. Armitage Robinson, *The Times of St Dunstan* (Oxford).

1923   K. Jost, 'Wulfstan und die angelsächsische Chronik' (47 *Anglia* 105–123).

1925   F. M. Stenton, 'The South-Western Element in the Old English Chronicle' (*Essays in Medieval History presented to Thomas Frederick Tout*, 15–24, Manchester).

1925   F. P. Magoun, Jr, Two Lexicographical Notes' (40 *MLN* 411–12).

1926   Bruce Dickins, 'The Peterborough Annal for 1137' (2 *RES* 341–3).

1928   R. W. Chambers, *England Before the Norman Conquest* (London).

1928   R. R. Darlington, *The Vita Wulfstani of William of Malmesbury* (III/40 Camden (Royal Historical Society) London).

1929   S. J. Crawford, *Byrhtferth's Manual* (EETS, Original Series, 177, London). An important scientific treatise on the reckoning of time.

1930   Margaret Ashdown, *English and Norse Documents, relating to the Reign of Ethelred the Unready* (Cambridge). Translation of Norse documents.

1930   T. D. Kendrick, *A History of the Vikings* (London).

1932   R. W. Chambers, *On the Continuity of English Prose from Alfred to More and his School* (EETS, Oxford).

1933   F. M. Stenton, 'Medeshamstede and its Colonies' (*Historical Essays in Honour of James Tait* 313–26, Manchester).

1933   F. P. Magoun, Jr, 'Cynewulf, Cyneheard, and Osric' (57 *Anglia* 361–70).

1934   N. R. Ker, 'Some Notes on the Peterborough Chronicle' (3 *Medium Ævum* 136–8).

1934   Heinrich Henel, *Studien zum altenglischen Computus* (Leipzig).

1935   R. H. Hodgkin, *A History of the Anglo-Saxons*, 3rd ed. 1953 (Oxford). 2 vols. Excellent illustrations.

1935   A. H. Smith, 'The Sons of Ragnar Lothbrok' (11 *Saga-Book of the Viking Society* 173–91).

1935   A. Hamilton Thompson (editor), *Bede, His Life, Times and Writings* (Oxford).

1936   R. G. Collingwood and J. N. L. Myres, *Roman Britain and the English Settlements*, 2nd ed. 1937 (Oxford).

1937   E. V. Gordon, *The Battle of Malden* (London).

1937   C. H. Fernquist, 'Study on the O.E. Version of the Anglo-Saxon Chronicle in Cott. Domitian A viii' (13 *Studier modern Språk-vetenskap* 38–103, Uppsala).

1938   Alistair Campbell, *The Battle of Brunanburh* (London).

1938   T. D. Kendrick, *Anglo-Saxon Art to A.D. 900* (London).

1939   C. E. Wright, *The Cultivation of Saga in Anglo-Saxon England* (Edinburgh).

1940   Bruce Dickins, 'The Cult of S. Olave in the British Isles' (12 *Saga Book of the Vikings Society* 53–80).

1940   Dom David Knowles, *The Monastic Order in England*, reprinted 1950 (Cambridge).

1943   F. M. Stenton, *Anglo-Saxon England*, 3rd ed. 1971 (Oxford). Indispensable, with extensive bibliography.

1943   C. W. Jones, *Bedae Opera de Temporibus* (41 *The Mediaeval Academy of America*, Cambridge, Mass.). Essential for the understanding of dating, chronology, etc.

1945   F. P. Magoun, Jr, 'The Domitian Bilingual of the *Old-English Annals*: Notes on the F-Text' (6 *Modern Language Quarterly* 371–380, Harvard).

1945   F. P. Magoun, Jr, 'The Domitian Bilingual of the *Old-English Annals*: The Latin Preface' (20 *Speculum* 65–72).

1946   Wilhelm Levison, *England and the Continent in the Eighth Century* (Oxford).

1947   F. P. Magoun, Jr, '*Annales Domitiani Latini*: An Edition' (9 *Medieval Studies* 235–95, Toronto).

1947 C. W. Jones, *Saints' Lives and Chronicles in Early England* (Ithaca, N.Y.).

1947 Eleanor S. Duckett, *Anglo-Saxon Saints and Scholars* (New York).

1949 Alistair Campbell, *Encomium Emmae Reginae* (III/72 Camden (Royal Historical Society) London).

1949 T. D. Kendrick, *Late Saxon and Viking Art* (London).

1950 M. Charlesworth and M. D. Knowles (editors), *The Heritage of Early Britain* (London).

1951 D. M. Stenton, *English Society in the Early Middle Ages*, 2nd ed. 1952 (London).

1951 A. L. Poole, *From Domesday Book to Magna Carta* (Oxford).

1951 C. E. Wright, 'The Dispersal of the Monastic Libraries and the Beginnings of Anglo-Saxon Studies' (1 *Transactions of the Cambridge Bibliographical Society* 208–37).

1951 G. Turville-Petre, *The Heroic Age of Scandinavia* (London). Brilliant, compressed account.

1952 F. E. Harmer, *Anglo-Saxon Writs* (Manchester). Definitive edition.

1952 F. Wormald, *English Drawings of the Tenth and Eleventh Centuries* (London).

1952 Dorothy Whitelock, *The Beginnings of English Society* (London). The best brief account of Anglo-Saxon life and thought.

1952 D. Talbot Rice, *English Art 871–1100* (Oxford).

1952 Bruce Dickins, *The Genealogical Preface to the Anglo-Saxon Chronicle*, Occasional Papers: No. II (Department of Anglo-Saxon, Cambridge).

1954 Bede, *Ecclesiastical History*, Everyman edition (London). A companion volume.

1954 Cecily Clark, 'Studies in the Vocabulary of the *Peterborough Chronicle*, 1070–1154' (5 *English and Germanic Studies* 67–89).

1954 Cecily Clark, 'Notes on MS. Laud Misc. 636' (23 *Medium Ævum* 71–5).

1955 Dorothy Whitelock, *English Historical Documents*, vol. I (c. 500–1042) (London).

1955 C. E. Wright, *Bald's Leechbook* (Early English Manuscripts in Facsimile, vol. V. Rosenkilde and Bagger, Copenhagen).

1956 P. Hunter Blair, *An Introduction to Anglo-Saxon England* (Cambridge).

1956 A. J. Robertson, *Anglo-Saxon Charters* (Cambridge). Valuable introduction and notes.

1957 N. R. Ker, *Catalogue of Manuscripts containing Anglo-Saxon* (Oxford). Indispensable for any advanced study.

1957 E. Duckett, *Alfred the Great and his England* (London).

1957 *The Bayeux Tapestry*, ed. F. M. Stenton (London). Comprehensive survey by leading authorities.

1959 Dorothy Whitelock, 'The Dealings of the Kings of England with Northumbria in the Tenth and Eleventh Centuries' (*The Anglo-Saxons*, ed. P. Clemoes).

1959 P. Clemoes (ed.), *The Anglo-Saxons* (London).

1960 J. Brøndsted, *The Vikings* (London).

1960 D. M. Wilson, *The Anglo-Saxons*, revised edition (London). Up-to-date account of the archaeological evidence.

1962 A. Campbell, *The Chronicle of Æthelweard* (London).

1962 C. J. Godfrey, *The Church in Anglo-Saxon England* (Cambridge). Background for the ecclesiastical material.

1962 H. R. Loyn, *Anglo-Saxon England and the Norman Conquest* (London).

1962 P. H. Sawyer, *The Age of the Vikings* (London).

1963   P. H. Blair, *Roman Britain and Early England 58 B.C.–A.D. 371* (London).
1963   C. Green, *Sutton Hoo* (London).
1963   C. Brooke, *The Saxon and Norman Kings* (London).
1964   G. N. Garmonsway, *Canute and his Empire* (London).
1966   R. L. S. Bruce-Mitford, *The Sutton Hoo Ship Burial* (British Museum).
1968   Gwyn Jones, *A History of the Vikings* (Oxford).
1969   P. H. Sawyer, 'The Two Viking Ages of Britain', *Medieval Scandinavia*, vol. ii (Odense U.P.).
1970   P. C. Foote and D. M. Wilson, *The Viking Achievement* (London). Comprehensive with beautiful plates.

(b) Place-Names

1924 ff.   Publications of the English Place-Name Society (Cambridge).
1925   A. Mawer, 'Some Place-Name Identifications in the Anglo-Saxon Chronicles' (147 *Palaestra* 41–54, Leipzig).
1935   Eilert Ekwall, *The Concise Oxford Dictionary of English Place-Names*, revised ed. 1960 (Oxford). Essential for the understanding of the geography of the *Chronicle*.
1935   F. P. Magoun, Jr, 'Territorial, Place-, and River-Names in the Old-English Chronicle, A-Text' (18 *Harvard Studies and Notes in Philology and Literature* 69–111).
1938   F. P. Magoun, Jr, 'Territorial, Place-, and River-Names in the Old-English Annals, D-Text' (20 *Harvard Studies and Notes in Philology and Literature* 147–80).
1956   A. H. Smith, *English Place-Name Elements*, 2 vols. (London).
1956   A. H. Smith, 'Place-Names and the Anglo-Saxon Settlement', *Proceedings of the British Academy*.
1960   P. H. Reany, *The Origin of English Place-Names* (London).
1961   K. Cameron, *English Place-Names* (University of Nottingham). Maps and well-chosen illustrations.

(c) Chronology

1901   R. L. Poole, 'The Beginning of the Year in the Anglo-Saxon Chronicles' (16 *EHR* 719–21).
1917   M. L. R. Beaven, 'The Regnal Dates of Alfred, Edward the Elder, and Athelstan' (32 *EHR* 517–31).
1918   M. L. R. Beaven, 'The Beginning of the Year in the Alfredian Chronicle' (33 *EHR* 328–42).
1918   R. L. Poole, *Medieval Reckonings of Time* (Helps for Students of History, No. 3, London).
1924   R. H. Hodgkin, 'The Beginning of the Year in the English Chronicle' (39 *EHR* 497–510).
1926   R. L. Poole, *Chronicles and Annals* (Oxford).
1933   A. E. Stamp, *Methods of Chronology* (92 Hist. Ass. pamphlet, London).
1934   R. L. Poole, *Studies in Chronology and History* (Oxford).
1938   W. S. Angus, 'The Chronology of the Reign of Edward the Elder' (53 *EHR* 194–210).
1939   F. M. Powicke (editor), *Handbook of British Chronology* (Royal Historical Society).
1945   C. R. Cheney, *Handbook of Dates* (Royal Historical Society).
1945   F. T. Wainwright, 'The Chronology of the *Mercian Register*' (60 *EHR* 385–92).
1952   Dorothy Whitelock, 'On the Commencement of the Year in the Saxon Chronicles' in a reprint of C. Plummer, *Two of the Saxon Chronicles Parallel* II. cxxxix–cxliid (Oxford).

1953 K. Sisam, 'Anglo-Saxon Royal Genealogies' (Proc. Brit. Acad. xxxix).
1954 R. Vaughan, 'The Chronology of the Parker Chronicle 890–970' (69 *EHR* 59–66).

III. TRANSLATIONS

1643 A. Wheloc, *Chronologie Anglo-Saxonica* (in Latin).
1692 E. Gibson, *Chronicon Saxonicum* (in Latin).
1819 Anna Gurney, *Saxon Chronicle* (privately circulated).
1823 J. Ingram, *The Saxon Chronicle* (reprinted in Everyman's Library, 1912).
1947 J. A. Giles, *Bede's Ecclesiastical History and the Anglo-Saxon Chronicle* (London).
1853 J. Stevenson, *The Church Historians of England* (vol. II, i).
1861 B. Thorpe, *The Anglo-Saxon Chronicle* (vol. II).
1909 E. E. C. Gomme, *The Anglo-Saxon Chronicle* (London).
1922 F. Viglione, *Studio critico-filologico su l'Anglo-Saxon Chronicle* (Pavia).
1933 Marie Hoffmann-Hirtz, *Une chronique anglo-saxonne, traduite d'après le manuscrit 173 de Corpus Christi College, Cambridge* (Strasbourg).
1951 H. A. Rositzke, *The Peterborough Chronicle* (*Records of Civilization, Sources, and Studies* XLIV, Columbia University Press, New York).
1953 Susie I. Tucker, 'The Anglo-Saxon Chronicle (1042–1154)' in vol. II of *English Historical Documents* (ed. D. C. Douglas).
1955 Dorothy Whitelock, 'The Anglo-Saxon Chronicle (*c.* 500–1042)' in vol. I of *English Historical Documents* (ed. D. C. Douglas).
1960 Gwyn Jones, *Egils Saga* (New York).
1961 P. Foote, *Heimskringla. Sagas of the Norse Kings* (London).
1962 Dorothy Whitelock, with David C. Douglas and Susie I. Tucker, *The Anglo-Saxon Chronicle*. A Revised Translation (London).
1964 Jacqueline Simpson, *Heimskringla. The Olaf Sagas* (London). Olaf Tryggvason in England and the capture of London by St. Olaf.

THE ANGLO-SAXON CHRONICLE

In the year [1] of Christ's Nativity 494, Cerdic and Cynric his son landed at *Cerdicesora* with five ships. That Cerdic was the son of Elesa, the son of Esla, the son of Gewis, the son of Wig, the son of Freawine, the son of Frithugar, the son of Brand, the son of Bældæg, the son of Woden.

Six years after they landed they conquered the kingdom of Wessex. These were the first kings who conquered the land of Wessex from the Welsh. He held the kingdom sixteen years, and when he died his son Cynric succeeded to the kingdom and held it ⟨twenty-six years. When he passed away, his son Ceawlin succeeded and held it⟩ [2] seventeen years. When he died Ceol succeeded to the kingdom and held it six years. When he died his brother Ceolwulf succeeded and ruled seventeen years, and their ancestry goes back to Cerdic. Then Cynegils, Ceolwulf's brother's son, succeeded to the kingdom and ruled thirty-one years, and he was the first of the West Saxon kings to receive baptism. Then Cenwalh succeeded and held it thirty-one years; and that Cenwalh was the son of Cynegils. Then his queen, Seaxburh, held the kingdom one year after him. Then Æscwine, whose ancestry goes back to Cerdic, succeeded to the kingdom and held it two years. Then Centwine, the son of Cynegils, succeeded to the kingdom of Wessex and ruled seven years. Then Caedwalla, whose ancestry goes back to Cerdic, succeeded to the kingdom and held it three years. Then Ine, whose ancestry goes back to Cerdic, succeeded to the kingdom of Wessex and held it thirty-seven years. (*continued on p.* 4)

[1] This Genealogical Preface appears as a separate document in several other manuscripts, which show slight variations from the above, particularly in the regnal years. Some of these versions have recently been conveniently printed by Bruce Dickins, *The Genealogical Preface to the Anglo-Saxon Chronicle* (*Four texts edited to supplement Earle-Plummer*), Occasional Papers: No. II (printed for the Department of Anglo-Saxon, Cambridge 1952).

[2] Supplied from β. Material wanting in any MS., and supplied from other sources, is enclosed in ⟨ ⟩ brackets. Passages in F in round brackets are insertions in that MS. on the margin or above the line. Square brackets are used to enclose explanatory matter.

The [3] island of Britain is eight hundred miles long and two hundred miles broad; and here in this island are five languages: English, British or Welsh, Irish, Pictish, and Latin.[4] The first inhabitants of this land were the Britons, who came from *Armenia* [an error for *Armorica* = Brittany], and took possession at first of the southern part of Britain. Then it happened that Picts came from the south from Scythia with warships, not many, and landed at first in northern Ireland, and there asked the Scots [5] if they might dwell there. But they would not allow them, for they ⟨said that they could not all live together there. And then⟩ [6] said the Scots, 'We can nevertheless give you good advice. We know another island to the east of this where you can settle if you wish, and if anyone resists you, we will help you to conquer it.' Then went the Picts and took possession of the northern part of this land; the southern part was held by the Britons, as we said before. And the Picts asked the Scots for wives, and they were given to them on condition that they always chose their royal race in the female line, and they observed this for a long time afterwards. Then it happened after the course of years that a part of the Scots went from Ireland into Britain (*continued on p. 5*)

---

[3] This preface is in D E F; in C, however, the text is prefaced by a metrical calendar followed by Gnomic Verses.

[4] *English, Welsh, Irish, Pictish, and Latin* D; F follows E, but omits *Latin*; F Lat has *Angli, Britoni, Waloni, Scithi et Picti*. 'By breaking up D's *BrytWylsc* into *Brittisc 7 Wilsc*, E has apparently made six languages.' (Plummer).

[5] Down to the time of Alfred this term *Scottas* refers either to the Scots of Ireland or of the Irish kingdom of Argyll. On the settlement of the 'Scots' in Britain, see C. Plummer, *Baedae Opera* II. 9.

[6] From D

A
from
p. 2 Then Æthelheard, whose ancestry goes back to Cerdic, succeeded and held it fourteen years. Then Cuthred, whose ancestry goes back to Cerdic, succeeded and held it seventeen years. Then Sigeberht, whose ancestry goes back to Cerdic, succeeded and held it one year. Then Cynewulf, whose ancestry goes back to Cerdic, succeeded and held it thirty-one years. Then Beorhtric, whose ancestry goes back to Cerdic, succeeded and held it sixteen years. Then Egbert succeeded to the kingdom and held it thirty-seven years and seven months. Then his son Æthelwulf succeeded and held it eighteen and a half years. That Æthelwulf was the son of Egbert, the son of Ealhmund, the son of Eafa, the son of Eoppa, the son of Ingeld, the son of Cenred; and Ine, Cuthburh and Cwenburh were also children of Cenred. Cenred was the son of Ceolwald, the son of Cuthwulf, the son of Cuthwine, the son of Celin [1] [= Ceawlin], the son of Cynric, the son of Cerdic.

Then Æthelbald his [Æthelwulf's] son succeeded to the kingdom and held it five years. Then his brother Æthelberht succeeded and held it five years. Then their brother Æthelred succeeded and held it five years. Then their brother Alfred succeeded to the kingdom when he was twenty-three years old, and it was three hundred and ninety-six years since his ancestors had first conquered the land of Wessex from the Welsh.

SIXTY years before the Incarnation of Christ, the emperor Julius Caesar was the first of the Romans to come to Britain, and hard pressed the Britons in battle and overcame them, but could not gain a kingdom there.

ANNO 1. Octavian reigned fifty-six years, and in the forty-second year of his reign Christ was born.

2. The astrologers from the east came to show honour to Christ; and, because of Herod's persecution of Christ, the children in Bethlehem were slain.

3. In this year Herod died, stabbed by his own hand, and his son Archelaus succeeded to the kingdom. (continued on p. 6)

---

[1] MS. *celming·celm* in error for *celining·celin.*

and conquered part of the land; the leader of their army was
called Reoda, from this they are named Dæl Reodi.

E

from
p. 3
Sixty years before Christ was born, Julius Caesar, emperor
of the Romans, came to Britain with eighty ships. At first
he was harassed by fierce fighting, and led a great part of his
host to destruction. Then he left his host to remain with the Irish,[1]
and went into Gaul and there gathered six hundred ships, and with
them he went back into Britain. And when they first joined battle,
the emperor's tribune, who was called Labienus, was slain. Then
went the British and staked all the ford of a certain river with great
sharp piles [2] under the water: that river was called the Thames. When
the Romans became aware of this, they would not cross over that ford.
Then the Britons fled to the protection of the woods.[3] The emperor
took very many of the principal strongholds with great labour, and
went back into Gaul.

ANNO 1. Octavian reigned fifty-six years, and in the forty-second year
of his reign Christ was born.

2. The astrologers from the east came to show honour to Christ;
and, because of Herod's persecution, the children in Bethlehem were
slain; and he died, stabbed by his own hand, and his son Archelaus
succeeded to the kingdom. (*continued on p.* 7)

F
3. In this year Herod passed away, and the Christ Child
was carried back from Egypt. (*continued on p.* 6)

---

[1] 'A mistake due to a misreading found in several manuscripts of Bede of
Hibernia for *hiberna*, "winter-quarters."' (Plummer)
[2] *stakes* D
[3] *to the wild woodlands* D

Ā 6
from
p. 4

6. From the beginning of the world to this year had passed away five thousand and two hundred years.

11. *In this year Herod Antipas*[1] *succeeded to the kingdom in Judæa.*[2]

12. Philip and Herod and Lysanias[3] divided Judæa [i.e. the Holy Land] into four tetrarchies.

16. In this year Tiberius succeeded to the kingdom.

27 [26]. *In this year Pilate became procurator over the Jews.*

30. In this year Christ was baptized, and Peter and Andrew converted, and James and John and Philip and the twelve apostles.

33. In this year Christ was crucified, five thousand two hundred and twenty-six years from the beginning of the world.

34. In this year was Paul converted, and St Stephen pelted to death.

35. In this year the blessed apostle Peter occupied the episcopal see in the city of Antioch.

39. In this year Gaius obtained the kingdom.

45. In this year the blessed apostle Peter occupied the episcopal see in Rome.

46. In this year Herod died, he who had slain James one year before his own death.

47. In this year Claudius was the second Roman emperor to come to Britain, and took possession of most of the island, and likewise made the Orkney islands subject to the Roman empire. *This was in the fourth year of his reign; and in this same year arose the great famine in Syria which Luke speaks of in the book of the Acts of the Apostles.*

(*continued on p.* 8)

F
from
p. 5

38. In this year Pilate killed himself with his own hand.

39. Gaius succeeded to the kingdom.

40. Matthew in Judea began to write his gospel.

44. In this year the apostle Peter occupied the episcopal see in Rome. (*continued on p.* 7)

---

[1] The text has *Herod, son of Antipater.* Herod Antipas was the grandson of Antipater, the father of Herod the Great.

[2] The text of Ā has been considerably interpolated. The bulk of these interpolations, probably due to a scribe or scribes of the twelfth century, are printed in *small italics*. Some additions, however, by earlier hands, are printed in small romans, not in *small italics*.

[3] The text misunderstood Luke iii. 1 which refers to the fifteenth year of the reign of Tiberius, when Pilate was governor of Judæa, Herod tetrarch of Galilee, and Philip tetrarch of Iturea and Trachonitis; Lysanias, tetrarch of Abilene, being transformed into the country Lycia.

**E 11
from
p. 5**

11. From the beginning of the world to this year had passed away five thousand and two hundred years.

12. Philip and Herod divided Judæa [the Holy Land] into four kingdoms.

16. In this year Tiberius succeeded to the kingdom.

26. In this year Pilate became procurator over the Jews.

30. In this year Christ was baptized, and Peter and Andrew converted, and James and John and the twelve apostles.

33. In this year Christ was crucified, five thousand two hundred and twenty-six years from the beginning of the world.

34. In this year was St Paul converted, and St Stephen pelted to death.

35. In this year the blessed apostle Peter occupied the episcopal see in the city of Antioch.

39. In this year Gaius obtained the kingdom.

45. In this year the blessed apostle Peter occupied the episcopal see in Rome.

46. In this year Herod died, he who had slain James one year before his own death.

47. In this year Claudius, emperor of the Romans, went with an host to Britain and conquered the island and made all the Picts and Welsh subject to the Roman empire. He finished this campaign in the fourth year of his reign. In this year arose the great famine in Syria which was foretold in the Acts of the Apostles by Agabus the prophet. Then, after Claudius, Nero succeeded to the kingdom, he who in the end lost the island of Britain because of his inactivity. (*continued on p.* 9)

**F 45
from
p. 6**

45. In this year James, the brother of John, was slain by Herod.

46. In this year the emperor Claudius came to Britain and conquered a great part of the island; he also reduced the island of Orkney to Roman rule.

47. Mark the evangelist in Egypt begins to write the gospel.

(*continued on p.* 8)

THE PARKER CHRONICLE (Ā) 62

Ā 62
from
p. 6

62. In this year James, the brother of the Lord, suffered martyrdom.
63. In this year Mark the evangelist passed away.
69. In this year Peter and Paul suffered martyrdom.
70. In this year Vespasian obtained the kingdom.

71. In this year Titus, son of Vespasian, slew one hundred and eleven thousand Jews in Jerusalem.

81. In this year Titus succeeded to the kingdom, he who said that he lost the day on which he did no good.

83.[1] In this year Domitian, brother of Titus, succeeded to the kingdom.

84.[1] In this year John the evangelist in the island of Patmos wrote the Book of the Apocalypse.

99. *In this year Simon the apostle was crucified, and John the evangelist fell asleep in Ephesus.*

101. *In this year pope Clement passed away.*

110. In this year bishop Ignatius suffered martyrdom.

155. *In this year Marcus Antonius and his brother Aurelius succeeded to the kingdom.*

167. In this year Eleutherius received the episcopal see in Rome, and held it gloriously for fifteen years. To him Lucius, king of Britain, sent letters and asked that he might be made a Christian, and he obtained his request, *and they remained afterwards in the true faith until the reign of Diocletian.*

189. In this year Severus obtained the kingdom and reigned seventeen years. In Britain he carried an earthwork from sea to sea; *and then ended his days in York, and his son Bassianus succeeded to the kingdom.*[2] (*continued on p.* 10)

F
from
p. 7

48. In this year was a very severe famine.
49. In this year Nero began to rule.
50. In this year Paul was sent bound to Rome.
62. In this year James, the brother of Christ, suffered martyrdom.
63. Mark the evangelist passed away.

69. In this year Peter suffered martyrdom on the cross and Paul was slain (beheaded).

116. In this year the emperor Hadrian began to rule.

137. In this year Antoninus began to rule. (*continued on p.* 10)

[1] 'The annals 83 and 84 have been altered into 84 and 87. At 90–92 something has been erased. It would seem that the first scribe entered here the notices which the corrector has entered under 99 and 101. The annal 96 has been entered twice.' (Plummer)
[2] 'From 262 to 693 there is a chasm in MS. D.' (Plummer)

8

62. In this year James, the brother of the Lord, suffered martyrdom.

62.[3] In this year Mark the evangelist passed away.

69. In this year Peter and Paul suffered martyrdom.

70. In this year Vespasian obtained the kingdom.

71. In this year Titus, ⟨son of⟩ Vespasian, slew one hundred and eleven thousand Jews in Jerusalem.

81. In this year Titus succeeded to the kingdom, he who said that he lost the day on which he did no good.

84. In this year Domitian, brother of Titus, succeeded to the kingdom.

87. In this year John the evangelist in the island of Patmos wrote the Book of the Apocalypse.

100. In this year Simon the apostle [4] was crucified, and John the evangelist fell asleep [5] in Ephesus.

101. In this year pope Clement passed away.

110. In this year bishop Ignatius suffered martyrdom.

114. Alexander hic constituit aquam benedictam fieri.

124. Syxtus papa hic constituit ymnum decantare Sanctus, Sanctus, Sanctus in officio missæ.

134. Telesphorus papa hic constituit ymnum angelicum cantari GLORIA IN EXCELSIS DEO diebus festis.

155. In this year Marcus Antonius and his brother Aurelius succeeded to the kingdom.

167. In this year Eleutherius received the episcopal see in Rome, and held it gloriously [6] for fifteen years. To him Lucius, king of the Britons, sent men and asked for baptism, and he straightway sent to him, and they remained afterwards in the true faith until the reign of Diocletian.

189. In this year Severus succeeded to the kingdom, and proceeded with a host into Britain, and by battle conquered a great part of the island, and then constructed (continued on p. 10)

---

[3] Altered by a later hand into 63.
[4] F adds the kinsman of Christ.
[5] B C add on that day.
[6] uiriliter regit   F Lat

200. *Two hundred years.*

Ā 200
from
p. 8

283. *In this year St Alban, the martyr, suffered martyrdom.*

300. *Three hundred years.*

379. *In this year Gratian succeeded to the kingdom.*

381. In this year the emperor Maximus succeeded to the kingdom. He was born in Britain and then went into Gaul, *and there he slew the emperor Gratian, and drove his brother, who was called Valentinian, from the country. That Valentinian later gathered an army and slew Maximus and succeeded to the kingdom. At that time arose the heresy of Pelagius throughout the world.*

409. In this year the Goths took the city of Rome by storm, and never afterwards did the Romans rule in Britain: *that was eleven hundred and ten years after it was built. In all they had reigned in Britain four hundred and seventy years since Julius Caesar first came to the country.*

418. In this year the Romans collected all the treasures which were in Britain and hid some in the earth so that no one afterwards could find them, and some they took with them into Gaul.

423. *In this year Theodosius the younger succeeded to the kingdom.*

430. In this year bishop Palladius (*vel Patricius*) was sent by pope Celestine to the Scots to strengthen their faith. (*continued on p.* 12)

a wall of sods and a palisade on the top from sea to sea[1] as a

E 189
from
p. 9

protection for the Britons. He reigned seventeen years and then ended his days in York. His son Bassianus succeeded to the kingdom, his other son who was called Geta perished [at his brother's hands].

202. Victor papa hic constituit ut Pascha die dominico celebretur, sicut predecessor eius Eleutherius.

254. Cornelius papa hic de catacumbas leuauit per noctem corpora apostolorum, et posuit Pauli quidem uia Ostensi ubi decollatus est. Petri autem iuxta locum ubi crucifixus est. (*continued on p.* 11)

F 200
from
p. 8

200. In this year the Holy Cross was found.

(*continued on p.* 12)

---

[1] *Severus in Brittannia magnam fossam firmissimamque vallem crebris turribus communitum per CXXII milia passuum a mari ad mare eduxit* F Lat

286. In this year St Alban, the martyr, suffered martyrdom.

E 286
from
p. 9
311. St Silvester, the twenty-third pope. Huius tempore celebratur Nicenum concilium, Arelatense quoque primum, in quo fuit Auitianus Rotomagi archiepiscopus.

379. In this year Gratian succeeded to the kingdom.

379. Hoc tempore celebratur Constantinopolitanum concilium ·cl· patrum aduersus Macedonum et Eunomium sub Damaso.

380. In this year Maximus succeeded to the kingdom. He was born in Britain and thence went into Gaul, and there he slew the emperor Gratian, and drove his brother, who was called Valentinian, from the country. That Valentinian later gathered an army and slew Maximus and succeeded to the kingdom. At that time arose the heresy of Pelagius throughout the world.

403. Innocentius papa hic misit decretalem epistolam Victricio Rotomagensi archiepiscopo. Hic constituit sabbato ieiunare quia eo die Dominus iacuit in sepulchro.

409. In this year the city of the Romans was taken by assault by the Goths, eleven hundred and ten years after it was built. Afterwards, beyond that, the kings of the Romans ruled no longer in Britain; in all they had reigned there four hundred and seventy years since Julius Caesar first came to the country.

418. In this year the Romans collected all the treasures which were in Britain and hid some in the earth so that no one afterwards could find them, and some they took with them into Gaul.

423. In this year Theodosius the younger succeeded to the kingdom.

425. Huius temporis ætate extitit exordium regnum Francorum, primus Faramundus.

430. In this year Patrick was sent by pope Celestine to preach baptism to the Scots.

431. Hoc tempore diabolus, in Creta Iudeis in specie Moysi apparens, ad terram repromissionis per mare pede sicco perducere promittit; sicque plurimis necatis, reliqui ad Christi gratiam conuertuntur.

433. Celestinus papa: huius tempore aggregata est Ephesina synodus ducentorum episcoporum; cui prefuit Cirillus Alexandrinus presul aduersus Nestorium Constantinopolitanum episcopum.

439. Leo papa: hic sanciuit Calcedonensem sinodum.

(continued on p. 13)

11

Ā 443
from
p. 10

443. *In this year the Britons sent to Rome and asked them for troops against the Picts, but they had none there because they were at war with Attila, king of the Huns; and then they sent to the Angles and made the same request to the princes of the Angles.*

Marcian

449. In this year Mauricius and Valentinian obtained the kingdom and reigned seven years. In their days Hengest and Horsa, invited by Vortigern, king of the Britons, came to Britain at a place which is called *Ypwinesfleot* [Ebbsfleet, K] at first to help the Britons, but later they fought against them. *The king ordered them to fight against the Picts, and so they did and had victory wherever they came. They then sent to Angel; ordered (them) to send them more aid and to be told of the worthlessness of the Britons and of the excellence of the land. They then sent them more aid. These men came from three nations of Germany: from the Old Saxons, from the Angles, from the Jutes. From the Jutes came the people of Kent and the people of the Isle of Wight, that is the race which now dwells in the Isle of Wight, and the race among the West Saxons which is still called the race of the Jutes. From the Old Saxons came the East Saxons and South Saxons and West Saxons. From Angel, which has stood waste ever since between the Jutes and the Saxons, came the East Angles, Middle Angles, Mercians, and all the Northumbrians.*

455. In this year Hengest and Horsa fought against king Vortigern at a place which is called *Agælesþrep* [1] [*Aylesford, K*], and his brother Horsa was slain. And after that Hengest succeeded to the kingdom and Æsc, his son.

457. In this year Hengest and Æsc fought against the Britons at a place which is called *Crecganford* [2] [*Crayford, K*] and there slew four thousand men; and the Britons then forsook Kent and fled to London in great terror.

465. In this year Hengest and Æsc fought against the Welsh near *Wippedesfleot* [2] and there slew twelve Welsh nobles;

(*continued on p.* 14)

444. In this year St Martin passed away.

F 444
from
p. 10

448. In this year John the Baptist showed his head to two monks who came from the east to worship in Jerusalem, at a place which once was Herod's residence. At that same time came the Marcian and Valentinian reigned; and at that time came the Angles to this land, invited by king Vortigern, to help him overcome his enemies. They came to this land with three warships, and their leaders were Hengest and Horsa. First of all they slew the enemies of the king and drove them away, and afterwards they turned against the king and against the Britons, and destroyed them by fire and by the edge of the sword. (*continued on p.* 14)

[1] *Ægelesford* W
[2] The Old English forms of some of the place-names in the earliest annals are given as a matter of interest, and in all cases where they cannot now be identified. The modern form of the place-name is given in *italic* if there is some doubt about the identification. The county abbreviations are those used by the English Place-Name Society.

443. In this year the Britons sent oversea to Rome and
asked them for troops against the Picts, but they had none
there because they were at war with Attila, king of the Huns;
and then they sent to the Angles and made the same request to
the princes of the Angles.

449. Huius tempore celebratur Calcedonense concilium ·dcxxx·
episcoporum aduersus Euticem abbatem et Dioscorum.   In this year
Marcian and Valentinian obtained the kingdom and reigned seven
years.   In their days Vortigern invited the Angles hither, and they then
came hither to Britain [3] in three ships at a place *Heopwinesfleot* [Ebbs-
fleet, K].   King Vortigern gave them land to the south-east of this land
on condition that they fought against the Picts.   They then fought
against the Picts and had victory wherever they came.   Then they sent
to Angel; ordered (them) to send more aid and to be told of the worthlessness of the Britons and of the excellence of the land.   They then at
once sent hither a larger force to help the others.   These men came from
three nations of Germany: from the Old Saxons, from the Angles, from
the Jutes.   From the Jutes came the people of Kent and the people of
the Isle of Wight, that is the race which now dwells in the Isle of Wight,
and the race among the West Saxons which is still called the race of the
Jutes.   From the Old Saxons came the East Saxons and South Saxons
and West Saxons.   From Angel, which has stood waste ever since
between the Jutes and the Saxons, came the East Angles, Middle Angles,
Mercians and all the Northumbrians.   Their leaders were two brothers,
Hengest and Horsa; they were sons of Wihtgils.   Wihtgils was the son
of Witta, the son of Wecta, the son of Woden; from this Woden sprang
all our [4] royal family and that of the peoples dwelling south of the
Humber.

455. In this year Hengest and Horsa fought against king Vortigern
at a place which is called *Ægelesþrep* [*Aylesford, K*], and his brother
Horsa was slain.   And after that Hengest succeeded to the kingdom
and Æsc, his son.

456. In this year Hengest and Æsc fought against the Britons at a
place which is called *Crecganford* [*Crayford, K*], and there slew four
companies; and the Britons then forsook Kent and fled to London in
great terror.

465. In this year Hengest and Æsc fought against the Welsh near
Wippedesfleot,[5] (continued on p. 15)

---

[3] For an excellent account of the invasion, see J. N. L. Myres in *Roman
Britain and the English Settlements* (Oxford 1936), Bk. V.
    [4] i.e. the Northumbrian, cf. Plummer II. § 68.
    [5] *in loco qui dicitur Uuippedes-* (gloss. *vel Wippedes-*) *fleot*   F Lat

and one of their thanes, whose name was Wipped, was slain
there.

473. In this year Hengest and Æsc fought against the Welsh and captured innumerable spoils, and the Welsh fled from the English like fire.[1]

477. In this year Ælle came to Britain and his three sons Cymen, Wlencing, and Cissa with three ships at the place which is called *Cymenesora* [The Owers to the south of Selsey Bill], and there slew many Welsh and drove some to flight into the wood which is called *Andredesleag* [Sussex Weald].

485. In this year Ælle fought against the Welsh near the bank of [the stream] *Mearcrædesburna*.

488. In this year Æsc succeeded to the kingdom, and was king of the people of Kent twenty-four years.

491. In this year Ælle and Cissa besieged *Andredescester* [the Roman fort of Anderida, Pevensey], and slew all the inhabitants; there was not even one Briton left there.

495. In this year two princes,[2] Cerdic and Cynric his son, came to Britain with five ships [arriving] at the place which is called *Cerdicesora*, and the same day they fought against the Welsh.

501. In this year Port and his two sons, Bieda and Mægla, came with two ships to Britain at the place which is called *Portesmuþa* [Portsmouth, Ha], and slew a young Briton, a very noble man.

508. In this year Cerdic and Cynric slew a Welsh king, whose name was Natanleod, and five thousand men with him. The district was afterwards [*or* in consequence] called *Natanleag* as far as *Cerdicesford*.[3]

514. In this year the West Saxons, Stuf and Wihtgar, came to Britain with three ships [arriving] at the place which is called *Cerdicesora*, and fought against the Britons and put them to flight.

(*continued on p.* 16)

482. In this year the blessed abbot Benedict became illustrious throughout this world through the glory of his miracles, as the blessed Gregory tells in the book of Dialogues.

509. In this year St Benedict the abbot, the father of all monks, went to heaven. (*continued on p.* 17)

A 465
from
p. 12

F 482
from
p. 12

---

[1] *as one flies from fire* F

[2] MSS. *aldormen*, perhaps a translation of *principes* (H. M. Shadwick, *The Origin of the English Nation*, p. 20, note 1); *duces duo* F Lat

[3] The *Oxford Dictionary of Place-Names* gives Netley Marsh Ha and Charford Ha for *Natanleag* and *Cerdicesford* respectively.

and there slew twelve Welsh nobles; and one of their own thanes, whose name was Wipped, was slain there.[3]

E 465 from p. 13

473. In this year Hengest and Æsc fought against the Welsh and captured innumerable spoils, and the Welsh fled from the English as fast as possible.

477. In this year Ælle came to Britain and his three sons Cymen, Wlencing, and Cissa with three ships at the place which is called *Cymenesora* [The Owers to the south of Selsey Bill], and there slew many Welsh and drove some to flight into the wood which is called *Andredesleg* [Sussex Weald].

485. In this year Ælle fought against the Welsh near the bank of [the stream] *Mearcredesburna*.

488. In this year Æsc succeeded to the kingdom, and was king thirty-four years.

490. Hoc tempore beatus Mamertus, episcopus Uiennensis, solennes letanias instituit rogationum.

491. In this year Ælle and Cissa besieged *Andredesceaster* [the Roman fort of Anderida, Pevensey], and slew all the inhabitants; there was not even one Briton left there.

495. In this year two princes,[2] Cerdic and Cynric his son, came to Britain with five ships [arriving] at the place which is called *Certicesora*, and the same day they fought against the Welsh.

501. In this year Port and his two sons, Bieda and Mægla, came with two ships to Britain at the place which is called *Portesmuða* [Portsmouth, Ha], and immediately seized land and slew a young Briton, a very noble man.

508. In this year Cerdic and Cynric slew a Welsh king, whose name was Nazaleod, and five thousand men with him. The district was afterwards [*or* in consequence] called *Nazanleog* all the way to *Certicesford*.

514. In this year the West Saxons, Stuf and Wihtgar, came to Britain with three ships [arriving] at the place which is called *Certicesora*, and fought against the Britons and put them to flight.

(*continued on p. 17*)

---

[3] *Ibi etiam quidam perdives nomine Uuipped ex parte Hengest occiditur* F Lat

519. In this year Cerdic and Cynric obtained

A 519 *of the West Saxons*
from the kingdom; and the same year they fought against the
p. 14 Britons at a place now called *Cerdicesford. And from that day on the princes of the West Saxons have reigned.*

527. In this year Cerdic and Cynric fought against the Britons at the place which is called *Cerdicesleag.*

530. In this year Cerdic and Cynric obtained possession of the Isle
many
of Wight and slew a few men at *Wihtgaræsburh.*

534. In this year Cerdic passed away, and his son Cynric continued to
all the Isle of Wight
reign twenty-six years. They gave the Isle of Wight to their two *nefan,*[1] Stuf and Wihtgar.

538. In this year the sun was eclipsed on 16 February from early morning until nine in the morning.

540. In this year the sun was eclipsed on 20 June, and the stars appeared very nearly half an hour after nine in the morning.

544. In this year Wihtgar passed away and was buried at *Wihtgaraburh.*

547. In this year Ida, from whom sprang the royal race of the
and reigned
Northumbrians, succeeded to the kingdom. [2] ⟨Ida was the son of *twelve years. He built Bamburgh, which was first enclosed by a stockade* Eoppa, the son of Esa, the son of Ingui, the son of Angenwit, the *and thereafter by a rampart.* son of Aloc, the son of Benoc, the son of Brand, the son of Bældæg, the son of Woden, the son of Freotholaf,[3] the son of Frithuwulf, the son of Finn, the son of Godwulf, the son of Geat.⟩

552. In this year Cynric fought against the Britons at the place called *Searoburh* [Old Sarum, W], and put the Britons to flight. Cerdic was Cynric's ⟨father. Cerdic was the son of Elesa, the son of Esla, the son of Gewis, the son of Wig, the son of Freawine, the son of Frithugar, the son of Brand, the son of Bældæg, the son of Woden.⟩

556. In this year Cynric and Ceawlin fought against the Britons at *Beranburh* [Barbury castle, W]. (*continued on p.* 18)

---

[1] 'Since *nefa* means both *grandson* and *nephew* it may here correctly denote relationship to two persons who were themselves father and son.' (Chadwick)

[2] 'The original text of A has been erased by a later scribe in order to make room for matter more interesting to himself. His substituted text is given in interlined italics. The same is the case at 560, 565, 603, 604, 626. At 552 and 611 the genealogy has been erased, but nothing put in its place. In all these cases the text in brackets is that of B and C, and various readings are given from W.' (Plummer)

[3] *Freotholaf* for *Frealaf.*

16

519. In this year Cerdic and Cynric obtained the kingdom
E 519 of the West Saxons, and the same year they fought against the
from Britons at a place now called *Certicesford*. And from that day
p. 15 on the princes of the West Saxons have reigned.

527. In this year Cerdic and Cynric fought against the
Britons at the place which is called *Certicesford*.

528. Hoc tempore Dionisius in urbe *Romae* circulum paschalem
composuit. Tunc Priscianus profunda grammatica rimatus est.

530. In this year Cerdic and Cynric obtained possession of the Isle of
Wight, and slew many men at *Wihtgarasburh*.

534. In this year Cerdic passed away, and his son Cynric continued
to reign twenty-six years. They gave all the Isle of Wight to their
two *nefan*, Stuf and Wihtgar.

538. In this year the sun was eclipsed on 16 February from early
morning until nine in the morning.

540. In this year the sun was eclipsed on 20 June, and the stars
appeared very nearly half an hour after nine in the morning.

544. In this year Wihtgar passed away and was buried at *Wihtgarasburh*.

547. In this year Ida, from whom originally sprang the royal race of
the Northumbrians, succeeded to the kingdom and reigned twelve
years. He built Bamburgh, which was first enclosed by a stockade
and thereafter by a rampart.

552. In this year Cynric fought against the Britons at the place called
Searoburh [Old Sarum, W], and put the Britons to flight.

556. In this year Cynric and Ceawlin fought against the Britons at
Beranburh [Barbury Castle, W]. (*continued on p.* 19)

552. In this year Cynric fought against the Britons at the
F 552 place called *Sælesberi* [Salisbury, W]. And Æthelberht was
from born in the . . ., the son of Eormenric, and in the . . . tenth
p. 14 year of his reign he was the first of the kings in Britain to
receive baptism. (*continued on p.* 20)

17

Æ 560
from
p. 16
reigned thirty years.

560. In this year Ceawlin succeeded to the kingdom in Wessex, and Ælle succeeded to the kingdom of the North- *Ida having died, and each of them* umbrians.[1] ⟨Ælle was the son of Yffe, the son of Uxfrea, the son of Wilgisl, the son of Westerfalca, the son of Sæfugl, the son of Sæbald, the son of Sigegeat, the son of Swebdæg, the son of Sigegar, the son of Wægdæg, the son of Woden.⟩

In this year Æthelberht succeeded to the kingdom of Kent and ruled fifty-three years. In his days Gregory sent baptism to us, and the priest Columba 565. ⟨In this year Columba the priest came from Ireland to Britain to instruct the Picts, and made a monastery on the island of Iona.⟩ *came to the Picts, and converted them to the faith of Christ—they are inhabitants along the northern mountains—and their king gave him the island which is called Iona where there are five 'hides' of land, according to what men say. There that Columba built a monastery, and he was abbot there thirty-two years, and there he passed away when he was seventy-seven years old. His heirs still have that holy place. The South Picts had been baptized by bishop Ninian who had been educated in Rome. His church is Whithorn, consecrated in the name of St Martin; there he rests with many holy men. Now there must always be an abbot in Iona, not a bishop, and all the bishops of the Scots must be subject to him, because Columba was an abbot, not a bishop.*

568. In this year Ceawlin and Cutha fought against Æthelberht and drove him into Kent; and they slew two princes,[2] Oslaf [3] and Cnebba, at Wibbandun.

571. In this year Cuthwulf fought against the Britons at *Bedcanford* and captured four villages,[3] Limbury, Aylesbury, Benson, and Eynsham; and in the same year he passed away.

577. In this year Cuthwine and Ceawlin fought against the Britons and slew three kings, Coinmail, Condidan, and Farinmail, at the place which is called Dyrham; and they captured three cities,[4] Gloucester, Cirencester, and Bath.

583. *In this year Maurice succeeded to the empire of the Romans.*

(continued on p. 20)

---

[1] i.e. Deira.   [2] MSS. *aldormen* cf. p. 14, note 2.
[3] So B C, *Oslac* F as E

18

E 560 from p. 17

560. In this year Ceawlin obtained the kingdom in Wessex, and Ælle succeeded to the kingdom of the Northumbrians, Ida having died, and each of them reigned thirty years.

565. In this year Æthelberht succeeded to the kingdom of Kent and ruled fifty-three years. In his days Gregory sent baptism to us, and the priest Columba came to the Picts and converted them to the faith of Christ—they are inhabitants along the northern mountains—and their king gave him the island which is called Iona where there are five 'hides' of land according to what men say. There that Columba built a monastery, and he was abbot there thirty-two years, and there he passed away when he was seventy-seven years old. His heirs still have that holy place. The South Picts had been baptized much earlier: bishop Ninian, who had been educated in Rome, preached baptism to them. His church and collegiate minster is at Whithorn, consecrated in the name of St Martin; there he rests with many holy men. Now there must always be an abbot in Iona, not a bishop, and all the bishops of the Scots must be subject to him, because Columba was an abbot, not a bishop.

568. In this year Ceawlin and Cutha fought against Æthelberht and drove him into Kent; and they slew two princes,[1] Oslac and Cnebba, at *Wibbandun.*

571. In this year Cutha fought against the Britons at *Biedcanford* and captured four villages,[4] Limbury, Aylesbury, Benson, and Eynsham; and in the same year he passed away. That Cutha was the brother of Ceawlin.

577. In this year Cuthwine and Ceawlin fought against the Britons and slew three kings, Coinmail, Condidan, and Farinmail, at the place which is called Dyrham; and they captured three cities,[5] Gloucester, Cirencester, and Bath.

583. In this year Maurice succeeded to the empire of the Romans.

(*continued on p. 21*)

---

[4] MSS. *tunas*   [5] MSS. *ceastra*; *tres civitates*   F Lat

19

584. In this year Ceawlin and Cutha fought against the
Ā 584 Britons at the place which is called *Feþanleag* [*nr. Stoke Lyne,*
from *O*], and Cutha was slain; and Ceawlin captured many villages
p. 18 and countless booty, and departed in anger to his own [terri-
tories].

588. In this year king Ælle passed away, and Æthelric reigned five
years after him.

ric   six

591. Ceol reigned five years.

592. In this year there was great slaughter at Adam's Grave [in
Alton Priors, W], and Ceawlin was expelled. *Gregory succeeded to the
papacy in Rome.*

593. In this year Ceawlin and Cwichelm and Crida perished. Æthelfrith succeeded to the kingdom *of Northumbria.*

595. *In this year pope Gregory sent Augustine to Britain with very many
monks who preached God's word to the English nation.*

597. In this year Ceolwulf began to reign in Wessex, and ever fought
and made war either against the Angles, or against the Welsh, or against
the Picts, or against the Scots. He was the son of Cutha, the son of
Cynric, the son of Cerdic, the son of Elesa, the son of Esla, the son of
Gewis, the son of Wig, the son of Freawine, the son of Frithugar, the
son of Brand, the son of Bældæg, the son of Woden.

601. In this year pope Gregory sent the pallium to archbishop'
Augustine in Britain, and very many religious teachers to help him, and
Bishop Paulinus [who] converted Edwin, king of Northumbria, to
Christianity.

Aedan, king of the Irish [*in W. Scotland*], *fought against Dælreoda* [1]
603. In this year ⟨was a battle at *Egesanstan.*⟩
*and against Æthelfrith, king of Northumbria, at Dægstan; and almost all his
host was slain.*

Augustine consecrated two bishops, Mellitus and Justus. He sent
604. In this year ⟨the East Saxons received the faith and baptism
Mellitus to preach Christianity to the East Saxons; there the king was called
at the font at the hands of king Sæberht and bishop Mellitus.⟩
*Sæberht, the son of Ricole, Æthelberht's sister, whom Æthelberht appointed
as king. Æthelberht gave Mellitus an episcopal see in London, and to Justus
a see in Rochester which is twenty-four miles from Canterbury.*

(*continued on p.* 22)

F 597 597. In this year came Augustine and his companions to
from England.
p. 17
(*continued on p.* 22)

[1] Aedan was king of the Dalreodi, the people of the Scottish (Irish)
kingdom of Dalriada, roughly co-extensive with the modern county of
Argyll. E and the inset Ā misunderstood Bede's account of the battle.
(*EH* I. 34)

20

584. In this year Ceawlin and Cutha fought against the
Britons at the place which is called *Feþanlea* [*nr. Stoke Lyne, O*],
and Cutha was slain; and Ceawlin captured many villages and
countless booty.

588. In this year king Ælle passed away, and Æthelric
reigned five years after him.

591. Ceolric [2] ruled six years. Gregorius papa hic augmentauit in
predicatione canonem: Diesque nostros in tua pace disponas.

592. In this year Gregory succeeded to the papacy in Rome. There
was great slaughter in Britain this year at Adam's Grave [in Alton
Priors, W], and Ceawlin was expelled.

593. In this year Ceawlin and Cwichelm and Crida perished.
Æthelfrith succeeded to the kingdom of Northumbria. He was the
son of Æthelric, the son of Ida.

596. Hoc tempore monasterium sancti Benedicti a Longobardis
destructum est. In this year pope Gregory sent Augustine to Britain
with very many monks who preached God's word to the English nation.

597. In this year Ceolwulf began to reign in Wessex, and ever fought
and made war either against the Angles, or against the Welsh, or against
the Picts, or against the Scots.

601. In this year pope Gregory sent the pallium to archbishop
Augustine in Britain, and very many religious teachers to help him, and
Bishop Paulinus [who] converted Edwin, king of Northumbria, to
Christianity.

603. In this year Aedan, king of the Irish [in W. Scotland], fought
against Deolreda [1] and against Æthelfrith, king of Northumbria, at
Dægsanstan; and almost all his host was slain. There Theodbald,
Æthelfrith's brother, was slain with all his retinue. Thereafter no
king of the Scots dared lead a host against this nation. Hering, son of
Hussa, led the host thither.

604. In this year Augustine consecrated two bishops, Mellitus and
Justus. He sent Mellitus to preach Christianity to the East Saxons;
there the king was called Sæberht, the son of Ricole, Æthelberht's

(*continued on p.* 23)

---

[2] Ceol, the original reading of A, is no doubt correct. The source of the
error is evident in the Anglo-Saxon: Ceol ricsode (Ā) has become Ceolric
rixade (E) by repetition of the syllable -*ric*.

606. In this year Gregory passed away, ten years after he had
Ā **606** sent us Christianity.[1]
from 607. In this year Ceolwulf fought against the South Saxons.
p. 20 *In this year Æthelfrith led his levies to Chester and there slew a
countless number of Welsh: and so was Augustine's prophecy fulfilled
which he spoke, 'If the Welsh refuse peace with us, they shall perish at the
hands of the Saxons.' Two hundred priests were also slain there who had
come thither to pray for the Welsh host. Their leader was called Scrocmail
[Bede recte Brocmail], who was one of the fifty who escaped thence.*

611. In this year Cynegils succeeded to the kingdom in Wessex and
ruled thirty-one years. ⟨That Cynegils was the son of Ceol, the son of
Cutha, the son of Cynric.⟩

614. In this year Cynegils and Cwichelm fought at *Beandun,*[2] and slew
two thousand and sixty-five Welsh.[3]

616. In this year Æthelberht, king of Kent, passed away, and Eadbald, his son, succeeded to the kingdom.[4] *He abandoned Christianity
and followed heathen custom, having his father's widow to wife. Then
Laurentius, who was archbishop in Kent, decided to go south oversea* [5] *and
abandon all, but the apostle Peter came to him at night and fiercely scourged
him because he wished to forsake God's flock; and ordered him to go to the
king and preach the true faith to him. And so he did, and the king was converted to the true faith. In the days of this king the archbishop Laurentius,
who succeeded Augustine in Kent,*

(*continued on p.* 24)

614. ... Laurentius became archbishop, he whom Augustine
F 614 in his holy lifetime [had consecrated] to be archbishop there.[6]
from 616. In this year Æthelberht, king of Kent, passed away (he
p. 20 was the first of the English kings to receive baptism; he was the
son of Eormenric): he reigned fifty-three years. After him his
son Eadbald succeeded to the kingdom. He abandoned Christianity,
having his father's widow to wife. At that time Laurentius was archbishop, and because of the grief he had on account of the king's
unbelief, he had decided to abandon all this land and go oversea.
But the apostle Peter scourged him fiercely one night, because he wished
so to forsake God's flock; and ordered him to teach the true faith boldly
to the king. And so he did, and the king was converted to the true
faith. In the time of this same king Eadbald, the same Laurentius
passed away. The holy Augustine (while alive and in health) had consecrated him bishop in order that Christ's congregation, which was still
young in England, should not be without an archbishop for any length
of time after his decease. After him Mellitus, who had been bishop of
London, succeeded to the archiepiscopal see; and within five years of the
decease of Laurentius, while Eadbald was reigning, Mellitus departed to
Christ.

619. In this year archbishop Laurentius passed away.

(*continued on p.* 28)

[1] *His father was called Gordianus and his mother Silvia* B C
[2] *Beamdun* B C

**E 604
from
p. 21**

sister, whom Æthelberht appointed as king. Æthelberht gave Mellitus an episcopal see in London, and to Justus a see in Rochester which is twenty-four miles from Canterbury.

605. In this year pope Gregory passed away. In the same year Æthelfrith led his levies to Chester and there slew a countless number of Welsh; and so was Augustine's prophecy fulfilled which he spoke, 'If the Welsh refuse peace with us, they shall perish at the hands of the Saxons.' Two hundred priests were also slain there who had come thither to pray for the Welsh host. Their leader was called Brocmail, who was one of the fifty who escaped thence.[7]

607. In this year Ceolwulf fought against the South Saxons.

611. In this year Cynegils succeeded to the kingdom in Wessex and ruled thirty-one years.

614. In this year Cynegils and Cwichelm fought at *Beandun*, and slew two thousand and sixty-five Welsh.

616. In this year Æthelberht, king of Kent, passed away; he reigned fifty-six years. After him his son Eadbald succeeded to the kingdom, who abandoned Christianity and followed heathen custom, having his father's widow to wife. Then Laurentius, who was archbishop in Kent, decided to go south to Rome and abandon everything, but the apostle Peter came to him at night and fiercely scourged him because he wished so to forsake God's flock; and ordered him to go to the king and preach the true faith to him. And so he did, and the king was converted and was baptized. In the days of this king, archbishop Laurentius, who succeeded Augustine in Kent, passed away, and was buried beside Augustine on 2 February. After him Mellitus, who had been bishop of London, succeeded to the archiepiscopal dignity. At that time the people of London, where Mellitus had been, were heathen;

(*continued on p.* 24)

---

[3] *forty-five* B C; *forty-six* W

[4] *and from the beginning of the world to this same year had passed away five thousand and eight hundred years* B C; *and six hundred and sixteen* W

[5] suð ofer sæ, cf. Dorothy Whitelock, *Chadwick Memorial Studies* 270.

[6] Cropped by the binder. The Latin is *Hoc anno vii Kalendas Iunii beatus Augustinus, finito labore huius erumnosæ vitæ, adeptus est consortium angelorum; qui fuit apostolus Anglorum, anno Dominicæ Incarnationis DCXIIII. Cui successit Laurentius, quem ipse adhuc vivens Augustinus ad hoc consecravit, ut ei succederet in archiepiscopatu.*

[7] *Scrocmagil* F Lat

23

passed away on 2 February, and was buried beside Augustine. After
Ā 616 *him Mellitus, who was bishop of London, succeeded to the archi-*
from *episcopal dignity, and within five years of this Mellitus passed away.*
p. 22 *Then after him Justus succeeded to the archiepiscopal dignity: he was*
bishop of Rochester, and he consecrated Romanus bishop there.

625. In this year Paulinus was consecrated bishop of Northumbria by archbishop Justus.

626. In this year Eanfled, daughter of king Edwin, was baptized on the holy eve of Whit Sunday [6 June]. Penda ruled for thirty years: he was fifty when he succeeded to the kingdom. ⟨Penda was the son of Pybba, the son of Creoda, the son of Cynewald, the son of Cnebba, the son of Icel, the son of Eomer,[1] the son of Angeltheow, the son of Offa,[1] the son of Wermund,[1] the son of Wihtlæg,[1] the son of Woden.⟩

627. In this year king Edwin and his court [2] were baptized at Easter.

628. In this year Cynegils and Cwichelm fought against Penda at Cirencester, and then they came to an agreement.

632. In this year Eorpwald was baptized.

633. In this year Edwin was slain, and Paulinus returned to Kent and occupied the episcopal see in Rochester. (*continued on p.* 26)

and five years after, while Eadbald was reigning, Mellitus went
E 616 to Christ. Then Justus succeeded to the archiepiscopal
from dignity, and he consecrated Romanus to Rochester, where he
p. 23 had formerly been bishop.

617. In this year Æthelfrith, king of Northumbria, was slain by Rædwald, king of East Anglia, and Edwin, son of Ælle, succeeded to the kingdom, and conquered all Britain except Kent alone, and drove out the princes, the sons of Æthelfrith: the eldest was Eanfrith, [then] Oswald, Oswy, Oslac, Oswudu, Oslaf, and Offa.

624. In this year archbishop Mellitus passed away.

625. In this year archbishop Justus consecrated Paulinus bishop on 21 July. Hic ciclus Dionisii quinque decennouenalibus constans, hoc est ·xcv· (*continued on p.* 25)

---

[1] On these personages see H. M. Chadwick, *op. cit.* 131–3.
[2] On the meaning of *þeod*, 'warriors old and young in the personal service of the king,' see H. M. Chadwick, *The Origin of the English Nation* 156–7. For a similar use of the word, see annals 794, 823.

annis, sumitque exordium a xxx° anno Incarnationis Domini,
E 625 et desinit in ·dc·xxvi· anno. Hic ordo decennouenalis quem
from Græci Ennia kaith Iohannes papa Kaderida uocat, a *Sanctis*
p. 24 patribus in Nicea Sinodo fuit constitutus, in quo ·xiiii· luna
Paschalis omni anno sine ulla dubitatione.[3]

626. In this year Eomer came from Cwichelm, king of Wessex: he
meant to stab king Edwin, but he stabbed Lilla, his thane, and Forthhere,
and wounded the king. That same night a daughter was born to
Edwin, who was called Eanfled. Then the king promised Paulinus to
give his daughter to God, if he by his prayers would obtain from God
that he might overthrow his enemy who had sent the assassin there.
And he went into Wessex with levies and slew five kings there and
killed a great number of the people. And Paulinus baptized his
daughter on Whit Sunday with eleven others, and within a twelve-
month the king was baptized at Easter with all his nobility; that year
Easter was on 12 April. This was done in York, where previously he
had ordered a church to be built of wood; it was consecrated in the
name of St Peter. There the king gave Paulinus an episcopal see, and
afterwards ordered a larger church to be built there of stone. In this
year Penda succeeded to the kingdom, and reigned thirty years.

627. In this year king Edwin was baptized by Paulinus; and this
same Paulinus also preached Christianity in Lindsey, where the first
to be converted was a certain powerful man called Blecca [4] with all his
chief men. At this time Honorius, who sent the pallium here to
Paulinus, succeeded Boniface to the papacy. And archbishop Justus
died on 10 November, and Honorius was consecrated by Paulinus at
Lincoln; to Honorius this pope also sent the pallium, and he sent a
letter to the Scots enjoining them to adopt the correct Easter.

628. In this year Cynegils and Cwichelm fought against Penda at
Cirencester, and then they came to an agreement.

632. In this year Eorpwald was baptized.

633. In this year king Edwin was slain by Cadwallon and Penda at
Hatfield Chase on 14 October; and he had ruled seven [*recte* seven-
teen] years. His son Osfrith was also slain with him. Then afterwards went Cadwallon and Penda and laid waste the whole of Northumbria. When Paulinus saw this, then he took Æthelburh, Edwin's
widow, and went (*continued on p.* 26)

---

[3] The Easter Table (the Cycle) of Dionysius ran from 532 to 626, extending
for 95 years. It was, as the Latin annal states, a nineteen-year cycle, called
in Greek *enneakaidekaetērida* (the words *Iohannes papa* appear in the middle
of the word in error), in Latin *decemnovenalis*; the OE phrase is *þa
nigontynlican hringas* (cf. O.E. Bede v. 21, and Byrhtferth's *Manual* (ed.
Crawford) 146). It was widely adopted after the Council of Nicea, A.D. 325.

In adopting a cycle of 19 years, the lunar and solar years are reconciled by
intercalating 7 lunar months every 19 years. The solar year is longer by
10·875 days each year [365·2422 days as against 354·3672 (12 × 29·5306
days)]. In 19 years, longer by 206·625 days, which is almost exactly 7 lunar
months [7 × 29·5306 = 206·7142 days]. See C. W. Jones, *op. cit.* 11, 31,
and R. L. Poole, *Studies in Chronology and History* (Oxford 1934), 28–37.

[4] *praefectus* (*EH* II. 16), translated *gerefa* 'reeve' in the OE version.

634. In this year bishop Birinus preached Christianity to the
Ā **634** West Saxons.
from   **635.** In this year Cynegils was baptized by Birinus, bishop of
p. 24   Dorchester, and Oswald stood sponsor for him.
          636. In this year Cwichelm was baptized at Dorchester, and
the same year he passed away.   And bishop Felix preached the faith of
Christ to the East Anglians.[1]
          639. In this year Birinus baptized Cuthred at Dorchester and stood
sponsor for him.
          640. In this year Eadbald, king of Kent, passed away; he had reigned
twenty-five years.[2]   *He had two sons Eormenred and Eorcenberht, and
Eorcenberht reigned there after his father.   Eormenred begat two sons, who
were afterwards martyred by Thunor.*
          642. In this year Oswald, king of Northumbria, was slain.[3]
          643. In this year Cenwalh succeeded to the kingdom of Wessex, and
ruled thirty-one years; and that Cenwalh ordered the church at Winchester to be built.
          644. In this year Paulinus passed away: he was archbishop of York
and later (bishop) of Rochester.
          645. In this year Cenwalh was expelled by king Penda.
          646. In this year Cenwalh was baptized. (*continued on p.* 28)

          by ship to Kent, and Eadbald and Honorius received him very
E 633 honourably and gave him the episcopal see at Rochester, and
from   he remained there until his death.
p. 25   **634.** In this year Osric, whom Paulinus had baptized, suc-
                                              Deira
          ceeded to the kingdom of the Deirans (*continued on p.* 27)

---

[1] *Hic de Burgundiæ partibus uenit episcopus quidam nomine Felix, qui
predicauit fidem populis Orientalium Anglorum, hic accersitus a Sigeberto
rege suscepit episcapatum* (sic) *in Domuce: in quo sedit ·xvii· annis*   F Lat
          [2] So B C; *xxiiii*   F
          [3] 'B and C place the death of Oswald *and* the succession of Cenwalh
under 641; and the building of the *old* church at Winchester under 642.'
(Plummer) Oswald was defeated and killed on 5 August 641.   Cenwalh's
accession was probably in 643.   The founding of the Old Minster at Winchester must have been after 645 since Cenwalh was still a heathen when
expelled from Wessex in that year.

E 634
from
p. 26 he was the son of Ælfric, Edwin's paternal uncle: and to Bernicia succeeded Æthelfrith's son, Eanfrith. Also in this year Birinus first preached Christianity to the West Saxons under king Cynegils. That Birinus came thither at the command of pope Honorius, and he was bishop there until his life's end. And also in this year Oswald succeeded to the kingdom of Northumbria, and he reigned nine years. That ninth year was assigned to him on account of the heathen practices which had been performed by those who had reigned that one year between him and Edwin [i.e. Osric and Eanfrith].[4]

635. In this year Cynegils was baptized by Birinus, bishop of Dorchester, and Oswald, king of Northumbria, stood sponsor for him.

636. In this year Cwichelm was baptized at Dorchester-on-Thames, and the same year he passed away. And bishop Felix preached the faith of Christ to the East Anglians.

639. In this year Birinus baptized Cuthred at Dorchester and stood sponsor for him.

639 [640]. In this year Eadbald, king of Kent, passed away; he had been king twenty-four years. Then his son Eorcenberht succeeded to the kingdom; he put down all heathen practices [5] in his realm, and was the first of the English kings to enforce the observance of Lent. His daughter was called Eorcengota, a holy virgin and a remarkable person, whose mother was Seaxburh, daughter of Anna, king of the East Anglians.

641. In this year Oswald, king of Northumbria, was slain by Penda the Mercian at *Maserfeld* [*Oswestry, Sa*], on 5 August, and his body was buried at Bardney. His holiness and miracles were afterwards abundantly made manifest throughout this island, and his hands are at Bamburgh uncorrupted. And in this year Cenwalh succeeded to the kingdom of Wessex and ruled twenty-one years. That Cenwalh ordered the church at Winchester to be built; and he was the son of Cynegils. And the same year that Oswald was slain, his brother Oswy succeeded to the Northumbrian kingdom, and he reigned twenty-eight years.

643 [644].[6] In this year archbishop Paulinus passed away in Rochester on 10 October; he was a bishop for nineteen years two months and twenty-one days. And in this year Oswine, the son of Osric, the son of Edwin's paternal uncle, succeeded to the kingdom of the Deirans, and reigned seven years.

644 [645]. In this year Cenwalh was expelled by king Penda.

645 [646].[6] In this year Cenwalh was baptized.

(*continued on p.* 28]

---

[4] On the regnal years of the Northumbrian kings, see Peter Hunter Blair, 'The Moore Memoranda on Northumbrian History' (*Chadwick Memorial Studies, esp.* pp. 248 ff.).

[5] Or possibly 'idols': Bede has *idola*.

[6] 'From 642 to 647, E is one year behind Ā. Then by the omission of 647 in E harmony is restored; but they diverge again immediately.' (Plummer)

648. In this year Cenwalh gave his kinsman Cuthred [1] 'three
Ā 648 thousands' of land [2] by Ashdown: [3] that Cuthred was the son
from of Cwichelm, the son of Cynegils.
p. 26 650. In this year Agilbert of Gaul received the episcopal see
of Wessex after Birinus, the Roman bishop.

651. In this year king Oswine was killed, and bishop Aidan passed
away.

652. In this year Cenwalh fought at Bradford on Avon.

653. In this year the Middle Saxons [*recte* Angles [4]] under Peada
the ealdorman received the true faith.

654. In this year king Anna was killed; and Botwulf began to build a
monastery at *Icanhoh*.

655. In this year Penda perished, and the Mercians became Christians. Then five thousand eight hundred and fifty years had passed
away from the beginning of the world. And Peada, son of Penda,
succeeded to the kingdom of Mercia. (*continued on p.* 32)

648. In this year was built the church at Winchester which
F 648 king Cenwalh had made and consecrated in St Peter's name.
from 650. In this year bishop Birinus passed away, and Agilbert
p. 22 the Frank was consecrated.

(*continued on p.* 38)

648. In this year Cenwalh gave his kinsman Eadred 'three
E 648 thousands' of land by Ashdown.
from 649. In this year Agilbert of Gaul received the episcopal sees [5]
p. 27 of the Saxons after Birinus, the Roman bishop.

650. In this year, on 20 August, king Oswy ordered king
Oswine to be killed; and twelve days later bishop Aidan passed away on
31 August.

652. In this year the Middle Angles under Penda [*recte* Peada] the
ealdorman received the true faith.

653. In this year king Anna was killed, and Botwulf began

(*continued on p.* 29)

---

[1] So B C
[2] *three thousand 'hides' of land* B C. 'Is it possible that the grant in
question was the origin of Berkshire?' (H. M. Chadwick, *Studies on
Anglo-Saxon Institutions* 287 *q.v.*)
[3] i.e. the line of the Berkshire Downs. Cf. A Mawer, *Some Place-Name
Identifications in the Anglo-Saxon Chronicle* (147 *Palaestra* 43).
[4] So B C; cf. E
[5] *biscopdomas*, probably a proleptic use of the plural. The West-Saxon
diocese was not divided till 705. There is nothing in Bede to account for
the plural.

28

E 653
from
p. 28

to build a monastery at *Icanhoh*. And in this year archbishop Honorius passed away on 30 September.

654. In this year Oswy slew Penda at *Winwidfeld* and thirty princes with him, and some of them were kings; one of them was Æthelhere, brother of Anna, king of East Anglia. Then five thousand eight hundred years had passed away from the beginning of the world. And Peada, son of Penda, succeeded to the kingdom of Mercia.

In his time they came together, he and Oswy, brother of king Oswald, and declared that they wished to establish a monastery to the glory of Christ and to the honour of St Peter. And they so did, and gave it the name *Medeshamstede* [Peterborough], because there is a spring [6] there called *Medeswæl*. And then they began the foundations and built upon them, and then entrusted it to a monk who was called Seaxwulf. He was a great friend of God, and all people loved him, and he was very nobly born in the world and powerful. He is now much more powerful with Christ.

But that king Peada did not reign for long, for he was betrayed by his own queen at Eastertide.

655. In this year Ithamar, bishop of Rochester, consecrated Deusdedit to Canterbury on 26 March.

656. In this year Peada was killed, and Wulfhere, son of Penda, succeeded to the kingdom of Mercia.

In his [7] time the abbey of *Medeshamstede*, which his brother Peada had begun, grew very wealthy. The king loved it much for love of his brother Peada, and for love of his sworn brother, Oswy, and for love of Seaxwulf, its abbot. He said that he wished to honour and reverence it according to the advice of his brothers Æthelred and Merewala, and according to the advice of his sisters, Cyneburh and Cyneswith, and according to the advice of the archbishop who was called Deusdedit, and according to the advice of all his councillors, both spiritual and temporal, who were in his realm: and he so did.

Then sent the king for the abbot to come quickly to him, and he did so. Then spake the king to the abbot, 'O beloved Seaxwulf, I have sent for you for my soul's need, and I wish freely to tell you why. My brother Peada and my dear friend Oswy began a monastery to the glory of Christ and St Peter, but my brother, as Christ willed it, has departed this life, but I wish to ask you, O beloved friend, (continued on p. 30)

---

[6] *Est enim ibi fons ut dicunt unde ebullit aqua* (Chronicle of Hugh Candidus, ed. W. T. Mellows) (Peterborough 1949), 6.
[7] i.e. Wulfhere's.

to have them labour quickly at the work, and I will provide
E 656 you with gold and silver, land and property, and all that is
from needed for it.' The abbot went home and began to work. As
p. 29 Christ granted him so he succeeded, so that in a few years the
monastery was finished. When the king heard tell of this, then
he was very glad. He bade send throughout his kingdom for all his
thanes, for the archbishop, for bishops, for his earls, and for all those
who loved God, that they should come to him; and he appointed a
day when the monastery was to be consecrated.

When the monastery was consecrated, there were present king
Wulfhere and his brother Æthelred, and his sisters Cyneburh and Cyneswith; and archbishop Deusdedit of Canterbury consecrated the
monastery, and the bishop of Rochester, Ithamar, and the bishop of
London who was called Wine, and the bishop of the Mercians who was
called Jaruman, and bishop Tuda; present also was the priest Wilfrid
who afterwards was a bishop, and there too were all the thanes in his
kingdom.

When the monastery had been consecrated in the name of St Peter,
and of St Paul, and of St Andrew, then the king stood up before all his
thanes and spoke in a loud voice, 'Thanks be to the High Almighty
God for this ceremony which has been performed here, and I intend this
day to honour Christ and St Peter, and I wish that ye all approve my
words. I, Wulfhere, to-day freely give to St Peter and to the abbot
Seaxwulf and the monks of the monastery these lands and these waters
and meres and fens and weirs and all the lands that are situated thereabout which belong to my kingdom, so that no man shall have any
authority there except the abbot and the monks. This is the gift: from
Medeshamstede to Northborough and so to the place called *Folies*, and
so all the fen straight to Asendike, and from Asendike to the place called
Feðermude, and so along the main road for ten miles to *Cuggedic*,
and so to *Raggewilh*, and from *Raggewilh* five miles to the main
stream [1] that goes to Elm and to Wisbech, and so three miles about to
Throckenholt, and from Throckenholt straight through all the fen to
Dereuord, a distance of twenty miles and so to *Grætecros*, and from
Grætecros through a clear stream [2] which is called *Bradanæ*, and from
thence six miles to *Paccelad*, and so on through all the meres and fens
that lie (*continued on p. 31*)

---

[1] *magistram aquam quae ducit ad Elme et ad Wisebeche* in the Latin
version of Hugh Candidus. Identified as 'the river Nene. It flowed *usque
ad Trokenholt* on what is now called the Shire Drain.' (19 EPN xxviii–xxix)

[2] *pulchra aqua Bradanea nomine;* 'the original Ouse, now represented by
"Old Course of the Nene" on which lie Bradney Farm in March and
Bradney House in Benwick.' (*ibid*. xxix, and 254.)

toward the town of Huntingdon and these meres and lakes
Scælfremere and Whittlesey Mere, and all the others that lie
thereabout, with the land and houses that are on the east side of
Scælfremere, and from thence all the fens to *Medeshamstede*,
and from *Medeshamstede* all the way to Wansford, and from
Wansford to King's Cliffe, and from thence to Easton, and from Easton
to Stamford, and from Stamford following the course of the stream
[? R. Welland] to the aforesaid Northborough.' These are the lands
and the fens which the king gave to St Peter's monastery.

E 656 from p. 30

Then spake the king, 'This is but a small benefaction, but I desire
that they hold it so royally and freely that neither tax nor rent be taken
from it except for the monks alone. Thus I desire to free this monastery so that it be subject only to Rome; and I desire that all of us who
cannot go to Rome come to visit St Peter here.'

Amongst other matters discussed the abbot desired that he would
grant to him what he had desired from him, and the king granted it:
'I have here God-fearing monks who would like to spend their lives in
an anchorite's cell if they knew where: but here is an island called
Ancarig, and I desire that we may build there a monastery to the glory
of St Mary, so that those who wish to lead their lives in peace and quiet
may dwell there.'

Then answered the king and spake thus, 'O beloved Seaxwulf, thus I
approve and grant not only what you desire, but all those things that I
know you desire on our Lord's behalf. And I ask you, brother
Æthelred, and my sisters Cyneburh and Cyneswith, for your souls'
salvation, to be witnesses and to write it [i.e. the cross] with your finger.[3]
And I enjoin all my successors, be they my sons, be they my brothers, or
kings that shall succeed me, that our benefaction may stand, according
as they desire to be partakers of the life everlasting and escape eternal
punishment. Whosoever shall diminish our benefaction or the bene-
factions of other good men, may the heavenly doorkeeper diminish him
in the kingdom of heaven; and whosoever shall make it greater, may
the heavenly doorkeeper make him greater in the kingdom of heaven.'

These are the witnesses who were there present, and who attested it
with their finger on Christ's cross and agreed to it verbally. That
was first the king Wulfhere who first confirmed it by his

(*continued on p. 32*)

---

[3] I am indebted to Dr F. E. Harmer for advice on the translation of this
formula of attestation which occurs three times in this annal. She writes:
'It is probable that the terms *writan, gewritan* sometimes refer to the making
of the sign of the cross on the parchment, whether in ink, or by tracing over
a cross already made by the scribe, since the evidence suggests that the
documents were normally written by the scribe and not by the grantor or the
witnesses.'

657. In this year Peada passed away, and Wulfhere, son of Penda, succeeded to the Mercian kingdom.

658. In this year Cenwalh fought at Penselwood against the Welsh, and drove them in flight as far as the Parret. This battle was fought after his return from East Anglia, where he was for three years in exile. Penda had expelled him and deprived him of his kingdom because he had repudiated his [Penda's] sister.

660. In this year bishop Agilbert departed from Cenwalh, and Wine held the episcopal see three years; and that Agilbert received the episcopal see of Paris on the Seine in Gaul.

661. In this year, at Easter, Cenwalh fought at *Posentesburh*; and Wulfhere, son of Penda, ravaged as far as [1] Ashdown. Cuthred, son of Cwichelm, and king Cœnberht passed away in the one year. Wulfhere, son of Penda, ravaged in the Isle of Wight, and gave the people of Wight to Æthelwald, king of Sussex, because Wulfhere had stood sponsor for him at baptism. And Eoppa, the priest,

(continued on p. 34)

word and afterwards attested it with his finger on Christ's cross and thus spake: I, king Wulfhere, in conjunction with these kings and earls, leaders of the army and thanes, the witnesses of my benefaction, do confirm it before archbishop Deusdedit with a cross +. And I, Oswy, king of Northumbria, friend of this monastery and of abbot Seaxwulf, approve it with a cross +. And I, king Sigehere, grant it with a cross +. And I, king Sebbi sign it with a cross +. And I, Æthelred, the king's brother, grant the same with a cross +. And we, the king's sisters, Cyneburh and Cyneswith, we approve it. And I, Deusdedit, archbishop of Canterbury, grant it. After that all the others who were present agreed to it with a cross +. They were, by name, Ithamar, bishop of Rochester, and Wine, bishop of London, and Jaruman, who was bishop of Mercia, and bishop Tuda, and Wilfrid the priest who was afterwards bishop, and Eoppa the priest whom king Wulfhere sent to preach Christianity in the Isle of Wight, and abbot Seaxwulf, and ealdorman Immine, and ealdorman Eadberht, and ealdorman Herefrith, and ealdorman Wilberht, and ealdorman Abo, Æthelbald, Brorda, Wilberht, Ealhmund, Frithugis; these and many (continued on p. 33)

(continued on p. 33)

[1] *in Ashdown* B C

others who were present of the king's retainers all agreed to it.
E 656 This charter was written six hundred and sixty-four years after
from the birth of our Lord, the seventh year of king Wulfhere, the
p. 32 ninth year of archbishop Deusdedit.   Then they laid the curse
of God and the curse of all his saints and of all Christian people
upon anyone who should abrogate anything that was done there.   So
be it, say all.   Amen.

When this matter was brought to a conclusion, the king sent to
Rome to Vitalian, who was then pope, and desired that he would grant
with his bull and with his blessing all this proceeding aforesaid.   And
the pope sent his bull, saying thus: I, pope Vitalian, grant to you, king
Wulfhere, and to archbishop Deusdedit and to abbot Seaxwulf all the
things which you ask, and I forbid any king or any man to have any
authority there except the abbot alone, and that he obey no man except
the pope of Rome and the archbishop of Canterbury.   If anyone
violates this in any respect, may St Peter destroy him with his sword: if
anyone observes it, may St Peter with the key of heaven open to him the
kingdom of heaven.   Thus was the monastery at *Medeshamstede*
begun, which afterwards was called *Burh*.

Afterwards came another archbishop to Canterbury who was called
Theodore, a very good man and wise, and he held his synod with his
bishops and with the clergy.   Then was Winfrith, bishop of Mercia,
deprived of his bishopric, and abbot Seaxwulf was elected to be bishop
there, and Cuthbald, a monk from the same monastery, was elected
abbot.   This synod was held six hundred and seventy-three years after
the birth of our Lord.

658. In this year Cenwalh fought at Penselwood against the Welsh,
and drove them in flight as far as the Parret.   This battle was fought
after his return from East Anglia, where he was for three years in exile.
Penda had expelled him and deprived him of his kingdom because he had
repudiated his [Penda's] sister.

660. In this year bishop Agilbert departed from Cenwalh, and Wine
held the episcopal see three years; and that Agilbert received the
episcopal see of Paris on the Seine in Gaul.

661. In this year at Easter Cenwalh fought at *Posentesburh*; and
Wulfhere, son of Penda, ravaged from [2] Ashdown.   Cuthred, son of
Cwichelm, and king Cœnberht passed away in the one year.   Wulfhere,
son of Penda, ravaged in the Isle of Wight, and gave the people of Wight
to Æthelwald, king of Sussex, because Wulfhere had stood sponsor for
him (*continued on p.* 34)

[2] *in* B C

Ā 661
from
p. 32

at the command of Wilfrid and king Wulfhere, was the first to bring Christianity to the inhabitants of the Isle of Wight. 664. In this year there was an eclipse of the sun. Eorcenberht, king of Kent, passed away. Colman with his companions went to his native land.[1] In this same year there was a great pestilence. Ceadda and Wilfrid were consecrated, and the same year Deusdedit passed away.

668. In this year Theodore was consecrated archbishop.

669. In this year king Egbert gave Reculver to Bass the priest to build a church there.

670. Oswy, king of Northumbria, passed away, and Ecgfrith reigned after him. Hlothhere, nephew of bishop Agilbert, succeeded to the episcopal see of Wessex and held it for seven years. Bishop Theodore consecrated him. And that Oswy was the son of Æthelfrith, the son of Æthelric, the son of Ida, the son of Eoppa.

671. In this year there was the great mortality of birds.

672. In this year Cenwalh passed away, and Seaxburh, his queen, reigned one year after him.

673. In this year Egbert, king of Kent, passed away. The same year there was a synod at Hertford, and St Æthelthryth founded the monastery at Ely.

674. In this year Æscwine succeeded to the kingdom of Wessex: he was the son of Cenfus, the son of Cenfrith, the son of Cuthgils, the son of Ceolwulf, the son of Cynric, the son of Cerdic.

675. Wulfhere, son of Penda, and Æscwine fought at *Biedanheafod*, and the same year Wulfhere passed away, and Æthelred succeeded to the kingdom. (*continued on p.* 36)

E 661
from
p. 33

at baptism. Eoppa, the priest, at the command of Wilfrid and king Wulfhere, was the first to bring Christianity to the inhabitants of the Isle of Wight. 664. In this year there was an eclipse of the sun on 3 May, and in this year (*continued on p.* 35)

---

[1] 'It should be noted that even E omits all mention of the Synod of Whitby, and merely gives the departure of Colman, which was the result of it. The same omission is made in the Anglo-Saxon version of Bede.' (Plummer)

came a great pestilence to the island of Britain. In the pesti-
E 664 lence passed away bishop Tuda; he was buried at *Wagele*, and
from Eorcenberht, king of Kent, passed away and Egbert, his son,
p. 34 succeeded to the kingdom. Colman with his companions went
to his native land. Ceadda and Wilfrid were consecrated, and
in the same year archbishop Deusdedit passed away.

667. In this year Oswy and Egbert sent Wigheard the priest to Rome
to be consecrated archbishop, but he passed away as soon as he arrived
there.

668. In this year pope Vitalian consecrated Theodore archbishop,
and sent him to Britain.

669. In this year king Egbert gave Reculver to Bass the priest to
build a church there.

670. In this year Oswy, king of Northumbria, passed away on 15
February, and Ecgfrith, his son, reigned after him. Hlothhere,
nephew of bishop Agilbert, succeeded to the episcopal see of Wessex
and held it for seven years. Bishop Theodore consecrated him.

671. In this year there was the great mortality of birds.

672. In this year Cenwalh passed away, and Seaxburh, his queen,
reigned one year after him.

673. In this year Egbert, king of Kent, passed away. Archbishop
Theodore summoned a synod at Hertford, and St Æthelthryth[2] founded
the monastery at Ely.

674. In this year Æscwine succeeded to the kingdom of Wessex.

675. In this year Wulfhere, son of Penda, and Æscwine, son of
Cenfus, fought at *Bedanheafod*, and the same year Wulfhere passed
away, and Æthelred succeeded to the kingdom. In his days he sent
bishop Wilfrid to Rome to the pope that then was, who was called
Agatho, and made known to him by letters and verbally how his
brothers, Peada and Wulfhere, and the abbot Seaxwulf had built a
monastery which was called *Medeshamstede*, and that they had freed it
of all service to king and bishop, and asked him to confirm this with his
bull and with his blessing. And the pope sent his bull then to England,
thus saying: 'I, Agatho, pope of Rome, greet well the noble Æthelred,
king of Mercia, and the archbishop Theodore of Canterbury

(*continued on p.* 36)

---

[2] She was the daughter of Anna, king of the East Angles. Bede, *EH*
IV. 17 (19), tells how after her death, perhaps from goitre, her bones were
disinterred by her sister and successor, Abbess Seaxburh, and buried in a
white marble coffin from Cambridge. Bede tells how she bore her
infirmity stoically, and was wont to say: 'I know that I deservedly bear the
weight of my sickness on my neck, for I remember, when I was very young,
I bore there the needless weight of jewels.' (*Everyman* translation.)

Ā 676
from
p. 34 676. In this year Æscwine passed away, and Hedde succeeded to

(continued on p. 38)

E 675
from
p. 35 and the Mercian bishop Seaxwulf who was formerly abbot, and all the abbots who are in England, with God's greeting and my blessing. I have heard the petition of king Æthelred and of archbishop Theodore and of bishop Seaxwulf and of abbot Cuthbald, and I desire that it shall obtain in every particular as you have said. And I enjoin, in the name of God and of St Peter and of all saints and of all the dignitaries of the Church, that neither king nor bishop nor earl nor any man shall have any authority there or rent or tax or military service, nor shall anyone exact any kind of service from the abbey of *Medeshamstede*. Moreover I command that the diocesan bishop be not so presumptuous as to perform ordination or consecration within this abbey, except the abbot ask it of him; neither shall it be liable to the bishop's fine, nor shall synod, nor any kind of assembly, have any authority there.

'I also desire that the abbot be considered as legate from Rome over the whole island; and whatever abbot be there elected by the monks that he be consecrated by the archbishop of Canterbury. I desire and grant that whatever man may have made a vow to make a pilgrimage to Rome and be unable to fulfil it, whether on account of sickness or his lord's need or because of poverty or some other exigency which prevents his going, whether he come from England or from whatever other island, let him come to the monastery at *Medeshamstede* and have the same forgiveness from Christ and St Peter and from the abbot and from the monks that he would have if he went to Rome.

'Now I ask you, brother Theodore, that you have it proclaimed throughout all England that the synod be assembled and this bull be read and observed. Likewise I command you, bishop Seaxwulf, that just as you wish the monastery to be free, so I forbid you and all those bishops that succeed you, by Christ and by all his saints, to have any authority over the monastery except in so far as the abbot shall permit. Now I declare that whoever observes this bull and this mandate, may he ever dwell with God *(continued on p. 37)*

Almighty in the kingdom of heaven, and whoever breaks it
E 675 may he be excommunicated and cast down into hell with Judas
from and with all devils unless he make amends. AMEN.'
p. 36 This bull pope Agatho and a hundred and twenty-five
bishops sent by archbishop Wilfrid of York to England. This
was done six hundred and eighty years after the birth of our Lord, in the
sixth year of king Æthelred. Then the king ordered archbishop
Theodore to appoint an assembly of all the councillors at the place
called Hatfield. When they were gathered there, he had the bull read
which the pope had sent thither, and they all agreed to it and fully confirmed it.

Then said the king, 'All those things that my brother Peada and my
brother Wulfhere and my sisters Cyneburh and Cyneswith gave and
granted to St Peter and the abbot, these I desire to remain undisturbed,
and I wish in my day to increase it for the salvation of their souls and
mine. Now give I to St Peter to-day to his monastery *Medeshamstede*
these lands and all that belongs thereto; namely Breedon on the Hill
[Lei], *Hrepingas* [*Rippingale, L*], *Cedenac*, Swineshead [L], *Heanbyrig*,
Lodeshac, Shifnal [Sa], *Costesford*, Stratford, Wattlesborough [Sa],
the Lizard [Sa], *Æthelhuniglond*, Bardney [L].[1] These lands I give St
Peter with the same freedom from control as when I held them, and so
that none of my successors take anything therefrom. If anyone do so,
may he have the curse of the pope of Rome and the curse of all bishops
and of all those who here are witnesses, and I confirm this with a
cross +.'

I, Theodore, archbishop of Canterbury, am witness to this charter of
Medeshamstede, and I confirm it with my signature, and I excommunicate all those who break it in any particular, and I bless all those
who observe it +. I, Wilfrid, archbishop of York, I am a witness to
this charter and I agree to this same curse +. I, Seaxwulf, who was
first abbot and now am bishop, I give him who breaks this my curse
and that of all my successors. I, Osthryth, Æthelred's queen, grant it.
I, Adrian, legate, agree to it. I, Putta, bishop of Rochester, I subscribe
to it. I, Waldhere, bishop of London, confirm it. I, abbot Cuthbald,
agree to it so that whoever breaks it may he have the malediction of all
bishops and of all Christian people. Amen.

676. In this year Æscwine passed away, and Hedde succeeded to the
episcopal see (*continued on p.* 38)

---

[1] For the place-name identifications see F. M. Stenton, 'Medeshamstede
and its Colonies' (*Historical Essays in Honour of James Tait*, 314, Manchester 1933). The possible identification of *Hrepingas* with *Rippingale*
(L) was suggested by Eilert Ekwall (*DEPN*), but Stenton (*op. cit.* 319 note 3)
thinks it unlikely.

the episcopal see, and Centwine succeeded to the kingdom.
Centwine was the son of Cynegils, the son of Ceolwulf. Æthelred, king of Mercia, ravaged Kent.

678. In this year the star 'comet' appeared. Bishop Wilfrid was driven from his bishopric by king Ecgfrith.

679. In this year Ælfwine was slain, and St Æthelthryth passed away.

680. In this year archbishop Theodore presided over a synod at Hatfield because he wished to amend the doctrines of the Christian faith. The same year Hild, abbess of Whitby, passed away.

682. In this year Centwine drove the Britons as far as the sea.

685. In this year Cædwalla began to contend for the kingdom. That Cædwalla was the son of Cœnberht, the son of Cadda, son of Cutha, the son of Ceawlin, the son of Cynric, the son of Cerdic. Mul was the brother of Cædwalla, and later he was burned to death in Kent. This same year king Ecgfrith was slain: that Ecgfrith was the son of Oswy, the son of Æthelfrith, the son of Æthelric, the son of Ida, the son of Eoppa. This same year Hlothhere passed away.

686. In this year Cædwalla and Mul laid waste Kent and the Isle of Wight.

687. In this year Mul was burned to death in Kent and twelve other men with him; and that year Cædwalla again laid waste Kent.

(*continued on p.* 40)

F 685
from
p. 28

685. In this year in Britain it rained blood, and milk and butter were turned into blood. (*continued on p.* 42)

E 676
from
p. 37

and Centwine succeeded to the kingdom of Wessex. Æthelred, king of Mercia, overran Kent.

678. In this year the star 'comet' appeared in August, and for three months every morning shone like sunshine. Bishop Wilfrid was driven from his bishopric by king Ecgfrith, and

(*continued on p.* 39)

two bishops were consecrated in his place, Bosa to Deira and
E 678 Eata to Bernicia. Eadhed was consecrated bishop to the
from people of Lindsey: he was the first of the bishops of Lindsey.
p. 38 679. In this year Ælfwine was slain beside the Trent, at the
place where Ecgfrith and Æthelred fought. In this year passed
away St Æthelthryth; and Coldingham was consumed by fire which
came down from heaven.[1]

680. In this year archbishop Theodore presided over a synod at
Hatfield because he wished to amend the doctrines of the Christian
faith. The same year Hild, abbess of Whitby, passed away.

681. In this year Trumberht was consecrated bishop of Hexham;
and Trumwine was consecrated bishop to the Picts, because then they
were subject to us.[2]

682. In this year Centwine drove the Britons as far as the sea.

684. In this year Ecgfrith sent a host to Ireland and Beorht, his
ealdorman, with it, and they pitiably laid waste and burned God's
churches.

685. In this year king Ecgfrith had Cuthbert consecrated bishop, and
archbishop Theodore consecrated him bishop of Hexham at York on
the first day of Easter, for Trumberht had been removed from the
episcopal see. This same year king Ecgfrith was slain to the north of
the sea [the Firth of Forth] on 20 May, and a great host with him. He
was king for fifteen years, and Aldfrith, his brother, succeeded to the
kingdom. In this year Cædwalla began to contend for the kingdom,
and the same year Hlothhere, king of Kent, passed away. John was
consecrated bishop in Hexham,[3] and was there until the return of
Wilfrid. John was afterwards appointed to the episcopal see of York
because bishop Bosa had passed away. Thereafter Wilfrid, his priest,[4]
was consecrated bishop of York, and John retired to his monastery at
Beverley.[5]

686. In this year Cædwalla and Mul, his brother, laid waste Kent and
the Isle of Wight. This Cædwalla gave to St Peter's monastery of
Medeshamstede the place Hoo, which is on an island called Avery.[6]
The abbot of the monastery was then Egbalth: he was the third abbot
after Seaxwulf. Theodore was then archbishop in Kent.

687. Mul was burned in Kent, and twelve other men with him; and
that year Cædwalla again laid waste Kent. (*continued on p. 41*)

---

[1] *celico igni* F Lat

[2] *Trumuini ad prouinciam Pictorum, quae tunc temporis Anglorum erat
imperio subiecta* (Bede, *EH* IV. 12). 'As the *Angli* to whose *imperium* the
Picts were then subject were of course the Northumbrians, the use of this
word *hither* betrays a northern point of view, and it is noteworthy that F,
a Canterbury chronicle, alters the phrase into "farþan hi hyraþ þider inn."'
(Plummer)

[3] *on Agust*', usually translated 'in August,' but *Agust*' is the abbreviated
form of the place-name *Hagustaldesea*, Hexham.

[4] Not the famous Wilfrid, but Wilfrid II of York, a pupil of abbess Hild
of Hartlepool and Whitby (see Bede, *EH* IV. 23).

[5] On these episcopal appointments see F. M. Stenton, *Anglo-Saxon
England* 139, and B. Colgrave, *Two Lives of St Cuthbert* 18–19.

[6] For Avery Farm see J. K. Wallenberg, *Kentish Place-Names* (Uppsala
1931), 19–21, and the map in R. Arnold, *The Hundred of Hoo* (London 1947).

688. In this year Ine succeeded to the kingdom of Wessex and ruled thirty-seven years: *he built the monastery at Glastonbury.* The same year Cædwalla went to Rome and received baptism at the hands of the pope who named him Peter, and seven days after he passed away. The aforementioned Ine was the son of Cenred, the son of Ceolwald; Ceolwald was the brother of Cynegils: they were the sons of Cuthwine, the son of Ceawlin, the son of Cynric, the son of Cerdic.

690. In this year archbishop Theodore passed away, and Berhtwald succeeded to the episcopal see. Before this time the [arch]bishops had been Roman, but afterwards they were English.

694. In this year the Kentishmen came to terms with Ine and gave him 'thirty thousands'[1] because they had burned Mul to death. Wihtred succeeded to the kingdom of Kent and ruled thirty-three years: that Wihtred was the son of Egbert, the son of Eorcenberht, the son of Eadbald, the son of Æthelberht.

703. In this year bishop Hedde passed away: he held the episcopal see of Winchester twenty-seven years.

704. In this year Æthelred, son of Penda, king of Mercia, became a monk: he had ruled that kingdom twenty-nine years. He was succeeded by Cœnred.

705. In this year Aldfrith, king of Northumbria, passed away, and bishop Seaxwulf also.

709. In this year bishop Aldhelm passed away: he was bishop 'to the west of the wood.'[2] In the early days of Daniel, Wessex was divided into two dioceses—previously it had been one—Daniel held one, Aldhelm the other. After Aldhelm, Forthhere succeeded. Ceolred succeeded to the kingdom of Mercia, and Cœnred went to Rome, and Offa with him. (*continued on p.* 42)

(in the left margin)
Ā 688
from
p. 38

---

[1] *thirty thousand pounds* B; *thirty pounds* C; *thirty thousand pounds in friendship* F; *xxx milia librarum* F Lat. Ā D E leave the denomination unexpressed. Despite these readings, there is no doubt that *sceattas* is implied. At 4 sceattas to the shilling in Kent in Ine's time, this wergild would be equal to 7,500 sh., six times the value of the thane's wergild at 1,200 sh.—a king's wergild according to *Be Myrcna Lage*; the extra amount (7,500 instead of 7,200) due to compensation for loss in weighing. (Cf. H. M. Chadwick, *Studies on Anglo-Saxon Institutions* 17 f.)

[2] *to the west of Selwood* B; *in parte Occidentis Silue* F Lat. See F. M. Stenton, *Anglo-Saxon England* 64–5 on Selwood.

688. In this year king Cædwalla went to Rome and received
A 688 baptism at the hands of Sergius the pope, who gave him the
from name Peter. But seven days afterwards, on 20 April, he
p. 39 passed away in his baptismal robes, and he was buried within
St Peter's church. Ine succeeded to the kingdom of Wessex
after him, and reigned twenty-seven years: afterwards he went to
Rome, and remained there until the day of his death.

690. In this year archbishop Theodore passed away: he had been
bishop twenty-two years, and was buried inside Canterbury.

692. In this year Berhtwald was elected archbishop on 1 July: he was
previously abbot of Reculver. Before this time the [arch]bishops had
been Roman, and afterwards they were English. There were then two
kings in Kent, Wihtred and Wæbheard.

693. In this year Berhtwald was consecrated archbishop by Godun,
a bishop of Gaul, on 3 July. Meanwhile Bishop Gifemund passed
away, and Berhtwald consecrated Tobias in his stead; and Berhthelm
[*recte* Dryhthelm ³] was led from this life.

694. In this year the Kentishmen came to terms with Ine and gave
him 'thirty thousands' because they had burnt Mul to death. Wihtred
succeeded to the kingdom of Kent and ruled twenty-three years.

697. In this year the Mercians ⁴ slew Osthryth, Æthelred's queen,
sister of Ecgfrith.

699. In this year the Picts slew Beorht the ealdorman.

702. In this year Cœnred succeeded to the Mercian ⁴ kingdom.

703. In this year bishop Hedde passed away: he held the episcopal
see of Winchester twenty-seven years.

704. In this year Æthelred, son of Penda, king of Mercia, became
a monk: he had ruled that kingdom twenty-nine years when Cœnred
succeeded.

705. In this year Aldfrith, king of Northumbria, passed away on 14
December at Driffield, and Osred, his son, succeeded to the kingdom.

709. In this year bishop Aldhelm passed away: he was bishop 'to
the west of the wood'.⁵ In the early days of Daniel, Wessex was divided
into two dioceses—previously it had been one—Daniel held one,
Aldhelm the other. After Aldhelm, Forthhere succeeded. Ceolred
succeeded to the kingdom of Mercia, and Cœnred went to Rome, and
Offawith him: Cœnred was there until his life's end. The same year
bishop Wilfrid passed away at Oundle and his body was taken to Ripon.
He had been a bishop forty-five years: king Ecgfrith had formerly
driven him to Rome. (*continued on p.* 43)

---

³ So D correctly. See Bede, *EH* IV. 12, for the account of the vision.
Dryhthelm lived in a monastic cell on the Tweed near Melrose. He used to
stand up to his neck in the river during winter to mortify the flesh, and to
remember the lost souls whom he had seen in his vision tormented by
extremes of alternate heat and cold.
⁴ Literally 'Southumbrians' (annal 697), 'Southumbrian' (annal 702),
indicative of the northern origin of the entries.
⁵ Selwood, which divided East and West Wessex.

A 710 from p. 40

710. In this year ealdorman Beorhtfrith fought against the Picts; and Ine and Nunna, his kinsman, fought against Geraint, king of the Britons [of Cornwall].

714. In this year passed away St Guthlac.[1]

715. In this year Ine and Ceolred fought at Adam's Grave [in Alton Priors, W].

716. In this year Osred, king of Northumbria, was killed: he had ruled the kingdom seven [2] years after Aldfrith. Then Cœnred succeeded to the kingdom, and ruled two years; then Osric ruled eleven years. In this same year Ceolred,[3] king of Mercia, passed away, and his body rests in Lichfield, and that of Æthelred, son of Penda at Bardney. Then Æthelbald succeeded to the kingdom of Mercia, and ruled forty-one years. Æthelbald was the son of Alweo, the son of Eawa, the son of Pybba, whose ancestry is written down above. And that venerable man Egbert rightly induced the monks on the island of Iona to celebrate Easter at the proper time, and to adopt the Roman tonsure.

718. In this year Ingeld, brother of Ine, passed away, and their sisters were Cwenburh and Cuthburh; and that Cuthburh founded the monastic community at Wimborne; she was given in marriage to Aldfrith, king of Northumbria, but they parted during their lifetime.

721. In this year Daniel went to Rome. And the same year Ine killed Cynewulf.

722. In this year queen Æthelburh destroyed Taunton, which Ine had built, and Ealdberht the exile fled into Surrey and Sussex, and Ine fought against the South Saxons.

725. In this year Wihtred, king of Kent, passed away; his ancestry *and Eadberht succeeded to the kingdom of Kent.* is above. And Ine fought against the South Saxons, and there slew Ealdberht.

and there gave up his life

728. In this year Ine went to Rome; and Æthelheard succeeded to the kingdom of Wessex and ruled fourteen years. In this year fought Æthelheard and prince Oswald; and that Oswald was the son of Æthelbald, the son of Cynebald, the son of Cuthwine, the son of Ceawlin. (*continued on p.* 44)

F 714 from p. 38

714. In this year passed away St Guthlac, and Pippin the king.

715. In this year passed away king Dagobert.

(*continued on p.* 44)

---

[1] An OE poem on the life of St Guthlac is to be found in *The Exeter Book*. A Latin life of the saint, probably by a fellow monk at Crowland, was written in the early eighth century, and was probably the source of the OE prose life written in the eleventh century.

[2] *eight* D

[3] *Ceolwold* B C

710. In this year Acca, Wilfrid's chaplain, succeeded to
E 710 the episcopal see which Wilfrid had held; and the same year
from ealdorman Beorhtfrith fought against the Picts between *Hæfe*
p. 41 [*R. Avon, Linlithgow*] and *Cære* [*R. Carron, Stirlingshire*].
Ine and Nunna, his kinsman, fought against Geraint, king
of the Britons, and this same year Hygebald [4] was killed.

714. In this year St Guthlac passed away.

715. In this year Ine and Ceolred fought at Adam's Grave [in Alton
Priors, W].

716. In this year Osred, king of Northumbria, was killed to the south
of the border [5]: he had ruled seven years after Aldfrith. Then Cœnred
succeeded to the kingdom and ruled two years. After him Osric
ruled eleven years. In this same year Ceolred, king of Mercia, passed
away, and his body rests in Lichfield, and that of Æthelred, son of
Penda, at Bardney. Then Æthelbald succeeded to the kingdom of
Mercia and ruled forty-one years. That venerable man Egbert
converted the religious community of Iona to the correct Easter and
the Petrine tonsure.

718. In this year Ingeld, the brother of Ine, passed away, and their
sisters were Cwenburh and Cuthburh; and that Cuthburh founded the
monastic community at Wimborne: she was given in marriage to Aldfrith, king of Northumbria, but they parted during their lifetime.

721. In this year Daniel went to Rome. And the same year prince
Cynewulf was killed. In this year passed away the holy bishop John,
who was bishop thirty-three years eight months and thirteen days:
his body rests at Beverley.

722. In this year queen Æthelburh destroyed Taunton, which Ine had
built; and Ealdberht the exile fled into Surrey and Sussex.

725. In this year Wihtred, king of Kent, passed away on 23 April:
he had reigned thirty-four years. [6] And Ine fought against the
South Saxons, and there slew Ealdberht, the prince whom he had
banished.

726. In this year Ine went to Rome, [7] and Æthelheard, his kinsman,
succeeded to the kingdom of Wessex and ruled fourteen years.

727. In this year passed away Tobias, bishop of Rochester, and in his
place archbishop Berhtwald consecrated Ealdwulf bishop.

(*continued on p.* 45)

---

[4] *Sigbald* D correctly.
[5] i.e. south of the border between Northumbria and Mercia.
[6] *and Eadberht reigned after him in Kent* F; *Obitus Wihtredi gloriosi regis Cantiæ* F Lat
[7] *In this year king Ine passed away* F; *Obitus Ina rex* F Lat

729. In this year the star 'comet' showed itself; and St
Ā 729 Egbert passed away.
from 730. In this year Oswald the prince passed away.
p. 42 731. In this year Osric, king of Northumbria, was slain, and
   Ceolwulf succeeded to the kingdom and ruled eight years.[1]
That Ceolwulf was the son of Cutha, the son of Cuthwine, the son of
Leodwald, the son of Ecgwald, the son of Aldhelm, the son of Ocga, the
son of Ida, the son of Eoppa. Archbishop Berhtwald died, and the
same year Tatwine was consecrated archbishop.

733. In this year Æthelbald captured Somerton: and the sun was
eclipsed.

734. In this year the moon was as if it were suffused with blood; and
Tatwine and Bede passed away.

736. In this year archbishop Nothhelm received the pallium from the
'bishop of the Romans.'

737. In this year bishop Forthhere and queen Frithugyth journeyed
to Rome.

738. In this year Eadberht succeeded to the Northumbrian kingdom:
he was the son of Eata, the son of Leodwald and he ruled twenty-one
years. His brother was archbishop Egbert, son of Eata, and they both
rest in York in the same chapel.[2]

741. In this year king Æthelheard passed away; and Cuthred succeeded to the kingdom of Wessex and ruled sixteen [3] years, and resolutely made war against king Æthelbald. Cuthbert was consecrated
archbishop, and Dunn bishop of Rochester. (continued on p. 46)

F 742 742. In this year there was a great synod at *Cloueshoh*, and
from present were Æthelbald, king of Mercia, and archbishop
p. 42 Cuthbert and many other learned men. (continued on p. 46)

---

[1] 'D inserts the death of Osric and the accession of Ceolwulf, both under
729 (as E and F), and under 731 as Ā B C.' (Plummer) The correct date
is 729. 'Bede's *Ecclesiastical History*, which king Ceolwulf of Northumbria
read and criticized in draft, is the response of a great scholar to a great
opportunity.' (Stenton)
[2] On the use of the *porticus*, or side-chapel, as a place of burial, see A. W.
Clapham, *English Romanesque Architecture before the Conquest* (London
1930) 28.
[3] *twenty-six* B C

729. In this year two comets appeared; and the same year Osric passed away, who had been king eleven years; and St Egbert passed away in Iona. Then Ceolwulf succeeded to the kingdom and ruled eight years.

730. In this year prince Oswald passed away.

731. In this year archbishop Berhtwald passed away on 13 January: he had been bishop thirty-seven years six months and fourteen days. The same year Tatwine was consecrated archbishop: he had been a priest at Breedon on the Hill, in Mercia. He was consecrated by Daniel, bishop of Winchester and Ingwald, bishop of London, and Ealdwine, bishop of Lichfield, and Ealdwulf, bishop of Rochester, on 10 June.[4]

733. In this year Æthelbald captured Somerton; and in the same year the sun was eclipsed;[5] and Acca was driven from his bishopric.

734. In this year the moon was as if it were suffused with blood, and archbishop Tatwine passed away, and also Bede; and Egbert was consecrated bishop.

735. In this year bishop Egbert received the pallium from Rome.

736. In this year archbishop Nothhelm received the pallium from the 'bishop of the Romans.'[6]

737. In this year bishop Forthhere and queen Frithugyth journeyed to Rome. King Ceolwulf received the Petrine tonsure;[7] and gave his kingdom to Eadberht, the son of his paternal uncle: he reigned twenty-one years. And bishop Æthelwald[8] and Acca passed away, and Cynewulf was consecrated bishop. In this same year Æthelwald [recte Æthelbald] harried Northumbria.

738. In this year Eadberht succeeded to the Northumbrian kingdom: he was the son of Eata, the son of Leodwald, and he ruled twenty-one years. His brother was archbishop Egbert, son of Eata, and they both rest in York in the same chapel.

740. In this year king Æthelheard passed away; and Cuthred, his kinsman, succeeded to the kingdom of Wessex and ruled sixteen years, and resolutely made war against Æthelbald, king of Mercia. Eadberht [recte Cuthbert] was consecrated archbishop, and Dunn bishop of Rochester.

741. In this year York was burnt down. (continued on p. 47)

---

[4] *He held the archiepiscopal see three years* F

[5] *and all the circle of the sun became like a black shield* F; *totus orbis solis quasi nigerrimo et horrendo scuto uidebatur esse coöperatus circa tertiam horam diei* F Lat

[6] *et tenuit v. annos* F Lat

[7] *and became a secular priest* F

[8] Æthelwald, bishop of Lindisfarne, pressed and bound the Lindisfarne Gospels, which had been written by his predecessor, Eadfrith.

45

A 743
743. In this year Æthelbald and Cuthred fought against the Welsh.

from p. 44
744. In this year Daniel retired from the bishopric of Winchester, and Hunferth succeeded to the episcopal see.

745. In this year Daniel passed away; forty-three years had elapsed since he succeeded to the episcopal see.

746. In this year king Selred was slain.

748. In this year Cynric, prince of Wessex, was slain, and Eadberht, king of Kent, passed away, *and Æthelberht, son of king Wihtred, succeeded to the kingdom.*

750. In this year king Cuthred fought against Æthelhun, the presumptuous ealdorman.

752. In this year, in the twelfth year of his reign, Cuthred fought against Æthelbald at *Beorgfeord.*

753. In this year Cuthred fought against the Welsh.

754 [756].[1] In this year Cuthred passed away; and Cyneheard succeeded to the episcopal see of Winchester after Hunferth; and this year Canterbury was burnt down, and Sigeberht succeeded to the kingdom of Wessex and ruled one year.

755 [757].[2] In this year Cynewulf and the councillors of Wessex deprived Sigeberht of his kingdom for unlawful actions, with the exception of Hampshire; and this he kept until he slew the ealdorman who remained faithful to him longer than the rest. And Cynewulf then drove him away into the Weald, and he lived there until a herdsman stabbed him at the stream at Privett, thereby avenging the ealdorman Cumbra. And that Cynewulf frequently fought great battles against the Welsh; and after ruling thirty-one [3] years he wished to expel a prince called Cyneheard; and that Cyneheard was the brother of that Sigeberht. And then he learnt that the king was visiting a mistress at *Merantun,* with but a small retinue; and he surprised him there, and surrounded the bower [4] before the men who were with the king became aware of him. (*continued on p.* 48)

F 755 [757] from p. 44
755 [757]. In this year Cynewulf deprived king Sigeberht of his kingdom; and Cyneheard, Sigeberht's brother, slew Cynewulf at *Merantun*; he had reigned thirty-one years. In this same year Æthelbald, king of Mercia, was murdered at Repton.[5] Offa seized the kingdom of Mercia, having put Beornred to flight.[6] (*continued on p.* 50)

---

[1] From this annal to 845, in all extant versions of the *Chronicle*, there is a chronological dislocation, the majority of the events being dated two years too early. This dislocation is the result of a mistake made by a scribe who was copying mechanically the common original from which these annals spring. The corrected dates are put in square brackets.

[2] 'The story of the deaths of Cynewulf and Cyneheard gave rise to what seems to be the earliest known piece of English narrative prose.' (F. M. Stenton, *Anglo-Saxon England* 208 note 3, *q.v.*).

[3] So B C; *twenty-one* D

[4] *þa burh* B C. 'In this circumstantial narrative the reader should bear in mind the arrangements of a Saxon residence. The chief building was the *hall*, around which were grouped the other apartments, each entered from the court; the whole surrounded by a *wall* or rampart of earth, and therefore

743. In this year Æthelbald, the Mercian king, and Cuthred,
E 743 king of Wessex, fought against the Welsh.

from 744. In this year Daniel retired from the bishopric of
p. 45 Winchester, and Hunferth succeeded to the episcopal see. In
this year there were many shooting stars. Wilfrid the Young
[i.e. Wilfrid II], bishop of York, passed away on 29 April: he was
bishop thirty years.

745. In this year Daniel passed away: forty-six years had elapsed
since he succeeded to the episcopal see.

746. In this year king Selred was slain.

748. In this year Cynric, prince of Wessex, was slain, and Eadberht,
king of Kent, passed away.

750. In this year Cuthred, king of Wessex, fought against Æthelhun,
the presumptuous ealdorman.

752. In this year, in the twenty-second year of his reign, Cuthred,
king of Wessex, fought at *Beorhford* against Æthelbald, king of Mercia,
and put him to flight.

753. In this year Cuthred, king of Wessex, fought against the Welsh.

754 [756].[7] In this year Cuthred, king of Wessex, passed away, and
Cyneheard succeeded to the episcopal see of Winchester after Hunferth;
and this year Canterbury was burned down and Sigeberht, his [Cuth-
red's] kinsman, succeeded to the kingdom of Wessex and ruled one year.

755 [757]. In this year Cynewulf and the councillors of Wessex
deprived Sigeberht, his kinsman, of his kingdom for unlawful actions,
with the exception of Hampshire; and this he kept until he slew the
ealdorman who remained faithful to him longer than the rest. And
Cynewulf then drove him away into the Weald, and he lived there until
a herdsman stabbed him at the stream at Privett, thereby avenging the
ealdorman Cumbra. And that Cynewulf frequently fought great
battles against the Welsh; and after ruling sixteen years he wished to
expel a prince called Cyneheard, and that Cyneheard was the brother of
that Sigeberht. And then he learnt that the king was visiting a mistress
at *Merantun*, with but a small retinue; and he surprised him there, and
surrounded the bower (*continued on p.* 49)

---

named a *burh*. The common external entrance was the gate (*geat*), which
was an opening in the *wall*; but the entrance to any of the enclosed buildings
was a door (*duru*). The description in this annal seems to imply that the
residence at Merton covered a considerable area. The king was in the
lady's chamber (*bur*—the 'bower' of medieval romance).' (Earle, quoted
by Plummer.) In other places in the *Chronicle* the word *burh* has the
meaning of a defensible centre for the neighbouring population, and in
Alfred's reign and after as a fortress or strongpoint permanently manned
for national defence. (On the *burh* and its development, see F. M. Stenton,
Anglo-Saxon England 261–3, 288–9, 331–2, 518–21.)

[5] *at Seckington, and his body rests in Repton* D.   Cf. E (p. 49).

[6] *fugato Bernredo rege herede Adelb[aldi]* F Lat

[7] See note 1 opposite. Sometimes the scribe of E had the correct date for
some of his northern material, but in taking over the incorrect dating of the
copy of the Alfredian chronicle before him, he introduced chronological
discrepancies into some annals. In these cases a correction of dating is
attempted: for example, *s.a.* 759 E, Bregowine was consecrated in 761
(cf. Ā, *s.a.* 759), but Æthelwald Moll's accession was in 759.

A 755
[757]
from
p. 46

And then the king perceived this, and he went to the door and then gallantly defended himself until he caught sight of the prince, and then rushed out on him and severely wounded him; and they all set on the king until they had slain him. And then from the woman's cries the king's thanes became aware of the disturbance, and whoever then was ready and quickest ran thither; and the prince offered each of them money and life, and none of them would accept it, but they went on fighting continuously until they all lay slain, except one Welsh hostage, and he was badly wounded. When in the morning the king's thanes who had been left behind heard that the king was slain, they rode thither, and his ealdorman Osric and Wigfrith his thane and the men whom he had left behind, and found the prince in the fortified place where the king lay slain, and they had closed the gates upon themselves, and then they went thereto. And then he offered them their own choice of money and land if they would grant him the kingdom, and they told them that kinsmen of theirs were with them who would not desert them;[1] and then they replied that no kinsman was dearer to them than their lord, and they never would follow his slayer; and then they offered to let their kinsmen depart unharmed. And they replied that the same had been offered to their comrades who had been with the king; then they said that they themselves did not care for this 'any more than your comrades who were slain with the king.' And they went on fighting around the gates until they forced their way in and slew the prince and the men who were with him, all except one who was the ealdorman's godson, and he spared his life, although he was wounded many times.[2]

And that Cynewulf reigned thirty-one years, and his body lies at Winchester, and that of the prince at Axminster; and their direct paternal ancestry goes back to Cerdic. And the same year Æthelbald, king of Mercia, was murdered at Seckington, and his body lies in Repton. And Beornred succeeded to the kingdom, and ruled a short time (*continued on p.* 50)

---

[1] or *kinsmen of theirs were with him who would not desert him*
[2] On the implications of this story see H. M. Chadwick, *Studies on Anglo-Saxon Institutions* 363 f. See also F. P. Magoun, Jr, 'Cynewulf, Cyneheard and Osric' (57 *Anglia* 361–76).

E 755
[757]
from
p. 47

before the men who were with the king became aware of him. and then the king perceived this, and he went to the door, and then gallantly defended himself until he caught sight of the prince, and then rushed out on him and severely wounded him; and they all set on the king until they had slain him. And then from the woman's cries the king's thanes became aware of the disturbance, and whoever then was ready the quickest ran thither; and the prince offered each of them money and life, and none of them would accept, but they went on fighting continuously until they were all slain, except one Welsh hostage, and he was badly wounded. When in the morning the king's thanes who had been left behind heard that the king was slain, they rode thither, and his ealdorman Osric and Wigfrith his thane and the men whom he had left behind, and found the prince in the fortified place where the king lay slain, and they had closed the gates upon themselves, and then they went thereto. And then he offered them their own choice of money and land if they would grant him the kingdom, and he told them that kinsmen of theirs were with him who would not desert him; and then they replied that no kinsman was dearer to them than their lord, and they never would follow his slayer; and then they offered to let their kinsmen go away from them unharmed. And they replied that the same had been offered to their comrades who had been with the king. Then they said this that they would not consider it any more than their comrades who were slain with the king. And they went on fighting around the gates until they fled [3] inside, and they slew the prince and the men who were with him, all except one who was the ealdorman's godson, and he spared his life, and he was wounded many times. And that Cynewulf reigned thirty-one years, and his body lies in Winchester, and that of the prince in Axminster; and their direct paternal ancestry goes back to Cerdic. And the same year Æthelbald, king of Mercia, was murdered at Seckington, and his body rests at Repton; he reigned forty-one years. And then Beornred succeeded to the kingdom, and ruled a short time

(*continued on p.* 50)

---

[3] *fled inside*, so E, which has *in flugon*, possibly a mistake for *fulgon* $\overline{A}$ C D, although it could possibly mean that they gave up defending the gates and fled to seek new defensive positions inside the residence: the change of subject necessary for what follows is of frequent occurrence in the annal.

A 755
[757]
from
p. 48

and unhappily; and the same year Offa succeeded to the kingdom and ruled thirty-nine years; and his son Ecgfrith ruled one hundred and forty-one days. That Offa was the son of Thingfrith, the son of Eanwulf, the son of Osmod, the son of Eawa, the son of Pybba, the son of Creoda, the son of Cynewald, the son of Cnebba, the son of Icel, the son of Eomer, the son of Angeltheow, the son of Offa, the son of Wermund, the son of Wihtlæg, the son of Woden.

758 [760]. In this year archbishop Cuthbert passed away.[1]

759 [761]. In this year Bregowine was consecrated archbishop at Michaelmas.[2]

760 [762]. In this year Æthelberht, king of Kent,[3] passed away; *who was the son of king Wihtred.*

761 [763–4]. In this year was the hard winter.

763 [765]. In this year [4] Jænberht was consecrated archbishop on the fortieth day after Christmas [Candlemas Day].[5]

764 [766]. In this year archbishop Jænberht received the pallium.

768. *In this year king Eadberht, son of Eata, passed away.*

772 [774]. In this year bishop Milred passed away.

773 [776]. In this year a red cross appeared in the sky after sunset. This same year the Mercians and the Kentishmen fought at Otford; and strange adders were seen in Sussex.

777 [779]. In this year Cynewulf and Offa fought round Benson, and Offa took the village. (*continued on p. 52*)

E 755
[757]
from
p. 49

and unhappily; and this same year Offa put Beornred to flight and succeeded to the kingdom, and ruled thirty-nine years: and his son Ecgfrith ruled one hundred and forty-one days. That Offa was the son of Thingfrith. (*continued on p. 51*)

F 777
from
p. 46

777. In this year Æthelberht was consecrated bishop of Whithorn at York.

(*continued on p. 52*)

---

[1] (*and he held the archbishopric eighteen years*) F. Passages from F in round brackets are insertions in the manuscript on the margin or above the line.

[2] (*and he held it four years*) F

[3] (*son of king Wihtred*) F

[4] (*passed away archbishop Bregowine*) F

[5] (*and he held it twenty-six years*) F

757. In this year Eadberht, king of Northumbria, received **E 757** the tonsure,[6] and Oswulf, his son, succeeded to the kingdom **from** and reigned one year: and the members of his household killed **p. 50** him on 24 July.

758 [760]. In this year archbishop Cuthbert passed away.

759 [761]. In this year Bregowine was consecrated archbishop at Michaelmas; and [759] Æthelwald Moll succeeded to the Northumbrian kingdom and reigned six years, and then abdicated.

760 [762]. In this year Æthelberht, king of Kent, passed away, and [764] Ceolwulf also passed away.

761 [763–4]. In this year was the hard winter; and [761] Moll, the Northumbrian king, slew Oswine at *Ædwinesclif* on 6 August.

762 [765]. In this year Jænberht was consecrated archbishop on the fortieth day after Christmas [Candlemas]; and [763] bishop Frithuwald of Whithorn passed away on 7 May: he was consecrated at York on 15 August in the sixth year of the reign of Ceolwulf: he had been bishop twenty-nine years: then Peohtwine was consecrated bishop of Whithorn at Elvet on 17 July.

765. In this year Alhred succeeded to the kingdom of Northumbria and reigned eight[7] years.

766. In this year archbishop Egbert passed away in York on 19 November: he had been bishop thirty-six years; also Frithuberht, bishop of Hexham: he had been bishop thirty-four years. And [767] Æthelberht was consecrated bishop of York and Ealhmund bishop of Hexham.

768. In this year passed away Eadberht, son of Eata, on 19 August.[8]

769. Initium regni Karoli regis.

772 [774]. In this year bishop Milred passed away.

774. In this year the Northumbrians expelled their king Alhred from York at Eastertide, and took Æthelred, son of Moll, as their lord, and he reigned four years. And [776] a red cross was seen in the sky after sunset. In the same year the Mercians and the Kentishmen fought at Otford; and strange adders were seen in Sussex.

776. In this year bishop Peohtwine passed away on 19 September: he had been bishop fourteen years.

777 [779]. In this year Cynewulf and Offa contended round Benson, and Offa took the village. And this same year [777] Æthelberht was consecrated bishop of Whithorn on 15 June at York.

(*continued on p.* 52)

[6] *suscipit clericalem coronam* F Lat
[7] *nine* D
[8] 20 August D

Ā 780
[782]
from
p. 50

780 [782]. In this year the Old Saxons and the Franks fought.

784 [786]. In this year Cyneheard slew king Cynewulf, and he [too] was slain and eighty-four men with him, and then Beorhtric succeeded to the kingdom of Wessex, and reigned sixteen years, and his body lies at Wareham, and his direct paternal ancestry goes back to Cerdic. *At this time king Ealhmund reigned in Kent.*

785 [787]. In this year there was a contentious synod at Chelsea, and Jænberht gave up a part of his jurisdiction as metropolitan; and

(*continued on p.* 54)

F 778
[779]
from
p. 50

778 [779]. In this year Ælfwald succeeded to the kingdom, and reigned ten years.

779 [780]. In this year archbishop Æthelberht passed away, and Eanbald had been consecrated [778] in his place. Cynebald [*recte* Cynewulf] resigned in Lindisfarne.

780 [782]. In this year Ealhmund, bishop of Hexham, passed away; and Tilberht was appointed thereto, and Hygebald to Lindisfarne;[1] and king Ælfwald sent to Rome for the pallium for the use of archbishop Eanbald.

782. In this year Cynewulf, bishop of Lindisfarne, passed away; and there was a synod at *Acleah*.

784. [Hic tunc temporis fuit in Cantia rex Ealhmundus: this king Ealhmund was the father of Egbert, the father of Æthelwulf.][2]

785 [787]. In this year a full synod sat at Chelsea, and Jænberht gave up a part of his jurisdiction as a metropolitan, and Hygeberht was appointed [archbishop of Lichfield] by king Offa. Ecgfrith was consecrated king. At this time legates (*continued on p.* 54)

E 777
[779]
from
p. 51

In the time of this king Offa there was an abbot of *Medeshamstede* called Beonna. This same Beonna, on the advice of all the monks of the monastery, leased[3] to ealdorman Cuthbert ten farms[4] at Swineshead [L], with pasture and with meadow and all appurtenances, on condition that the aforesaid Cuthbert gave the abbot fifty pounds for it, and each year a day's supply of food or thirty shillings in money; and on condition moreover that the said land should revert to the monastery on his decease. At this attestation were present the king Offa, the king Ecgfrith, the archbishop Hygeberht, and bishop Ceolwulf, (*continued on p.* 53)

---

[1] *qui fuit apud Soccabyri* F Lat. It was to Hygebald that Alcuin wrote his now famous letter (*Quid Hinieldus cum Christo?*) in 797. See H. M. Chadwick, *The Heroic Age* (Cambridge 1912) 41.

[2] Added by later scribes.

[3] See F. M. Stenton, 'Medeshamstede and its Colonies' 313–14 on this lease and that by Ceolred (*s.a.* 852 E).

[4] *bondeland*, 'land held by a *bonda* as tenant' (BT Suppl); possibly equivalent to a 'hide' of land, the normal peasant holding.

E 777
[779]
from
p. 52
and bishop Unwona, and abbot Beonna, and many other bishops and abbots, and many other prominent men. In the time of this same Offa there was an ealdorman called Brorda [5] who petitioned the king for love of him to free a church of his called Woking, because he wished to give it to *Medeshamstede* and to St Peter and the abbot that then was, who was called Pusa. That Pusa succeeded Beonna, and the king loved him well. And the king freed the church of Woking from all obligations due to king and to bishop and to earl and to all men, so that no one should have any authority there, except St Peter and the abbot. This was ratified in the royal manor of *Freoricburna*.

778. In this year Æthelbald and Heardberht slew three 'high-reeves' [6] on 22 March: Ealdwulf, son of Bosa, at Coniscliffe, and Cynewulf and Ecga at *Helaþyrne*. And then Ælfwald succeeded to the kingdom and drove Æthelred out of the country, and he reigned for ten years. Karolus in Hispanias intrauit. Karolus Saxoniam uenit. Karolus Pampileniam urbem destruxit, atque Cesar Augustam, exercitum suum coniunxit, et acceptis obsidibus, subiugatis Sarracensis, per Narbonam Wasconiam Franciam rediit.

779 [782]. In this year the Old Saxons and the Franks fought. And [780] the Northumbrian 'high-reeves' burned Beorn the ealdorman to death in *Seletun* on 24 December. And archbishop Æthelberht passed away in York, and Eanbald had been consecrated [778] in his place. And bishop Cynebald [*recte* Cynewulf] resigned in Lindisfarne.

780. In this year Ealhmund, bishop of Hexham, passed away on 8 September, and Tilberht was consecrated in his place on 2 October. And Hygebald was consecrated bishop of Lindisfarne at Sockburn-on-Tees; and king Ælfwald sent a man [7] to Rome for the pallium, and made Eanbald archbishop.

782. In this year passed away Wærburh, Ceolred's queen, and Cynewulf, bishop of Lindisfarne; and there was a synod at *Acleah*.

784 [786]. In this year Cyneheard slew king Cynewulf, and he [too] was slain and eighty-four men with him; and then Beorhtric, king of the West Saxons, succeeded to the kingdom and ruled sixteen years: his body lies at Wareham, and his direct paternal ancestry goes back to Cerdic.

785. In this year passed away Botwine, abbot of Ripon; and the same year [787] there was a contentious synod at Chelsea and archbishop Jænberht gave up a part (*continued on p. 55*)

---

[5] Offa's *prefectus*. See Stenton, *op. cit.* 323 on this grant of immunities to the church of Woking.

[6] The 'high-reeve' was probably an official responsible for the administration of a royal estate or large district, probably not very different in status from the ealdorman: 'high-reeves' are not known in the south of England until later in the period, when the term may mean the reeve of a large borough-district. (Cf. H. M. Chadwick, *Studies in Anglo-Saxon Institutions* 237)

[7] Alcuin.

A 785
[787]
from
p. 52

Hygeberht was appointed by king Offa [to be archbishop of Lichfield]; and Ecgfrith was consecrated king.

787 [789]. In this year king Beorhtric took to wife Eadburh, daughter of Offa. And in his days came for the first time three ships: and then the reeve rode thither and tried to compel them to go to the royal manor, for he did not know what they were, and they slew him. These were the first ships of the Danes to come to England.

790 [792]. In this year archbishop Jænberht passed away, and the same year abbot Æthelheard was elected bishop.

792 [794]. In this year king Offa, king of the Mercians, ordered king Æthelberht's head to be struck off. (*continued on p.* 56)

F 785
[787]
from
p. 52

were sent by pope Adrian to England to renew the faith which St Gregory had sent to us: and they were received with ceremony.

787 [789]. In this year king Beorhtric took to wife Eadburh, daughter of king Offa; and in his days came for the first time three ships of Norwegians [1] from Hörthaland [around Hardanger Fjord]: these were the first ships of the Danes to come to England.[2]

788 [787]. In this year a synod assembled at *Pincanhalh* in Northumbria.

789 [788]. In this year Ælfwald, king of Northumbria, was slain, and a light was frequently seen in the sky where he was slain. (And Osred, Alhred's son, succeeded to the kingdom, because he was the nephew of Ælfwald. And there was a great synod at *Acleah*.)

790 [792]. In this year archbishop Jænberht passed away, and the same year abbot Æthelheard (of the monastery of Louth) was elected archbishop. [790] And Osred, king of Northumbria, was driven from the kingdom, and Æthelred, son of Æthelwald, was restored to the kingdom.

791. In this year Baldwulf was consecrated bishop of Whithorn by archbishop Eanbald and bishop Æthelberht.

792 [794]. In this year king Offa ordered king Æthelberht's head to be struck off.[3]

793. In this year terrible portents appeared in Northumbria, and miserably afflicted the inhabitants: these were exceptional flashes of lightning, and fiery dragons were seen flying in the air, and soon followed (*continued on p.* 56)

---

[1] *de Danis* F Lat. 'The *Chronicle* frequently uses "Northmen" and "Danes" as convertible terms.' (Plummer)

[2] *Primæ fuerunt quia nunquam ante has postquam Angli intrauerunt Britanniam uenerant aliæ* F Lat. According to the Annals of St Neot's the pirates landed at Portland. In Æthelweard's account of the event the reeve is described as *exactor regis iam morans in oppido quod Dorceastre nuncupator.* Dorchester was a *uilla regalis*; and 'the story leads us to infer that external jurisdiction, reaching as far as the sea, was attached to it.' (H. M. Chadwick, *Studies in Anglo-Saxon Institutions* 257). In Alfred's *Laws* § 34 it is decreed 'with regard to traders: they shall bring before the king's reeve, at a public meeting, the men they are taking up into the

of his jurisdiction as a metropolitan, and Hygeberht was
E 785 appointed [archbishop of Lichfield] by king Offa. And Ecgfrith
from was consecrated king. At this time messengers were sent from
p. 53 Rome by pope Adrian to England to renew the faith and the
peace which St Gregory had sent to us by bishop Augustine:
they were received with ceremony.[4]

787 [789]. In this year Beorhtric took to wife Eadburh, daughter of
king Offa. And in his days came first three ships of Norwegians [5] from
Hörthaland [around Hardanger Fjord]: and then the reeve rode thither
and tried to compel them to go to the royal manor, for he did not know
what they were: and then they slew him. These were the first ships
of the Danes to come to England.[6]

788 [787]. In this year a synod assembled at *Pincanhalh* [7] in Northumbria on 2 September, and abbot Aldberht passed away.[8] Karolus
per Alemanniam uenit ad fines Bauuarie.

789 [788]. In this year Ælfwald, king of Northumbria, was slain by
Sicga on 23 September, and a light was frequently seen in the sky where
he was slain: he was buried at Hexham inside the church. And a
synod assembled at *Acleah*. And Osred, son of Alhred, succeeded to
the kingdom after him, and he was his nephew.

790 [792]. In this year archbishop Jænberht passed away, and the
same year abbot Æthelheard was elected archbishop. [790] And Osred,
king of Northumbria, was betrayed and driven from the kingdom; and
Æthelred, son of Æthelwald, was restored to the kingdom.

791. In this year Baldwulf was consecrated bishop of Whithorn by
archbishop Eanbald and bishop Æthelberht on 17 July.

792 [794]. In this year Offa, king of Mercia, ordered Æthelberht's
head to be struck off. And Osred, who had been king of Northumbria,
on his return from exile was seized and slain on 14 September; and his
body lies at Tynemouth. And king Æthelred married again on 29
September, and the lady was called Ælfled.

793. In this year terrible portents appeared over Northumbria, and
miserably frightened the inhabitants: these were exceptional flashes of
lightning,[9] and fiery dragons were seen flying in the air.

(*continued on p.* 57)

country, and declare how many of them there are' (F. L. Attenborough,
The Laws of the Earliest English Kings, Cambridge 1922, 78–9). Evidently
the reeve thought the pirates were merchants.
[3] See M. R. James, 'Two Lives of St Ethelbert, King and Martyr' (32
EHR 214–44), and C. E. Wright, *The Cultivation of Saga in Anglo-Saxon
England* 95–106.
[4] *and sent back in peace* D
[5] So B C D F
[6] For a translation of Æthelweard's account of the incident see R. H.
Hodgkin, *A History of the Anglo-Saxons* II. 473.
[7] *Wincanheale* D; *Pincanheale* E F
[8] *in Ripon* D
[9] *exceptional high winds and flashes of lightning* D

Ā 794
[796]
from
p. 54

794 [796]. In this year [795][1] pope Adrian and king Offa passed away. Æthelred, king of Northumbria, was killed by his own court; and bishop Ceolwulf and bishop Eadbald left the country. And Ecgfrith succeeded to the Mercian kingdom, and passed away that same year. And Eadberht, whose nickname was Præn, took possession of the kingdom of Kent.

796 [798]. In this year Ceolwulf [recte Cœnwulf], king of Mercia, harried the Kentishmen as far as Romney Marsh, and they seized Præn, their king, and led him bound into Mercia.

797 [799]. In this year the Romans cut off the tongue of pope Leo and put out his eyes, and banished him from his see: and soon afterwards, by God's help, he could see and speak, and became pope again as he had been. (continued on p. 58)

F 793
from
p. 54

a great famine, and after that in the same year the harrying of the heathen miserably destroyed God's church in Lindisfarne by rapine and slaughter.[2]

794 [796]. In this year pope Adrian and king Offa passed away; and Æthelred, king of Northumbria, was slain. And bishop Ceolwulf and bishop Eadbald left the country. And king Ecgfrith succeeded to the Mercian kingdom, and in that year passed away. And Eadberht Præn took possession of the kingdom of Kent.

795 [796]. In this year there was an eclipse of the moon between cock-crow and dawn.[3] And Eardwulf succeeded to the Northumbrian kingdom, and was consecrated king by archbishop Eanbald and bishop Æthelberht and Hygebald and bishop Baldwulf.

796 [798]. In this year Ceolwulf [recte Cœnwulf], king of Mercia, harried Kent, and seized Eadberht Præn, their king; he led him bound into Mercia (and had his eyes put out and his hands cut off). And Æthelheard, archbishop of Canterbury, called a synod, and confirmed and ratified, by command of pope Leo, all the ordinances concerning God's monasteries which were decreed during the reign of Wihtgar and during the reign of other kings.

798. [As 797 E] ... and bishop Æthelberht passed away. (And bishop Alfhun passed away at Sudbury and was buried at Dunwich, and Tidfrith was elected in his place. And Sigeric, king of Essex, journeyed to Rome. In the same year the body of Wihtburh was found quite sound and free from corruption [4] at Dereham, fifty-five years after she departed this life.) (continued on p. 58)

---

[1] Pope Adrian I died on 25 December 795.

[2] *uastauit terram rapinis et homicidiis.* *Translatio Sancti Albani martyris* F Lat

[3] *inter galli cantum et auroram. vi. Kalendas Iunii* F Lat

[4] *sine corruptione* F Lat

A great famine soon followed these signs; and a little after
E 793 that in the same year on 8 January [5] the harrying of the heathen
from miserably destroyed God's church in Lindisfarne by rapine and
p. 55 slaughter. And Sicga passed away on 22 February.

794 [796]. In this year pope Adrian and king Offa passed
away. Æthelred, king of Northumbria, was killed by his own court on
19 April. And bishop Ceolwulf and bishop Eadbald left the country.
And Ecgfrith succeeded to the Mercian kingdom, and that same year
passed away. Eadberht, whose nickname was Præn, took possession
of the kingdom of Kent. [794] And ealdorman Æthelheard passed
away on 1 August. And Northumbria was ravaged by the heathen,
and Ecgfrith's monastery at *Donemup* [Jarrow] looted; and there one
of their leaders was slain, and some of their ships besides were shat-
tered by storms: and many of them were drowned there, and some
came ashore alive and were at once slain at the river mouth.

795 [796]. In this year there was an eclipse of the moon between
cock-crow and dawn on 28 March. And Eardwulf came to the throne
of Northumbria on 14 May; he was afterwards consecrated and
enthroned on 26 May in York by archbishop Eanbald and Æthelberht
and Hygebald and Baldwulf.

796. In this year Offa, king of Mercia, passed away on 10 August; [6]
he reigned forty years; and archbishop Eanbald on 10 August of the
same year, and his body lies in York; and this same year passed away
bishop Ceolwulf; and a second Eanbald was consecrated in the other's
place on 14 August. And in the same year [798] Ceolwulf [*recte*
Cœnwulf], king of Mercia, harried the Kentishmen and the people of
Romney Marsh, and seized Præn, their king, and led him bound into
Mercia.

797 [799]. In this year the Romans cut off the tongue of pope Leo
and put out his eyes, and banished him from his see: and soon afterwards by God's help he could see and speak, and became pope again as
he had been. [797] And Eanbald received the pallium on 8 September;
and bishop Æthelberht passed away on ⟨16 October, and Heardred was
consecrated bishop in his stead on⟩ [7] 30 October.

798. In this year in spring, on 2 April, there was a great battle at
Whalley in Northumbria, and there was slain Alric, the son of Heardberht, and many others with him. (*continued on p.* 59)

---

[5] The Ides of January, probably a mistake for the Ides of June (8 June)
which is the date given by Simeon of Durham. 'The vikings would not cross
the sea at midwinter.' (Plummer)

[6] *29 July* D (correctly)

[7] 'From D. The omission in E is due to the recurrence of the words:
on . . . k Nov.' (Plummer)

Ā 799
[801]
from
p. 56

799 [801]. In this year archbishop Æthelheard and Cyneberht, bishop of Wessex, went to Rome.

800 [802]. In this year king Beorhtric passed away, and ealdorman Worr. And Egbert succeeded to the kingdom of Wessex: and the same day ealdorman Æthelmund rode from the Hwicce [1] over [the Thames] at Kempsford, and was met by ealdorman Weohstan with the men of Wiltshire. There was a great battle, and both the ealdormen were slain there, and the men of Wiltshire won the victory.

802 [804]. In this year Beornmod was consecrated bishop of Rochester.

803 [805]. In this year archbishop Æthelheard passed away, and Wulfred was consecrated archbishop, and abbot Forthred passed away.

804 [806]. In this year archbishop Wulfred received the pallium.

805 [807]. In this year king Cuthred passed away in Kent, and abbess Ceolburh and ealdorman Heahberht.[2]

812 [814]. In this year king Charlemagne passed away: he reigned forty-five years. And archbishop Wulfred and Wigberht, bishop of Wessex, both went to Rome.

813 [815]. In this year archbishop Wulfred returned home to his own see, with the blessing of pope Leo; and this same year king Egbert harried in Cornwall from east to west.

814 [816]. In this year Leo, the noble and holy pope, passed away, and Stephen succeeded to the papacy after him. (*continued on p.* 60)

F 806
from
p. 56

806 [*As E*]. . . . (Also in this same year, on 4 June, the sign of the holy cross appeared in the moon one Wednesday at dawn; and again this year, on 30 August, a marvellous ring appeared around the sun.[3])

809. In this year there was an eclipse of the sun at the beginning of the fifth hour of the day, on 16 July, on Tuesday, the twenty-ninth day of the moon. (*continued on p.* 63)

[1] . . . a people who in the seventh century occupied the territory now represented by Gloucestershire, Worcestershire, and the western half of Warwickshire.' (F. M. Stenton, *Anglo-Saxon England* 43)

[2] *Heabryht* Ā; *Heabriht* B C; *Heardbryht* D

[3] *Hoc anno etiam ·ii· Nonas Iunii, luna ·xiiii·, signum Crucis mirabili modo in luna apparuit feria ·v· aurora incipiente, hoc modo* ✚ *Eodem anno ·iii· Kalendas Septembris, luna ·xii·, die Dominica hora ·iiii·, corona mirabilis in circuitu solis apparuit* F Lat

E 799
[801]
from
p. 57

799 [801]. In this year archbishop Æthelred [4] and Cyneberht, bishop of Wessex, went to Rome.

800. In this year there was an eclipse of the moon at the second hour of the eve of 16 January. And [802] king Beorhtric passed away, and ealdorman Worr. And Egbert succeeded to the kingdom of Wessex: and the same day ealdorman Æthelmund rode from the Hwicce over [the Thames] at Kempsford, and was met by ealdorman Weohstan with the men of Wiltshire. There was a great battle, and both the ealdormen were slain there, and the men of Wiltshire won the victory. [800] Karolus rex imperator factus est, et a Romanis appellatus Augustus; qui illos qui Leonem papam dehonestauerant morte damnauit, sed precibus papæ morte indulta exilio retrusit. Ipse enim papa Leo imperatorem eum sacrauerat.

802. In this year there was an eclipse of the moon at dawn on 20 December [recte 21 May]. And [804] Beornmod was consecrated bishop of Rochester the same year.

803. In this year Hygebald, bishop of Lindisfarne, passed away on 24 June; and Egbert was consecrated in his place on 11 June. And [805] archbishop Æthelheard passed away in Kent, and Wulfred was consecrated archbishop.

804 [806]. In this year archbishop Wulfred received the pallium.

805 [807]. In this year king Cuthred passed away in Kent, and abbess Ceolburh and Heardberht.

806. In this year there was an eclipse of the moon on 1 September. And Eardwulf, king of Northumbria, was driven from his kingdom, and Eanberht, bishop of Hexham, passed away.

810. Karolus cum Niceforo imperatore Constantinopoli*tano* pacem fecit.

812 [814]. In this year king Charlemagne passed away; he reigned forty-five years. And archbishop Wulfred and Wigberht, bishop of Wessex, went to Rome. Cireneius [5] Karolo imperatori legatos suos cum pace mittit. Karolus imperator obiit.

813 [815]. In this year archbishop Wulfred returned home to his own see, with the blessing of pope Leo; and this same year king Egbert harried in Cornwall from east to west.

814 [816]. In this year Leo, the noble and holy pope, passed away, and Stephen succeeded to the papacy after him. (*continued on p.* 61)

---

[4] for *Æpelheard* of the other manuscripts
[5] Cireneius: A ghost name, 'derived probably from the original through several intermediate steps. The Annales Uticenses 811 have: *Niceforus obiit. Michael imperator, gener eius, qui Karolo . . . pace mittit.*' (Plummer)

A 816
[893]
from
p. 58

816 [817]. In this year pope Stephen passed away, and after him Paschal was consecrated pope. And in the same year 'the English Quarter' [1] was burnt down.

819 [821]. In this year Cœnwulf, king of Mercia, passed away, and Ceolwulf succeeded to the kingdom, and ealdorman Eadberht passed away.

821 [823]. In this year Ceolwulf was deprived of his kingdom.

822 [824]. In this year two ealdormen, Burhhelm and Muca, were slain: and there was a synod at *Clofeshoh*.

823 [825]. In this year there was a battle at Galford between the Britons [of Cornwall] and the men of Devon. And the same year king Egbert and king Beornwulf fought at *Ellendun*, and Egbert was victoriousi and great slaughter was made there. Then he sent his son Æthelwulf from his levies and Ealhstan, his bishop, and Wulfheard, his ealdorman, to Kent with a great force, and they drove king Baldred north over Thames, and the Kentishmen submitted to him, and the men of Surrey and Sussex and Essex, because formerly [2] they had been wrongly forced away from [their allegiance to] his kinsmen. And the same year the king of the East Angles and the court turned to king Egbert as their protector and guardian against the fear of Mercian aggression; and the same year the East Angles slew Beornwulf, king of the Mercians.

825 [827]. In this year Ludeca, king of Mercia, was slain and his five ealdormen with him, and Wiglaf succeeded to the kingdom.

827 [829]. In this year [828] [5] there was an eclipse of the moon on Christmas morning. And the same year king Egbert conquered Mercia, and all that was south of the Humber, and he was the eighth king to be 'Ruler of Britain' [3]: the first to rule so great a kingdom was Ælle, king of Sussex; the second was Ceawlin, king of Wessex; the third was Æthelberht, king of Kent; the fourth was Rædwald, king of East Anglia; the fifth was Edwin, king of Northumbria; the sixth was Oswald who reigned after him: the seventh was Oswy, Oswald's brother; the eighth was Egbert, king of Wessex. This Egbert led his levies to Dore against the Northumbrians, where they offered him submission and peace; thereupon they parted. (*continued on p.* 62)

---

[1] Literally 'School,' but not in any modern sense of the word. It was on the Vatican Hill and was inhabited by ecclesiastics, pilgrims and others whose business took them to Rome. Cf. W. Levison, *England and the Continent in the Eighth Century* (Oxford 1946), 40–1.

[2] At this point begins the fragment of MS. A

[3] *Bretwalda;* on this title see F. M. Stenton, *op. cit.* 33–4.

E 815
[817]
from
p. 59

815 [817]. In this year pope Stephen passed away, and after him Paschal was consecrated pope. And in the same year 'the School of the English' was burnt down.

819 [821]. In this year Cœnwulf, king of Mercia, passed away, and Ceolwulf succeeded to the kingdom, and ealdorman Eadberht passed away.

821 [823]. In this year Ceolwulf was deprived of his kingdom.

822 [824]. In this year two ealdormen, Burhhelm and Muca, were slain; and there was a synod at *Clofeshoh*.

823 [825]. In this year there was a battle at Galford between the Britons [of Cornwall] and the men of Devon. And this same year Egbert, king of Wessex, and Beornwulf, king of Mercia, fought at *Ellandun*, and Egbert was victorious, and great slaughter was made there. Then he sent his son Æthelwulf from his levies [4] and Ealhstan, his bishop, and Wulfheard, his ealdorman, to Kent with a great force, and they drove king Baldred north over Thames, and the Kentishmen submitted to him, and the men of Surrey and Sussex and Essex, because formerly they had been wrongly forced away from [their allegiance to] his kinsmen. And the same year the king of the East Angles and his court turned to king Egbert as their protector and guardian against the fear of Mercian aggression; and the same year the East Angles slew Beornwulf, king of the Mercians.

825 [827]. In this year Ludeca, king of Mercia, was slain and his five ealdormen with him, and Wiglaf succeeded to the kingdom.

827 [829]. In this year [828] [5] there was an eclipse of the moon on Christmas morning. And the same year king Egbert conquered Mercia and all that was south of the Humber, and he was the eighth king to be 'Ruler of Britain': the first to rule so great a kingdom was Ælle, king of Sussex; the second was Ceawlin, king of Wessex; the third was Æthelberht, king of Kent; the fourth was Rædwald, king of East Anglia; the fifth was Edwin, king of Northumbria; the sixth was Oswald who reigned after him: the seventh was Oswy, Oswald's brother; the eighth was Egbert, king of Wessex. This Egbert led his levies to Dore against the Northumbrians, where they offered him submission and peace; thereupon they parted. (*continued on p. 63*)

---

[4] I have used this expression for OE *fyrd*. On fyrd service see F. M. Stenton, *Anglo-Saxon England* 287–8.

[5] The eclipse was at 2 a.m. on 25 December 828, and opens the annal for 829 which begins the year at 24 September.

Ā 828
[830]
from
p. 60 828 [830]. In this year Wiglaf obtained again the kingdom of Mercia; and bishop Æthelwald passed away; and the same year king Egbert led his levies into Wales, and reduced them to humble submission.

829 [832]. In this year archbishop Wulfred passed away.

830 [833]. In this year Ceolnoth was elected [arch]bishop and consecrated; and abbot Feologild passed away.

831 [834]. In this year archbishop Ceolnoth received the pallium.

832 [835]. In this year the heathen devastated Sheppey.

833 [836]. In this year king Egbert fought against thirty-five ships' companies at Carhampton;[1] and great slaughter was made there, and the Danes had possession of the place of slaughter. And Herefrith and Wigthegn, two bishops, passed away; and Dudda and Osmod, two ealdormen, passed away.

835 [838]. In this year came a great pirate host to Cornwall, and they [the Danes and the Britons of Cornwall] united, and continued fighting against Egbert, king of Wessex. Then he heard this and proceeded with his levies and fought against them at Hingston Down, and there put to flight both Britons and Danes.

836 [839]. In this year king Egbert passed away; and [on an earlier occasion], thirteen[2] years before he became king, Offa, king of Mercia, and Beorhtric, king of Wessex, had expelled him from England to the land of the Franks; and Beorhtric supported Offa because he had his daughter as his queen. And that Egbert reigned thirty-seven years and seven months; and Æthelwulf, son of Egbert, succeeded to the kingdom of Wessex, and he gave his son Athelstan the kingdom of Kent and Essex and of Surrey and of Sussex.

837 [840]. In this year ealdorman Wulfheard fought at Southampton against thirty-three ships' companies, and made great slaughter there and won the victory; and the same year Wulfheard passed away. And the same year ealdorman Æthelhelm fought against a Danish host[3] at Portland with the men of Dorset, and for a considerable time they drove back the host, but the Danes had possession of the place of slaughter and slew the ealdorman.

838 [841]. In this year ealdorman Hereberht[4] was slain by the heathen and many with him among the people of Romney Marsh, and

(continued on p. 64)

---

[1] See Bruce Dickins, *The Times Literary Supplement* (22 September 1921).

[2] All manuscripts read *three* here, probably in error. Dr Whitelock, however, suggests to me that what is implied is that of his exile Egbert spent three years in the Frankish kingdom.

[3] OE *here*, the usual term in the *Chronicle* for the Scandinavian invaders. For the original meaning of the word, cf. Ine's *Laws* § 13, 1: 'We use the term "thieves" if the number of men does not exceed seven, "band of marauders" (*hlop*) for a number between seven and thirty-five. Anything beyond this is a "raid" (*here*)' (translation by F. L. Attenborough, *op. cit.* 40–1).

[4] Dr Whitelock informs me that an ealdorman of this name witnesses Æthelwulf's Kentish charters.

E 828
[830]
from
p. 61

828 [830]. In this year Wiglaf obtained again the kingdom of Mercia; and bishop Æthelbald [*recte* Æthelwald] passed away; and the same year king Egbert led his levies into Wales, and reduced them all to humble submission.

829 [832]. In this year archbishop Wulfred passed away.

830 [833]. In this year Ceolnoth was elected [arch]bishop and consecrated; and [832] abbot Feologild passed away.

831 [834]. In this year archbishop Ceolnoth received the pallium.

832 [835]. In this year the heathen devastated Sheppey.

833 [836]. In this year king Egbert fought against twenty-five ships' companies at Carhampton; and great slaughter was made there, and the Danes had possession of the place of slaughter. And Herefrith and Wigfrith [*recte* Wigthegn], two bishops, passed away; and Dudda and Osmod, two ealdormen, passed away.

835 [838]. In this year came a great pirate host to Cornwall, and they [the Danes and the Britons of Cornwall] united, and continued fighting against Egbert, king of Wessex. Then he made an expedition against them, and fought against them at Hingston Down, and there put to flight both Britons and Danes.

836 [839]. In this year king Egbert passed away; and [on an earlier occasion], thirteen [2] years before he became king, Offa, king of Mercia, and Beorhtric, king of Wessex, had expelled him from England to the land of the Franks. And that Egbert reigned thirty-seven years and seven months, and Æthelwulf, his son, succeeded to the kingdom of Wessex, and Athelstan, his second son,[5] succeeded to the kingdom of Kent and to Surrey and to the kingdom of Sussex.

837 [840]. In this year ealdorman Wulfheard fought at Southampton against thirty-three ships' companies and made great slaughter there and won the victory; and the same year Wulfheard passed away. And ealdorman Æthelhelm fought against the Danes at Portland with the men of Dorset, and the ealdorman was slain, and the Danes had possession of the place of slaughter. (*continued on p. 65*)

F 829
[832]
from
p. 58

829 [832]. In this year archbishop Wulfred passed away (and abbot Feologild was elected to succeed him in the archiepiscopal see on 25 April. He was consecrated on Sunday, 9 June, but he died on 30 August). (*continued on p. 67*)

---

[5] So D E F against A̅ B C. Athelstan was the son of Æthelwulf, not of Egbert.

Ā 838
[841]
from
p. 62

the same year, again in Lindsey and in East Anglia and in Kent, many men were slain by the host.

839 [842]. In this year there was great slaughter in London, and in *Cwantawic* [a lost place near Étaples], and in Rochester.

840 [843]. In this year king Æthelwulf fought at Carhampton against thirty-five ships' companies, and the Danes had possession of the place of slaughter.

845 [848]. In this year ealdorman Eanwulf with the men of Somerset and bishop Ealhstan and ealdorman Osric with the men of Dorset fought against a Danish host at the mouth of the Parret, and made great slaughter there and won the victory.

851 [850]. In this year ealdorman Ceorl with the men of Devon fought against the heathen at *Wiceganbeorg*, and made great slaughter there and won the victory. And this same year king Athelstan and ealdorman Ealhhere destroyed a great host at Sandwich in Kent, captured nine ships, and drove off the rest. And the heathen for the first time remained over the winter. And the same year [851] came three hundred and fifty ships to the mouth of the Thames, and stormed Canterbury and London, and put to flight Beorhtwulf, king of Mercia, with his levies, and went then south over Thames into Surrey; and king Æthelwulf and his son Æthelbald, with the West Saxon levies, fought against them at *Acleah*, and there made the greatest slaughter of a heathen host that we have heard tell of up to this present day, and there won the victory.

853. In this year Burhred, king of Mercia, and his councillors besought king Æthelwulf that he would help them to subject the Welsh. He then did so, and with his levies went through Mercia into Wales, and they made them all obedient to them. And the same year king Æthelwulf sent his son Alfred to Rome. At that time lord Leo was pope in Rome and he consecrated him as king, and stood sponsor to him at confirmation. Then that same year Ealhhere with the Kentishmen and Huda with the men of Surrey fought in Thanet against a heathen host, (*continued on p.* 66)

E 839
[842]
from
p. 63

839 [842]. In this year there was great slaughter in London, and in *Cantwic*, and in Rochester.

840 [843]. In this year king Æthelwulf fought at Carhampton against thirty-five ships' companies, and the Danes had possession of the place of slaughter.

845 [848]. In this year ealdorman Earnwulf [*recte* Eanwulf] with the men of Somerset and bishop Ealhstan and ealdorman Osric with the men of Dorset fought against a Danish host at the mouth of the Parret, and made great slaughter there and won the victory.

851 [850]. In this year ealdorman Ceorl with the men of Devon fought against the heathen at *Wicgeanbeorg*, and there made great slaughter and won the victory. And the heathen stayed in Thanet over the winter. And the same year [851] came three hundred and fifty ships to the mouth of the Thames, and stormed Canterbury, and put to flight Beorhtwulf, king of Mercia, with his levies, and went then south over Thames into Surrey; and king Æthelwulf and his son Æthelbald, with the West Saxon levies, fought against them at *Acleah*, and there made the greatest slaughter of a heathen host that we have ever heard tell of, and there won the victory. And the same year king Athelstan and ealdorman Ealhhere fought in ships, and destroyed a great host at Sandwich, and captured nine ships and drove off the rest.

852.[1] At this time Ceolred, abbot of *Medeshamstede*, and the monks leased to Wulfred the estate at Sempringham, on condition that on his decease the said estate should revert to the monastery, and Wulfred should give the estate at Sleaford to *Medeshamstede*, and he should give every year to the monastery sixty wagon loads of wood and twelve wagon loads of brushwood and six wagon loads of faggots, and two casks full of clear ale and two cattle for slaughter and six hundred loaves and ten measures of Welsh ale, and each year a horse and thirty shillings and a day's supply of food. Parties to the transaction were king Burhred, archbishop Ceolred [*recte* Ceolnoth], and bishop Tunberht, and bishop Cenred [*recte* Ceolred], and bishop Ealhhun, and bishop Beorhtred, and abbot Wihtred, and abbot Werheard, ealdorman Æthelheard, ealdorman Hunberht, and many others.

852 [853]. In this year Burhred, king of Mercia, made the Welsh subject to him with the assistance of king Æthelwulf. And the same year Ealhhere with the Kentishmen and Huda with the men of Surrey fought (*continued on p.* 67)

---

[1] A fuller version of this grant exists and is printed, with translation, in A. J. Robertson, *Anglo-Saxon Charters* (Cambridge 1939), 12–13. See also her notes (271–2) on *foper* (a wagon load), *mitta* (measure), and Welsh ale 'frequently recommended in potions for the relief of various illnesses and diseases.'

and at first were victorious, and there many men were slain
Ā 853 and drowned on either side. And after Easter of the same
from year, king Æthelwulf gave his daughter in marriage to king
p. 64 Burhred, as from Wessex to Mercia.

855. In this year the heathen for the first time wintered
in Sheppey. And the same year king Æthelwulf granted the tenth part
of his land over all his kingdom by charter [1] for the glory of God and
his own eternal salvation. And the same year he proceeded to Rome in
great state, and remained there twelve months and then made his way
towards home. And Charles, king of the Franks, gave him his daughter
as queen, and after that he came to his people and they were glad
thereof. And two years after he came from the Franks he died, and his
body lies at Winchester, and he reigned eighteen years and a half. And
that Æthelwulf was the son of Egbert, the son of Ealhmund, the son of
Eafa, the son of Eoppa, the son of Ingeld: Ingeld was the brother of Ine,
king of Wessex, who afterwards went to St Peter's [Rome] and there
gave up his life afterwards; and they were the sons of Cenred, and
Cenred was the son of Ceolwald, the son of Cutha, the son of Cuthwine,
the son of Ceawlin, the son of Cynric, the son of Cerdic,[2] the son of
Elesa, the son of Esla, the son of Gewis, the son of Wig, the son of
Freawine, the son of Frithugar, the son of Brand, the son of Bældæg,
the son of Woden, the son of Frithuwald, the son of Freawine, Frealaf,[3]
the son of Frithuwulf, the son of Finn, the son of Godwulf, the son of
Geat, the son of Tætwa, the son of Beaw, the son of Sceldwea, the son
of Heremod, the son of Itermon, the son of Hrathra, who [4] was born in
the ark: Noah, Lamech, Methuselah, Enoch, Jared, Mahalaleel,
Cainan, Enos, Seth, Adam the first man, and our father who is Christ.
Amen. And then Æthelwulf's two sons succeeded to the kingdom:
Æthelbald to Wessex, and Æthelberht to Kent and to Essex and to
Surrey and to Sussex: and then Æthelbald reigned five years.

860. In this year king Æthelbald passed away, and his body lies at
Sherborne; and Æthelberht, his brother, succeeded to the entire kingdom, *(continued on p. 68)*

---

[1] See F. M. Stenton, *op. cit.* 304–5. For text and translation of one of
these charters of King Æthelwulf, see A. J. Robertson, *op. cit.* 14–15.

[2] 'Cynric, the son of Creoda, the son of Cerdic.' B C D

[3] Cf. 547A where Freotholaf = Frealaf; here an additional name, Frithuwald, has been inserted before Frealaf.

[4] The original reading was probably as preserved in B C (see p. 67): the
person born in the ark is Sceaf. On King Æthelwulf's mythical ancestors,
see H. M. Chadwick, *The Origin of the English Nation*, chap. xi. Æthelweard's version of this genealogy follows Tætwa with Beo, Scyld, Scef, and
stops there. As Chadwick says (*loc. cit* 272), 'it would seem that he has
acquired it from some unknown source in a more primitive form than that
contained in the *Chronicle*.' F. M. Stenton, 'The South-Western Element
in the Old English Chronicle' 23 note 3, goes further and suggests that the
descent from Adam, which occurs in all existing versions of the *Chronicle*
at this point, was substituted after the work had passed into monastic hands,
thus lending support for his view that the original chronicle (750–891) was
a secular work.

Kenneth Sisam's important article, 'Anglo-Saxon Royal Genealogies'
(Proceedings of the British Academy (1953) 287–346), should also be noted.

E 852
[853]
from
p. 65

in Thanet against a heathen host; and there many were slain and drowned on either side, and the ealdormen both dead. And Burhred, king of Mercia, received in marriage the daughter of Æthelwulf, king of Wessex.

855. In this year the heathen for the first time wintered in Sheppey. And the same year king Æthelwulf granted the tenth part of his land over all his kingdom by charter for the glory of God and his own eternal salvation. And this same year he proceeded to Rome in great state, and remained there twelve months. And he received in marriage the daughter of Charles, king of the Franks, when on the way home,[5] and returned home in good health, and then two years afterwards he passed away, and his body lies in Winchester, and he had reigned nine years. He was the son of Egbert. And then his two sons succeeded to the kingdom,[6] Æthelbald to Wessex and to Surrey, and he [Æthelbald] reigned five years.

860. In this year king Æthelbald passed away, and his body lies at Sherborne. And Æthelberht, his brother, succeeded to the entire kingdom. And in his reign a great pirate host landed and stormed Winchester. And against the host fought ealdorman Osric with the men of Hampshire and ealdorman Æthelwulf with the men of Berkshire, and put the host to flight, (*continued on p.* 69)

B and C
855

855 [*As Æ*]. . . . Itermon, the son of Hathra, the son of Hwala, the son of Bedwig, the son of Sceaf, who is the son of Noah and was born in Noah's Ark; Lamech, Methuselah, Enoch, Jared, Mahalaleel, Cainan, Enos, Seth, Adam the first man, and our father who is Christ.

F 855
from
p. 63

855 [*As Æ*]. . . . to Sussex. (Alfred his third son he [Æthelwulf] had sent to Rome, and when the pope Leo heard tell that he had passed away, then he consecrated Alfred as king, and stood sponsor for him at confirmation,[7] just as his father Æthelwulf had requested when he sent him thither.)

(*continued on p.* 69)

---

[5] *she was called Judith* F
[6] 'The division of the kingdoms is given more correctly in Æ. The confusion in E is due to the use of a double source in its prototype, which D has retained. E has endeavoured to correct it, but unskilfully.' (Plummer)
[7] *benedixit et unxit eum in regem, et eum ad confirmandum tenuit* F Lat

and he ruled it in good peace and in great tranquillity. And
Ā 860 in his reign a great pirate host landed and stormed Winchester;
from and against the host fought ealdorman Osric with the men of
p. 66 Hampshire and ealdorman Æthelwulf with the men of Berkshire, and they put the host to flight and had possession of
the place of slaughter. And that Æthelberht reigned five years, and his
body lies at Sherborne.

865. In this year a heathen host remained in Thanet, and made peace
with the Kentishmen; and the Kentishmen promised them money in
return for the peace. And, under cover of the peace and the promise of
money, the host went secretly inland by night and devastated all the
eastern part of Kent.

866 [865].[1] In this year Æthelred, brother of Æthelberht, succeeded
to the kingdom of Wessex. And this same year came a great host to
England and took winter-quarters in East Anglia, and there were
provided with horses, and they made peace with them.

867 (866). In this year the host went from East Anglia over the
mouth of the Humber to York in Northumbria; and there was great
dissension of the people among themselves; and they had repudiated
their king Osberht and accepted Ælla, a king not of royal birth; and it
was late in the year when they set about making war against the host,
nevertheless they gathered great levies and went to attack the host at
York and stormed the city [21 March 867], and some of them got
inside; and immense slaughter was made of the Northumbrians there,
some inside, some outside, and both the kings were slain, and the
remnant made peace with the host. And in the same year died bishop
Ealhstan, and he held the episcopal see at Sherborne fifty years; and his
body lies there in the churchyard.

868 [867]. In this year the same host went into Mercia to Nottingham, and there took winter-quarters. And Burhred, king of Mercia,
and his councillors begged Æthelred, king of Wessex, and his brother
Alfred to help them fight against the host; and then [868] they proceeded
with the West Saxon levies into Mercia as far as Nottingham, and there
came upon the host in (*continued on p.* 70)

[1] The adjustments are necessary because here the chronology is based on
a year which probably began on 24 September before midwinter. (See
M. L. R. Beaven, 33 *EHR* 328–42)

and had possession of the place of slaughter. And that
E 860 Æthelberht reigned five years, and his body lies at Sherborne.
from 865. In this year the heathen host remained in Thanet, and
p. 67 made peace with the Kentishmen; and the Kentishmen
promised them money in return for the peace. And under
cover of the promise of money, the host went secretly inland by night
and devastated all the eastern part of Kent.

866 [865]. In this year Æthelred, brother of Æthelberht, succeeded
to the kingdom of Wessex. And this same year came a great heathen
host to England and took winter-quarters from the East Anglians, and
there were provided with horses, and they made peace with them.

867 [866]. In this year the host went from East Anglia over the
mouth of the Humber to York in Northumbria; and there was great
dissension of the people among themselves; and they had repudiated
their king Osberht and accepted Ælla, a king not of royal birth; and it
was late in the year when they set about making war against the host,
nevertheless they gathered great levies and went to attack the host at
York and stormed the city [21 March 867], and some of them got inside;
and immense slaughter was made of the Northumbrians there, some
inside, some outside, and both the kings were slain, and the remnant
made peace with the host. And in the same year died bishop Ealhstan,
and he held the episcopal see at Sherborne fifty years; and his body lies
there in the churchyard.

868 [867]. In this year the same host went into Mercia to Nottingham, and there took winter-quarters. And Burhred, king of Mercia,
and his councillors begged Æthelred, king of Wessex, and his brother
Alfred to help them fight against the host; and then they proceeded
with the West Saxon levies into Mercia as far as Nottingham,

(*continued on p.* 71)

861. In this year passed away St Swithin the bishop; also
F 861 king Æthelbald, and he lies in Sherborne. And Æthelbert his
from brother succeeded to the entire kingdom. And in his reign
p. 67 came a great pirate host and stormed Winchester; and against
that host fought the men of Hampshire and Berkshire, and put
the host to flight. And this Æthelberht reigned five years, and his body
lies at Sherborne. (*continued on p.* 74)

69

Ā 868
[867]
from
p. 68

the fortification, but there was no serious engagement, and the Mercians made peace with the host.

869. In this year the host went back to York, and remained there a year.

870 [869]. In this year the host rode across Mercia into East Anglia, and took winter-quarters at Thetford; and the same winter king Edmund fought against them, and the Danes won the victory, and they slew the king and overran the entire kingdom. And the same year [870] died archbishop Ceolnoth;[1] and Æthelred, bishop of Wiltshire, was elected archbishop of Canterbury.

871 [870]. In this year came the host to Reading in Wessex, and three days afterwards two jarls rode up-country; then ealdorman Æthelwulf opposed them at Englefield and fought against them and won the victory.[2] Four days[3] afterwards [871] king Æthelred and Alfred, his brother, led great levies there to Reading, and fought against the host; and great slaughter was made there on either side, and ealdorman Æthelwulf was slain, and the Danes had possession of the place of slaughter. And four days later king Æthelred and Alfred, his brother, fought against the entire host at Ashdown; and they were in two divisions: in the one were Bagsecg and Halfdan, the heathen kings, and in the other were the jarls. And then fought the king Æthelred against the division of the kings, and there the king Bagsecg was slain; and Alfred, his brother, against the division of the jarls, and there jarl Sidroc the Old was slain and jarl Sidroc the Young and jarl Osbern and jarl Fræna and jarl Harold, and both the hosts were put to flight, and there were many thousands of slain; and fighting went on till nightfall. And a fortnight later king Æthelred and Alfred, his brother, fought against the host at Basing, and there the Danes won the victory. And two months later king Æthelred and Alfred, his brother, fought against the host at *Meretun,* and they (*continued on p.* 72)

---

[1] In D there is the mistaken addition *to Rome*; the Anglo-Saxon verb *gefor* having been given its other meaning of *went*.

[2] *and one of them, whose name was Sidroc, was slain there* B C D

[3] See M. L. R. Beaven, *op. cit.* 334–5 for an attempt to date the events of this annal 'with something approaching precision.'

E 868
[867]
from
p. 69 and came upon the host there in the fortification, and besieged
it therein, but there was no serious engagement, and the
Mercians made peace with the host.

869. In this year the host went back to York, and remained
there a year.

870 [869]. In this year the host went across Mercia into East Anglia,
and took winter-quarters at Thetford; and the same winter St Edmund
the king fought against them, and the Danes won the victory, and they
slew the king [4] and overran the entire kingdom, and destroyed all the
monasteries to which they came. At that same time they came to the
monastery at *Medeshamstede* and burned and demolished it, and slew
the abbot and monks and all that they found there, reducing to nothing
what had once been a very rich foundation. And in this year died
archbishop Ceolnoth.

871 [870]. In this year rode the host to Reading in Wessex, and three
days afterwards two jarls rode up-country; then ealdorman Æthelwulf
opposed them at Englefield and fought against them and won the
victory; and one of the jarls, whose name was Sidroc, was slain there.
Then four days later [871] king Æthelred and Alfred, his brother, led
great levies there to Reading, and fought against the host; and great
slaughter was made there on either side, and ealdorman Æthelwulf was
slain, and the Danes had possession of the place of slaughter. And
four days later king Æthelred and Alfred, his brother, fought against the
entire host at Ashdown; [5] and they were in two divisions: in the one
were Bagsecg and Halfdan, the heathen kings, and in the other were the
jarls. And then fought the king Æthelred against the division of the
kings, and there the king Bagsecg was slain; and Alfred, his brother,
against the division of the jarls, and there jarl Sidroc the Old was slain
and jarl Sidroc the Young and jarl Osbern and jarl Fræna and jarl
Harold, and both the hosts were put to flight, and there were many
thousands of slain; and fighting went on till nightfall. And a fortnight
later king Æthelred and Alfred, his brother, fought against the host at
Basing,[6] and there the Danes won the victory. And two months later
Æthelred and Alfred, his brother, fought against the host at *Mæredun*,
and they were (*continued on p.* 73)

(*continued on p.* 73)

---

[4] *and slew the king (St Edmund) and overran the entire kingdom (the names
of the leaders who slew the king were Ingware and Ubba)* F

[5] . . . *Ashdown; and the Danes were overcome; and they had two heathen
kings, Bagsecg and Halfdan, and many jarls* F; *Halden* F Lat

[6] *ad Basingas dimicat, set peccatis exigentibus Dani campum ceperunt* F Lat

A 871
[870]
from
p. 70 were in two divisions, and they put both to flight and far into the day were victorious; and there was great slaughter on either side, but the Danes had possession of the place of slaughter; and bishop Heahmund was slain there and many good men. And after this fight came a great summer [1] host. And afterwards, after Easter, king Æthelred died, and he reigned five years; and his body lies at Wimborne.

Then his brother Alfred, son of Æthelwulf, succeeded to the kingdom of Wessex. And one month later king Alfred fought with a small force against the entire host at Wilton, and for a long time during the day drove them off, and the Danes had possession of the place of slaughter. And in the course of the year nine general engagements were fought against the host in the kingdom to the south of the Thames, besides those innumerable forays which Alfred, the king's brother, and a single ealdorman and king's thanes rode on, which were never counted. And in the course of this year were slain nine jarls and one king; and this year the West Saxons made peace with the host.

872 [871]. In this year went the host to London from Reading, and there took winter-quarters, and the Mercians [2] made peace with the host.

873 [872]. In this year went the host into Northumbria. And it took winter-quarters at Torksey in Lindsey, and then the Mercians made peace with the host.

874 [873]. In this year the host went from Lindsey to Repton, and there took winter-quarters, and [874] drove the king Burhred oversea twenty-two years after he succeeded to the kingdom; and conquered the entire kingdom. And he went to Rome and there resided, and his body lies in St Mary's church in 'the English Quarter.' And the same year they gave the government of the kingdom of Mercia into the hands of a foolish king's thane, and he swore them oaths and gave hostages that the kingdom should be at their disposal whenever they might require it, and that he should hold himself in readiness to serve the needs of the host with all who would follow him.

875 [874]. In this year went the host from Repton, and Halfdan went with a part of the host into Northumbria, and took winter-quarters (*continued on p.* 74)

---

[1] i.e. one with its base abroad.
[2] 'In 871 the fate of London would be a Mercian, not a West Saxon, concern.' (Beaven, *op. cit.* 341)

E 871
[870]
from
p. 71

in two divisions, and they put both to flight and for a long time during the day were victorious; and there was great slaughter on either side, but the Danes had possession of the place of slaughter; and bishop Heahmund was slain there and many good men. And after this fight came a great summer host to Reading. And afterwards, after Easter, king Æthelred died, and he reigned five years; and his body lies at the monastery of Wimborne.[3]

Then his brother Alfred, son of Æthelwulf, succeeded to the kingdom of Wessex. And one month later king Alfred fought with a small force against the entire host at Wilton, and for a long time during the day drove them off, and the Danes had possession of the place of slaughter. And in the course of the year nine general engagements were fought against the host in the kingdom to the south of the Thames, besides those innumerable forays which Alfred, the king's brother, and ealdormen and king's thanes rode on, which were never counted. And in the course of this year were slain nine jarls and one king; and this year the West Saxons made peace with the host.

872 [871]. In this year went the host to London from Reading, and there took winter-quarters, and the Mercians made peace with the host.

873 [872]. In this year the host took winter-quarters at Torksey.

874 [873]. In this year the host went from Lindsey to Repton, and there took winter-quarters, and drove the king Burhred oversea twenty-two years after he succeeded to the kingdom; and conquered the entire kingdom. And he went to Rome and there resided, and his body lies in St Mary's church in 'the School of the English.' And the same year they gave the government of the kingdom of Mercia into the hands of Ceolwulf, a foolish king's thane, and he swore them oaths and gave hostages that the kingdom should be at their disposal whenever they might require it, and that he should hold himself in readiness to serve the needs of the host with all who would follow him.

875 [874]. In this year went the host from Repton, and Halfdan went with a part of the host into Northumbria, and took winter-quarters (*continued on p.* 75)

Ā 875
[874]
from
p. 72

on the river Tyne; and the host overran that land, and made frequent raids against the Picts and against the Strathclyde Britons; and Guthrum and Oscytel and Anund, the three kings, went from Repton to Cambridge with a great host, and remained there a year. And in the summer [875] king Alfred sailed out to sea with a fleet, and fought against seven ships' companies, and captured one of them and put the others to flight.

876 [875]. In this year the host eluded the West Saxon levies and got into Wareham. And [876] the king made peace with the host, and they swore him oaths on the sacred ring, which before they would never do to any nation, that they would quickly leave his kingdom; and then under cover of this agreement they evaded the English levies by night, and the mounted host got into Exeter. And in this year Halfdan shared out the lands of Northumbria, and they were engaged in ploughing and in making a living for themselves.

877 [876]. In this year came the host into Exeter from Wareham, and the pirate host sailed west about, and they were caught in a great storm at sea, and there off Swanage one hundred and twenty ships were lost. And Alfred the king rode after the mounted host with his levies as far as Exeter, but could not overtake them before they were in the fortress where they could not be got at. And there they gave him preliminary hostages, as many as he would have, and swore solemn oaths, and then kept a firm peace. And then in autumn [877] the host departed into Mercia, and some of it they shared out and some they gave to Ceolwulf.

878. In this year the host went secretly in midwinter after Twelfth Night to Chippenham, and rode over Wessex and occupied it, and drove a great part of the inhabitants oversea, and of the rest the greater part they reduced to submission, except Alfred the king; and he with a small company moved under difficulties through woods and into inaccessible places in marshes. And in the same winter a brother of Ivar and Halfdan was in Wessex in Devon with twenty-three ships,
(*continued on p.* 76)

F 876
from
p. 69

876. In this year Rollo invaded Normandy with his host and he reigned fifty years. (*continued on p.* 93)

E 875
[874]
from
p. 73

on the river Tyne; and the host overran that land, and made frequent raids against the Picts and against the Strathclyde Britons; and Guthrum and Oscytel and Anund, the three kings, went from Repton to Cambridge with a great host, and remained there a year. And in the summer [875] king Alfred sailed out to sea with a fleet, and fought against seven ships' companies, and captured one of them and put the others to flight.

876 [875]. In this year the host eluded the West Saxon levies and got into Wareham. And afterwards the king made peace with the host, and they gave to him as hostages the most distinguished men next to the king in the host, and swore him oaths on the sacred ring,[1] which before they would never do to any nation, that they would quickly leave his kingdom; and then under cover of this agreement they evaded the English levies by night, and the mounted host got into Exeter. And in this year Halfdan shared out the lands of Northumbria, and they were engaged in ploughing and in making a living for themselves. *Rollo cum suis Normaniam penetrauit et regnauit annis ·liii·*

877 [876]. In this year came the host to Exeter from Wareham, and the pirate host sailed west about, and they were caught in a great storm at sea, and there off Swanage one hundred and twenty ships were lost. And Alfred the king rode after the mounted host with his levies as far as Exeter, but could not overtake them before they were in the fortress where they could not be got at. And there they gave him preliminary hostages, as many as he would have,[2] and swore solemn oaths, and then kept a firm peace. And then in autumn [877] the host departed into Mercia, and some of it they shared out, and some they gave to Ceolwulf.

878. In this year the host went secretly in midwinter after Twelfth Night to Chippenham, and rode over Wessex and occupied it, and drove a great part of the inhabitants oversea, and reduced the greater part of the rest, except Alfred the king; and he with a small company moved under difficulties through woods and into inaccessible places in marshes. And in the same winter a brother of Ivar and Halfdan was in Wessex in (*continued on p. 77*)

---

[1] *iusiurandum super sacrum armillum fecerunt* F Lat. Cf. *Eyrbyggja Saga,* chap. 4: 'on the altar [in the temple] lay a penannular ring weighing 20 oz.; on it all oaths were to be sworn, and the temple-priest was to wear it at all assemblies.'

[2] *Quos iterum sequenti anno insequitur rex usque Exoniam, et iterum sacramenta ab eis magna et obsides plures prioribus accepit; et non post multum temporis a regno eius, uidelicet Occidentalium Saxonum discedunt* F Lat

and there he was slain and eight hundred men with him and
forty men of his retinue.[1] And the Easter after, king Alfred
with a small company built a fortification at Athelney, and
from that fortification, with the men of that part of Somerset
nearest to it, he continued fighting against the host. Then
in the seventh week after Easter he rode to *Ecgbryhtesstan*, to the east
of Selwood, and came to meet him there all the men of Somerset
and Wiltshire and that part of Hampshire which was on this side of the
sea,[2] and they received him warmly. And one day later he went from
those camps to Iley Oak, and one day later to Edington; and there he
fought against the entire host, and put it to flight, and pursued it up
to the fortification,[3] and laid siege there a fortnight; and then the host
gave him preliminary hostages and solemn oaths that they would leave
his kingdom, and promised him in addition that their king would
receive baptism; and they fulfilled this promise in the following manner.
And three weeks later the king Guthrum came to him, one of thirty of
the most honourable men in the host, at Aller which is near Athelney,
where the king stood sponsor to him at baptism; and the ceremony of
the removal of the baptismal fillet took place at Wedmore, and he was
twelve days with the king, who greatly honoured him and his companions with riches.

879 [878]. In this year the host went to Cirencester from Chippenham, and remained there one year. And this year a band of pirates
gathered and took up quarters at Fulham on Thames. And the same
year the sun was eclipsed for one hour of the day.

880 [879]. In this year the host went from Cirencester into East
Anglia, and occupied that land, and shared it out. And the same year
the host which had occupied Fulham went oversea to Ghent in the land
of the Franks, and remained there one year.

881. In this year the host went deeper into the land of the Franks,
and the Franks fought [4] against them, and there the host were supplied
with horses after the fight.

882 [881]. In this year the host went up along the Meuse far into the
land of the Franks, and there remained one year. And the same year
[882] king Alfred went out to sea with ships and fought against four

(*continued on p.* 78)

---

[1] The text has *his heres*, 'of his host'; but, as Bruce Dickins suggests, this
is perhaps a mistake for *his hiredes*, 'of his retinue.'

[2] The reference is either to Southampton Water or to the English Channel.
If, as Sir Frank Stenton thinks, this part of the *Chronicle* was composed in
the south-west and not at Winchester, it is probable that Southampton
Water and the western part of Hampshire is meant. Otherwise the reference is to the men of Hampshire who had not fled beyond the sea.

[3] Probably Chippenham.

[4] This battle is the subject of the Old High German poem *Ludwigslied*.
(See A. H. Smith, *The Parker Chronicle* 34)

E 878
from
p. 75

Devon, and there he was slain and eight hundred men with him and forty men of his retinue; and there the banner which they called the Raven[5] was captured. And the Easter after, king Alfred with a small company built a fortification at Athelney, and from that fortification, with the men of that part of Somerset nearest to it, he continued fighting against the host. Then in the seventh week after Easter he rode to *Ecgbrihtesstan*, to the east of Selwood, and came to meet him there all the men of Somerset and Wiltshire and that part of Hampshire which was on this side of the sea, and they received him warmly. And one day later he went from those camps to Iley Oak, and one day later to Edington; and there he fought against the entire host, and put it to flight, and pursued it up to the fortification, and laid siege there a fortnight; and then the host gave him hostages and solemn oaths that they would leave his kingdom, and promised him in addition that their king would receive baptism, and they fulfilled this promise. And three weeks later the king Guthrum came to him, one of thirty of the most honourable men in the host, at Aller which is near Athelney, where the king stood sponsor to him at baptism; and the ceremony of the removal of the baptismal fillet took place at Wedmore, and he was twelve days with the king, who greatly honoured him and his companions with riches.

879 [878]. In this year the host went to Cirencester from Chippenham, and remained there one year. In this year a band of pirates gathered and took up quarters at Fulham on Thames. And the same year the sun was eclipsed for one hour of the day.

880 [879]. In this year the host went from Cirencester into East Anglia, and occupied that land, and shared it out. And the same year the host which had occupied Fulham went oversea to Ghent in the land of the Franks, and remained there one year.

881. In this year the host went deeper into the land of the Franks, and the Franks fought against them, and there the host were supplied with horses after the fight.

882 (881). In this year the host went up along the Meuse deeper inland into the land of the Franks, and there remained one year. And the same year [882] king Alfred went out to sea with ships and fought against four ships' companies of Danes, (*continued on p.* 79)

---

[5] Ā alone omits this remark about the Raven Banner. The Annals of St Neot (*s.a.*) give a fuller account: *dicunt enim quod tres sorores Hungari et Habbae, filiae uidelicet Lodebrochi [Ragnar Lothbrok] illud uexillum texuerunt, et totum parauerunt illud uno meridiano tempore. Dicunt etiam, quod in omni bello, ubi praecederet idem signum, si uictoriam adepturi essent, appareret in medio signi quasi coruus uluus uolitans; sin uero uincendi . . . fuissent, penderet directe nihil mouens, et hoc saepe probatum est.* Cf. the Raven Banner of Sigurðr, Earl of the Orkneys (*Orkneyinga Saga*, chaps. xi–xii, translated by A. B. Taylor, pp. 148–9, 150), and his death at the Battle of Clontarf, 1014 (*The Story of Burnt Njal*, Everyman's Library, pp. 322–7). Cnut, too, had a Raven Banner, cf. A. Campbell, *Encomium Emmae* 24.

Ā 882
[881]
from
p. 76

ships' companies of Danes, and captured two of the ships, and the men aboard were slain; and two ships' companies surrendered to him,[1] and they were badly cut about and severely wounded before they surrendered.

883 [882]. In this year the host went up the Scheldt to Condé [dép. Nord], and there remained one year.

884 [883]. In this year the host went up the Somme to Amiens [dép. Somme], and there remained one year.

885 [884]. In this year the above-mentioned host separated into two, one part east and the other part to Rochester, and besieged the city; and they built another fortification around themselves; and the citizens, however, defended the city until Alfred came to their relief [885] with levies. Then went the host to their ships and abandoned that encampment, and were there deprived of their horses,[2] and soon the same summer went oversea. And the same year king Alfred sent a naval force into East Anglia. As soon as they came to the mouth of the Stour,[3] then they met sixteen ships of pirates and fought against them, and captured all the ships, and slew the crews. When they were on their way home with the booty, they met a great fleet of pirates, and fought against them the same day, and the Danish were victorious. And the same year [884], before midwinter, Carloman, king of the Franks, passed away, and a wild boar killed him; and one year earlier his brother [Louis] had passed away; he also had ruled that western kingdom [France] and they were both sons of Louis [the Stammerer], who also had ruled that western kingdom and had passed away the year [879] in which the sun was eclipsed;[4] he was the son of Charles [the Bald] whose daughter [Judith] Æthelwulf, king of Wessex, had as queen. And the same year a great pirate host assembled among the Old Saxons, and great battles took place there, twice in the year,[5] and the Saxons were victorious, and there were Frisians with them. The same year Charles [the Fat] succeeded to the western kingdom, and to all the western kingdom between the Mediterranean and the North Sea and English Channel, even as his great-grandfather had had it, except for Brittany; (*continued on p.* 80)

---

[1] *two escaped* F; *et duas fugauit* F Lat

[2] Asser's *Life* of King Alfred has *equis, quos de Francia secum adduxerant, derelictis*

[3] Reading *Sture* as D E; A Ā B C *Stufe* corrected to *Sture* in A.

[4] The eclipse was on 29 October 878 (cf. p. 77); Louis died on 10 April 879—both dates within the same annalistic year beginning 24 September.

[5] i.e. within the year beginning 24 September 884; probably at Norden in Frisia (December 884), and in Saxony (May 885).

E 882
[881]
from
p. 77

and captured two of the ships, and slew the men; and two surrendered to him, and the men were badly cut about and severely wounded before they surrendered.

883 [882]. In this year the host went up the Scheldt to Condé [dép. Nord], and there remained one year. And pope Marinus sent the *lignum Domini* [6] to king Alfred; and the same year Sigehelm and Athelstan took to Rome, and also to India to St Thomas and to St Bartholomew, the alms which king Alfred had vowed to send thither when they besieged the host in London; and, by the mercy of God, they were there very successful in their prayers in accordance with those vows.[7]

884 [883]. In this year the host went up the Somme to Amiens [dép. Somme], and there remained one year.

885 [884]. In this year the above-mentioned host separated into two, one part east and the other part to Rochester, and besieged the city; and they built another fortification around themselves; and the citizens, however, defended the city until king Alfred came to their relief [885] with levies. Then went the host to their ships and abandoned that encampment, and were there deprived of their horses, and at once the same summer went back oversea. And the same year king Alfred sent a naval force from Kent into East Anglia. As soon as they came to the mouth of the Stour, then they met sixteen ships of pirates and fought against them, and captured all the ships, and slew the crews. When they were on their way home with the booty, they met a great fleet of pirates, and fought against them the same day, and the Danish were victorious. And the same year [884], before midwinter, Carloman,[8] king of the Franks, passed away, and a wild boar killed him; and one year earlier his brother [Louis] had passed away; he also had ruled that western kingdom [France]; and he [Louis the Stammerer] had passed away the year [879] in which the sun was eclipsed; he was the son of Charles [the Bald] whose daughter [Judith] Æthelwulf, king of Wessex, had as queen. And the same year [884] passed away the good pope

(*continued on p. 81*)

[6] See note 1, p. 80.
[7] 'As there is no specific record of any operations undertaken by Alfred against London before 886, it is highly probable that this passage is really a misplaced allusion to the events preceding his occupation of the city in the latter year.' (F. M. Stenton, *Anglo-Saxon England* 256 note)
[8] MSS. *Carl*.

Ā 885
[884]
from
p. 78

that Charles was the son of Louis [the German], who was the brother of Charles [the Bald], who was the father of Judith whom king Æthelwulf married; they were sons of Louis [the Pious], who was son of Charles the Old [the Great], who was the son of Pippin [the Short]. And this same year passed away the good pope Marinus who freed 'the School of the English' from payment of dues at the request of Alfred, king of Wessex; and he sent him great gifts and a fragment of the Cross[1] on which Christ suffered. And the same year the host in East Anglia broke peace with king Alfred.

886 [885]. In this year the host, which before this had arrived in the east [at Louvain], went again west, and then up the Seine and there took winter-quarters. The same year [886] king Alfred occupied London, and all the English people submitted to him, except those who were in captivity to the Danes; and he then entrusted the city to ealdorman Æthelred to rule.

887 [886–7].[2] In this year the host went up through the bridge at Paris, and then along the Seine and up the Marne as far as Chézy-sur-Marne;[3] and they encamped there and in the valley of the Yonne, two winters in those two places. And the same year [888] passed away Charles [the Fat], king of the Franks; and Arnulf, his brother's son, deprived him of the kingdom six weeks before his death. And then the kingdom was divided into five, and five kings were consecrated thereto; that, however, was done with the consent of Arnulf; and they declared they ought to hold it [their kingdom] from him as overlord because not one of them was born thereto on the paternal side, except him alone. Arnulf then remained in the territory to the east of the Rhine, and Rudolf succeeded to the Middle Kingdom [Burgundy], and Odo to the western part [Neustria], and Berengar and Guido to Lombardy and to the lands on that side of the Alps, which they ruled in great enmity, and fought two pitched battles, many a time and oft laying waste that country, and each frequently drove out the other. And in the same year in which the host went up country over the bridge at Paris, ealdorman Æthelhelm took the alms of the West Saxons and of king Alfred to Rome.

888. In this year ealdorman Beocca took the alms of the West Saxons

(continued on p. 82)

---

[1] 'It is just conceivable that the Brussels Cross preserves the fragment of the True Cross sent to Alfred by Pope Marinus.' (Bruce Dickins and A. S. C. Ross, *The Dream of the Rood* (London 1934), 15); cf. also *ibid.* 19: 'It may also be suggested that the occasion for the revision of the poem (*The Dream of the Rood*) was the gift of a piece of the True Cross to Alfred in 885.'

[2] On the chronology of the continental campaigns of this annal see A. H Smith, *op. cit.* 37.

[3] Reading *Caziei* as D E F; *Cariei* Ā B C

E 885
[884]
from
p. 79

Marinus, who freed 'the School of the English' from payment of dues at the request of Alfred, king of Wessex; and he sent him great gifts and a fragment of the Cross on which Christ suffered.[4] And the same year the host went to East Anglia, and broke peace with king Alfred.

886 [885]. In this year the host which before this had arrived in the east, went again west, and then up the Seine and there took winter-quarters in the city of Paris. The same year [886] king Alfred occupied London, and all the English people submitted to him, except those who were in captivity to the Danes; and he then entrusted the city to ealdorman Æthelred to rule.

887 [886–7]. In this year the host went up through the bridge at Paris, and then along the Seine as far as the Marne, and then up the Marne to Chézy-sur-Marne; and they encamped there [and] in the valley of the Yonne, two winters in those two places. And the same year [888] passed away Charles [the Fat], king of the Franks; and Arnulf, his brother's son, deprived him of the kingdom six weeks before his death. And then the kingdom was divided into five, and five kings were consecrated thereto; that, however, was done with the consent of Arnulf; and they declared they ought to hold it [their kingdom] from him as overlord because not one of them was born thereto on the paternal side, except him alone. Arnulf remained in the territory to the east of the Rhine, and Rudolf succeeded to the Middle Kingdom [Burgundy], and Odo to the western part [Neustria], and Berengar and Guido to Lombardy and to the lands on that side of the Alps, which they ruled in great enmity, and fought two pitched battles, many a time and oft laying waste that country, and each frequently drove out the other. And in the same year in which the host went up country over the bridge at Paris, ealdorman Æthelhelm took the alms of the West Saxons and of king Alfred to Rome.

888. In this year ealdorman Beocca and queen Æthelswith, who was king Alfred's sister, took the alms of the West Saxons

(*continued on p.* 83)

---

[4] *many gifts of relics* F; *plura donaria, scilicet de Cruce Domini et de reliquiis sanctorum* F Lat

81

Ā 888
from
p. 80

and of king Alfred to Rome. And queen Æthelswith, who was king Alfred's sister, passed away, and her body lies at Pavia. And this same year archbishop Æthelred and ealdorman Æthelwald passed away in one month.

889. In this year no journey was made to Rome, except by two couriers whom king Alfred sent with letters.

890. In this year abbot Beornhelm took the alms of the West Saxons and of king Alfred to Rome. And Guthrum, the northern kind, whose baptismal name was Athelstan, passed away; he was the godson of king Alfred, and he dwelt in East Anglia and was the first to take possession of that country. And the same year [889] the host went from the Seine to St Lô [dép. Manche], which lies between the Bretons and the Franks; and [890] the Bretons fought against them and were victorious, and drove them out into a river and drowned many.

In this year Plegmund was chosen [as archbishop] by God and by all His saints.[1]

891. In this year the host went east; and king Arnulf fought against the mounted host, before the ships came, with the East Franks and the Saxons and the Bavarians, and put it to flight. And three Irishmen came to king Alfred in a boat without any oars,[2] from Ireland, whence they had stolen away because they wished for the love of God to be on pilgrimage, they cared not where.[3] The boat in which they set out was made of two and a half hides,[4] and they had taken with them provisions for a week [5] and after a week they came to land in Cornwall, and soon went to king Alfred. Thus were they named: Dubhslaine and Macbeathadh and Maelinmhain.[6] And Suibhne, the best teacher among the Scots [from Ireland], died.[7]

892.[8] And the same year after Easter, during Rogationtide or earlier, appeared the star which in Latin is called 'cometa'; likewise [9] men say in English that a comet is a long-haired star, because long beams of light shine therefrom, sometimes on one side, sometimes on every side. (*continued on p.* 84)

(*continued on p.* 84)

---

[1] *by the whole nation to the archiepiscopal see of Canterbury* F

[2] *sine omni gubernatione humana* F Lat

[3] On the *peregrinatio pro amore Dei* see Dorothy Whitelock, 'The Interpretation of *The Seafarer*' (*Chadwick Memorial Studies* 267 ff.)

[4] *in nauicula facta de duobus coriis et dimidio* F Lat

[5] *septimo die* F Lat

[6] *Dublasne* D, *Dubslana* F Lat; *Maccbethath* B, *Machbethu* C D, *Maccbethu* F; *Maelinmuin* B, *Maelinmumin* C, *Maelmumin* D, *Maelinmun* F.

[7] . . . *Maelinmun. Nam quartus socius eorum obiit nomine Suifneh qui uit peritissimus doctor. Et eodem anno apparuit cometa stella circa Ascensionem Domini* F Lat

[8] The handwriting of the first scribe of Ā finishes here near the foot of folio 16a. The rest of the annal was added on folio 16b by the second scribe, who omitted to cross out the numeral 892. A later scribe, misled by this into thinking that the appearance of the comet was in 892, proceeded to add 1 to the following numerals, making the year 892 into 893 (p. 84 top), and so on with each annal to 929.

[9] *some men* B C D with more probability.

and of king Alfred to Rome; and she passed away [10] and her
E 888 body lies at Pavia.   And this same year archbishop Æthelred
from and ealdorman Æthelwald passed away in one month.
p. 81   889. In this year no journey was made to Rome, except
by two couriers whom king Alfred sent with letters.

890. In this year abbot Beornhelm took the alms of the West Saxons
and of king Alfred to Rome.   And Guthrum, the northern king, whose
baptismal name was Athelstan, passed away; he was king Alfred's
godson, and he dwelt in East Anglia, and was the first to take possession
of that country.   And this same year [889] the host went from the
Seine to St Lô [11] [dép. Manche], which lies between the Bretons and the
Franks; and [890] the Bretons fought against them and were victorious,
and drove them out into a river, and drowned many.[12]   Hic Plegemundus
archiepiscopus a Deo et omni populo electus est. (*continued on p.* 85)

---

[10] *on the way to Rome*   F;   *in itinere Romæ*   F Lat
[11] *Sand Loðan* B; *Sant Loðdan* C; *Scan Leoðan* D; *Scandlaudan* F
[12] *et est locus inter Brittanes* (corrected from *Brittas*) *et Francigenas.
Audientes hoc, Brytones exeuntes dimicabant contra eos et, victis Danis,
propulsabant in quandam aquam, ubi plures eorum demersi sunt*   F Lat

Ā 893
[892]
from
p. 82
893 [892]. In this year the great host about which we formerly spoke went again from the east kingdom [the kingdom of the East Franks] westward to Boulogne, and were there provided with ships so that they crossed in one voyage, horses and all, and then came up into the mouth of the Lympne with two hundred and fifty ships. That estuary is in east Kent, at the east end of the great forest which we call Andred [the Weald]. This forest from east to west is a hundred and twenty miles long or longer, and thirty miles broad. The river which we mentioned before flows out from the forest; they rowed their ships up as far as the forest, four miles from the entrance to the estuary, and there stormed a fort within the fen; [1] occupying it were a few peasants and it was half built.

Then soon after this Hæsten came with eighty ships into the mouth of the Thames, and made himself a fort at Milton Royal, and the other host at Appledore.

894 [893]. In this year, twelve months from the time that they had made the fort in the east kingdom [at Louvain], the Northumbrians and East Anglians had given oaths to king Alfred, and the East Angles six preliminary hostages, yet, contrary to the pledge, as often as the other hosts sallied forth in full force, then went they either with them or alone on their own account. And then king Alfred gathered his levies and marched so that he was encamped between the two hosts, at a convenient distance from the stronghold in the forest [Appledore] and the stronghold on the water [Milton], so that he could overtake either if they wished to make for any open country. Then afterwards they moved through the woods in gangs and bands, wherever the margin was left unguarded; and almost every day other troops, both from the levies and also from the forts, went to attack them ⟨either by day⟩[2] or by night. And the king had divided his levies into two sections, so that there was always half at home and half on active service, with the exception of those men whose duty it was to man the fortresses. Only twice did the host come out from the camps in full force; on the one occasion when they first landed, before the levies were mustered,

(continued on p. 85)

---

[1] *fenne* Ā F, *fænne* E; *fæsten(n)e* B C D is usually the reading adopted, and the passage repunctuated. As A. H. Smith, *The Parker Chronicle* 42, points out, 'this introduces a redundant preposition *on*. The fen is between Rye and Appledore.'

[2] Omitted by Ā B, supplied from C D

892. In this year the great host about which we formerly
E 892 spoke went again from the east kingdom [the kingdom of the
from East Franks] westward to Boulogne, and were there provided
p. 83 with ships so that they crossed in one voyage, horses and all,
and then came up into the mouth of the Lympne with two
hundred and fifty ships. That estuary is in east Kent, at the east end of
the great forest which we call Andræd [the Weald]. This forest from
east to west is a hundred and twenty miles long or longer, and thirty
miles broad. The river which we mentioned before flows out from the
forest; they pulled their ships upstream as far as the forest, four miles
from the entrance to the estuary, and there stormed a fort within the fen;
occupying it were a few peasants and it was half built. Then soon after
this Hæsten came with eighty ships into the mouth of the Thames, and
made himself a fort at Milton Royal, and the other host at Appledore.
Hic obiit Wulfhere Northanhymbrorum archiepiscopus.

(continued on p. 91)

Ā 894 and on the other occasion when they wished to evacuate
[893] those positions. They had then seized much plunder, and
from wished to carry that northwards across the Thames into
p. 84 Essex to meet the ships. Then the levies rode and intercepted them and fought against them at Farnham, and put
the host to flight and recovered the plunder; and they fled across
Thames without using any ford, then up by the Colne on to an island.
Then the levies surrounded them there as long as their provisions lasted;
but they had *(continued on p. 86)*

Ā 894
[893]
from
p. 85

completed their tour of duty and had come to an end of their food, and the king was on his way thither [to relieve them] with the division which was campaigning with him. When he was on his way thither and the other levies were on their way home—the Danes remaining behind in their position because their king had been wounded in the fight and could not be moved—the Danes dwelling in Northumbria and East Anglia assembled about a hundred ships which sailed south about and about forty ships which sailed north about and besieged a fort in Devonshire on the Bristol Channel: and those which sailed south about besieged Exeter. When the king learnt of this, he marched west towards Exeter with all the levies, with the exception of a very inconsiderable part who continued eastward.

They went on until they came to London, and then with the citizens and the help which came to them from the west, they went east to Benfleet. Hæsten had come there with his host, which had been encamped at Milton; and in addition the great host had arrived there, which had been encamped at Appledore at the mouth of the Lympne. Hæsten had made that fort at Benfleet before this, and was then off on a plundering raid while the great host was in occupation. Then they [the English] advanced and put that host to flight, stormed the fort, and seized everything inside it, both property and women and also children, and conveyed them all into London: and all the ships they either broke up or burned up or brought to London or to Rochester. And Hæsten's wife and his two sons were brought to the king, and he restored them to him, because one of them was his godson and the other the godson of ealdorman Æthelred. They had stood sponsors for them before Hæsten had come to Benfleet,[1] and he had given him hostages and oaths, and the king in addition had presented him with much property, and he did likewise when he restored the boy and the lady. But as soon as they came to Benfleet and the fort was built (*continued on p.* 87)

---

[1] MS. *Bleamfleote*

Ā 894
[893]
from
p. 86 he [Hæsten] went harrying in that very quarter of Alfred's kingdom that his son's godfather Æthelred had to rule over: and again on this second occasion he was away harrying in that very kingdom when his fort was stormed.

Then the king was on his way west with the levies towards Exeter, as I said before, and the host had besieged the town; when he had arrived there they retired to their ships.

When the king was occupied against the host there in the west, both the hosts were concentrated at Shoebury in Essex, and there they made a fort and marched in company up along the Thames, joined by great reinforcements both from East Anglia and from Northumbria. They went up along the Thames until they reached the Severn, then up along the Severn. Then assembled ealdorman Æthelred and ealdorman Æthelhelm and ealdorman Æthelnoth, and the king's thanes who were occupying the forts, from every fortress east of the Parret, both west and east of Selwood, and also north of Thames and west of Severn, together with a section of the Welsh. When they were all assembled they overtook the host at Buttington on Severn shore, and surrounded them on every side in a stronghold. When they had been encamped for many weeks on the two sides of the river, the king being occupied west in Devon against the pirate host, they became distressed for lack of food, and had devoured most of their horses, the remainder perishing with hunger; then they sallied forth against the men encamped on the east side of the river and fought against them, and the Christians had the victory. And there Ordheh, the king's thane, was slain, and also many other king's thanes were slain: ⟨and very great slaughter was made there of the Danes⟩, and the remnant that escaped

(*continued on p.* 88)

Ā 894
[893]
from
p. 87
were saved by flight. When they came to their fort and to their ships in Essex, the remainder again gathered together a great host from East Anglia and Northumbria before winter; and placing their women, their ships and their property in safety in East Anglia, they marched without a halt by day and night, until they arrived at a deserted Roman site in Wirral, called Chester. The levies were unable to overtake them before they got inside that fort, but they besieged it some two days, and seized all the cattle in the vicinity, slaying all the men they could intercept outside the fort: they burnt up all the corn, and with their horses ate all the neighbourhood bare. That was twelve months after they had come hither oversea.

895 [894]. Soon after this, in this year, the host moved from Wirral into Wales: they were unable to remain there because they had been deprived of both the cattle and corn which had been plundered. Then again they moved from Wales with the plunder they had taken there, marching across Northumbria and East Anglia so that the levies were unable to get at them, until they reached east Essex, on an island out at sea called Mersea. When the host which had besieged Exeter sailed back on its way home, it harried inland in Sussex near Chichester, but the garrison put them to flight and slew many hundred of them, capturing some of their ships.

Then the same year before winter, the Danish who occupied Mersea pulled their ships up Thames and then up (*continued on p.* 89)

A 895
[894]
from
p. 88

the Lea. That was two years after they had come hither oversea.

896 [895]. In the same year the aforementioned host built a fort by the Lea, twenty miles above the city of London. Then later in the summer, a large body of the garrison and of other forces set out and reached the Danish fort, and there they were repulsed and some four king's thanes were slain. Then the following autumn the king encamped in the neighbourhood of the fortress while the corn was being reaped, so that the Danish men could not keep them back from the reaping. One day the king rode up along the river and looked to see where the river could be blocked, so that they would not be able to bring out their ships. This they proceeded to do: they made two forts on the two sides of the river, but when they had just begun that operation and had encamped thereby, the host saw that they could not bring out their ships. Thereupon they abandoned them and went across country until they reached Bridgnorth on Severn, and there built a fort. Then the levies rode west after the host, and the men of London fetched the ships, and all that they could not take away they broke up, and those that were serviceable they brought into London. The Danish men had placed their women in safety in East Anglia before they went out from that fort. They remained at Bridgnorth for the winter. That was three years since they had arrived hither at the mouth of the Lympne from oversea.

897 [896]. Then the following summer, in this year, the host dispersed, some to East Anglia, some to Northumbria, and those without stock got themselves ships there, and sailed south oversea to the Seine.

The host, by the mercy of God, had not altogether utterly crushed the English people; but they were much more severely crushed

(*continued on p.* 90)

Ā 897
[896]
from
p. 89
during those three years by murrain and plague, most of all by the fact that many of the best of the king's servants in the land passed away during those three years: one of these was Swithwulf, bishop of Rochester, and Ceolmund, ealdorman in Kent, and Beorhtwulf, ealdorman in Essex, and Wulfred, ealdorman in Hampshire, and Ealhheard, bishop at Dorchester, and Eadwulf, the king's thane in Sussex, and Beornwulf, reeve in Winchester, and Ecgwulf, the king's marshal, and many others in addition to them, though I have named the most distinguished.

This same year the hosts in East Anglia and Northumbria greatly harassed Wessex along the south coast with predatory bands, most of all with the warships they had built many years before. Then king Alfred ordered warships to be built to meet the Danish ships: they were almost twice as long as the others, some had sixty oars, some more; they were both swifter, steadier, and with more freeboard than the others; they were built neither after the Frisian design nor after the Danish, but as it seemed to himself that they could be most serviceable. Then on one occasion the same year came six ships to the Isle of Wight and did much harm there, both in Devon and almost everywhere along the coast. Then the king ordered nine of the new ships to put out, and they blockaded the entrance from the open sea against their escape. Then the Danes sailed out with three ships against them, and three of their ships were beached on dry land at the upper end of the harbour,[1] and the crews had gone off inland. Then the English seized two of the three ships at the entrance to the estuary, and slew the men, but the other escaped; in her also all but five were slain; and they escaped because the ships of the others were aground: they were also very awkwardly aground; (*continued on p.* 91)

---

[1] Poole Harbour (Dorset) has been suggested as the scene of this engagement (A. J. Wyatt, *An Anglo-Saxon Reader* 206, note to I. 312), but see F. P. Magoun, Jr, 'King Alfred's Naval and Beach Battle with the Danes' (37 *MLR* 409–14) for a full discussion of the incident.

E 901
[899]   901 [899].[2] In this year king Alfred died on 26 October:
from   he ruled (*continued on p.* 93)
p. 85

D 901   901 [899]. In this year king Alfred died on 26 October:
[899]   he ruled (*continued on p.* 93)

A 897   three had gone aground on the side of the channel where
[896]   the Danish ships were aground, and the others all on the
from   other side, so that none of them could reach the others.
p. 90   But, when the tide had ebbed many furlongs from the ships,
the Danes went from the three ships to the other three which
were stranded on their side, and then there they fought. There were
slain Lucumon, the king's reeve, and Wulfheard the Frisian, and Æbbe
the Frisian, and Æthelhere the Frisian, and Æthelfrith of the king's
household,[3] totalling sixty-two killed of English and Frisians, and one
hundred and twenty of the Danes. The tide, however, came first to the
Danish ships, before the Christians could push off theirs, and hence they
rowed away out to sea. They were so sorely crippled that they were
unable to row past Sussex, but there the sea cast two of them ashore;
the men were led to the king at Winchester, and he had them hanged
there. The men who were on the single ship reached East Anglia badly
wounded. This same summer no less than twenty ships perished with
all hands along the south coast. The same year Wulfric, the king's
marshal, passed away: he had also been the Welsh reeve.[4]

898 [897]. In this year died Æthelhelm, ealdorman of Wiltshire, nine
nights before midsummer: and in this year passed away Heahstan, who
was bishop of London.

901 [899]. In this year died Alfred, son of Æthelwulf, six nights
before All Hallows' Day [1 November]. He was king over all England
except that part which was under Danish domination, and he ruled the
kingdom (*continued on p.* 92)

[2] On the date of Alfred's death see M. L. R. Beaven, 'The Regnal Dates of
Alfred, Edward the Elder, and Athelstan' (32 *EHR* 517–31).

[3] *cynges geneat:* the word *geneat* originally meant 'companion,' and 'the
geneatas formed a peasant aristocracy' (Stenton); the *cynges geneat* was a
member of the royal household, with the same wergild as that of the king's
thane. (Cf. H. M. Chadwick, *Studies on Anglo-Saxon Institutions* 136 f.)

[4] Cf. Chadwick, *op. cit.* 233: 'The *Wealhgerefa* mentioned in the *Chronicle*
(897) was probably an official entrusted with the duty of collecting tribute
from the Welsh. He may also have commanded auxiliary Welsh troops in
time of war. The text has *gefera*; the confusion of these two words is very
common and sometimes causes considerable difficulty.'

twenty-eight and a half years. Then Edward, his son, succeeded
Ã 901 to the kingdom.

[899] Then Æthelwold, son of his paternal uncle, seized the
from manor at Wimborne and at Christchurch without the consent
p. 91 of the king and his councillors. Then the king and his levies
rode until he encamped at Badbury Rings, near Wimborne,
and Æthelwold remained inside the manor with the men who had given
him their allegiance: he had barricaded all the gates against them,
declaring that he meant to stay there live or dead; then under cover of
this he slipped away by night and came to the host in Northumbria.
The king ordered a pursuit, but they were unable to overtake him.
Then was the lady arrested whom he had abducted without the king's
consent, and in defiance of the command of the bishops, because she
had taken the vows of a nun. In this same year passed away Æthelred,
ealdorman in Devon, four weeks before king Alfred.

903 [902]. In this year died ealdorman Æthelwulf, the brother of
Ealhswith; also died Virgilius, an abbot from Ireland, and Grimbald
the priest on 8 July.

904 [903]. In this year Æthelwold came hither from oversea to
Essex with the fleet which was accompanying him.

905 [904]. In this year Æthelwold seduced the host in East Anglia
to begin hostilities, with the result that they harried across Mercia until
they came to Cricklade and there crossed the Thames: they seized all
that they could, both in Braydon Forest and in the surrounding countryside, and then returned home. Then king Edward

(*continued on p.* 94)

92

E 901
[899]
from
p. 91

twenty-eight and a half years. Then Edward, his son, succeeded to the kingdom. (*continued on p.* 95)

F 903
from
p. 74

903. In this year died Grimbald the priest; and the same year was consecrated the New Minster at Winchester, and the relics of St Judoc were translated there. (*continued on p.* 105)

D 901
[899]
from
p. 91

twenty-eight and a half years. Then Edward, his son, succeeded to the kingdom.
Then Æthelwold, son of his paternal uncle, seized the manor at Wimborne, and at Christchurch without the consent of the king and his councillors. Then the king and his levies rode until he encamped at Badbury Rings, near Wimborne, and Æthelwold remained inside the manor with the men who had given him their allegiance: he had barricaded all the gates against them, declaring that he meant to stay there live or dead; then under cover of this the prince rode off by night and came to the host in Northumbria which received him as king and submitted to him. Then was the lady arrested whom he had abducted without the king's consent, and in defiance of the commands of the bishops, because she had taken the vows of a nun. In this year passed away Æthelred, ealdorman in Devon, four weeks before king Alfred.

903. In this year died ealdorman Æthelwulf, the brother of Ealhswith, the mother of king Edward; also died Virgilius, an abbot from Ireland, and Grimbald the priest.

904. In this year Æthelwold came hither from oversea to Essex with all the ships he could muster and which had given him allegiance.

905. In this year a comet appeared on 20 October.

In this year Æthelwold led the host in East Anglia to begin hostilities, with the result that they harried across the whole of Mercia until they came to Cricklade and there crossed the Thames: they seized all that they could, both in Braydon Forest and in the surrounding countryside, and then went east homewards. Then king Edward marched after them as quickly as he could (*continued on p.* 95)

C 902

902.[1] In this year Ealhswith passed away, and the same year was fought that battle at *the Holm* between the Kentishmen and the Danes.

904. In this year was the moon eclipsed.

905. In this year a comet appeared. (*continued on p.* 94)

---

[1] 'B and C after closing the year 915 (918 Ā) fetch back to 896 (the annals 896 to 901 being blank) and introduce the present episode, which may be considered to close at 924 (925 Ā). Both are then barren to 934 (935 Ā) where they fall in with the usual current of history. The episode forms therefore a little Mercian Register of about twenty years, and might be styled the "Annals of Æthelflæd."' (Plummer) No attempt is made here to reconcile the discrepancies in the chronology, except to correct the mechanical error in the dating of Ā up to 929.

marched after them as quickly as he could gather his levies
Ā 905 together, and ravaged all their territory between the [Cam-
[904] bridgeshire] dikes and the Wissey, all of it as far north as the
from fens. When he wished to withdraw, he had the order given
p. 92 throughout the levies for a general retirement; then the Kentishmen remained behind disobeying the order, and seven messengers he had sent to them. Then they were caught there by the host
and a battle was fought. Among the slain were ealdorman Sigewulf,
and ealdorman Sigehelm, and Eadwold the king's thane, and abbot
Cenwulf, and Sigeberht, son of Sigewulf, and Eadwold, son of Acca,
and many others besides these, though I have named the most distinguished. On the Danish side were slain their king Eohric and prince
Æthelwold, who had incited him to this rebellion, and Beorhtsige, son
of prince Beornnoth, and the Scandinavian barons[1] Ysopa and
Oscytel, and many others besides these whom we cannot name here:
on each side there was great slaughter made, and although the Danes
had possession of the place of slaughter they suffered greater losses.

And Ealhswith died this same year.

906 [905]. In this year died Alfred, who was reeve at Bath: and in the
same year peace was ratified at Tiddingford,[2] as king Edward ordained,
both with the host from East Anglia and with the Northumbrians.

909 [908]. In this year died Denewulf, who was bishop of Winchester.

910 [909]. In this year Frithustan succeeded to the see of Winchester,
and Asser, bishop of Sherborne, died afterwards. And this same
year king Edward sent levies from both Wessex and Mercia, and
severely harried the host in the north, destroying both people

(*continued on p.* 96)

907. In this year Chester was rebuilt.
C 907 909. The body of St Oswald was translated from Bardney
from into Mercia.
p. 93 910. In this year English and Danes fought at Tettenhall,
and the English had the victory. This same year Æthelflæd
built the fortress at *Bremesburh*. (*continued on p.* 96)

---

[1] In Scandinavia (cf. *Haralds Saga hins Hárfagra*, Heimskringla cap. 6)
the *hold* was ranked below the *jarl* and was probably a landowner in hereditary possession of land. In England he holds the more exalted position of a
nobleman, equal to that of an important English king's thane. See H. M.
Chadwick, *Studies on Anglo-Saxon Institutions* 393 ff.
[2] 2EPN 81.

906. In this year king Edward was compelled to make peace
E 906 both with the host from East Anglia and with the Northumbrians.
from 910. In this year the English army and the Danes fought
p. 93 at Tettenhall, and Æthelred, lord of Mercia, passed away, and
king Edward occupied London and Oxford, and all the lands
which belonged thereto. A great host of pirates came hither from the
south, from Brittany, and severely harried along the Severn, but almost
all of them afterwards perished there. (*continued on p.* 103)

gather his levies together, and ravaged all their territory
D 905 between the [Cambridgeshire] dikes and the Wissey, all of it as
from far north as the fens. When he wished to withdraw, he had the
p. 93 order given throughout the levies for a general retirement; then
the Kentishmen remained behind disobeying the order, and
seven messengers he had sent to them. Then they were caught there by
the host and a battle was fought. Among the slain were ealdorman
Sigewulf, and ealdorman Sigehelm, and Eadwold the king's thane, and
abbot Cenwulf, and Sigeberht, son of Sigewulf, and Eadwold, son of
Acca, and many others besides these, though I have named the most
distinguished. On the Danish side were slain king Eohric and prince
Æthelwold, whom they had elected as their king, and Beorhtsige, son of
prince Beorhtnoth, and the Scandinavian barons Ysopa and Oscytel,
and many others besides these whom we cannot name here: on each
side there was great slaughter made, and although the Danes had
possession of the place of slaughter they suffered greater losses. And
Ealhswith died the same year.

906. In this year the body of St Oswald was translated from Bardney
[to Gloucester]. In this year died Alfred, who was reeve at Bath:
and in the same year peace was ratified at Tiddingford,[2] as king Edward
ordained, both with the host from East Anglia and with the Northumbrians.

909. In this year the Mercians and West Saxons fought against the
host near Tettenhall on 6 August and were victorious. And this same
year Æthelflæd built the fortress at *Bremesburh*. In this year died
Denewulf, bishop of Winchester.

910. In this year Frithustan succeeded to the see of Winchester, and
Asser, bishop of Sherborne, died afterwards. And this same year king
Edward sent levies from both (*continued on p.* 97)

Ā 910
[909]
from
p. 94

and every kind of cattle: they slew many Danes and were five weeks in their territory.

911 [910]. In this year the host in Northumbria broke the truce, and rejecting with scorn whatever peace king Edward and his councillors offered them, harried across Mercia. And the king, who was then in Kent, had mustered about a hundred ships which sailed east along the south coast to meet him. The host, believing that the chief strength of the king lay in his ships, thought that they could range unchecked wherever they pleased. When the king learnt that they had gone out harrying, he sent his levies both from Wessex and from Mercia, and they intercepted the host as it was on its way home, and fought and put it to flight, slaying many thousands thereof, including their king Eowils.[1]

912 [911]. In this year died Æthelred, ealdorman of Mercia, and king Edward took over London and Oxford and all the lands which belonged thereto.

913 [912]. In this year, about Martinmas, king Edward had the more northerly fortress at Hertford built [i.e. north of the Lea], between the Maran and the Beane and the Lea. Then afterwards, the summer after, between Rogation days and midsummer, king Edward went with part of his forces to Maldon in Essex, and encamped there whilst the earthwork at Witham was being built and stockaded: and a good number of people who had earlier been under Danish domination submitted to him. Another part of his forces built the fortress at Hertford meanwhile on the southern bank of the Lea.

(*continued on p.* 98)

C 911
from
p. 94

911. Then in this, the following year, Æthelred, lord of the Mercians, died.

912. In this year, on the holy eve of the Invention of the Holy Cross [2 May], Æthelflæd, the 'Lady of the Mercians,' came to *Scergeat* and built a fortress there, and the same year that at Bridgnorth.

913. In this year, by the grace of God, Æthelflæd, the 'Lady of the Mercians,' went with all the Mercians to Tamworth, and built the fortress there early in the summer, and afterwards that at Stafford before Lammas. (*continued on p.* 98)

---

[1] *Eowils* B C; *Eowilisc* D; *Ecwils* Ā

Wessex and Mercia, and severely harried the host in the north,
D 910 destroying both people and every kind of cattle: they slew
from many Danes, and were five weeks in their territory.
p. 95   In this year English and Danes fought at Tettenhall, and
Æthelred, lord of Mercia, passed away, and king Edward took
over London and Oxford, and all the lands which belonged thereto.
And a great pirate host came hither from the south, from Brittany, and
severely harried along the Severn, but almost all of them afterwards
perished there.

911. In this year the host in Northumbria broke the truce, and
rejecting with scorn whatever fair terms king Edward and his councillors
offered them, harried across Mercia.   The king, who was then in Kent,
had mustered about a hundred ships which sailed east along the south
coast to meet him.   The host, believing that the chief strength of the
king lay in his ships, thought that they could range unchecked wherever
they pleased.   When the king learnt that they had gone out harrying,
he sent his levies both from Wessex and from Mercia, and they intercepted the host as it was on its way home, and fought and put it to flight,
slaying many thereof.   And there was slain king Eowils, king Halfdan,
jarl Ohtor, jarl Scurfa, and the Scandinavian barons Athulf[2] and
Agmund.

912. In this year died Æthelred, ealdorman of Mercia, and king
Edward took over London and Oxford and all the lands which belonged
thereto.

913. In this year Æthelfled fortified Tamworth and Stafford.   After
Martinmas this year, king Edward had the northern fortress at Hertford
built, between the Maran and the Beane and the Lea.   Then afterwards,
the summer after, between Rogation days and midsummer, king
Edward went with part of his forces to Maldon in Essex, and encamped
there whilst the earthwork at Witham was being built and stockaded:
and a good number of people who had earlier been under Danish
domination submitted to him.   Another part of his forces built the
fortress at Hertford on the southern bank of the Lea.

(*continued on p.* 99)

---

[2] 'and baron Benesing, and Anlaf the Black, and baron Thurferth, and
Osferth Hlytte, and baron Guthferth, and baron Agmund, and Guthferth.'
B C

Ā 917
[916]
from
p. 96

917 [916]. In this year after Easter the host rode out from Northampton and from Leicester and broke the peace, slaying many men at Hook Norton and thereabout; and very quickly after this, as these first raiders were on their way home, they came across a second troop of marauders riding out in the direction of Luton. And then the people of the country became aware of it, and fought against them and routed them completely, recovering all that they had taken and also a great part of their horses and their weapons.

918 [917]. In this year a great pirate host came over hither from the south from Brittany under two jarls Ohtor and Hroald, and sailed west about until they reached the estuary of the Severn, and harried at will everywhere along the Welsh coast. They seized Cyfeiliog, bishop of Archenfield [on the borders of Herefordshire and Gloucestershire], and took him with them to the ships, but king Edward ransomed him afterwards for forty pounds. Then after this the whole host went inland with the intention of renewing their raids in the direction of Archenfield: they were opposed by the men from Hereford and Gloucester and from the nearest fortresses who fought against them and put them to flight. They slew the jarl Hroald and the other jarl Ohtor's brother and a great part of the host, and drove them into an enclosure and besieged them there until they gave them hostages and promised to depart from king Edward's dominion. The king had arranged that the coast should be guarded along the southern shore of the Severn estuary, from Cornwall in the west eastwards as far as the mouth of the Avon, with the result that they durst not land anywhere in that region. However, they landed secretly by night on two separate occasions, once east of Watchet and again at Porlock, and on each occasion the English struck them so that only those few escaped who swam out to the ships. They encamped out on the island of Flatholme until the time came that they were very short of food, and many men perished of hunger, since they were unable (*continued on p.* 100)

C 914
from
p. 96

914. Then in this, the following year, [was fortified] that [fortress] at Eddisbury [Cheshire] in early summer; and later in the same year, late in autumn, that at Warwick.

(*continued on p.* 99)

914. In this year after Easter the host rode out from North-
D 914 ampton and from Leicester and broke the peace, slaying many
from men at Hook Norton and thereabout; and very quickly after
p. 97 this, as these first raiders were on their way home, they came
across a second troop of marauders riding out in the direction
of Luton. And then the people of the country became aware of it, and
fought against them and routed them completely, recovering all that
they had taken and also a great part of their horses and their weapons.

915. In this year Warwick was fortified and a great pirate host came
over hither from the south from Brittany under two jarls Ohtor and
Hraold, and sailed west about until they reached the estuary of the
Severn, and harried in Wales at will everywhere along its banks.   They
seized Cyfeiliog, bishop of Archenfield [on the borders of Herefordshire
and Gloucestershire], and took him with them to the ships, but king
Edward ransomed him afterwards for forty pounds.   Then after this
the whole host went inland with the intention of renewing their raids in
the direction of Archenfield: they were opposed by the men from
Hereford and Gloucester and from the nearest fortresses who fought
against them and put them to flight.   They slew the jarl Hraold and the
other jarl Ohtor's brother and a great part of the host, and drove them
into an enclosure and besieged them there until they gave them hostages
and promised to depart from the king's dominion.   The king had
arranged that the coast should be guarded against them along the
southern shore of the Severn estuary, from Cornwall in the west eastwards as far as the mouth of the Avon, with the result that they durst
not land anywhere in that region.   However, they landed secretly by
night on two separate occasions, once east of Watchet and again at
Porlock, and on each occasion the English struck them so that only
those few escaped who were able to swim out to the ships.   They
encamped out on the island of Steepholme until the time came that they
were very short of food, and many men perished of hunger, since they
were unable to obtain provisions: then they went (continued on p. *(continued on p.* 100)

C 915 915. Then in this, the following year after Christmas, [was
from built] that fortress at Chirbury [Shropshire], and then that
p. 98 at *Weardburh*; and in this same year before Christmas that at
Runcorn [Cheshire]. *(continued on p.* 100)

Ā 918
[917]
from
p. 98

to obtain provisions. They went thence to Dyfed [S. Wales] and then out to Ireland, and this was in the autumn. Then afterwards, in the same year before Martinmas [11 November], king Edward went to Buckingham with his levies and was there for four weeks, constructing both of the fortifications, one on each side of the river, before he left; and jarl Thurcytel submitted to him, and all the [Scandinavian] barons, and almost all of the chief men who owed allegiance to Bedford, besides many of those who owed allegiance to Northampton.[1]

919 [918]. In this year, before Martinmas [11 November], king Edward went with his army to Bedford and occupied the fortress: most of the garrison who had previously occupied it submitted to him. He remained there for four weeks, and before he left he ordered the fortress on the south bank of the river to be built.

920 [919]. In this year, before midsummer, king Edward went to Maldon and built the fortress and garrisoned it before he left. In this same year jarl Thurcytel went oversea to France with men who wished to follow him, under the protection of king Edward and with his assistance. (*continued on p.* 101)

D 915
from
p. 99

thence to Dyfed [S. Wales], and thence to Ireland, and this was in the autumn. Then afterwards, in the same year before Martinmas [11 November], king Edward went to Buckingham with his levies and was there for four weeks, constructing both of the fortifications, one on each side of the river, before he left; and jarl Thurcytel submitted to him, and all the jarls, and the chief men who owed allegiance to Bedford, besides many of those who owed allegiance to Northampton.[2] (*continued on p.* 105)

C 916
from
p. 99

916. In this year before midsummer, on 16 June, the day of the festival of St Quiricus the Martyr,[3] abbot Ecgberht, who had done nothing to deserve it, was slain together with his companions. Three days later Æthelflæd sent an army into Wales and stormed *Brecenanmere* [at Llangorse lake, near Brecon], and there captured the wife of the king and thirty-three other persons. (*continued on p.* 101)

---

[1] 'At this point B and C insert the Mercian Register of the years 902–24 which is given above.' (Plummer)

[2] 'The annals 917, 918, 919, 921 have been borrowed by D direct from the Mercian Register. They are therefore omitted here from D' (Plummer)

[3] On St Cyr see Alban Butler, *Lives of the Saints* I. 795.

A 921
[921]
from
p. 100

921 [920]. In this year before Easter king Edward had the fortress at Towcester occupied and fortified; then afterwards, at Rogationtide in the same year, he had the fortress built at *Wigingamere.*

The same summer, between Lammas and midsummer, the host from Northampton and Leicester and north from there, broke the peace and went to Towcester and besieged the fortress the whole day, thinking that they would be able to take it by storm: but the garrison inside defended it until reinforcements came up, so the Danes gave up the siege and went away. Very soon after that, however, they sallied forth in marauding bands at night, and waylaid unsuspecting folk, taking considerable spoil both in captives and cattle between Bernwood and Aylesbury.

At the same time the host went from Huntingdon and from East Anglia and built the fortress at Tempsford: they occupied it after its construction, abandoning the other fortress at Huntingdon, thinking that by operating from there they could in the future dominate a wider area by war and hostility. They went out and reached Bedford, but the garrison sallied out to meet them, fought against them and put them to flight, slaying a good part of them.

Yet again after this a great host assembled from East Anglia and Mercia, and went to the fortress at *Wigingamere* and besieged it: they fought against it until far into the day and carried off the cattle thereabouts: but the garrison defended (*continued on p.* 102)

C 917
from
p. 100

917. In this year before Lammas, Æthelflæd, the 'Lady of the Mercians,' won the borough called Derby with God's help, together with all the region which it controlled: four of her thanes, who were dear to her, were slain there within the gates.
(*continued on p.* 105)

Ā 921
[920]
from
p. 101

the fortress with the result that the Danes gave up the siege and went away.

Then after this, in the same summer, a great force assembled in king Edward's dominion, and all the men from the nearest fortresses who could reach it marched to Tempsford and besieged the fortress: they attacked it until they took it by storm, and slew the king, and jarl Toglos, and his son, jarl Manna, and his brother, and all the garrison who put up a resistance, making prisoners of the rest and seizing everything inside the fortress.

Then very quickly after this a great force gathered together in the autumn, from Kent, Surrey, and Essex, and from all parts from the nearest fortresses, and marched on Colchester and surrounded the fortress and attacked until they had captured it: they slew all the inhabitants, and seized everything inside, except the men who escaped over the wall.

Yet again after this, the same autumn, a great host assembled from East Anglia, composed of Danes then in the country and pirates whom they had enticed to their aid: their intention was to avenge the reverses they had suffered. They went to Maldon, surrounded the fortress, and attacked it until reinforcements came from without to their relief; thereupon they gave up the siege and went away. Then sallied out the garrison in pursuit; and, with the assistance of the reinforcements, put the host to flight and slew many hundreds of them, both pirates and others.

Then very quickly after this the same autumn, king Edward went with the levies of Wessex to Passenham, and encamped there whilst the fortress at Towcester was being reinforced by a stone wall. Jarl Thurferth and the [Scandinavian] barons submitted to him, together with the entire host (*continued on p.* 103)

E 918
from
p. 95

918. In this year passed away Æthelflæd, the 'Lady of the Mercians.'

921. In this year king Sihtric slew Niall, his brother.[1]

(*continued on p.* 105)

Ā 921
[920]
from
p. 102

which owed allegiance to Northampton, as far north as the Welland, and made their submission to him as their lord and protector.

When this division of the English levies went home, the other came out on military service and occupied the fortress at Huntingdon: acting on orders from king Edward, they repaired and rebuilt it where it had been destroyed; and all the original inhabitants who had survived in the district submitted to king Edward, and sought his peace and protection.

Yet again after this, before Martinmas in the same year, king Edward went with West Saxon levies to Colchester, and repaired and rebuilt the fortress where it had been destroyed. Many people, both from East Anglia and from Essex, who had previously been under Danish domination, submitted to him: and the entire Danish host in East Anglia swore union with him, 'that they wished all that he wished, protecting all that he protected, by sea and land.' The host which owed allegiance to Cambridge independently chose him as lord and protector: the treaty was ratified with oaths exactly as he drew it up.

922 [921]. In this year, between Rogation days and midsummer, king Edward marched with his levies to Stamford, and had a fortress built on the south bank of the river: all the people who owed allegiance to the more northerly fortress submitted to him and sought him for their lord. During the stay he made there his sister Æthelflæd died at Tamworth, twelve days before midsummer: thereupon he took over the fortress at Tamworth, and all the people of Mercia who had been under allegiance to Æthelflæd turned in submission to him. The kings of Wales, Hywel, Clydog, and Idwal, (*continued on p.* 104)

---

[1] Sihtric killed his brother Sigefrith in 888, and Niall Glundubh, king of Ireland, in 919. The annal is a conflation of these two events.

Ā 922
[921]
from
p. 103

and all the people of Wales, gave him their allegiance. Then he went thence to Nottingham and occupied the borough: he had it repaired and garrisoned both by Englishmen and Danes, and all the people settled in Mercia, both Danish and English, submitted to him.

923 [922]. In this year, in late autumn, king Edward went with his levies to Thelwall, and had the fortress built, settled and garrisoned. Whilst he was encamped there he ordered other levies, also drawn from Mercia, to occupy Manchester in Northumbria, and had it repaired and garrisoned. In this year passed away archbishop Plegmund.

924 [923]. In this year before midsummer, king Edward went to Nottingham with his levies, and had a fortress built on the south side of the river, opposite to the other, and made a bridge over the Trent to connect the two forts. From thence he went to Bakewell in the Peak of Derbyshire, and had a fortress built in the neighbourhood and garrisoned. Then the king of Scots and the whole Scottish nation accepted him as 'father and lord': so also did Rægnald and the sons of Eadwulf and all the inhabitants of Northumbria, both English and Danish, Norwegians and others; together with the king of the Strathclyde Welsh and all his subjects.

925 [924]. In this year passed away king Edward, and Athelstan, his son, came to the throne. St Dunstan was born,[1] *and Wulfhelm became archbishop of Canterbury, (continued on p.* 106)

(continued on p. 106)

---

[1] For arguments in favour of 909, instead of 925, see Abbot [F. A.] Gasquet and E. Bishop, *The Bosworth Psalter* (Appendix by A. L. St L. Toke); and J. A. Robinson, *The Saxon Bishops of Wells* (Brit. Acad. Suppl. Papers, No. 4, 1919).

E 923
from
p. 103

923. In this year king Rægnald won York.
924. [In this year king Edward passed away and Athelstan, his son, came to the throne.] [2]
925. In this year bishop Wulfhelm was consecrated, and the same year king Edward passed away. (*continued on p.* 107)

F 924
from
p. 93

924. In this year king Edward was accepted as 'father and lord' by the king of the Scots and his people, by king Rægnald and all the Northumbrians, also by the king of the Strathclyde Welsh and all his subjects.
925 [924]. In this year king Edward passed away and Athelstan, his son, came to the throne. Wulfhelm was consecrated archbishop of Canterbury, and St Dunstan was born.

(*continued on p.* 107)

D 923
from
p. 100

923. In this year king Rægnald stormed York.
924. King Edward died at Farndon-on-Dee in Mercia; and very soon, sixteen days after, his son Ælfweard died at Oxford; they were buried at Winchester. Athelstan was accepted as king by the Mercians and was consecrated at Kingston: he gave his sister in marriage oversea [3] to the son of the king of the Old Saxons [Otto the Great].
925. King Athelstan and Sihtric, king of Northumbria, met at Tamworth on 30 January, and Athelstan gave him his sister in marriage.

(*continued on p.* 107)

C 918
from
p. 101

918. In the early part of this year, with God's help, she secured possession of the borough of Leicester by peaceful means; and the majority of the Danish forces that owed allegiance to it became subject to her. The people of York had promised her to accept her rule, some of them engaged themselves to do so by pledge, others ratifying it with oaths. But very soon after they had agreed to this she died, twelve days before midsummer [12 June] at Tamworth, and in the eighth year of her rule over Mercia as its rightful lord. She was buried at Gloucester in the east chapel of St Peter's Church.
919. In this year too the daughter of Æthelred, lord of the Mercians, was deprived of all authority in Mercia: she was taken to Wessex three weeks before Christmas. Her name was Ælfwynn.
921. In this year king Edward built the fortress at the mouth of the Clwyd.[4]
924. King Edward died at Farndon-on-Dee in Mercia. His son, Ælfweard, died very soon after at Oxford: they were buried at Winchester. Athelstan was accepted as king by the Mercians, and was consecrated at Kingston. He gave his sister . . . (*continued on p.* 113)

---

[2] This annal was crossed out by a later hand; probably because of the next annal.
[3] MS. *ofsæ*. For the marriages of Athelstan's sisters see F. M. Stenton, *Anglo-Saxon England* 342.
[4] Cf. F. T. Wainwright, '*Cledemutha*' (65 *EHR* 203–12).

931. In this year, on 29 May, Beornstan was consecrated
bishop of Winchester: he was bishop two and a half years.

932. In this year bishop Frithustan passed away.

933. In this year king Athelstan invaded Scotland with a
land and naval force, and harried much of the country. Bishop
Beornstan passed away at Winchester on All Saints' day [1 November].

934. In this year Ælfheah was made bishop [of Winchester].

937.   In this year king Athelstan, lord of warriors,
Ring-giver of men, with his brother prince Edmund,
Won undying glory with the edges of swords,
In warfare around *Brunanburh*.
With their hammered blades, the sons of Edward
Clove the shield-wall and hacked the linden bucklers,
As was instinctive in them, from their ancestry,
To defend their land, their treasures and their homes,
In frequent battle against each enemy.
The foemen were laid low: the Scots
And the host from the ships fell doomed. The field
Grew dark [1] with the blood of men [2] after the sun,
That glorious luminary, God's bright candle,
Rose high in the morning above the horizon,
Until the noble being of the Lord Eternal
Sank to its rest. There lay many a warrior
Of the men of the North, torn by spears,
Shot o'er his shield; likewise many a Scot

(*continued on p.* 108)

Ā 931
from
p. 104

---

[1] Reading *dunnade*. For editions of the poem see Alistair Campbell,
The Battle of Brunanburh (London 1938), and N. Kershaw, *Anglo-Saxon and
Norse Poems* (Cambridge 1922) 59–71.

[2] Ā has *bold warriors*; the above translates B C D

E 927
from
p. 105

927. In this year Athelstan drove out king Guthfrith: and archbishop Wulfhelm went to Rome.

928. Willelm suscepit regnum, et ·xv· annis regnauit.

933. In this year prince Edwin was drowned at sea.

934. In this year king Athelstan invaded Scotland both with a land and a naval force, and harried much of the country.

937. In this year king Athelstan led levies to *Brunanburh*.

(*continued on p. 111*)

F 927
from
p. 105

927. In this year king Athelstan drove out king Guthfrith: and archbishop Wulfhelm went to Rome.[3]

928. In this year William [Longsword] became duke of Normandy, and ruled fifteen years.

931. In this year Frithustan, bishop of Winchester, passed away, and Beornstan was consecrated in his stead.

934. In this year Athelstan invaded Scotland both with a land and a naval force, and harried much of the country.

935. In this year Ælfheah became bishop of the see of Winchester.

937. In this year Athelstan (and Edmund, his brother), led levies to *Brunanburh*,[4] and there fought against Anlaf: with the help of Christ they had the victory (and there slew five kings and eight jarls).

(*continued on p. 125*)

D 926
from
p. 105

926. In this year fiery rays of light appeared in the northern sky. Sihtric died and king Athelstan annexed the kingdom of Northumbria: he brought into submission all the kings in this island: first Hywel, king of the West Welsh, and Constantine, king of Scots, and Owain, king of Gwent, and Ealdred Ealdulfing from Bamburgh. They established a covenant of peace with pledges and oaths at a place called Eamont Bridge on 12 July: they forbade all idolatrous practices, and then separated in concord.

934. In this year king Athelstan invaded Scotland both with a land and naval force, and harried much of the country. (*continued on p. 111*)

---

[3] *pro pallio* adds F Lat
[4] *Hic factum est illud magnum et famosum bellum in Brunanbyri* F Lat

107

Sated with battle, lay lifeless.

Ā 937
from
p. 106

All through the day the West Saxons in troops
Pressed on in pursuit of the hostile peoples,
Fiercely, with swords sharpened on grindstone,
They cut down the fugitives as they fled.
Nor did the Mercians refuse hard fighting
To any of Anlaf's warriors, who invaded
Our land across the tossing waters,
In the ship's bosom, to meet their doom
In the fight.   Five young kings,
Stretched lifeless by the swords,
Lay on the field, likewise seven
Of Anlaf's jarls, and a countless host
Of seamen and Scots.   There the prince
Of Norsemen, compelled by necessity,
Was forced to flee to the prow of his ship
With a handful of men.   In haste the ship
Was launched, and the king fled hence,
Over the waters grey, to save his life.

There, likewise, the agèd Constantine,
The grey-haired warrior, set off in flight,
North to his native land.   No cause
Had he to exult in that clash of swords,[1]
Bereaved of his kinsmen, robbed of his friends
On the field of battle, by violence deprived
Of them in the struggle.   On the place of slaughter

(*continued on p.* 109)

---

[1] So B C, possibly *clash of men* so D, and apparently originally Ā.   See Alistair Campbell, *op. cit.* 110–11.

He left his young son, mangled by wounds,
Received in the fight. No need to exult
In that clash of blades had the grey-haired warrior,
That practised scoundrel, and no more had Anlaf
Need to gloat, amid the remnants of their host,
That they excelled in martial deeds
Where standards clashed, and spear met spear
And man fought man, upon a field
Where swords were crossed, when they in battle
Fought Edward's sons upon the fateful field.

The sorry Norsemen who escaped the spears
Set out upon the sea of Ding, making for Dublin
O'er deep waters, in ships with nailèd sides,
Ashamed and shameless back to Ireland.[2]

Likewise the English king and the prince,
Brothers triumphant in war, together
Returned to their home, the land of Wessex.

To enjoy the carnage, they left behind
The horn-beaked raven with dusky plumage,
And the hungry hawk of battle, the dun-coated
Eagle, who with white-tipped tail shared
The feast with the wolf, grey beast of the forest.

Never before in this island, as the books

(*continued on p.* 110)

---

[2] *their land* A; the reading is that of B C D

Of ancient historians tell us, was an army
Ā 937 Put to greater slaughter by the sword
from Since the time when Angles and Saxons landed,
p. 109 Invading Britain across the wide seas
From the east, when warriors eager for fame,
Proud forgers of war, the Welsh overcame,
And won for themselves a kingdom.

941. In this year passed away king Athelstan, on 27 October, forty years all but a day after king Alfred. Prince Edmund came to the throne at the age of eighteen. King Athelstan had ruled fourteen years and ten weeks. *At this time Wulfhelm was archbishop of Canterbury.*

942.   In this year king Edmund, lord of the English,
Guardian of kinsmen, loved doer of deeds, conquered Mercia
As far as Dore and Whitwell Gap the boundary form
And Humber river, that broad ocean-stream;
The Boroughs Five he won, Leicester and Lincoln,
Nottingham, Derby and Stamford too.[1]
Long had the Danes under the Norsemen
Been subjected by force to heathen bondage,
Until finally liberated by the valour of Edward's son,
King Edmund, protector of warriors.

He stood sponsor for king Anlaf at baptism, and the same year, after some length of time, he also stood sponsor for king Rægnald. ⟨In this year passed away Wulfhelm⟩ the archbishop.

943. ⟨In this year King Edmund gave Glas⟩tonbury into the charge of St Dunstan, who later became its first abbot.

944. In this year king Edmund brought all Northumbria under his sway, and drove out two kings, Anlaf Sihtricson and Rægnald Guthfrithson.

945. In this year king Edmund ravaged all Strathclyde, and ceded it to Malcolm, king of Scots, on the condition that he would be his fellow worker both by sea and land. (*continued on p.* 112)

---

[1] See A. Mawer, 'The Redemption of the Five Boroughs' (38 *EHR* 551–7).

940. In this year king Athelstan passed away, and Edmund, his brother, succeeded to the throne.

E 940 from p. 107

942. In this year king Anlaf passed away. Et Ricardus uetus suscepit regnum et regnauit an*nos* ·lii·

944. In this year king Edmund conquered all Northumbria, and drove out two men of royal blood, Anlaf and Rægnald.

945. In this year king Edmund ravaged all Strathclyde.

(*continued on p.* 113

940. In this year king Athelstan passed away at Gloucester on 27 October, forty years all but a day after king Alfred. Prince Edmund came to the throne at the age of eighteen. King Athelstan had ruled fourteen years and ten weeks.

D 940 from p. 107

941. In this year the Northumbrians were false to their pledges, and chose Anlaf from Ireland as their king.

942.

In this year king Edmund, lord of the English,
Guardian of kinsmen, loved doer of deeds, conquered Mercia
As far as Dore and Whitwell Gap the boundary form
And Humber river, that broad ocean-stream;
The Boroughs Five he won, Leicester and Lincoln,
Nottingham, Derby and Stamford too.
Long had the Danes under the Norsemen
Been subjected by force to heathen bondage,
Until finally liberated by the valour of Edward's son,
King Edmund, protector of warriors.

943.[2] In this year Anlaf stormed Tamworth and there was great slaughter on both sides: the Danes had the victory and carried great booty away with them. On this raid Wulfrun was taken prisoner.

In this year king Edmund besieged king Anlaf and archbishop Wulfstan in Leicester, and might have captured them had they not escaped from the city by night. Afterwards Anlaf obtained king Edmund's friendship, and king Edmund stood sponsor for him at baptism and bestowed royal gifts upon him. The same year, after a very long time, he stood sponsor for king Rægnald.

944. In this year king Edmund brought all Northumbria under his sway, and drove out two kings, Anlaf Sihtricson and Rægnald Guthfrithson.

945. In this year king Edmund ravaged all Strathclyde, and ceded it to Malcolm, king of Scots, on the condition that he would be his fellow worker both by sea and land. (*continued on p.* 112)

---

[2] On the events of this annal see Alistair Campbell, *op. cit.* 50 note 4.

946. In this year king Edmund passed away on St Augustine's
Ā 946 day [26 May], after ruling six and a half years. He was
from succeeded by his brother prince Eadred who reduced all
p. 110 Northumbria to subjection: and Scots gave him oaths and
promised to do his will in all things.

951. In this year Ælfheah, bishop of Winchester, passed away on St
Gregory's day [12 March].

955. In this year king Eadred passed away on St Clement's day
[23 November] at Frome: he had ruled nine and a half years. He
was succeeded by Eadwig, the son of king Edmund.

956. and [king Eadwig] drove St Dunstan out of the country.

958. In this year king Eadwig passed away on 1 October, and was
succeeded by Edgar, his brother.

959. In this year he sent for St Dunstan and gave him the bishopric of
Worcester, and afterwards the bishopric of London.

(*continued on p.* 114)

946. In this year king Edmund passed away on St Augus-
D 946 tine's day [26 May]. It was widely known how he met his
from end, that Liofa stabbed him at Pucklechurch. Æthelflæd of
p. 111 Damerham, daughter of ealdorman Ælfgar, was then his queen.

He had ruled six and a half years, and was succeeded by his
brother, prince Eadred, who reduced all Northumbria to subjection:
the Scots gave him oaths and promised to do his will in all things.

947. In this year king Eadred came to Tanshelf, and there archbishop
Wulfstan and all the councillors of Northumbria pledged their allegiance to the king, but within a short while they were false both to their
pledges and oaths.

948. In this year king Eadred harried all Northumbria, because they
had taken Eric [1] for their king: on the raid the famous minster at Ripon,
which St Wilfrid built, was destroyed by fire. Then when the king
was on his way home, the host from out of York overtook the
king's rearguard at Castleford, and there was great slaughter. Then
was the king so enraged that he would have invaded that land a second
time and completely devastated it, but when the council of the Northumbrians heard of it they abandoned Eric and made reparation to king
Eadred for their action.

952. In this year king Eadred had Wulfstan imprisoned in the stronghold at *Iudanburh* because he had been frequently accused to the king;
in this year too the king had many put to death in the borough of
Thetford, to avenge the death of abbot Eadhelm whom they had slain.

(*continued on p.* 113)

[1] Possibly Eric 'Bloodaxe,' late king of Norway. See N. Kershaw, *op.
cit.* 93 ff., and for text and translation of the *Eiríksmál.*

948. In this year king Edmund was stabbed to death, and
E 948 Eadred, his brother, succeeded him; and straightway he reduced
from all Northumbria to subjection: and Scots swore him oaths and
p. 111 promised to do his will in all things.

949. In this year Anlaf Cuaran [2] came to Northumbria.

952. In this year the Northumbrians drove out king Anlaf and accepted Eric, son of Harold, as their king.

954. In this year the Northumbrians drove out Eric, and Eadred succeeded to the Northumbrian kingdom.

955. In this year king Eadred passed away, and Eadwig, son of Edmund, succeeded to the kingdom.

956. In this year archbishop Wulfstan passed away.

959. In this year king Eadwig passed away, and was succeeded by Edgar, his brother. (*continued on p.* 114)

954. In this year the Northumbrians drove out Eric, and
D 954 Eadred succeeded to the Northumbrian kingdom. Arch-
from bishop Wulfstan was restored to the bishopric of Dorchester.
p. 112 955. In this year king Eadred passed away, and he rests in the
Old Minster [Winchester]. Eadwig succeeded to Wessex, and his brother Edgar to Mercia: they were sons of king Edmund and St Ælfgifu.

957. In this year archbishop Wulfstan passed away on 16 December, and he was buried at Oundle: in the same year abbot Dunstan was driven oversea.

958. In this year archbishop Oda dissolved the marriage of king Eadwig and Ælfgifu on grounds of consanguinity.

(*continued on p.* 119)

956. In this year king Eadred passed away, and Eadwig
B 956 succeeded him.
and 957. In this year prince Edgar came to the throne of Mercia.
C 956 959. In this year king Eadwig passed away, and was suc-
ceeded by Edgar, his brother, who ruled over Wessex, Mercia, and Northumbria: he was then sixteen years old.

(*continued on p.* 119)

---

[2] i.e. Olaf Sihtricson. See W. G. Collingwood, *Scandinavian Britain* (London 1908) *passim*, and Alistair Campbell, *op. cit.* 44 ff.

961. In this year archbishop Oda died, and St Dunstan suc-
Ā 961 ceeded to the archbishopric.

from 962. In this year Ælfgar, the king's kinsman, passed away
p. 112 in Devonshire and his body rests at Wilton. King Sigferth
killed himself, and his body lies at Wimborne. In this year
there was a very great pestilence, and a destructive fire in London burnt
down St Paul's: it was rebuilt the same year.

In this same year Æthelmod the priest went to Rome, and there
passed away on 15 August.

963. In this year Wulfstan the deacon passed away on Holy Innocents' day [28 December], and later Gyric the priest passed away.

In this same year abbot Æthelwold became bishop of Winchester;
he was consecrated on the vigil of St Andrew's day [29 November],
which was a Sunday. (*continued on p.* 116)

His reign was prosperous, and God granted him
E 959 To live his days in peace: he did his duty,
from And laboured zealously in its performance.
p. 113 Far and wide he exalted God's praise
And delighted in His law, improving the security
Of his people more than all the kings
Who were before him within the memory of man.

God helped him moreover to subdue kings and earls,
Who cheerfully submitted to his will.
So that without opposition he was able to subdue
All to his wishes.   (*continued on p.* 115)

114

E 959
from
p. 114

> He was greatly honoured far and wide throughout the
> nations,
> For he zealously honoured God's name,
> And continually pondered God's law,
> And exalted God's praise far and wide,
> And constantly counselled all his people wisely,
> On both religious and secular matters.
>> One grave fault, however, was all too characteristic of him,
> Namely he was far too fond of foreign, vicious customs,
> And introduced heathen practices too eagerly
> Into this land: he invited foreigners hither,
> And encouraged harmful elements to enter this country;
>> But may God grant him that his virtues triumph over his
>> faults,
> And serve to shield his soul on its long journey.

963.[1] In this year St Æthelwold was chosen by king Edgar to be bishop of Winchester: and St Dunstan, archbishop of Canterbury, consecrated him on the first Sunday of Advent, which was 29 November.

In the year after he was consecrated he established many monasteries, and drove out the secular clergy from the cathedral because they would not observe any monastic rule, and replaced them with monks. He established two abbeys, one of monks and the other of nuns, both at Winchester. Then he came to king Edgar and asked him to give him all the monasteries which the heathen had destroyed, because he wished to restore them: and the king cheerfully granted it. The bishop went first to Ely, where St Æthelthryth is buried, and had the monastery built, giving it to one of his monks whose name was Byrhtnoth: he consecrated him abbot and peopled it with monks to serve God, where formerly there had been nuns. He bought many villages from the king and richly endowed it.

Afterwards came bishop Æthelwold to the monastery called *Medeshamstede*, which had been destroyed by the heathen, and found nothing there but old walls and wild woods. He found, hidden in the old walls, documents which had been written by abbot Hedde,

(*continued on p.* 116)

---

[1] 'This insertion is the basis of the narrative entitled "Relatio Heddæ Abbatis" given by Hugh Candidus (ed. Sparke, p. 23). It is unlikely to be older than the early twelfth century, and has no authority for the pre-Danish period.' (F. M. Stenton, 'Medeshamstede and its Colonies' 325 note 1.)

A 964
from
p. 114 964. In this year king Edgar drove out the priests from the Old Minster and from the New Minster of Winchester, and from Chertsey, and from Milton Abbas [Dorset], and planted monks in those churches. He appointed abbot Æthelgar

(continued on p. 118)

E 963
from
p. 115 telling how king Wulfhere and Æthelred, his brother, had built it and freed it from all obligations to king, to bishop, and from all secular service; and how pope Agatho had confirmed it with his bull, and archbishop Deusdedit also. Thereupon he had the monastery built, and appointed there an abbot who was called Ealdwulf, and placed monks there where nothing was before. He came then to the king and had him examine the documents which had been found, and the king answered and said: 'I, Edgar, before God'and before the archbishop Dunstan, grant and give to-day freedom to the monastery of St Peter, *Medeshamstede*, from the jurisdiction of king and bishop, and to all the villages which pertain thereto, namely Eastfield, Dogsthorpe, Eye, and Paston, and in such wise I exempt it that no bishop shall have any authority there, only the abbot of the monastery. Moreover I give the village called Oundle with everything pertaining thereto, namely the Eight Hundreds, and market and toll so freely that neither king nor bishop nor earl nor sheriff shall have any authority, nor any man but the abbot only and his officers. And I give to Christ and to St Peter, on account of the petition of the bishop Æthelwold, these lands: namely Barrow, Warmington, Ashton, Kettering, Castor, Ailsworth, Walton, Werrington, Eye, Longthorpe, and a moneyer in Stamford. These lands and all the others which belong to the monastery I declare free, that is with *sake* and with *soke*, with *toll* and with *team*, and with *infangenetheof*.[1] These rights and all others I declare free to Christ and to St Peter. And I give two-thirds of Whittlesey Mere, with its waters, weirs, and fens, and so through *Merelad* straight on to the river called Nene, and so eastward to King's Delph: and I desire that a market be created in the same town, and that there be no other between Stamford and Huntingdon. And I desire that the right of toll over the following area shall be given: first from Whittlesey Mere all the way to the king's toll (*continued on p. 117*)

---

[1] On these technical terms denoting judicial and financial rights, see F. E. Harmer, *Anglo-Saxon Writs* (Manchester 1952) 73–8, and *passim*.

of Norman Cross Hundreds, and then back in the opposite
E 963 direction from Whittlesey Mere through *Merelad* straight
from on to the Nene,[2] and so as the river runs to Crowland, and from
p. 116 Crowland to the Muscat,[3] and from the Muscat to King's
Delph and to Whittlesey Mere. And I desire that all the free-
doms and all the indulgences granted by my predecessors shall remain
in force; and I sign it and confirm it with the sign of Christ's cross.'

Then answered archbishop Dunstan of Canterbury and said: 'I
concede that all the things which here are given and mentioned, and all
those things that your predecessors and mine have granted—these I
will shall stand; and whosoever violates this I give him the curse of God
and of all saints and of all the dignitaries of the Church and mine too,
unless he repents: and I give in acknowledgment to St Peter my cope
and my stole and my robe for the service of Christ.'

'I, Oswald, archbishop of York, agree to all these words, by the holy
cross on which Christ suffered.'

'I, Æthelwold, bishop, bless all those who shall observe this, and I
excommunicate all who shall violate this, unless he repents.'

Here were present bishop Ælfstan, bishop Æthelwulf, and abbot
Æscwig, and abbot Osgar, and abbot Æthelgar, and ealdorman
Ælfhere, and ealdorman Æthelwine, Byrhtnoth, ealdorman Oslac, and
many other prominent men: and they all ratified it, and all signed it
with the sign of Christ. This was done nine hundred and seventy-two
years after the birth of our Lord, and in the sixteenth year of the king.

The abbot Ealdwulf bought many estates, and altogether richly
endowed the monastery. He was there until archbishop Oswald of
York passed away, and then was elected to succeed him. Another
abbot was speedily chosen from the same monastery: he was called
Cenwulf, who was afterwards bishop of Winchester. He was the first
to build the wall around the monastery, and gave it then the name
Burch,[4] although formerly it had been known as *Medeshamstede*. He
was there until he was appointed bishop of Winchester. Then another
abbot named Ælfsige was elected from the same monastery: this
Ælfsige was abbot afterwards for fifty years. He exhumed St Cyneburh
and St Cyneswith, who were buried at Castor, and St Tibba, who was
buried at Ryhall, and translated them to Peterborough and offered
them all to St Peter on the same day, and kept possession of their relics
while he was abbot there.

964. Hic expulsi sunt canonici de ueteri monasterio.

(*continued on p.* 119)

---

[2] Dr A. Bell in W. T. Mellows, *The Chronicle of Hugh Candidus XXIII*,
points out that the OE has skipped a whole section of the bounds—ad
aquam Nen, et inde sicut aqua currit *ad Welmesforde et de Welmesforde
ad Stanforde et de Stanford inxta cursum aque usque* ad Crulande.
[3] 19 EPN 7–9.
[4] Subsequently translated Peterborough, its modern equivalent.

abbot of New Minster, and Ordberht to Chertsey, and Cyneweard to Milton Abbas.

Ā 964
from
p. 116

971. ⟨In this year prince Edmund passed away, and his body
lies at Romsey.⟩[1]

973.   In this year, Edgar, ruler of the English,
Was consecrated king by a great assembly,
In the ancient city of *Acemannesceaster*,
Also called Bath by the inhabitants
Of this island.   On that blessed day,
Called and named Whit Sunday by the children of men,
There was great rejoicing by all.   As I have heard,
There was a great congregation of priests, and a goodly
     company of monks,
And wise men gathered together.
Then, as the books record, by numerical reckoning,
Had passed away ten hundred years, all but twenty-seven,
From the time of the birth of the renowned King,
Guardian of the heavenly bodies:
Almost one thousand years had elapsed
Since the time of the Lord of Victories when this happened.
Edmund's son, the valiant in warlike deeds,
Had spent twenty-nine years in the world when this took
     place.
He was in his thirtieth year when consecrated king.

975.   In this year Edgar, king of the English,
Brought to an end his earthly pleasures:
He chose another world, radiant and joyous,
Quitting this poor and transitory existence.

(*continued on p.* 120)

---

[1] 971, erased in Ā, is taken from Wheloc.

966. In this year Thored, son of Gunner, ravaged Westmor-
E 966 land, and the same year Oslac became earl [of Northumbria].
from 969. In this year king Edgar ordered the whole of the Isle of
p. 117 Thanet to be harried.

970. In this year passed away prince Edmund.

972. In this year prince Edgar was consecrated king on Whit Sunday [11 May] at Bath, in the thirteenth year after his accession, and when he was twenty-nine years old. Soon after this the king led all his fleet to Chester, and there six kings came to him to make their submission, and pledged themselves to be his fellow workers by sea and land.

975.[a]   In this year Edgar passed away,
                   Ruler of the English,
                   Friend of the West Saxons,
                   And protector of the Mercians.

(*continued on p.* 121)

D 965
from   965. In this year king Edgar took Ælfthryth for his queen:
p. 113   she was the daughter of ealdorman Ordgar.

(*continued on p.* 121)

971. In this year passed away archbishop Oscytel, who was
B 971 first consecrated diocesan bishop of Dorchester and later
from translated to York, by the consent of king Eadred and all his
p. 113 councillors. He had been a bishop for twenty-two years, and
passed away on the night of All Saints' day [1 November], ten days before Martinmas [11 November] at Thame. Abbot Thurcytel, his kinsman, carried the bishop's body to Bedford, since he was abbot there in those days.

---

[a] 'B and C have the longer poem as in $\overline{A}$; D (like E) has the shorter poem. F is content with the simple prose entry: *in this year king Edgar passed away*.' (Plummer)

The sons of men on earth, men everywhere in our native
land,
Those who have been correctly instructed in the art of
reckoning,
Give the name July to the month when the young Edgar,
The patron of men, departed this life on its eighth day.
His son, a stripling, succeeded then to the throne:
The name of the prince of earls was Edward.
　　Ten days before, the good bishop Cyneweard,
The glorious hero, good from native virtue,
Passed away from Britain.
　　Then, as I have heard, the praise of the Ruler
Fell away everywhere throughout the length and breadth
Of Mercia, and many wise servants of God were expelled.
This was great grief to those in whose hearts and minds
Reigned fervent love for the Creator. Then was the
Prince of Glories,
Lord of Victories, the Ruler of the Heavens,
Too frequently rejected, and his law violated.
Then too the bold-hearted Oslac was driven from the land,
Over the tossing waves where the gannet bathes.
The grey-haired hero, wise and sage in counsel,
Was driven into exile over the turmoil of the waves,
Over the home of the whale, and bereft of his lands.
　　Then, up in the heavens, a star in the firmament
Made its appearance, which confident sages,
Wise seers, astronomers, and sage scholars [1]
Everywhere call by the name of 'comet.'
Throughout the nation, the vengeance of the Lord
Was widely evident when hunger reigned
Over the earth. Thereafter the Keeper of the Heavens
(*continued on p.* 122)

---

[1] *prophets* B C
[2] Plummer does not print the beginning of this annal, but indicates that it
is identical with that of E by the use of an asterisk.

E 975
from
p. 119

That was known far and wide
Throughout many nations,
   Kings honoured the son of Edmund
Far and wide over the gannet's bath,
And submitted to the sovereign,
As was his birthright.
   No fleet however proud,
No host however strong,
Was able to win booty for itself
In England, while that noble king
Occupied the royal throne.

And in this year Edward, Edgar's son, succeeded to the throne: and soon in the autumn of the same year appeared that star known as 'comet.' The next year came a great famine and very many disturbances throughout England. Ealdorman Ælfhere had very many monasteries destroyed which king Edgar (*continued on p.* 122)

975.[2]   8 July

D 975
from
p. 119

In this year Edgar passed away,
Ruler of the English,
Friend of the West Saxons,
And protector of the Mercians.
That was known far and wide
Throughout many nations,
   Kings honoured the son of Edmund
Far and wide over the gannet's bath,
And submitted to the sovereign,
As was his birthright.
   No fleet however proud,
No host however strong,
Was able to win booty for itself
In England, while that noble king
Occupied the royal throne.

And in this year Edward, Edgar's son, succeeded to the throne: and soon in the autumn of the same year appeared that star known as 'comet.' The next year came a great famine and very many disturbances throughout England.

In his days, on account of his youth,
God's adversaries broke God's laws;
Ealdorman Ælfhere and many others
Hindered the monastic rule, and destroyed monasteries,
Dispersed monks, and put to flight God's servants,
Whom king Edgar had ordered the holy bishop
   Æthelwold to establish;
Widows were robbed many a time and oft,
And many injustices and evil crimes
Flourished thereafter.
And ever afterwards things went from bad to worse.
And at this time too was Oslac, the famous earl, banished from England.

(*continued on p.* 147)

The Lord of Angels remedied that, restoring happiness
To every islander by means of the fruits of the earth.

Ā 975
from
p. 120

978. In this year king Edward was murdered and prince Æthelred, his brother, came to the throne.

(*continued on p.* 124)

E 975
from
p. 121

had ordered the holy bishop Æthelwold to found. At this time too was Oslac, the famous earl, banished from England.

(*continued on p.* 123)

976. In this year was the great famine in England.

C 976

977. In this year was the great assembly at Kirtlington after Easter, and there passed away suddenly bishop Sideman, on 30 April: he was bishop of Devonshire, and his wish was to be buried at Crediton at his see. King Edward and archbishop Dunstan ordered him to be carried to St Mary's abbey at Abingdon, and this was done. He lies in honourable burial on the north side of St Paul's chapel.[1]

978. In this year king Edward was martyred, and his brother, prince Æthelred, came to the throne: he was consecrated king the same year. In this year passed away Ælfwold, bishop of Dorset, and he was buried at Sherborne, in the cathedral.

979. In this year Æthelred was consecrated king on the Sunday, a fortnight after Easter, at Kingston: at his consecration were present two archbishops and ten diocesan bishops. This same year a cloud red as blood was seen, frequently with the appearance of fire and it usually appeared about midnight: it took the form of rays of light of various colours, and at the first streak of dawn it vanished.

980. In this year, on 2 May, abbot Æthelgar was consecrated bishop to the see of Selsey (*continued on p.* 124)

[1] Here ends Chronicle B

978. In this year the leading councillors of England fell
E 978
from
p. 122
down from an upper storey [2] at Calne, all except the holy archbishop Dunstan, who alone remained standing on a beam: [3]
some were severely injured there, and some did not escape with
their lives.[4]

979 [978]. In this year on 18 March king Edward was murdered in
the evening, at Corfe 'passage': [5] he was buried at Wareham with no
royal honours.

No worse deed for the English was ever done
    Than this was,
Since first they came to the land of Britain.
Men murdered him, but God exalted him;
In life he was an earthly king,
But after death he is now a heavenly saint.
His earthly kinsmen would not avenge him,
Yet his Heavenly Father has amply avenged him.
Those earthly slayers would have destroyed
    His memory upon earth;
But the Celestial Avenger has spread his fame abroad,
    In the heavens and upon the earth.
Those who before would not bend in reverence to his
    living body,
They now humbly bend the knee to his dead bones.
    Now can we perceive that the wisdom of men,
    Their deliberations and their plots,
    Are as nought against God's purpose.

In this year Æthelred came to the throne,[6] and very quickly afterwards
amid great rejoicing of the councillors of England was consecrated king
at Kingston.

980. In this year ealdorman Ælfhere [7] fetched (*continued on p.* 125)

---

[2] *in uno solario* F Lat

[3] *in uno de laquearibus* F Lat

[4] *some paid for it with their lives* F

[5] *in loco qui dicitur Porta Corf* F Lat OE *æt Corfes geate*; *corf* =
'cutting,' and *geat* = 'passage' (cf. Symond's Yat, Herefordshire). See
A. Fägersten, *The Place-names of Dorset* (Uppsala 1933), 116.

[6] *Eodem anno Ædelredus successit fratri suo in regnum. Tempore suo
multa mala uenerunt in Angliam et postea semper hucusque creverunt*
F Lat

[7] *Ælferus dux cum beato Dunstano* F Lat; (St Dunstan) and Ælfhere F

983. In this year ealdorman Ælfhere passed away.

Ā 983
from
p. 122

984. In this year passed away the benevolent bishop Æthelwold. The consecration of his successor Ælfheah, who was also known as Godwine, was on 19 October: he was installed in the bishop's see at Winchester on the festival of the two apostles Simon and Jude. (*continued on p.* 126)

C 980
from
p. 122

and in the same year Southampton was ravaged by a pirate host and most of the citizens slain or taken prisoner. In the same year the island of Thanet was harried; and also in the same year Cheshire was harried by a pirate host from the north.

981. In this year Padstow[1] was laid waste; and in the same year much destruction was done everywhere along the coast, both in Devon and Cornwall. In the same year passed away Ælfstan, bishop of Wiltshire, and his body lies in the abbey at Abingdon, and Wulfgar succeeded to the bishopric. In the same year passed away Womær, abbot of Ghent.

982. In this year three pirate crews landed in Dorset and ravaged in Portland. The same year there was a great fire in London; and in the same year two ealdormen passed away, Æthelmær of Hampshire and Eadwine of Sussex: the body of Æthelmær rests in the New Minster at Winchester, and Eadwine's in the abbey at Abingdon. The same year passed away two abbesses in Dorset: Herelufu of Shaftesbury and Wulfwynn of Wareham. In the same year Otto, emperor of the Romans, went to Italy, and met a great host of the Saracens coming up from the sea with the intention of waging war on the Christian inhabitants. The emperor fought against them, and there was great slaughter on either side, but the emperor had possession of the place of slaughter: he was, however, hard pressed before he returned from thence. On his way home passed away his brother's son, whose name was Otto. He was the son of prince Liudolf, and this Liudolf was the son of Otto the elder by the daughter of king Edward.[2]

983. In this year passed away ealdorman Ælfhere, and Ælfric succeeded to the same ealdormanry; and pope Benedict passed away.

984. In this year passed away bishop Æthelwold on 1 August.

985. In this year ealdorman Ælfric was driven from the land, and in the same year Eadwine was consecrated abbot of the abbey at Abingdon. (*continued on p.* 125)

---

[1] Professor Bruce Dickins suggests Padstow, not Bodmin, since it is more accessible; and notes that the same point has recently been made by W. G. Hoskins and H. P. R. Finberg, *Devonshire Studies* (London 1952), 29.

[2] On English interest in these events see F. M. Stenton, *Anglo-Saxon England* 342.

the body of the holy king [Edward] from Wareham, and con-
E 980 veyed it with great ceremony to Shaftesbury.
from   981. In this year for the first time seven ships came and
p. 123 ravaged Southampton.
     983. In this year passed away ealdorman Ælfhere, and
Ælfric succeeded to the same ealdormanry.
     984. In this year passed away the holy bishop Æthelwold, father of
monks; and in this year, too, Eadwine was consecrated abbot of
Abingdon.
     985. In this year ealdorman Ælfric was banished.
     986. In this year the king laid waste the diocese of Rochester; and
the great pestilence among cattle came first to England.
     987. In this year Watchet was ravaged.
     988. In this year Goda, the Devonshire thane, was slain and many
with him. In this year, too, the holy archbishop Dunstan departed this
life and attained the heavenly. Bishop Æthelgar succeeded to the
archiepiscopal see after him, but lived for a short time afterwards, no
more than a year and three months.
     989. In this year abbot Eadwine passed away, and Wulfgar succeeded
him; in this year, too, was Sigeric consecrated archbishop.

(*continued on p.* 127)

     986. In this year the king laid waste the diocese of Rochester;
C 986 and the great pestilence among cattle came first to England.
from   988. In this year Watchet was ravaged, and Goda, the
p. 124 Devonshire thane, was slain and many with him. In this
     year died archbishop Dunstan, and bishop Æthelgar succeeded
to the archiepiscopal see after him, but lived for a short time afterwards,
no more than a year and three months. (*continued on p.* 126)

     989 [990]. In this year Sigeric was consecrated archbishop,
F 989 and afterwards, the same year, went to Rome [3] for his pallium.
(*continued on p.* 126)

[3] For Sigeric's travel-diary of this journey to Rome in Brit. Mus. MS.
Cott. Tib. B v, folios 22–3, see F. P. Magoun, Jr, 'The Rome of Two Northern
Pilgrims' (33 *Harvard Theological Review* 268–77), and 'An English Pilgrim-
Diary of the year 990' (2 *Medieval Studies* 231–52). On the dates of his
consecration and death see K. Sisam, 7 *RES* 15–16.

A 993
[991]
from
p. 124

993 [991]. In this year came Anlaf[1] with ninety-three ships to Folkestone, and harried outside, and sailed thence to Sandwich, and thence to Ipswich, overrunning all the countryside, and so on to Maldon. Ealdorman Byrhtnoth came to meet them with his levies and fought them, but they slew the ealdorman there [10 August] and had possession of the place of slaughter. Afterwards peace was made with them and the king stood sponsor for him [Anlaf] at confirmation: this was done on the advice of Sigeric, archbishop of Canterbury, and Ælfheah, bishop of Winchester.

994. In this year passed away archbishop Sigeric, and Ælfric, bishop of Wiltshire, succeeded him. (*continued on p.* 132)

C 990
from
p. 125

990. In this year Sigeric was consecrated archbishop: abbot Eadwine passed away and abbot Wulfgar succeeded to the abbacy [of Abingdon]. (*continued on p.* 157)

F 991
from
p. 125

991. In this year ealdorman Byrhtnoth was slain at Maldon, and in the same year it was decided for the first time to pay tribute to the Danes on account of the atrocities they wrought along the sea coast. On this first occasion it amounted to ten thousand pounds. This course was adopted on the advice of archbishop Sigeric.

992. In this year the blessed archbishop Oswald passed away, and abbot Ealdwulf succeeded to the sees of York and Worcester. In this year too the king and all his councillors decided that all the ships that were of any value should be collected at London in an attempt to entrap the host somewhere out at sea. But ealdorman Ælfric, one of those in whom the king had most trust, had the host warned; and the night before the morning on which they were to have joined battle, this same Ælfric fled from the levies, with the result that the host got away.

993. In this year Bamburgh was destroyed, and much plunder taken there. Afterwards the host came to the mouth of the Humber and did much damage there. Then great levies were gathered together, but when they should have joined battle, the leaders were the first to set the example of flight: these were Fræna, Godwine, and Frithugist.

994. In this year Anlaf and Swein[2] came to London with ninety-four ships, and kept up an unceasing attack on the city, and they

(*continued on p.* 128)

---

[1] i.e. Olaf Tryggvason, later king of Norway. The best translation of the famous poem on the battle of Maldon is by Margaret Ashdown, *English and Norse Documents* (Cambridge 1930), 23 ff. The most recent edition is by E. V. Gordon, *The Battle of Maldon* (London 1937).

[2] King of Denmark, son of Harold Bluetooth, father of Cnut.

E 991
from
p. 125

991. In this year Ipswich was harried, and very soon afterwards ealdorman Byrhtnoth was slain at Maldon. In this year it was decided for the first time to pay tribute to the Danes because of the great terror they inspired along the sea coast. On this first occasion it amounted to ten thousand pounds. This course was adopted on the advice of archbishop Sigeric.

992. In this year the blessed archbishop Oswald departed this life and attained the heavenly, and ealdorman Æthelwine died in the same year. Then the king and his councillors decided that all the ships that were of any value should be collected at London, and the king gave the command of the levies to ealdorman Ælfric, earl Thored, bishop Ælfstan, and bishop Æscwig, with instructions to try to entrap the host somewhere out at sea. Then ealdorman Ælfric sent and had the host warned; and the night before the day on which they were to have joined battle, he fled from the levies, to his own great disgrace, and the host got away, except for one single ship on which the crew was slaughtered. The host was engaged by ships from East Anglia and London, and they made great slaughter of them, capturing the ship, fully armed and equipped with sails, on which the ealdorman had been. After the death of archbishop Oswald, abbot Ealdwulf of Peterborough succeeded to the sees of York and Worcester, and Cenwulf to the abbacy of Peterborough.

993. In this year Bamburgh was destroyed, and much plunder taken there. Afterwards the host came to the mouth of the Humber and did much damage there, both in Lindsey and in Northumbria. Then great levies were gathered together, but when they should have joined battle, the leaders were the first to set the example of flight. These were Fræna, Godwine, and Frithugist. In this year the king ordered Ælfgar, son of ealdorman Ælfric, to be blinded.

994. In this year on the Nativity of St Mary [8 September] came Anlaf and Swein to London with ninety-four ships, and kept up an unceasing attack on the city, and they (*continued on p.* 129)

purposed, moreover, to set it on fire. But there, God be
F 994 thanked, they came off worse than they ever thought possible;
from so they went away thence, doing as much harm as any host was
p. 126 capable of, in all kinds of ways wherever they went. Then the
king and his councillors decided to offer them tribute: this was
done [1] and they accepted it, together with provisions which were given
them from the whole of the West Saxon kingdom, the sum amounting
to sixteen thousand pounds. Then the king sent bishop Ælfheah and
ealdorman Æthelweard [2] to seek king Anlaf, hostages being sent meanwhile to the ships; and king Anlaf was conducted with great ceremony
to the king at Andover. The king stood sponsor for him at confirmation, and gave him royal gifts; and Anlaf then promised, and also kept
his word, that he would never come again to England with warlike
intent.

995. In this year appeared the star called 'comet' (that is 'the long-
haired'); and archbishop Sigeric passed away, and Ælfric, bishop of
Wiltshire, was chosen to succeed him (on Easter day [21 April] at Ames-
bury by king Æthelred and all his councillors). This Ælfric was a very
wise man, and there was no wiser man in all England. Then went Ælfric
to his archiepiscopal see, and when he arrived thither he was received
by those of the clergy who were most distasteful to him, that is by
secular clergy. And straightway . . . everywhere for the most learned
men he knew, especially for well-informed men who knew how to give
the truest account concerning the state of things in this land in the days
of their ancestors, besides what he himself had learnt from books and
wise men. Men of great age, both cleric and lay, told him that their
fathers had told them what had been established by law immediately
after St Augustine had come to this land:

'When Augustine had received the episcopal see in the city, which
was ⟨the capital of all this⟩ kingdom of king Æthelberht, as can be read
in the "History of the English" [Bede's *Ecclesiastical History*] . . . he
made a see, with the king's help . . . they began on an old Roman site . . .
began to flourish. The first of that community were Mellitus, Justus,
Paulinus, Rufianus. The blessed pope sent the pallium by these men,
and in addition letters and instructions how he should consecrate
bishops and in which places in Britain they should be established. He
also sent letters and many temporal gifts of various kinds to king Ethel-
berht; and the church which had been prepared for him he ordered to
be consecrated in the name of the Lord Saviour Christ and in the name
of St Mary; and he should establish there a dwelling place for himself,
and for all his successors; and that he should place therein men of the
same regular [not secular] clergy as he himself was, and whom he had
sent hither to this country (*continued on p.* 129)

---

[1] See F. M. Stenton, *op. cit.* 372 note 1, and E. V. Gordon, *The Battle of
Maldon* (London 1937), 10–13.
[2] On Æthelweard, the first translator of the *Chronicle*, see F. M. Stenton,
op. cit. 455, and in *Essays presented to T. F. Tout* 19 ff.

E 994
from
p. 127

purposed moreover, to set it on fire, but there they suffered greater loss and injury than they ever thought possible that any garrison would inflict upon them. But in this [3] the holy Mother of God manifested her clemency to the garrison and delivered them from their foes. They went away, doing as much harm as any host was capable of doing in burning, harrying, and slaughter, both along the coast and in Essex, Kent, Sussex, and Hampshire. Finally they got themselves horses, and rode far and wide wherever they pleased, and continued to do unspeakable damage. Then the king and his councillors agreed to send to them, offering tribute and supplies, if they would desist from their harrying. This they agreed to, and the whole host came to Southampton, and there took up winterquarters, and were provisioned from the whole kingdom of Wessex and paid [4] sixteen thousand pounds. Then the king sent bishop Ælfheah and ealdorman Æthelweard to seek king Anlaf, hostages being sent meanwhile to the ships; and Anlaf was conducted with great ceremony to the king at Andover. The king stood sponsor for him at confirmation, and gave him royal gifts; and Anlaf then promised, and also kept his word, that he would never come again to England with warlike intent. Hic Ricardus uetus obiit, et Ricardus filius eius suscepit regnum et regnauit ·xxxi· an*nos*.

995. In this year appeared the star called 'comet'; and archbishop Sigeric passed away. (*continued on p.* 131)

F 995
from
p. 128

and moreover that each succeeding bishop who should occupy the archiepiscopal see of Canterbury should belong to a monastic order; and this should be for ever adhered to, by the consent and blessing of God, of St Peter, and of all his successors. When this embassy returned to king Æthelberht and Augustine, they were very happy because of such instructions. The archbishop then consecrated the church in Christ's name and in the name of St Mary, on the day which is known as the festival of the two martyrs, Primus and Felicianus [9 June], and monks, as St Gregory had ordered, were placed therein, who in purity performed the Divine Office. From these same monks bishops were appointed to every see, as you may read in the "History of the English." [5]

Then was archbishop Ælfric very happy that he had so many witnesses (*continued on p.* 130)

[3] *on this day* C D   [4] *paid in money* C D

who at that time were very influential with the king.

F 995　　Then those same councillors who were with the archbishop
from　　continued their testimony: 'Thus, as we have related, monks
p. 129　　have continued to live in Christ Church in the days of Augustine, Laurentius, Mellitus, Justus, Honorius, Deusdedit,
Theodore, Berhtwald, Tatwine, Nothhelm, Cuthbert, Bregowine, Jænberht, Æthelheard, Wulfred, and Feologild. But, in the year
when Ceolnoth succeeded to the archbishopric, there was so severe a
plague that no more than five monks were left in Christ Church. . . .
Moreover in his days there was strife and sorrow in this land, so that no
one could think about anything else but . . . Now, God be thanked, it
lies in the king's jurisdiction and in thine whether they [the secular
clergy] remain therein any longer, for no more opportune time could be
found to expel them than this, if it be the king's will and thine.'

Without delay the archbishop went straight to the king, accompanied
by all the wise men, and made known to him all just as we have set
forth above. The king was very glad when he heard these tidings, and
said to the archbishop and to the others: 'I think it advisable that first
of all you go to Rome for your pallium, and make all this known to the
pope, and then act according to his advice.' They all answered that
this was the best course of action. When those [secular] priests heard
of this, they decided to choose two of their number and send to the
pope, and offer him great treasure and silver, on condition he gave them
the pallium; but when they came to Rome the pope refused to do this,
since they brought no letter either from the king or from the nation,
and ordered them to depart wherever they wished. As soon as the
priests had turned back from thence, archbishop Ælfric arrived in
Rome, and the pope received him with great ceremony, and ordered
him to say mass in the morning at the altar of St Peter, where the pope
himself put on him his own pallium and did him great honour. When
this was done, the archbishop began to tell the pope all about the
secular priests, and how it had come about that they lived in the
cathedral church in his see: in return the pope told how the priests had
come to him offering great treasure so that he would give them the
pallium. 'But,' said the pope, 'return now to England, with God's
blessing, St Peter's, and mine, and on your return fill your cathedral
church with men of the same regular [not secular] clergy as those whom
the blessed Gregory ordered Augustine to place therein: do this by
God's command, St Peter's, and mine.' The archbishop returned
to England with this mandate, and as soon as he arrived he occupied
his archiepiscopal see, and afterwards went to see the king. The king
and all his people thanked God for his return (*continued on p.* 131)

996. In this year was Ælfric consecrated archbishop at Christ Church.

E 996
from
p. 129

997. In this year the host went round Devonshire into the mouth of the Severn, and there harried, both in Cornwall, Wales, and Devon, and landed at Watchet: they wrought great havoc by burning and killing people and then went back round Land's End to the south side, and entered the estuary of the Tamar, and so up it until they came to Lydford. There they burned and slew everything they met, and burnt to the ground Ordwulf's abbey church at Tavistock, carrying off an indescribable amount of plunder with them to the ships.

998. In this year the host turned eastward again, into the mouth of the Frome, and pushed up into Dorset in whatever direction they pleased. Many a time levies were gathered to oppose them; but, as soon as battle was about to begin, the word was given to withdraw, and always in the end the host had the victory. Then for another period they had their base in the Isle of Wight, and drew their supplies meanwhile from Hampshire and Sussex.

999. In this year the host again came round into the Thames, and so up the Medway to Rochester. They were opposed by the Kentish levies, and a sharp encounter took place: but alas! all too quickly they turned and fled, because they did not get the support they should have had, and the Danes had possession of the place of slaughter,

(*continued on p.* 133)

and that his mission had succeeded to their entire satisfaction. He then returned to Canterbury and drove away the priests from the cathedral church, replacing them by monks as the pope had commanded him.[1]

F 995
from
p. 130

996. In this year Wulfstan was consecrated bishop of London.

997. In this year archbishop Ælfric went to Rome for his pallium.

(*continued on p.* 134)

[1] 'This document is written in a very small hand on the margin and on an inserted leaf, and has been much injured by the use of galls.' (Plummer) The fuller, Latin version of F is printed by Plummer on pp. 285–7 of his edition. See also F. P. Magoun, Jr, *Annales Domitiani Latini:* An Edition, 262–4.

1001. In this year there were constant hostilities in England
Ā **1001** because of the pirate host, and they harried and burnt almost
from everywhere, so that in one continuous drive they penetrated
p. 126 inland as far as *Æthelingadene*.[1] They were opposed by the
men of Hampshire who fought against them: among the slain
were Æthelweard, the king's 'high-reeve,' Leofric, who lived at Whitchurch, Leofwine, the king's 'high-reeve,' Wulfhere, the bishop's officer,
Godwine, who lived at Worthy, the son of bishop Ælfsige, eighty-one men in all. The Danish casualties were heavier, but they had
possession of the place of slaughter.

Then they went west from thence until they came to Devon, where
Pallig joined them with the ships he could assemble, for he had
departed from the allegiance he owed to king Æthelred, contrary to all
the pledges he had given him, and regardless of the extreme generosity
of the king in giving him manors, gold, and silver. They burnt down
Kingsteignton, and also many other goodly manors of which we do not
know the names, and peace was made with them afterwards. They
went from thence to the mouth of the Exe, and in one continuous drive
penetrated inland as far as Pinhoe, where they were opposed by Kola,
the king's 'high-reeve,' and Eadsige, the king's reeve, with such levies as
could be mobilized; but they were put to flight and many of them slain,
and the Danes had possession of the place of slaughter. Next morning
they burnt down the manors of Pinhoe and Broad Clyst, and many
other goodly manors of which we do not know the names. Then they
went back eastward again until they reached the Isle of Wight, and the
next morning they burnt down the manor at Bishop's Waltham and
many other villages: soon after this terms were settled with them, and
they made peace. (*continued on p.* 134)

---

[1] Probably on or near the Hampshire boundary of Sussex. See Bruce
Dickins, 'The Day of the Battle of *Æthelingadene*' (6 *LSE* 25–7), i.e. 23 May.

and got horses and rode far and wide as they pleased, destroying
and laying waste almost the whole of West Kent. Then the
king with his councillors decided to advance against them with
both naval and land levies; but when the ships were ready there
was delay from day to day, which was very galling for the
unhappy sailors manning the vessels. Time after time the more urgent
a thing was the greater was the delay from one hour to the next, and all
the while they were allowing the strength of their enemies to increase;
and as they kept retreating from the sea, so the enemy followed close
on their heels. So in the end these naval and land preparations were a
complete failure, and succeeded only in adding to the distress of the
people, wasting money, and encouraging their enemy.

E 999
from
p. 131

1000. In this year the king marched into Cumberland and laid waste
very nearly the whole of it. His fleet went round by Chester, but were
unable to make contact with him as had been planned, so they harried
the Isle of Man. The enemy fleet had sailed away to Richard's realm
in the same summer.

1001. In this year the host came to the mouth of the Exe and so up
to the fortress: they made a determined attack upon it, but were met by
a solid and courageous resistance. They then overran the countryside,
and followed their usual tactics, slaying and burning. Then vast levies
of the men of Devon and Somerset were mustered, and they joined
battle at Pinhoe; but as soon as they met, the English levies gave ground
and the enemy inflicted great slaughter on them, and then went riding
over the countryside; and each inroad was worse than the last, and they
brought much plunder with them to their ships, and sailed thence for
the Isle of Wight, where they went about at will, encountering no resistance. No fleet by sea nor levies on land dared approach them, however far inland they went. In every way it was a hard time, for they
never ceased from their evil deeds.

1002. In this year the king and his councillors decided to pay tribute
to the fleet and to make peace, on condition they ceased from their evil
deeds. The king sent ealdorman Leofsige to the fleet and he, at the
command of the king and his councillors, arranged a truce with them,
and that they should receive maintenance and tribute. This was
accepted and they were paid twenty-four thousand pounds. Then in
the midst of these events (*continued on p.* 134)

A 1005
from
p. 132

1005. In this year passed away archbishop Ælfric.

1006. In this year Ælfheah was consecrated archbishop.

(continued on p. 154)

E 1002
from
p. 133

ealdorman Leofsige slew Æfic, the king's 'high-reeve,' and the king banished him from the realm. In the same spring the Lady,[1] Richard's daughter, came hither to this country. In the same summer archbishop Ealdwulf passed away, and in the same year the king *(continued on p.* 135)

F 1003
from
p. 131

1003. In this year Exeter was destroyed because of a French fellow, called Hugh, whom the Lady had appointed as reeve; the host utterly laid waste the borough. Then great levies were assembled, and it was ealdorman Ælfric's duty to lead them, but he was up to his old tricks; as soon as they were close enough for each force to see the other, he pretended to vomit, saying he was ill, thus leaving his men in the lurch. When Swein saw their lack of resolution he led his host into Wilton, and burnt down the village, then went to Salisbury and from there back to the sea.

1004. In this year Swein came with his fleet to Norwich, and completely sacked the borough and burnt it down. Then Ulfcytel and the chief men from East Anglia decided to make peace with the host, for they had come unexpectedly and he had not had time to gather his levies together. However, under cover of the truce, the host came up secretly from the ships and made their way to Hertford.[2] Ulfcytel gathered together his host *(continued on p.* 136)

---

[1] Used as a title, of a king's wife. F adds her name *Ymma* '*Ælfgiua.*'

[2] So F; C D E *Thetford.*

134

gave orders for all the Danish people who were in England to be slain on St Brice's day [13 November], because the king had been told that they wished to deprive him of his life by treachery, and all his councillors after him, and then seize his kingdom.[3]

1003. In this year Exeter was destroyed through Hugh, the French fellow, whom the Lady had appointed as her reeve: the host utterly laid waste the borough and seized much plunder there.[4] Then great levies were assembled from Wiltshire and Hampshire, firmly resolved to march against the host, and it was ealdorman Ælfric's duty to lead the levies, but he was up to his old tricks: as soon as they were close enough for each force to see the other, he pretended to be ill, and made violent efforts to vomit, saying he was taken ill, thus leaving in the lurch [5] the men it was his duty to lead: as the saying goes: **When the General grows faint-hearted then the whole Army suffers a severe check.**[6] When Swein saw their lack of resolution, and that they were all dispersing, he led his host into Wilton and sacked and burnt down the borough, and then went to Salisbury and from there back to the sea where he knew his 'wave-stallions' were.

1004. In this year Swein came with his fleet to Norwich, and completely sacked the borough and burnt it down. Then Ulfcytel and the chief men from East Anglia decided that it would be better for them to buy peace from the enemy before they did too much damage in that district, since they had come unexpectedly, and he had not had time to gather his levies together. However, under cover of the truce which was to have been observed between them, the host came up secretly from the ships and made their way to Thetford. When Ulfcytel discovered this, he sent men to hew their ships to pieces, but those detailed for it failed in their duty, so he mobilized in secret as strong a [7] force of levies as he could. The host reached Thetford within three weeks of sacking Norwich, and spent a night in the borough, pillaging and burning it to the ground. The next morning, when they planned to retire to their ships, Ulfcytel came up with his force [8] and there was a fierce encounter and great slaughter on each side. There were slain the chief men of East Anglia, but if they had been up to full strength

(*continued on p.* 136)

---

[3] F adds *without any opposition*
[4] C and D add *and in the same year the enemy went up into Wiltshire*
[5] *deceiving* C D
[6] Plummer notes a similar saying in one of Alcuin's letters: 'Si dux timidus erit, quomodo saluabitur miles.' Cf. also 1 Corinthians xiv. 8: 'For if the trumpet give an uncertain sound, who shall prepare himself to the battle?'
[7] or perhaps 'as quickly as he could'.
[8] C adds *so that they were compelled to give battle*

the enemy would never have got back to their ships, as they
E 1004 themselves admitted.[1]
from 1005. This was the year of the great famine throughout
p. 135 England, the most severe in living memory. During this year
the enemy fleet went from this country to Denmark, but allowed
only a short time to elapse before it returned.

1006. In this year passed away archbixhop Ælfric, and bishop
Ælfheah succeeded him in the metropolitan see. Bishop Beorhtwold
was appointed to the bishopric of Wiltshire. Wulfgeat was deprived
of all his property, and Wulfheah and Ufegeat were blinded; and
ealdorman Ælfhelm was slain and bishop Cenwulf passed away. Then
after midsummer the Danish fleet [2] came to Sandwich, and did as they
had been wont to do: they harried, burned, and slew as they went.
Then the king had the whole of the people of Wessex and Mercia called
out, and they were on service against the host all the autumn, but with
no more success than very often in the past. Despite all this the host
went where it pleased, and the campaign caused all manner of distress
to the inhabitants, so that neither the home levies nor the invading
host did them any good!

When it drew near to winter the levies went home, and after Martinmas [11 November] the host retired to its safe base in the Isle of Wight,
procuring everywhere there whatever they had need of. At Christmas
they proceeded out through Hampshire into Berkshire to their well-
stocked food depot [2a] (*continued on p.* 137)

and marched after them, and there was a fierce encounter in
F 1004 which many of the chief men of East Anglia were slain.
from 1005. This was the year of the great famine throughout
p.134 England, the most severe in living memory. During this year
the enemy fleet went from this country to Denmark, but soon

returned. (*continued on p.* 146)

---

[1] *they themselves admitted that they had never met with harder hand-play
in England than Ulfcytel gave them* C D
[2] *the great fleet* C D
[2a] Preferably, as Prof. Dorothy Whitelock translates, 'they betook themselves to the entertainment waiting them, but through Hampshire into
Berkshire to Reading.'

at Reading, and as usual kindled their beacons [3] as they went.
E 1006 They went to Wallingford and burned it to the ground.[4] and
from proceeded along the Berkshire Downs to ⟨Cuckhamsley Knob,
p. 136 and there awaited the great things that had been threatened,
for it had often been said that if ever they⟩ [5] got as far as Cuck-
hamsley Knob, they would never again reach the sea; but they went
back by another route. Then levies were mustered there at East
Kennet, and there they joined battle; but the Danes soon put that force
to flight, and bore their plunder to the sea. There the people of Winchester could watch an arrogant and confident [6] host passing their gates
on its way to the coast, bringing provisions and treasures from a distance
of more than fifty miles inland.

At that time the king had crossed the Thames on his way to Shropshire, and received entertainment there during the festival of Christmas.
Then the terror inspired by the host grew so great that everybody was
incapable of devising or drawing up a plan to get them out of the
country, or for holding this land against them, for with fire and sword
they had effectively left their mark on every shire in Wessex. The king
began to deliberate in earnest with his ministers to get agreement on the
best way to save this country before it was utterly destroyed. Then
the king and his councillors agreed that they were compelled by circumstances to pay tribute to the host for the good of all the people, however
distasteful it might be to them all. Then the king sent to the host and
ordered it to be made known to them that he desired a truce between
them, and that tribute should be paid and supplies granted, and they
all accepted it, and provisions were supplied from all parts of England.

(*continued on p.* 138)

---

[3] *their war-signals* C D
[4] *destroyed it* E; *and spent one night at Cholsey* C D
[5] The phrase in brackets was omitted in E because of the repetition of the place-name: it is restored from C D
[6] *proud* F; *strenuum et nichil timentem exercitum* F Lat

1007. In this year tribute money amounting to thirty [1]
E 1007 thousand pounds was paid to the hostile host. In this year
from also was Eadric [Streona] appointed ealdorman in [2] Mercia.
p. 137 1008. In this year the king gave orders that ships should be
speedily built throughout the whole of England: namely [one
large warship was to be provided from every] three hundred 'hides' and
a cutter from every ten 'hides,' [3] while every eight 'hides' were to
provide a helmet and a corselet.

1009. In this year the ships about which we spoke above were ready,
and there were more of them, according to what the books tell us, than
there had ever been before in England in the days of any king. They
were all brought together off Sandwich, to be stationed there to protect
this realm against every invading host. But no more than on previous
occasions were we to enjoy the good fortune or the honour of naval
operations which would be advantageous to this land. About this same
time or a little before, it happened that Beorhtric, the brother of the
ealdorman Eadric, made an accusation to the king against Wulfnoth, [4]
a nobleman of Sussex, and he then fled the country and succeeded in
winning over as many as twenty ships, and went harrying everywhere
along the south coast, and did all manner of evil. Then information
was brought to the fleet that they [Wulfnoth's ships] could easily be
surrounded if the opportunity were seized. Then the aforesaid
Beorhtric procured eighty ships, and thought to win great fame for
himself by taking Wulfnoth dead or alive. But when his ships were on
their way, he was met by a storm worse than anyone could remember:
the ships were all battered and knocked to pieces and cast ashore.
Then that Wulfnoth came (*continued on p.* 139)

---

[1] *thirty-six* C D
[2] *throughout* C D; *over all* F; *super totam Merciam* F; D adds *In this year bishop Ælfheah went to Rome for his pallium.*
[3] [*of*] *þrim hund hidum* 7 *of ·x· hidon ænne scegð* E; *of þrim hund hidum* 7 *of tynum ænne scegð* C; *of þrym hund scipum* 7 *·x· be tynum anne scægð* D; *hoc est de CCC hidis et ·x· unam magnam nauem quæ Anglice nominatur scegð* F Lat. See F. E. Harmer, *Anglo-Saxon Writs* 266–7 and the references given.
[4] *father of earl Godwine* F; *quendam nobilem uirum nomine Wlnoðum* (*patrem Godwini ducis*) F Lat

E 1009
from
p. 138
straightway and burned the ships. When news of the fate of
these ships reached the rest of the fleet under the command of
the king, then it was as if everything was in confusion, for the
king, the ealdormen, and the chief councillors went home,
abandoning the ships thus irresponsibly. Then those who
remained with the ships brought them back to London, thus incon-
siderately allowing the effort of the whole nation to come to naught,
so that the threat [5] to the Danes, upon which the whole of England had
set its hopes, turned out to be no more potent than this. When this
naval campaign was thus brought to a close, there came to Sandwich
immediately after Lammas [1 August], that immense hostile host,[6] and
made their way at once to Canterbury and would soon have taken the
borough if they had not forestalled them by suing for peace; and all
eastern Kent made a truce with the host, and paid them three thousand
pounds. Then immediately after this the host turned about until they
came to the Isle of Wight, and burned and harried, as their custom
was,[7] everywhere in Sussex, Hampshire, and also in Berkshire. Then
the king gave orders that the whole nation should be called out, so that
a stand should be made against them on all sides, but in spite of this
they went just where they pleased. Then on one occasion the king had
surrounded them with all the levies when they were making for their
ships, and everybody was ready to fall upon them; but, as was always
the case, it was ealdorman Eadric who prevented it. Then, after
Martinmas [11 November], they returned to Kent, and took up winter-
quarters on the Thames, and drew supplies from Essex and from the
neighbouring shires on both sides of the Thames. They made frequent
attacks on the borough of London, but praise be to God, she still
stands safe and sound, and the Danes always suffered heavy losses
there. Then, after Christmas they made an incursion away through
the Chilterns, and so came to Oxford, and burned down the borough,
and made their way back on both sides of the Thames towards

(*continued on p.* 140)

---

[5] *the victory* (*over the Danes*) C D
[6] C adds *to which we gave the name of Thurkil's host.* Thurkil is the
Thorkell the Tall of Scandinavian history (cf. Heimskringla *Óláfs saga
Tryggvasonar*, caps. 34 ff.), and the brother of jarl Sigvaldi, the commander
of the pirates of Jómsborg.
[7] *as their custom is* C D

their ships. Then when they had been warned that levies were waiting to oppose them at London, they crossed at Staines; and thus they moved about the whole winter through, and that spring [1010] they were in Kent, repairing their ships.

E 1009 from p. 139

1010. In this year came the aforesaid host after Easter to East Anglia, and landed at Ipswich, and went straight to where they had heard that Ulfcytel was with his levies. This was on the first day of Ascension [18 May]. The East Anglians soon took to flight, but Cambridgeshire [1] firmly resisted them. There was slain Athelstan, the king's son-in-law, and Oswy [2] and his son, and Wulfric, the son of Leofwine, and Eadwig, Æfic's brother, and many other good thanes and a countless number of people. It was Thurcytel 'Mare's Head' that instigated the flight, and the Danes had possession of the place of slaughter, and then got horses for themselves, and thereafter got control of East Anglia. For three months they harried and burnt that land, even penetrating into the uninhabited fens, slaying men and cattle, and burning throughout the fens. They destroyed Thetford and Cambridge by fire and then turned south again to the Thames. Those who had horses rode towards the ships, and then quickly turned westwards into Oxfordshire, and thence into Buckinghamshire, and so along the Ouse until they came to Bedford, and so on as far as Tempsford, destroying by fire ever as they went. Then they made their way back to the ships with their plunder: and when they were dispersing to the ships, then the levies should have been out, ready in case they should intend to go inland. Then, however, the levies were on their way home. And when the enemy was in the east, then our levies were mustered in the west; and when they were in the south, then our levies were in the north. Then all the councillors were summoned to the king, for a plan for the defence of the realm had to be devised then and there, but whatever course of action was decided upon it was not followed even for a single month. In the end there was no leader

(*continued on p.* 141)

[1] *but Cambridge alone stood firm* F Florence of Worcester gives the name of the battlefield as *Ringmere* and its date as 5 May, which date is confirmed by an obit recorded in a twelfth-century Ely Kalendar (cf. Bruce Dickins, 6 *LSE* 15 ff.). The site of the battle, in Norfolk, was either Ringmere adjoining the highway from Thetford to East Wretham, or Rymer 4 miles S. of Thetford. I am indebted to Prof. Dickins for the reference to W. G. Clarke, *In Breckland Wilds* (2nd ed., revised by R. R. Clarke, Cambridge 1937), who describes the former (p. 40) as 'a placid pool embosomed in a circular hollow with steeply-sloping sides, and when full has an area of 6¾ acres,' and gives two photographs of it. See also *ibid* 88–9 for an account of the battle, and translations of two stanzas from two Norse poems which refer to it as the battle of *Hringmaraheiðr* (Heimskringla *Óláfs saga Helga* cap. 14).

[2] The son-in-law of Byrhtnoth who was slain at Maldon. (See Bruce Dickins, 'The Day of Byrhtnoth's Death and other obits from a Twelfth-Century Ely Kalendar,' 6 *LSE* 15 ff.)

who was willing to raise levies, but each fled as quickly [3] as he
E 1010 could; nor even in the end would one shire help another.

from   Then before St Andrew's day [30 November], the host came
p. 140 to Northampton and immediately destroyed the town by fire,
and seized whatever they wanted in the neighbouring district,
and went thence across the Thames into Wessex, and so on towards the
marsh land at All and Bishop's Cannings [Vale of Pewsey, Wiltshire],
destroying everything with fire.   Then, when they had overrun as far
as they wished, they came at Christmas to their ships.

1011. In this year the king and his councillors sent to the host, and
craved peace, promising them tribute and provisions on condition that
they should cease their harrying.

They had by this time overrun (i) East Anglia, (ii) Essex, (iii) Middle-
sex, (iv) Oxfordshire, (v) Cambridgeshire, (vi) Hertfordshire, (vii)
Buckinghamshire, (viii) Bedfordshire, (x) [4] half of Huntingdonshire,
and to the south of the Thames all Kent, and Sussex, and the district
around Hastings, and Surrey, and Berkshire, and Hampshire, and a
great part of Wiltshire.

All these misfortunes befell us by reason of bad policy in that tribute
was not offered them in time; [5] but when they had done their worst,
then it was that peace was made with them.   And notwithstanding all
this truce and peace and tribute, they went about everywhere in bands,
and robbed and slew our unhappy people.   Then, in this same year,
between the Nativity of St Mary [8 September] and Michaelmas [29
September] they besieged Canterbury, and made their way in through
treachery, for Ælfmær, whose life archbishop Ælfheah had saved,
betrayed Canterbury to them.   And there they seized the archbishop
Ælfheah,[6] and Ælfweard, the king's reeve, and abbot Leofwine,[7] and
bishop of Godwine; and abbot Ælfmær [8] they let go free.   And they
seized all those in holy orders, both men and women, that were in the
borough, and it is impossible for any man to say how great a part of the
inhabitants that was. (*continued on p.* 142)

(*continued on p.* 142)

---

[3] or perhaps 'best.'

[4] So the manuscript; *and* (ix) *half of Huntingdonshire, and* (x) *a great part
of Northamptonshire*   C D

[5] C adds *or resistance made*.

[6] Known later as St Alphege.   On the churches dedicated to him see F.
Arnold-Forster, *Studies in Church Dedications* I. 344–5.

[7] C and D have, correctly, *Leofrun the abbess*.

[8] Probably not the same person as the traitor, who is styled *archidiaconus*
by Florence of Worcester.

E 1011
from
p. 141

And they remained in the borough as long as they wished; and when they had searched it thoroughly, then they went to their ships, taking the archbishop with them.

> Then was he a captive, he who had been
> The head of England and of Christendom.
> There might be seen wretchedness
> Where often bliss was seen before,
> In that unhappy city, whence came first to us
> Christendom, and both spiritual and earthly bliss.

And they kept the archbishop as their prisoner until the time when they martyred him.

1012. In this year, before Easter, there came to London ealdorman Eadric and all the chief councillors of England, spiritual and temporal. In this year Easter was on 13 April. And they remained there until after Easter, until all the tribute was paid, amounting to eight thousand [1] pounds. Then on the Saturday the host became greatly incensed against the bishop, because he was not willing to offer them any money, and forbade any ransom to be given for him. Moreover they were very drunk, for wine had been brought to them from the south. Then they took the bishop, and led him to their tribunal, on Saturday evening, within the octave of Easter [19 April], [2] and pelted him to death with bones and the heads of cattle; [3] and one of them smote him on the skull with the iron [head] [4] of an axe, so that with the blow he sank down and his holy blood fell upon the earth, and his holy soul was sent forth to God's kingdom. Then in the morning the bishops Eadnoth and Ælfhun and the citizens (*continued on p.* 143)

---

[1] *forty-eight thousand* C D
[2] C adds *and shamefully murdered him.*
[3] *mid hryþera neata heafedum* D
[4] The translation follows the suggestions of Bruce Dickins, *Runic and Heroic Poems* (Cambridge 1915) 22 (note on *yr* in the Anglo-Saxon Runic Poem), and F. P. Magoun, Jr, 'The Domitian Bilingual of the Old English Annals: Notes on the F-text' (6 *Modern Language Quarterly* 378–80).

received his holy body, and brought it to London with all **E 1012** reverence, and buried it in St Paul's church, where now God **from** makes manifest the miracles of the holy martyr. When the **p. 142** tribute was paid, and oaths of peace were sworn, then the host dispersed as widely as before it had been concentrated. Then forty-five ships transferred their allegiance to the king, and promised him to guard this land, on condition that he fed and clothed them.

1013. In the year following the archbishop's martyrdom, the king appointed bishop Lyfing to the metropolitan see of Canterbury; and in the same year, before the month of August, came king Swein with his fleet to Sandwich, and very soon after went round East Anglia into the mouth of the Humber, and so up along the Trent until he came to Gainsborough. Then earl Uhtred and all Northumbria straightway submitted to him, and all the people of Lindsey, and then the people belonging to the Five Boroughs, and soon afterwards all the Danes to the north of Watling Street; and he was given hostages from every shire. After he realized that all the people had submitted to him, he gave orders that his host should be provisioned and supplied with horses; he then turned southward with his whole force, committing his ships and the hostages into the charge of Cnut, his son. After he crossed Watling Street, they did the greatest mischief that any host was capable of, and made their way then to Oxford, and the citizens immediately surrendered and gave hostages; and from there to Winchester where they did the same. Thence they went east to London, and a great part of his host was drowned in the Thames, because they did not bother to look for any bridge. When he came to the borough, the citizens would not submit, but held out against them with the utmost valour, because king Æthelred was inside, and Thurkil with him. Then Swein turned (*continued on p.* 144) thence to Wallingford, and so over the Thames westward to Bath, and encamped there with his levies. Thither came ealdorman Æthelmær and the thanes from the west, and they all submitted to Swein and gave him hostages. Having made his way thus far, he turned northward to his ships, and the whole nation accepted him as their undisputed [1] king. Thereafter the citizens of London submitted and gave hostages, because they were afraid he would destroy them. Then Swein demanded tribute in full and supplies for his host during the winter, and Thurkil demanded the same for the host that lay at Greenwich, yet despite this they went harrying as often as they pleased. At this time nothing went right for this nation, neither in the south nor in the north. Then for a time the king was with the fleet in the Thames, and the Lady [2] [his queen] crossed the sea to her brother Richard, accompanied by Ælfsige, abbot of Peterborough. The king sent bishop Ælfhun across the sea in charge of the princes Edward and Alfred. Then at Christmas the king left the fleet for the Isle of Wight, and remained there for that festival, afterwards crossing the sea to Richard. He remained there with him until the opportunity presented by Swein's death.

[3] While the Lady was oversea with her brother, Ælfsige, abbot of Peterborough, who was with her there, went to the monastery which is called Bonneval, where the body of St Florentine lay. He found the foundation there was poor, and the abbot and the monks destitute, because they had been pillaged. Then he bought from the abbot and the monks there the body of St Florentine, all but the head, for five hundred pounds: and when he returned to this country he gave it as an offering to Christ and St Peter.

1014. In this year Swein ended his days at Candlemas [2 February]; [4] and the fleet [5] all chose Cnut as king. (*continued on p.* 145)

---

[1] See BT Suppl. *s.v. full*, 'entitled to all the privileges implied by a designation'; or, as Alistair Campbell, *Encomium Emmae Regina* (London 1949) liii, says, the words 'full king' imply kingly power without perfect constitutional standing.

[2] *the king sent his queen Ælfgifu Ymma across the sea to her brother Richard* F. On Ælfgifu Emma, later the wife of Cnut, see Alistair Campbell, *op. cit.* xl–l and *passim*.

[3] This paragraph is found only in E

[4] MS ·iii· N° Febř. *for* ·iiii· N° Febř. D adds *in this same year Ælfwig was consecrated bishop of London at York on St Juliana's day.*

[5] *Principes autem regis et qui cum eo uenerant in Angliam* F Lat

Then all the councillors,[6] both spiritual and temporal, advised
E 1014 that king Æthelred should be sent for, declaring that no lord
from was dearer to them than their rightful lord, if only he would
p. 144 govern his kingdom more justly than he had done in the past.
Then the king sent his son Edward hither with his messengers,
and bade greet [7] all his people, and said that he would be a gracious lord
to them, and would remedy each one of the things which they all
abhorred, and everything should be forgiven, that had been done or
said against him, on condition that they all unanimously and without
treachery returned to their allegiance. Then a complete and friendly
agreement was reached and ratified with word and pledge on either side,
and they declared every Danish king outlawed from England for ever.
Then during Lent of that year king Æthelred came home to his own
people, and was received with joy by them all. Now, after Swein's
death, Cnut stayed with his host in Gainsborough until Easter, and
an agreement was made between him and the people of Lindsey to
supply him with horses and then set out together and harry. Then king
Æthelred came with levies at full strength into Lindsey before they were
prepared, and they made raids and burned and slew every human being
they could find. Cnut put to sea with his fleet, and the unhappy people
were thus left in the lurch by him: he sailed southward until he came to
Sandwich, and there put ashore the hostages which had been given to
his father, and cut off their hands and noses.[8] In addition to all those
misfortunes the king gave orders to pay the host that lay at Greenwich
twenty-one thousand pounds. In this year, on St Michael's eve [28
September], the swollen incoming tide swept far and wide through many
places in this land; and it ran further inland than it had ever done
before, and submerged many homesteads and drowned a countless
number of human beings.

1015. In this year there was the great council at Oxford, and it was
there that ealdorman Eadric betrayed Siferth and Morcar,

(*continued on p.* 146)

---

[6] C adds *all those who were in England.*

[7] 'The wording of the *Chronicle* (*het gretan*) suggests that it was by writ
that king Æthelred II communicated with his subjects during the negotia-
tions for his return.' (F. E. Harmer, *Anglo-Saxon Writs* 16, cf. Appendix
IV note 3)

[8] *hands, ears, and noses* C D

the chief thanes belonging to the Seven Boroughs,[1] by enticing them into his chamber, where they were basely done to death. The king then confiscated all their property, and ordered Siferth's widow to be seized and brought to Malmesbury.

Then, after a short time, prince Edmund came and abducted the woman against the king's will, and made her his wife. Then, before the Nativity of St Mary [8 September], the prince proceeded from the west and went north to the Five Boroughs, and thereupon seized all the property of Siferth and Morcar, and the people all submitted to him. At the same time king Cnut came into Sandwich, and straightway sailed round Kent to Wessex, until he came to the mouth of the Frome, and harried in Dorset and Wiltshire and Somerset. At this time the king was lying sick at Cosham. Then ealdorman Eadric gathered levies, and prince Edmund gathered others in the north; and when they joined forces, the ealdorman intended to leave the prince in the lurch, and for this reason they parted without giving battle and left the field clear for their foes. Then ealdorman Eadric won over forty ships from their allegiance to the king, and then did homage to Cnut. And the West Saxons submitted and gave hostages, and supplied the host with horses, and it remained there until Christmas.

1016. In this year came Cnut with his host of one hundred and sixty ships, and with him ealdorman Eadric, and crossed the Thames into Mercia at Cricklade, and then during the season of Christmas turned into Warwickshire, and harried and burned and slew all

(continued on p. 147)

1016. In this year came Cnut with one hundred and sixty ships, and with him ealdorman Eadric, and crossed the Thames into Mercia at Cricklade, and then turned into Warwickshire, and in that county they burned and slew all that they found. And (continued on p. 148)

---

[1] See F. M. Stenton, *Anglo-Saxon England* 383 note 1, who suggests that this phrase, which does not occur again, clearly includes the five Danish boroughs of Lincoln, Stamford, Leicester, Nottingham, and Derby, with Torksey (L), and probably York.

that they found.   Then prince Edmund began to gather levies;
and when the levies were assembled nothing would satisfy
them but that the king should be with them, and that they
should have the support of the citizens from London.   So they
abandoned the expedition, and each man of them went off
home.   Then after the festival,[2] an order was issued to the levies calling
up again every man fit for military service on penalty of the full fine
for failure to report for duty; and word was sent to the king in London
asking him to join the levies with such reinforcements as he could
muster.   Then when they were all met, it came to nothing, as so often
before.   Then the king was informed that those who should have
supported him intended to betray him, so he abandoned the levies and
returned to London.

Then prince Edmund rode to Northumbria to earl Uhtred, and everybody imagined that they would collect levies to oppose king Cnut, but
they went into Staffordshire and to Shrewsbury and to Chester and
harried on their side (continued on p. 148)

1016. In this year came Cnut with his host, and with him
ealdorman Eadric, and crossed the Thames into Mercia at
Cricklade, and then during the season of Christmas turned into
Warwickshire, and harried and burned and slew all that they found.
Then prince Edmund began to gather levies; and when the levies were
assembled they would not be satisfied unless the king were there too
and they had the support of the citizens from London.   So they
abandoned the expedition and each man of them went off home.
Then after the festival,[2] an order was issued to the levies calling up again
every man fit for military service on penalty of the full fine for failure
to report for duty; and word was sent to the king in London asking him
to join the levies with such reinforcements as he could muster.   Then
when they were all met, it came to nothing, as so often before.   Then
the king was informed that those who should have supported him
intended to betray him, so he abandoned the levies and returned to
London.

Then prince Edmund rode to Northumbria to earl Uhtred, and everybody imagined that they would collect levies to oppose king Cnut, but
they went into Staffordshire, and to Shrewsbury and to Chester, and
harried on their side (continued on p. 149)

[2] i.e. of Christmas; see the beginning of the annal.

and Cnut on his. He went through Buckinghamshire into
E 1016 Bedfordshire, thence to Huntingdonshire, along by the fen to
from Stamford, then into Lincolnshire, and thence into Nottingham-
p. 147 shire, and so to Northumbria towards York. When Uhtred
learned of this, he gave up his harrying and hastened northwards, but had of necessity to submit, and all the Northumbrians with
him. He gave hostages, but nevertheless he was put to death,[1] and
Thurcytel, son of Nafena, with him. Then after this king Cnut appointed Eric as his earl in Northumbria just as Uhtred had been.
Thereafter he made his way southwards by another route, keeping well
to the west; and the whole host came to the ships before Easter. Prince
Edmund went to London to his father; and then, after Easter, king
Cnut made his way towards London with all his ships.

Then it happened that king Æthelred passed away before the ships
arrived. He ended his days on St George's day [23 April], after a life of
much hardship and many difficulties. Then, after his death, all the
councillors who were in London, and the citizens,

(*continued on p.* 149)

Prince Edmund went to his father in London, and Cnut made
F 1016 his way towards London with all his ships.
from But king Æthelred had passed away before the ships arrived.
p. 146 He departed this life on St George's day [23 April], after a life
of much hardship and many difficulties. Then, after his
death, all the councillors of England chose Edmund as king, and he
defended his kingdom valiantly during his lifetime.

Then at Rogation days [7–9 May] the Danish ships came to Greenwich, and soon went on to London. They dug a channel on the south
bank and dragged their ships to the west side of the bridge, and afterwards built earthworks outside the borough so that no one could
get in or out, and attacked the borough repeatedly, but they withstood
them valiantly. (*continued on p.* 150)

---

[1] C adds *on the advice of ealdorman Eadric.*

chose Edmund as king, and he defended his kingdom valiantly

E 1016 during his lifetime.

from Then at Rogation days [7–9 May], the [Danish] ships came

p. 148 to Greenwich, and within a short time went on to London.
They dug a great channel on the south bank and dragged their ships to the west side of the bridge, and afterwards built earthworks outside the borough so that no one could get in or out, and attacked the borough repeatedly, but they withstood them valiantly. Some time previous to this king Edmund had made his way out of the borough, and had taken possession of Wessex, and all the inhabitants submitted to him. Soon after this he fought against the host at Penselwood [Somerset], near Gillingham, and fought another battle

(*continued on p.* 150)

and Cnut on his. He went through Buckinghamshire into

D 1016 Bedfordshire, thence to Huntingdonshire, and so into North-

from amptonshire, and along by the fen to Stamford, then into

p. 147 Lincolnshire, and thence into Nottinghamshire, and so to
Northumbria towards York. When Uhtred learned of this he gave up his harrying, and hastened northwards, but had of necessity to submit, and all the Northumbrians with him. He gave hostages, but nevertheless he was put to death, and Thurcytel, son of Nafena, with him. Then after this the king appointed Eric as his earl in Northumbria, just as Uhtred had been. Thereafter he made his way southwards by another route, keeping well to the west; and the whole host came to the ships before Easter. Prince Edmund went to London to his father; and then, after Easter, king Cnut made his way towards London with all his ships.

Then it happened that king Æthelred passed away before the ships arrived. He ended his days on St George's day [23 April], after a life of much hardship and many difficulties. Then, after his death, all the councillors who were in London, and the citizens, chose Edmund as king, and he defended his kingdom valiantly during his lifetime.

Then at Rogation days [7–9 May], the [Danish] ships came to Greenwich, and within a short time went on to London. They dug a great channel on the south bank and dragged their ships to the west side of the bridge, and then afterwards built earthworks outside the borough so that no one could get in or out, and attacked the borough repeatedly, but they withstood them valiantly. Some time previous to this king Edmund had made his way out of the borough, and had taken possession of Wessex, and all the inhabitants submitted to him. Soon after this he fought against the host at Penselwood, near Gillingham, and fought another battle after midsummer (*continued on p.* 151)

E 1016
from
p. 149 after midsummer at Sherston, and there was great slaughter on both sides, and it was [not the leaders but] the armies themselves who broke off the fight. Ealdorman Eadric and Ælfmær Darling were assisting the host against king Edmund. Then he assembled levies for the third time, and marched to London and relieved the garrison, driving the enemy to their ships. Two days afterwards the king crossed the river at Brentford, and fought against the host and put it to flight; and a great number of the English were drowned through their own negligence, having gone on ahead of the main body in search of booty. After that the king went to Wessex and called up his levies; and immediately the host marched on London and besieged it, attacking it fiercely both by land and water, but the Almighty God delivered it.

After this the host left London, and went with their ships into the Orwell, and landed there and went into Mercia, destroying and burning everything in their path, as was their custom. They obtained supplies and sent both the ships and their livestock into the Medway. Then for the fourth time king Edmund called up all the people of England, and crossed the Thames (*continued on p.* 151)

F 1016
from
p. 148 After this the host left London, and went with their ships into the Orwell, and there went up into Mercia, destroying and burning as was their custom. Then king Edmund for the fourth time got together all the people of England, and went into Kent, and the host fled on their horses into Sheppey, and the king slew as many as he could overtake. Ealdorman Eadric turned over to the king's side at Aylesford. No greater error of judgment was ever made than this [to take him back into favour].

When the host was making its way back into Mercia the king learnt of it, and then for the fifth time got together all the English people, and pursued the host and overtook (*continued on p.* 153) at Brentford, and went into Kent, and the host fled before **E 1016** him with their horses into Sheppey, and the king slew as many **from** of them as he could overtake. Ealdorman Eadric turned over **p. 150** to the king's side at Aylesford. No greater error of judgment was ever made than this [to take him back into favour].

The host went back up into Essex, and made their way into Mercia, destroying everything before them. When the king learnt that the host had gone inland, then for the fifth time he called up all the people of England and followed them up, overtaking them in

(*continued on p.* 152)

at Sherston, and there was great slaughter on both sides, and it **D 1016** was [not the leaders but] the armies themselves who broke off the **from** fight. Ealdorman Eadric and Ælfmær Darling were assisting **p. 149** the host against king Edmund. Then he assembled levies for the third time, and marched to London [1] and relieved the garrison, driving the enemy to their ships. Two days afterwards the king crossed the river at Brentford, and fought against the host and put it to flight; and a great number of the English were drowned through their own negligence, having gone on ahead of the main body in search of booty. After that the king went to Wessex, and called up his levies; and the host marched on London and besieged it, attacking it fiercely both by land and water, but the Almighty God delivered it.

After this the host left London, and went with their ships into the Orwell, and landed there and went into Mercia, destroying and burning everything in their path, as their custom is. They obtained supplies and sent both the ships and their livestock into the Medway. Then for the fourth time king Edmund called up all the people of England, and crossed the Thames at Brentford, and went into Kent, and the host fled before him with their horses into Sheppey, and the king slew as many of them as he could overtake. Ealdorman Eadric turned over to the king's side at Aylesford. No greater error of judgment was ever made than this [to take him back into favour].

The host went back up into Essex, and made their way into Mercia, destroying everything before them. When the king learnt that the host had appeared on the scene, then for the fifth time he called up all the people of England and followed them up, overtaking them in Essex at

(*continued on p.* 152)

[1] C adds *keeping north of the Thames all the time, and coming out through the wooded slopes by Clayhill* (*Farm, in Tottenham*). Cf. 18 EPN 79.

Essex, at the hill called Ashingdon, and there a fierce battle was
E 1016 fought. Then ealdorman Eadric did as he had so often done
from before: he and the *Magesæte* [men from Herefordshire and
p. 151 south Shropshire] were the first to set the example of flight,
and thus he betrayed his royal lord and the whole nation. Cnut
was victorious, and won all England by his victory. Among the slain
were Eadnoth, abbot Wulfsige, ealdorman Ælfric, ealdorman Godwine,
Ulfcytel from East Anglia, and Æthelweard, son of ealdorman Æthelsige,[1] and all the flower of England.[2]
Then after this battle king Cnut proceeded with his host into
Gloucestershire, where he heard tell that Edmund the king was. Then
ealdorman Eadric and the *(continued on p.* 153)

the hill called Ashingdon, and there a fierce battle was fought.
D 1016 Then ealdorman Eadric did as he had so often done before: he
from and the *Magesæte* [men from Herefordshire and south Shrop-
p. 151 shire] were the first to set the example of flight, and thus he
betrayed his royal lord and all the people of England. Cnut
was victorious, and won all England by his victory. Among the slain
were bishop Eadnoth, abbot Wulfsige, ealdorman Ælfric, ealdorman
Godwine, Ulfcytel from East Anglia, and Æthelweard, son of ealdorman Ælfwine,[1] and all the flower of the English nation.
Then after this battle king Cnut proceeded with his host into
Gloucestershire, where he learnt that Edmund the king was. Then
ealdorman Eadric and the councillors who were present advised that
the kings should come to terms, and both kings met [3] at Alney, near
Deerhurst, and became comrades and sworn brothers, and made a
compact both with pledge and also with oaths, and fixed the amount of
money to be paid to the host, and then dispersed, king EDMUND to hold
Wessex and Cnut the country to the north. The host then went to
the ships with what they had taken, and the citizens of London came
to terms with the host and bought peace from them; and the host
brought their ships to London, and took up the winter-quarters there.
Then, on St Andrew's day [30 November] king EDMUND passed away,
and is buried with his grandfather Edgar at Glastonbury.

(continued on p. 154)

---

[1] *Æthelwine* C *recte.*
[2] *and all the flower of England perished there* C; Bruce Dickins (6 *LSE*
20 note 14) notes that 'Cambridgeshire suffered heavily at Ashingdon, as
six years earlier at *Ringmere* and fifty years later at Stamford Bridge.'
[3] *et colloquium habuerunt apud Olanige* F Lat

E 1016
from
p. 152
councillors who were present advised that the kings should come to terms; they exchanged hostages, and the kings met at Alney, and made a compact of mutual friendship, both with pledge and with oath, and fixed the amount of money to be paid to the host, and dispersed, having agreed that king Edmund should hold Wessex and Cnut Mercia.

Then the host went to the ships with the plunder they had taken, and the citizens of London came to terms with the host and bought peace from them; and the host brought their ships to London, and took up their winter-quarters therein.

Then, on St Andrew's day [30 November], king Edmund passed away, and is buried with his grandfather Edgar at Glastonbury. In this same year Wulfgar, abbot of Abingdon, passed away and Æthelsige [*recte* Æthelwine] succeeded. (*continued on p.* 155)

F 1016
from
p. 150
them at Ashingdon, and there a fierce battle was fought. Then ealdorman Eadric did as he had often done before: he and the *Magesæte* [men from Herefordshire and south Shropshire] were the first to set the example of flight, and thus he betrayed his royal lord and the whole nation. Cnut was victorious, and won all England by his victory. Among the slain were Eadnoth, abbot Wulfsige, ealdorman Ælfric, Ulfcytel from East Anglia, and Æthelweard, son of ealdorman Æthelsige,[1] and all the flower of England.

Then after this battle king Cnut proceeded with his host into Gloucestershire, where he heard tell that Edmund the king was. Then ealdorman Eadric and the councillors who were present advised that the kings should come to terms; they exchanged hostages, and the kings met at Alney, and made a compact of mutual friendship, both with pledge and with oath, and fixed the amount of money to be paid to the host, and dispersed, having agreed that king Edmund should hold Wessex and Cnut Mercia.

Then, on St Andrew's day [30 November], king Edmund passed away, and is buried with his grandfather Edgar at Glastonbury.

(*continued on p.* 177)

[1] See note 1, p. 152

153

A̅ 1017
from   1017. In this year Cnut was chosen as king.
p. 134   (continued on p. 156)

           1017. In this year king Cnut succeeded to the whole realm of
D 1017 England, and divided it into four parts, himself retaining
from   Wessex, and giving East Anglia to Thurkil, Mercia to Eadric,
p. 152   and Northumbria to Eric. In this year, too, was ealdorman
Eadric slain,[1] and Northman, son of ealdorman Leofwine, and
Æthelweard, son of Æthelmær the Stout, and Beorhtric, son of Ælfheah
of Devon. And king Cnut banished prince Eadwig,[2] and Eadwig,
'king of the peasants.' Then before 1 August the king commanded
the widow of the late king Æthelred, Richard's daughter, to be brought
to him so that she might become his wife.

           1018. In this year the following tribute was paid over all England: it
amounted in all to seventy-two thousand pounds, in addition to that
which the citizens of London paid, which was ten thousand five hundred
pounds. Part of the host returned to Denmark, and forty ships
remained with king Cnut. And Danes and English came to an agreement at Oxford to observe Edgar's law.

           1019 [1020]. In this year king Cnut went to Denmark with nine
ships, and remained there the whole winter. In this year passed away
archbishop Ælfstan, who was named Lyfing: he was a very prudent
man, both in ecclesiastical and secular matters.

           1020. In this year king Cnut returned to England. Then at Easter
there was a great council at Cirencester; then ealdorman Æthelweard
was banished. In this year the king and earl Thurkil went to Ashingdon, together with archbishop Wulfstan and other bishops and abbots
and many monks, and consecrated the church at Ashingdon. In this
same year, on 13 November, Æthelnoth, a monk, who was dean at
Christ Church [Canterbury], was consecrated bishop, with his see at
Christ Church [Canterbury].

           1021. In this year, at Martinmas [11 November], king Cnut outlawed
earl Thurkil; and the charitable bishop Ælfgar passed away at matins
on Christmas Day.

           1022. In this year king Cnut went out with his ships to the Isle of
Wight. Bishop Æthelnoth went to Rome, and was received there with
great ceremony by the venerable pope Benedict, who with his own hands
put the pallium on him, and (continued on p. 156)

---

[1] *in London very justly* inserts F
[2] C adds *and had him slain.* The expulsion of Eadwig, 'king of the
peasants,' is placed by C under the year 1020.

E 1017
from
p. 153

1017. In this year king Cnut succeeded to the whole realm of England, and divided it into four parts, himself retaining Wessex, and giving East Anglia to Thurkil, Mercia to Eadric, and Northumbria to Eric. In this year was ealdorman Eadric slain, and Northman, son of ealdorman Leofwine, and Æthelweard, son of Æthelmær the Stout, and Beorhtric, son of Ælfgeat [*recte* Ælfheah] of Devon. And king Cnut banished prince Eadwig, and Eadwig, 'king of the peasants.' Then before 1 August the king commanded the widow of the late king Æthelred, Richard's daughter, to be brought to him so that she might become his queen.[3]

1018. In this year the following tribute was paid over all England: it amounted in all to seventy-two thousand pounds, in addition to that which the citizens of London paid, which was eleven thousand pounds. Part of the host returned to Denmark, and forty ships remained with king Cnut. And Danes and English came to an agreement at Oxford. In this year abbot Æthelsige departed this life at Abingdon, and Æthelwine succeeded.[4]

1019. In this year king Cnut went to Denmark, and remained there the whole winter.

1020. In this year king Cnut came to England. Then at Easter there was a great council at Cirencester; then ealdorman Æthelweard was banished. In this year the king went to Ashingdon.[5] Archbishop Lyfing passed away, and Æthelnoth, monk and dean at Christ Church [Canterbury], was consecrated bishop thereto in that same year.[6]

1021. In this year, at Martinmas [11 November], king Cnut outlawed earl Thurkil.

1022. In this year king Cnut went out with his ships to the Isle of Wight. Bishop Æthelnoth went to Rome, and was received there with great ceremony by pope Benedict, who with his own hands put the pallium on him, and solemnly (*continued on p.* 157)

---

[3] *she was called Ælfgifu in English, and Emma in French* adds F

[4] Having invented an Æthelsige in annal 1016 E, the chronicler now summarily disposes of him to make way for the correct name of the abbot who succeeded in 1016.

[5] *and had a church built there of stone and lime for the souls of those men who had been slain there, and gave it to his own priest, whose name was Stigand* F

[6] *by Wulfstan archbishop* F; *a Wlstano archiepiscopo Eboracensi* F Lat

Ā 1031
from
p. 154

1031. In this year Cnut returned to England. As soon as
(continued on p. 158)

D 1022
from
p. 154

solemnly consecrated him archbishop on 7 October, and blessed him; and at the same time the archbishop straightway sang mass on the same day, and thereafter feasted with all honour in the company of the pope himself; he also took the pallium from the altar of St Peter, and then joyfully returned home to his native land.

1023. In this year, in St Paul's church in London, king Cnut gave full permission to archbishop Æthelnoth, bishop Beorhtwine, and to all the servants of God who were with them, that they might take up from the burial-place the body of archbishop St Ælfheah; and they did so on 8 June. The illustrious king, the archbishop, diocesan bishops, earls, and very many others, both clergy and laity, conveyed his holy body by ship over the Thames to Southwark, and there delivered the holy martyr to the archbishop and his companions, who then with a distinguished following and happy jubilation conveyed him to Rochester. Then on the third day came Emma the Lady with her royal son Harthacnut, and with great pomp and rejoicing and hymns of praise they conveyed the holy archbishop into Canterbury, and with equal ceremony brought him on 11 June into Christ Church [Canterbury]. Likewise afterwards on the eighth day, 15 June, archbishop Æthelnoth, bishop Ælfsige, bishop Beorhtwine, and all who were with them, buried the holy body of St Ælfheah on the north side of Christ's altar to the glory of God, and to the honour of the holy archbishop, and to the eternal salvation of all those who daily resort there to his holy body with devout heart and in all humility. May God Almighty have mercy on all Christian men because of the merits of the holy St Ælfheah.

1026. In this year bishop Ælfric went to Rome, and received the pallium from pope John on 12 November.

1028. In this year king Cnut sailed from England to Norway with fifty ships, and drove king Olaf from that country, and secured possession of all of it for himself.

1029. In this year king Cnut returned home to England.

1030. In this year king Olaf returned to Norway, and the people united to oppose him and fought against him, and he was there slain.[1]

1031 [1027]. In this year king Cnut went to Rome. As soon as he returned home (*continued on p.* 159)

---

[1] The battle of Stiklestad, near **Thrandheim Fiord** (cf. Heimskringla *Óláfs saga Helga,* caps. 205 ff.). For an account of England and the Scandinavian world at this period see F. M. Stenton, *op. cit.* 388 ff. Cf. Bruce Dickins, 'The Cult of S. Olave in the British Isles' (12 *Saga-book of the Viking Society* 53–80), and for the reference in C to Olaf as a saint, *ibid* 56 note 2.

E 1022
from
p. 155
consecrated him archbishop. Afterwards, invested with the pallium, he said mass there as the pope directed him, and after the service feasted with the pope: afterwards with his full blessing he returned home. Abbot Leofwine, who had been unjustly driven from Ely, was his companion; and there, on the testimony of the archbishop and of all those who had accompanied him [to Rome], he cleared himself, as directed by the pope, of all the charges that had been brought against him.

1023. In this year archbishop Wulfstan passed away, and Ælfric succeeded: [2] and the same year archbishop Æthelnoth conveyed the relics of St Ælfheah, the archbishop, to Canterbury from London.

1024. Hic Ricardus secundus obiit. Ricardus filius eius regnauit prope uno anno, et post eum regnauit Rodbertus frater eius ·viii· annis.

1025. In this year king Cnut went to Denmark with his ships to the battle-place at the Holy River, and Ulf and Eilaf met him with a great host, both a Swedish fleet and army; and there many men perished on king Cnut's side, both Danes and Englishmen; and the Swedes had possession of the place of slaughter.

1028. In this year king Cnut sailed from England to Norway with fifty ships,[3] and drove king Olaf from that country, and secured possession of it for himself.

1029. In this year king Cnut returned home to England.

1030. In this year king Olaf returned to Norway, and the people united to oppose him and fought against him, and he was there slain.

1031 [1027]. In this year king Cnut went to Rome. In the same year he went to Scotland, and Malcolm, the king of Scots, submitted to him

(*continued on p.* 159)

C 1023
from
p. 126
1023. In this year king Cnut returned to England, and Thurkil and he were reconciled. He delivered Denmark and his son into Thurkil's keeping, and the king took Thurkil's son with him to England. Afterwards he had the relics of St Ælfheah conveyed from London to Canterbury.

1028. In this year king Cnut sailed to Norway with fifty ships.

1030. In this year king Olaf was slain in Norway by his own people, and was afterwards canonized. Earlier in the same year Hakon, the valiant earl, perished at sea [4] (*continued on p.* 158)

---

[2] *archbishop Æthelnoth consecrated him in Canterbury* F
[3] *ships of English thanes* F; *de nobilibus Anglie* F Lat
[4] Hakon, son of Earl Eric of Hlathir, was drowned in the Pentland Firth.

he arrived in England, he gave to Christ Church [Canterbury]
Ā 1031 the port at Sandwich, together with all the dues that there
from accrue from both sides of the harbour, so that whenever the
p. 156 tide is at its highest and at the full, and a ship is afloat in closest
proximity to the shore, and a man is standing on that ship
with a small axe in his hand [the monastery shall receive the dues from
as far inland as can be reached by a small axe thrown from the ship] . . .

(The rest of the charter has been erased in the manuscript. The
phrase in brackets is taken from a fuller version in the Red Book of
Canterbury (No. 16 at Canterbury Cathedral), translated and edited by
A. J. Robertson, *Anglo-Saxon Charters*, p. 158.) (*continued on p.* 160)

1034. In this year died bishop Æthelric,[1] and he is buried at
C 1034 Ramsey.
from 1035. In this year king Cnut passed away on 12 November
p. 157 at Shaftesbury; and he was conveyed thence to Winchester and
there buried. And Ælfgifu Emma,[2] the Lady, was then residing
there. Harold, who claimed to be Cnut's son by the other Ælfgifu—
although it was quite untrue—sent thither and had all king Cnut's best
valuables that she could not keep back taken from her; she remained,
however, in residence there as long as she could.

1036. In this year Alfred, the blameless prince, son of king Æthelred,
came hither to this country, in order to visit his mother who was residing
in Winchester; but earl Godwine would not permit him to, neither
moreover would other men who wielded great power, because the
popular cry was greatly in favour of Harold, although it was unjust.

But then Godwine prevented him, and placed him in
    captivity,
Dispersing his followers besides, slaying some in various
    ways;
Some of them were sold for money, some cruelly murdered,
Some of them were put in chains, and some of them were
    blinded,
Some were mutilated, and some were scalped.[3]
No more horrible deed was done in this land
After the Danes came, and made peace with us here.
We can now but trust to the dear God
That they who without guilt were so pitiably killed
Rejoice joyfully in the presence of Christ,

(*continued on p.* 160)

---

[1] Bishop of Dorchester.
[2] *Imme* is written above *Ælfgyfu* in the manuscript.
[3] *and some blinded besides, and ignominiously scalped* D
[4] *And Robert, duke of Normandy, went to Jerusalem, and died there,
William, who was afterwards king of England, succeeded to Normandy.
although he was but a child* F
[5] E has misplaced the vacant annal for 1036.

E 1031
[1027]
from
p. 157

and two other kings, Mælbeth and Iehmarc. Rodbertus comes obiit in peregrinatione, et successit rex Willelmus in puerili ætate.[4]

1032. In this year wildfire appeared such as no man remembered before: it did damage everywhere, and in many places besides. In this same year Ælfsige, bishop of Winchester, passed away, and Ælfwine, the king's chaplain, succeeded to the bishopric.

1033. In this year Merehwit, bishop of Somerset, passed away, and he is buried at Glastonbury.

1034. In this year bishop Æthelric passed away.

1036 [1035].[5] In this year Cnut passed away at Shaftesbury, and he is buried in the Old Minster, Winchester. He was king over all England for very nearly twenty years. Soon after his passing there was a meeting of all the councillors at Oxford, and earl Leofric and almost all the thanes to the north of the Thames, and [Cnut's] household troops[6] in London, elected Harold as regent of all England on behalf of himself and his brother Harthacnut who was in Denmark. And earl Godwine and all the most prominent men in Wessex remained in opposition

(*continued on p.* 161)

D 1031
[1027]
from
p. 156

then he went to Scotland; and the king of Scots submitted to him and became his vassal, but maintained his allegiance for but a short time.

1033. In this year bishop Leofsige passed away, and his body rests at Worcester; and Beorhtheah was raised to his see.

1034. In this year bishop Ælfric [*sic*] passed away, and he is buried at Ramsey; and in the same year passed away Malcolm, king in Scotland.

1035. In this year king Cnut passed away, and his son Harold succeeded to the kingdom. He [Cnut] departed this life at Shaftesbury on 12 November, and he was conveyed to Winchester, and there buried. And Ælfgifu, the Lady, was then residing there. Harold claimed to be Cnut's son by Ælfgifu of Northampton, although it was not true. He sent thither, and had all king Cnut's best valuables taken from her; nevertheless she remained in residence there as long as she could.

1036. In this year Alfred, the blameless prince, son of king Æthelred, came hither to this country, in order to visit his mother who was residing in Winchester; but those who wielded great power in this land would not permit it, because the popular cry was greatly in favour of Harold, although it was unjust.

> Then he had him placed in captivity;
> Dispersing his followers besides, slaying some in various
> ways . . .

(Here follows the ballad on Alfred's death as in C, p. 158.)

(*continued on p.* 161)

---

[6] *þa liðsmen.* On the use of *lið, liðsmen* (*litsmen*) in the *Chronicle* see Appendix B. For these terms, which occur occasionally in following annals, I have used 'household troops' or 'troops.'

Ā 1040
from
p. 158
1040. In this year archbishop Eadsige went to Rome, and king Harold passed away.

(*continued on p.* 162)

C 1036
from
p. 158
Threatened with every kind of injury, the prince still lived,
Until the decision was taken to convey him
To the city of Ely, in chains as he was.
As soon as he arrived, his eyes were put out on board ship,
And thus sightless he was brought to the monks.
And there he remained as long as he lived.
Thereafter he was buried, as well became his rank,
With great ceremony, so honourable was he,
At the west end of the church, very near to the tower,
In the south aisle. His soul is with Christ.[1]

1037. In this year Harold was everywhere chosen as king, and Harthacnut repudiated because he remained too long in Denmark. His mother, queen Ælfgifu, was driven from the country without any mercy to face the raging winter. She went then to Bruges beyond the sea, and there count Baldwin received her well, and took care of her during her necessity. And earlier in this year Æfic, the noble dean of Evesham, passed away.

1038. In this year passed away the good archbishop Æthelnoth, also Æthelric, bishop of Sussex, and Ælfric, bishop of East Anglia, and on 20 December Beorhtheah, bishop of Worcestershire.

1039. This was the year of the great gale. Bishop Beorhtmær passed away at Lichfield. The Welsh slew Eadwine, the brother of earl Leofric, and Thurkil and Ælfgeat, together with very many other good men. In this year too came Harthacnut to Bruges, where his mother was.

1040. In this year died king Harold. Then, with the best intentions, they sent to Bruges for Harthacnut, and he came then to this country with sixty ships before midsummer, and then imposed a severe tax which was borne with difficulty: it was fixed at eight marks a rowlock; and all who had been zealous on his behalf now became disloyal to him. He never did (*continued on p.* 162)

---

[1] Alfred's obit was celebrated at Ely on 5 Feb. (6 *LSE* 18–19). On his burial place see A. W. Clapham, *op. cit.* 90.

**E 1036
[1035]
from
p. 159** as long as ever they could, but they could put no obstacle in the way.² Then it was decided that Ælfgifu, Harthacnut's mother, should reside in Winchester with the housecarles of the king her son, and hold all Wessex in trust for him, and earl Godwine was her ³ most devoted supporter. Some said of Harold that he was a son of Cnut by Ælfgifu, daughter of ealdorman Ælfhelm, but many thought this quite incredible; nevertheless he was undisputed king over all England.

1037. In this year Ælfgifu, king Cnut's widow, was driven from the country: she was the mother of king Harthacnut.⁴ She sought refuge across the Channel ⁵ with Baldwin, who gave her a dwelling in Bruges, and sheltered and took care ⁶ of her while she was there.

1038. In this year, on 1 November, archbishop Æthelnoth passed away, and shortly afterwards Æthelric, bishop of Sussex, and then before Christmas Beorhtheah, bishop of Worcestershire, and soon afterwards Ælfric, bishop of East Anglia. Then bishop Eadsige ⁷ succeeded to the archbishopric, and Grimcytel to the bishopric of Sussex, and bishop Lyfing to Worcestershire and Gloucestershire.

1039 [1040].⁸ In this year king Harold passed away at Oxford on 17 March, and he was buried at Westminster, and he had ruled England for four years and sixteen weeks. In his days sixteen ships [of the navy] were paid at the rate of eight marks a rowlock, just as had been done in king Cnut's time. In this same year came king Harthacnut to Sandwich, seven days before midsummer [17 June], and he was at once received by both English and Danes, though afterwards his councillors made a stiff recompense for it when they ordained that [Harthacnut's] sixty-two ships should be paid at the rate of eight marks a rowlock. And in this same year the 'sester' ⁹ of wheat rose in price to fifty-five pence and even higher.

1040 [1041]. In this year the tax for the payment of the fleet was paid; it amounted to twenty-one thousand (*continued on p.* 163)

**D 1038
from
p. 159** 1038. In this year passed away archbishop Æthelnoth the Good, also Æthelric, bishop of Sussex, who desired of God that He would not allow him to outlive his dear father Æthelnoth; and he too passed away within a week; and Beorhtheah, bishop of Worcestershire, on 20 December.

(*continued on p.* 163)

---

² *Earl Godwine and all the best men in Wessex opposed it, but met with no success* F
³ MS. *heora.*
⁴ *she was the mother of Edward and of Harthacnut* F
⁵ *in Flanders* F
⁶ *and honourably protected her* F
⁷ *the king's priest* F
⁸ E failed to leave blank annal 1039.
⁹ On the capacity of the *sester* see F. E. Harmer, *English Historical Documents* (Cambridge 1914) 79–80.

Ā 1042   1042. In this year king Harthacnut passed away.
from   1043. In this year was Edward consecrated king.
p. 160   (1050 *is the next annal in* Ā)

            anything worthy of a king while he reigned. He had the
C 1040 body of the dead Harold disinterred and cast into a marsh.
from   1041. In this year Harthacnut had all Worcestershire harried
p. 160 on account of his two housecarles who were collecting the
            heavy tax: the inhabitants slew them within the town, inside
the minster.   And early in the same year came Edward, his brother on
his mother's side, from abroad; he was the son of king Æthelred, and
had long been an exile from his country, but was nevertheless sworn in
as [future] king; and then he remained thus in his brother's court as long
as he [Harthacnut] lived.   And in this year also Harthacnut betrayed
earl Eadwulf, although he had guaranteed his safety, and thereby
became a breaker of his pledge.

    1042. In this year Harthacnut died as he stood at his drink and he
suddenly fell to the ground with a horrible convulsion; and those who
were near thereto took hold of him, but he never spoke again, and
passed away on 8 June.   And the whole nation then received Edward
as king, as was his right by birth.

    1043. In this year Edward was consecrated king at Winchester on
the first day of Easter with great ceremony: this year Easter was on
3 April.   Archbishop Eadsige consecrated him, and fully instructed
him before all the people, clearly reminding him of his duty as king
and his responsibility to the nation as a whole.   And Stigand the priest
was consecrated bishop of East Anglia.   Soon in this same year the
king had all the lands which his mother owned confiscated for his own
use, and took from her all she possessed, an indescribable number of
things of gold and silver, because she had been too tight-fisted with him.
Soon after Stigand was deprived of his see, and all that he possessed
was confiscated to the king, because he [Stigand] was his mother's
closest confidant, and she, as was supposed, followed his advice.

    1044. In this year archbishop Eadsige resigned from his bishopric
because of ill health (*continued on p.* 164)

162

E 1040
[1041]
from
p. 161

and ninety-nine pounds, and eleven thousand and forty-eight pounds was afterwards paid to thirty-two ships. In this same year Edward, son of king Æthelred, came hither to this country from France: he was the brother of king Harthacnut, and they were both sons of Ælfgifu, who was the daughter of duke Richard.

1041 [1042]. In this year died king Harthacnut at Lambeth on 8 June: he was king over all England for two years all but ten days.[1] He is buried in the Old Minster in Winchester with king Cnut, his father. Before he was buried, the whole nation chose Edward to be king in London; and may he reign as long as God grants him. In many and various ways this was a most disastrous year: the weather was severe and the crops suffered: during this same year more cattle died than anyone remembered before, either by reason of diseases of various kinds or because of the inclement weather. At this same time passed away Ælfsige, abbot of Peterborough, and Earnwig the monk was elected abbot because he was a very good man and very sincere.

1042 [1043]. In this year Edward was consecrated king in Winchester on Easter Sunday with great ceremony; this year Easter was on 3 April. Archbishop Eadsige consecrated him, and fully instructed him before all the people, clearly reminding him of his duty as king and his responsibility to the nation as a whole.[2] And Stigand the priest was consecrated bishop of East Anglia. Soon after the king had all the lands which his mother owned confiscated for his own use, and took from her all she possessed, an indescribable number of things of gold and silver, because she had been too tight-fisted with him.

1043 [1044]. In this year archbishop Eadsige resigned from his bishopric because of ill health (*continued on p.* 164)

1041. *As annal* 1041 *C* (p. 162) *with the addition:* In this year [1042] Æthelric was consecrated bishop at York on 11 January.

D 1041
from
p. 161

1042. *As annal* 1042 *C* (p. 162).

1043. In this year Edward was consecrated king at Winchester on the first day of Easter. And in the same year, a fortnight before St Andrew's day, the king was advised to ride from Gloucester, and [with] earl Leofric and earl Godwine and earl Siward and their band came to Winchester and took the Lady unawares, and deprived her of all the treasures which she possessed which were innumerable, because she had been too strict with the king, her son, in that she had done less for him than he wished, both before his accession and afterwards; and they allowed her to remain there in residence thereafter.

(*continued on p.* 165)

---

[1] F continues: *and he is buried in the Old Minster in Winchester; and his mother, for his soul's salvation, gave to the New Minster the head of St Valentine, the martyr. . . .* F Lat, however, has: *sepultus est Wentonia in ueteri monasterio. Pro cuius anima mater sua dedit caput Sancti Valentini martyris eidem ecclesiæ.*

[2] *and clearly reminding him of his duty as king, and of the welfare of all his subjects* F; *Edsinus . . . docuit eum coram omni populo ea, quæ sibi facienda erant ad honorem suum et ad utilitatem sibi subiecti populi* F Lat

E 1043
[1044]
from
p. 163
and consecrated Siward, abbot of Abingdon, to be his suffragan there, by permission and counsel of the king and earl Godwine: otherwise it was known to few before the appointment was made because the archbishop thought that somebody else, in whom he would have had far less confidence, and whom he would not have wished should have it, would get it either by asking or by purchase, if it had been more generally known. In this year there was a very great famine over England, and corn was dearer than anyone remembered, so that the (*continued on p.* 165)

C 1044
from
p. 162
and consecrated Siward, abbot of Abingdon, to be his suffragan there, by permission and counsel of the king and earl Godwine: otherwise it was known to few before the appointment was made, because the archbishop thought that somebody else, in whom he would have had far less confidence, and whom he would not have wished should have it, would get it either by asking or by purchase, if it had been more generally known. In this year there was a very great famine over the whole of England, and corn was dearer than anyone remembered, so that the 'sester' of wheat rose in price to sixty pence and even higher. This same year the king sailed out to Sandwich with thirty-five ships; and Athelstan, the sacristan, became abbot of Abingdon. In this same year [1045] [1] king Edward took to wife Edith, the daughter of earl Godwine, ten days before Candlemas [i.e. on 23 January].

1045. In this year bishop Beorhtwold passed away on 22 April, and king Edward gave the bishopric to Hereman, his chaplain. In the summer of this same year king Edward sailed out with his ships to Sandwich; and so large a host was gathered there that no man had ever seen a greater naval force in this land. In this same year [1046] bishop Lyfing passed away on 20 March, and the king gave the bishopric to Leofric, his chaplain.

1046. In this year earl Swein [2] marched into [South] Wales, and Gruffydd, the northern king, together with him, and hostages were given to him. When he was on his homeward way, he had the abbess of Leominster fetched to him, and kept her as long as he pleased, and then let her go home. In this same year Osgod Clapa [3] was outlawed before Christmas. After Candlemas [2 February] in this same year [1047] came the severe winter with frost and snow and widespread storms; it was so severe that no living man could remember another like it, because of the mortality of both men and cattle; both birds and fish perished because of the hard frost and from hunger.

1047. In this year bishop Grimcytel passed away: he was

(*continued on p.* 166)

---

[1] On this and subsequent adjustments in C's dating, see Introduction, p. xxix.

[2] Swein, the eldest son of Earl Godwine, was made an earl in 1043; his earldom bordered on S. Wales.

[3] i.e. 'goggle-eyed' (cf. ON *klápr*). Cf. also Dorothy Whitelock, 'Scandinavian Personal Names' (12 *Saga-Book of the Viking Society* 152)

E 1043 [1044] from p. 164 'sester' of wheat rose in price to sixty pence and even higher. This same year the king sailed out to Sandwich with thirty-five ships; and Athelstan, the sacristan, became abbot of Abingdon, and Stigand was restored to his bishopric.

1043 [4] [1045]. In this year king Edward made the daughter of earl Godwine his queen. And in this same year passed away bishop Beorhtwold, who had held the bishopric for thirty-eight years: and Hereman, the king's chaplain, succeeded to the bishopric. In this same year, at Christmas on St Stephen's day, Wulfric was consecrated abbot of St Augustine's [Canterbury], with the consent of the king and abbot Ælfstan, because of the latter's great infirmity.

1044 [1046]. In this year passed away Lyfing, bishop of Devonshire, and Leofric, who was the king's chaplain, succeeded to the see. In this same year, on 5 July, abbot Ælfstan passed away at St Augustine's [Canterbury]. In this same year Osgod Clapa was driven from the country.

1045 [1047]. In this year Grimcytel, bishop of Sussex, passed away, and Heca, the king's chaplain, succeeded to the see. And in this year passed away (*continued on p.* 166)

D 1045 [1044] from p. 163 1045 [5] [1044]. In this year, on 25 July, passed away Ælfweard, bishop of London. He was abbot of Evesham first, and had done much to promote the good of the abbey while he was there: then he retired to Ramsey, and gave up his life there. Manni was elected abbot, and consecrated on 10 August. This same year the noble lady Gunnhild, the kinswoman of king Cnut, was driven from the country: for a long time afterwards she resided at Bruges, and afterwards went to Denmark.

1046 [1045]. In this year died Beorhtwold, bishop of Wiltshire, and Hereman was appointed to his see. In this year king Edward gathered great naval force at Sandwich because of the threatened invasion of Magnus of Norway, but his warfare with Swein [6] in Denmark prevented his coming here.

1047 [1046]. In this year, on 23 March, the eloquent bishop Lyfing passed away: he held three sees, one in Devonshire, and in Cornwall and in Worcester. Leofric succeeded to the sees of Devonshire and Cornwall, and bishop Ealdred to Worcester. In this year Osgod, the staller, was outlawed, and Magnus conquered Denmark.

1048 [1047]. In this year was the winter cruel, and in this same year Ælfwine, (*continued on p.* 167)

---

[4] Thus manuscript: 1043 repeated, as in 1046. These errors, coupled with the failure to leave 1039 blank, puts the chronology out from one to three years.

[5] From here to 1052 D is a year in advance of the true chronology because the figure 1044 was left out. The error is put right when 1052 is put in twice (p. 176).

[6] Swein Estrithson, nephew of Cnut, king of Denmark.

[7] Magnus, son of St Olaf, king of Norway.

E 1045
[1047]
from
p. 165
Ælfwine, bishop of Winchester, on 29 August, and Stigand, bishop up north, succeeded thereto. In the same year earl Swein went abroad to Bruges in Flanders, where Baldwin ruled, and remained there the whole winter: towards summer he went abroad [to Scandinavia].

1046 [1048]. Bellum apud Uallium Dunas. In this year passed away Athelstan, abbot of Abingdon, and Spearhafoc, a monk from Bury St Edmund's, succeeded him. In this same year bishop Siward passed away, and archbishop Eadsige fully resumed his functions again. In this same year Lothen and Yrling came to Sandwich with twenty-five ships, and seized there indescribable booty, both in captives and in gold and silver, so that no one knew what it amounted to in all. They sailed then round Thanet, intending to do the same there, but the inhabitants bravely resisted, and refused to allow them to land and refused them water, and completely drove them off. They sailed thence to Essex, and harried here and took captives and whatever they could find, and sailed then (*continued on p.* 167)

C 1047
from
p. 164
bishop of Sussex. He is buried in Christ Church, Canterbury; and king Edward gave the bishopric to Heca, his chaplain. In this same year, on 29 August, passed away bishop Ælfwine and king Edward gave bishop Stigand the bishopric.[1] Athelstan, abbot of Abingdon, passed away in this same year [1048] on 29 March. In this year Easter Sunday was on 3 April, and there was very great mortality over all England in this same year.

1048. In this year there was a severe earthquake far and wide in England. In this same year Sandwich and the Isle of Wight were harried, and the best men that were there were slain; and king Edward and the earls put out to sea in their ships in pursuit of them. In this same year bishop Siward resigned his bishopric because of ill health, and went to Abingdon, and archbishop Eadsige resumed his functions; he [Siward] passed away on 23 October, within eight weeks of this.

1049. In this year the emperor [Henry III] gathered a countless host against Baldwin of Bruges, because he had taken by storm his palace at Nijmegen [Gelderland], besides doing him many other ill turns. The army which he had gathered was beyond number; and Leo, the pope from Rome, and many other famous men of many nations were present. He also sent to king Edward, asking him for naval support to prevent Baldwin's escape by sea. Thereupon he [Edward] sailed to Sandwich, and lay there with a great naval force until the emperor had obtained satisfaction from Baldwin. (*continued on p.* 168)

---

[1] Here begins a new scribe with the entry for 29 March, but puts it under 1047. He writes the number 1048 and the subsequent events for that year, and then stops. His entry, beginning on 29 March and passing on to Easter, shows clearly that he begins the year, not at Easter, but on 25 March (cf. R. L. Poole, 16 *EHR* 720–1).

E 1046
[1048]
from
p. 166

east to Flanders, and sold there the spoil they had taken, and thereafter sailed east whence they had come.

1046 [2] [1049]. In this year was held the great synod at Rheims: there were present pope Leo, the archbishop of Burgundy, the archbishop of Besançon, the archbishop of Trèves, and the archbishop of Rheims, and many men in addition, both ecclesiastics and laymen. King Edward sent thither bishop Duduc, and Wulfric, abbot of St Augustine's, and abbot Ælfwine, that they should be able to report to the king what was decided there on behalf of Christendom. In this same year king Edward sailed

(*continued on p.* 168)

D 1048
[1047]
from
p. 165

bishop of Winchester, passed away, and bishop Stigand was exalted to his see. Before this, in the same year, Grimcytel, bishop of Sussex, passed away, and Heca, the priest, succeeded to the bishopric. Also in this year Swein sent hither, and asked for help against Magnus, the Norwegian king, asking for fifty ships to be sent to his assistance: but it seemed to everybody a foolish plan, and the request was refused because Magnus had a powerful fleet. He then drove Swein out, and conquered that country with great slaughter, and the Danes paid him much money and accepted him as king: and in the same year Magnus passed away.

1049 [1048]. In this year Swein returned to Denmark; and Harold,[3] the uncle of Magnus on his father's side, went to Norway, after the death of Magnus, and the Norwegians accepted him as king, and he sent hither to make peace with this country. Swein likewise sent from Denmark, and asked king Edward for naval support of at least fifty ships, but the whole nation opposed it. In this year, too, on 1 May, there was an earthquake in many places, at Worcester, Droitwich, and Derby and elsewhere. There was also great mortality of men and cattle; and wildfire which spread over Derbyshire and some other places did much damage.

1050 [1049]. In this year the emperor [Henry III] gathered a countless host against Baldwin of Bruges, because he had taken by storm his palace at Nijmegen [Gelderland], besides doing him many other ill turns. The army which he had gathered was beyond number and the pope himself and the patriarch were present in it, together with many other famous men from every nation. He also sent to king Edward, asking him for naval support to prevent Baldwin's escape by sea. Thereupon he [Edward] sailed to Sandwich, and lay there with a great naval force until the emperor had obtained satisfaction from Baldwin.

(*continued on p.* 169)

---

[2] 1046 repeated.   [3] Harold Hardrada.

167

E 1046
[1049]
from
p. 167

out to Sandwich with a great naval force. Earl Swein came into Bosham with seven ships and made his peace with the king, and he was promised that his legal right to all his former possessions would be recognized. Then earl Harold, his brother, and earl Beorn objected [1] that he could not be regarded as having a legal right to any of the things which the king had granted them; but his safety was secured for four days to return to his ships. It was during this time that word came to the king that hostile ships lay off the west and were harrying. Then earl Godwine sailed west about with two ships of the royal navy with Harold in command of one and Tostig, his brother, in command of the other, together with forty-two ships manned by men on national service. Then Harold [recte Beorn] took over the king's ship which Harold had commanded, and they sailed west to Pevensey and lay there weather-bound. Then within two days earl Swein came thither and spoke with his father and with earl Beorn, and begged Beorn to go with him to the king

(continued on p. 169)

C 1049
from
p. 166

There earl Swein came back again to king Edward, and asked him for a grant of land to maintain himself on; but Harold, his brother, and earl Beorn opposed it, and refused to restore to him anything of what the king had bestowed on them. He came hither with dissimulation, saying he wished to be the king's vassal and begged earl Beorn to be his friend at court, but the king refused his every request. Then Swein went away to Bosham to his ships, and earl Godwine sailed from Sandwich with forty-two ships to Pevensey, and earl Beorn forth with him. The king then gave leave to all the Mercian contingent in the fleet to go home, and they did so. Then the king was informed that Osgod lay at Wulpe [Flanders] with twenty-nine ships; the king then sent after the ships that his summons could reach which were lying within the northern mouth [of the R. Stour, K.]. But Osgod placed his wife in Bruges, and came back again with six ships, and the others went to the Naze in Essex and did evil there, and went back to their ships. When earl Godwine and earl Beorn lay at Pevensey with their ships, then came earl Swein with deceit and begged earl Beorn accompany him to the king at Sandwich, declaring that he would be loyal to the king and swear him oaths; and Beorn, because of his kinship to him, never thinking that he would betray him, took then three followers with him, and they rode to Bosham, where Swein's ships lay, as if they were on their way to Sandwich.[2] He was immediately bound and led on board ship, and carried then to Dartmouth, where he had him slain and buried deep: but Harold, his kinsman, recovered his body there and conveyed it to Winchester, and buried him there beside Cnut, his uncle; (continued on p. 171)

---

[1] F continues: *so that he was ordered to leave the country within four days; and he went then and spoke with his father, who lay at Pevensey, and with earl Beorn, who was there with Godwine. And he begged . . .; ut si post triduum inueniretur in Anglia, deberet poni in custodia* F Lat

[2] It had probably been agreed to go to Sandwich via Bosham, west and north around the Weald, and then by the Pilgrims Way to Sandwich, via Canterbury.

E 1046
[1049]
from
p. 168
at Sandwich and help him to win the king's friendship, and Beorn agreed to it, and they set out as though they were going to the king. Then as they rode, Swein begged him to go with him to his ships, making out that his sailors would desert unless he went to them very quickly. Then they both went to where his ships lay; and when they arrived, earl Swein begged him to go on board, but he stubbornly refused until Swein's sailors seized him and threw him into the boat: they bound him and rowed to the ship and put him on board, hoisted their sails and ran west to Axmouth. They kept him with them until they slew him, and took the body and buried it in a church. Then came his friends and household troops from London and exhumed him, and carried him to Winchester to

(*continued on p.* 171)

D 1050
[1049]
from
p. 167
Thither too came earl Swein, who had been in exile in Denmark where he had cooked his goose with the Danes. He came hither with guile, declaring that he would return to his allegiance to the king, and earl Beorn promised that he would help him. Afterwards when peace was made between Baldwin and the emperor, many ships went home, and the king remained behind at Sandwich with a few ships, and earl Godwine also with forty-two ships sailed from Sandwich to Pevensey, and earl Beorn with him. Then the king was informed that Osgod lay at Wulpe [Flanders] with thirty-nine ships, and the king then sent after the ships that his summons could reach, which had gone home. Osgod placed his wife in Bruges, and he and his men came back with six ships, and the others went to the Naze in Sussex and did evil there, and went back to their ships. Then a violent gale came upon them so that all were destroyed, except four which were destroyed across the sea. While earl Godwine and earl Beorn lay at Pevensey, then came earl Swein and deceitfully begged earl Beorn, who was his uncle's son, to accompany him to the king at Sandwich and improve his relations with him. Because of his kinship Beorn went with him with three followers, and he led him then towards Bosham where his ships lay, and then he was bound and led on board ship. Thence he sailed with him to Dartmouth (*continued on p.* 170)

A 1050   In this year archbishop Eadsige passed away, and Robert
from succeeded to the archbishopric.
p. 162
(1053 *is the next annal*)

D 1050 and had him slain there and buried deep.   Later his body was
[1049] found and carried to Winchester and buried beside king Cnut,
from his uncle.   Just before this the men from Hastings and there-
p.160 about seized two ships of his [1] with their ships and slew all the
crews, and brought the ships to Sandwich to the king.   Eight
ships he had before he [1] betrayed Beorn, but afterwards all forsook him
but two.

In this same year thirty-six [Scandinavian] ships came from Ireland
up the Welsh Usk, and did evil thereabout, aided by Gruffydd, the
Welsh king.   Forces were gathered against them, and bishop Ealdred
went with them, but they had too few troops, and the enemy took them
by surprise when it was quite early morning and slew many good men
there, and the others made their escape with the bishop.   This happened on 29 July.

In this same year Oswy, abbot of Thorney, died in Oxfordshire, also
Wulfnoth, abbot of Westminster.   Ulf, the priest, was appointed as
pastor of the bishopric which Eadnoth had had, but later he was
expelled, because he did nothing worthy of a bishop while he occupied
the see, so that it brings shame to us to speak further about it.   And in
this year bishop Siward passed away, who is buried at Abingdon.

In this year the great cathedral at Rheims was consecrated, and there
present were pope Leo and the emperor; and they held a great synod
there about the service of God which was presided over by the holy
pope Leo.   It is difficult to know how many bishops attended, and
especially how many abbots; from this country two were sent, one from
St Augustine's and one from Ramsey.

1051 [1050]. In this year passed away Eadsige, archbishop of Canterbury, and the king gave the archbishopric to Robert the Frenchman
who had been bishop of London.   Spearhafoc, abbot of Abingdon,
became bishop of London, but later he was deprived of his see before he
had been consecrated.   In this year bishop Hereman and bishop
Ealdred went to Rome. (*continued on p.* 173)

[1] i.e. Swein.
170

E 1046
[1049]
from
p. 169

the Old Minster, and there he lies buried beside king Cnut, his uncle. Swein then sailed east to Baldwin's land [Flanders], and resided there all winter in Bruges under his full protection.

In the same year passed away Eadnoth, bishop [1] in the north [i.e. of Dorchester, which extended to the Humber], and Ulf was appointed to the bishopric.

1047 [1050]. In this year there was a great council in London at mid Lent, and nine ships of [king Edward's] household troops were paid off, and five remained behind.

In this same year earl Swein returned to England.

In this same year was the great synod in Rome, and king Edward sent thither bishop Hereman and bishop Ealdred, and they arrived thither on Easter eve. Afterwards the pope held a synod at Vercelli, which bishop Ulf attended, and it was said that they were very near to breaking his staff if he had not given exceptionally costly gifts, for he did not know how to perform his offices as well as he ought to have done. In this year archbishop Eadsige passed away on 29 October.

1048 [1051]. In this year in spring, king Edward appointed Robert, bishop of London, archbishop of Canterbury; [2] and in the same spring he went to Rome for his pallium, and the king (*continued on p.* 172)

C 1049
from
p. 168

and the king and the whole army declared Swein to be 'nithing' [a man without honour]. Eight ships he had before he murdered Beorn; afterwards all forsook him except two. Then he went to Bruges, and stayed with Baldwin.

In this year passed away Eadnoth, the good bishop of Oxfordshire, and Oswy, abbot of Thorney, and Wulfnoth, abbot of Westminster. King Edward gave the bishopric to Ulf, his chaplain, and made a bad appointment.

And in this same year [1050] king Edward paid off nine ships, and they went away with the ships and everything; five of the ships remained behind, and the king promised them twelve months' pay.

In this same year bishop Hereman and bishop Ealdred went to Rome to the pope, on a mission for the king.

1050. In this year the bishops returned from Rome, and the sentence of outlawry against earl Swein was revoked. On 29 October in this same year, archbishop Eadsige passed away; also in this same year [1051] on 22 January died Ælfric, archbishop of York, and he is buried at Peterborough. At mid Lent [1051] king Edward held a meeting of his council in London, and appointed Robert archbishop of Canterbury and abbot Spearhafoc bishop of London; and he gave to bishop Rudolf, his kinsman, (*continued on p.* 172)

---

[1] *episcopus Aquilonarium Saxonum* F Lat
[2] *Hic Eaduuardus rex dedit Rodberto, qui fuit abbas Gemeticæ, archiepiscopatum Cantuariæ* F Lat

E 1048 gave the bishopric of London to Spearhafoc, abbot of Abing-
[1051] don; and the king gave the abbacy to bishop Rudolf, his kins-
from man. Then the archbishop returned from Rome the day
p. 171 before the eve of St Peter's day [27 June], and was installed as
archbishop [1] at Christ Church [Canterbury] on St. Peter's day
[29 June], and at once went to the king. As he was on his way, abbot
Spaerhafoc met him with the king's letter and seal [2] to the effect that he
should consecrate him bishop of London, but the archbishop refused
and said that the pope had forbidden him to do it. Then the abbot
approached the archbishop again in the matter, and desired this consecration, but the archbishop resolutely refused him, and said that the
pope had forbidden him to have it. Then the abbot went to London,
and occupied the bishopric, which the king had granted him, all that
summer and that autumn with his full consent.

And then came Eustace [3] from oversea shortly after the bishop, and
went to the king and talked over with him what he wished, and then set
off on his way home. When he came east to Canterbury, he and his
men had a meal there, and went to Dover. When he was some miles
or more this side of Dover, he put on his coat of mail, and all his companions likewise, and went to Dover. When they arrived thither they
wanted to lodge where they pleased: then one of his men came and
wished to lodge at the house of a certain householder against his wish,
and wounded the householder, and the householder slew him. Then
Eustace got on his horse (*continued on p.* 173)

the abbacy of Abingdon. In this same year he paid off all his
C 1050 household troops.
from 1051. In this year archbishop Robert came hither from over-
p. 171 sea with his pallium; and in this same year earl Godwine and
all his sons were banished from England, and he went to
Bruges with his wife and his three sons, Swein, Tostig, and Gurth.
Harold and Leofwine went to Ireland, and stayed there the winter. In
this same year [1052] on 14 March passed away the Lady-dowager, the
mother of king Edward and of Harthacnut: she is called Emma. Her
body lies in the Old Minster [Winchester] beside king Cnut.

(*continued on p.* 178)

---

[1] *inthronizatur* (*in*) *cathedra archipresulatus sui* F Lat
[2] See F. E. Harmer, *Anglo-Saxon Writs*, Appendix IV note 6.
[3] For a delightful commentary on the Eustace incident and its conse-
quences, see R. W. Chambers, *On the Continuity of English Prose* (London
1932) lxi–lxiv. Sixteen years later the Kentishmen, in revolt against the
Conqueror, were to ask this same Eustace to cross from Boulogne and take
Dover by surprise. His expedition was a failure, and he escaped 'by having
the advantage of a fleet horse and his knowledge of the road' (Ordericus
Vitalis, trans. Forester II. 10–12).

E 1048
[1051]
from
p. 172
and his companions on theirs, and went to the householder and slew him upon his own hearth. Then they went up towards the town and slew both within and without more than twenty men;[4] and the townsmen slew nineteen men on the other side and wounded they knew not how many. And Eustace escaped with a few men, and went back to the king and gave a one-sided account of how they had fared;[5] and the king was greatly incensed against the townsmen, and summoned earl Godwine and ordered him to carry war into Kent to Dover, because Eustace had told the king that it was more the townsmen's fault than his; but it was not so. And the earl would on no account agree to the foray, because it was abhorrent to him to injure the people of his own province.[6]

Then the king sent for all his council, and ordered them to come to Gloucester about the second festival of St Mary [8 September]. At that time the foreigners [the French] had built a castle in Herefordshire

(*continued on p.* 174)

D 1052
[1051]
from
p. 170
1052 [1051]. In this year Ælfric, archbishop of York, passed away: he was a very venerable man and wise. And in this same year king Edward abolished that tax which king Æthelred had instituted to buy off the Danes: and this was in the thirty-ninth year since he had introduced it. This tax vexed the English nation for so long a time as is here written above; and it always had priority over the other taxes which were paid in various ways, and was the most generally oppressive.

In this same year Eustace landed at Dover; he was married to king Edward's sister. His men behaved foolishly when looking for quarters, and slew a man from the town; and another man from the town slew their companion, with the result that there lay dead seven of his

(*continued on p.* 175)

---

[4] *When he had talked over what he wished, then he turned back; and when his men came to Dover, one of his men wished to take up quarters at the house of a man against his will, with the result that he wounded the householder, and the householder slew the man. Then was Eustace very angry, and he and his men got on their horses, and went thither and slew this same householder, and in addition to him twenty men besides* F; *per superbiam uoluit ui accipere hospitium, et uulnerauit dominum domus, etc.* F Lat

[5] *told the king it was worse than it was* F; *aliter multo quam acta sit* F Lat

[6] *precepit Goduuino comiti Cantiæ ut congregaret exercitum et intraret Cantium, omnia deuastando, et maxime Dofris* (at foot of page: *et maxime Dofras*; in left margin: *ut deuastaret Dofras*). *Sed Goduuinus, nolens destruere comitatum suum, dissimulauit ire illuc* F Lat

E 1048
[1051]
from
p. 173

in earl Swein's territory and inflicted all the injuries and insults they possibly could upon the king's men in that region. Then earl Godwine, earl Swein, and earl Harold met at Beverstone, and many men with them for the purpose of approaching their royal lord and the whole council which was assembled with him, in order to obtain the advice and help of the king and all the council how they might avenge the insult to the king and the whole nation; but the foreigners [1] were first to gain the king's ear and accused the earls so that they could not get an audience with him,[2] for they made out that they wished to obtain it to betray the king. Earl Siward and earl Leofric and many people with them from the north had come there to the king, and earl Godwine and his sons were informed that the king and the men who were with him would take action against them; and they made a strong show of force in opposition, though it was hateful to them to be forced to oppose their royal lord. Then the council decreed that each party should desist from further wrong-doing; and the king gave God's peace [3] and his entire friendship to both sides.

Then the king and his council decreed that a second meeting of the full council should be held in London at the autumn equinox [24 September], and the king ordered levies to be called out, both to the south and to the north of the Thames, quite the best force that ever was. Then was earl Swein declared an outlaw, and earl Godwine and earl Harold were summoned to the assembly as soon as they could travel the distance. When they arrived out thither they were summoned to the assembly, and then Godwine required protection and hostages that he might come to the assembly and go from it without treachery. Then the king required the allegiance of all the thanes who had formerly been the earls', and they surrendered to him their lordship over them. Then the king sent again to them and ordered them to come

(*continued on p.* 175)

---

[1] *quidam de Normannis*   F Lat
[2] *near the king*   F; *ita ut rex interdiceret eis presentiam suam*   F Lat
[3] *the king gave the earls his entire friendship*   F

E 1048
[1051]
from
p. 174
with twelve men into the king's council. Then the earl again required protection and hostages, so that he might clear himself of each of the things with which he was charged. Then the hostages were refused him, (*continued on p.* 176)

D 1052
[1051]
from
p. 173
companions; and much evil was done on either side with horse and with weapons, until the townsfolk assembled, whereupon they fled away until they came to the king at Gloucester, and he gave them protection. Then was earl Godwine very indignant that such things should happen in his earldom, and began to gather forces together over all his earldom, and earl Swein, his son, over his, and Harold, his second son, over his earldom: and they all assembled in Gloucestershire at Longtree a great army and without number, all ready for war against the king, unless Eustace and his men were handed over to them, as well as the Frenchmen who were in the castle [in Herefordshire]. All this was done seven days before the later festival of St Mary [8 September]. King Edward was then residing in Gloucester. He sent then for earl Leofric and north for earl Siward and asked for troops from them; at first they came to him with moderate reinforcements, but after they knew the position there in the south, then they sent north over all their earldom and had great levies summoned to the assistance of their lord, and earl Ralph [4] did likewise throughout his earldom. And they all came to Gloucestershire to the king's assistance, late though it was, and were so resolute in support of the king that they were willing to attack Godwine's levies if the king had wished it. Then some of them considered it would be great folly if they joined battle, because wellnigh all the noblest in England were present in those two companies, and they were convinced they would be leaving the country open to the invasion of our enemies, and be bringing utter ruin upon ourselves. They then counselled that hostages should be exchanged, and they fixed times for coming to London, and the people over all these northern parts were called out thither in Siward's earldom, in Leofric's, and in some other places besides; and earl Godwine and his sons were to make their counter-plea there. Then they came to Southwark, and with them a great multitude from Wessex, but his host decreased in numbers more and more as time went on. And all the thanes of earl Harold, Godwine's son, were required to find sureties that they would become the king's men, and earl Swein, his other son, was outlawed. Then it did not suit him [Godwine] to come to meet the king and the host that was with him in order that his counter-plea should be heard. He fled away by night, and the following morning the king held a meeting of his council, and proclaimed him an outlaw, and all his host, him and all his sons. And he went south to Thorney [Thorney Island, off the coast of Sussex] with his wife and Swein, his son, together with Tostig and his wife, who was a kinswoman of Baldwin of Bruges, and Gurth, his son. And earl Harold and Leofwine went to Bristol in the ship which earl Swein (*continued on p.* 176)

[4] The nephew of king Edward.

175

E 1048
[1051]
from
p. 175
and he was granted five days' safe conduct to leave the country. Then earl Godwine and earl Swein went to Bosham, and launched their ships and went oversea and sought the protection of Baldwin,[1] and stayed there all winter. Earl Harold went west to Ireland, and stayed there all winter under the protection of the king. And soon after this happened, the king forsook the Lady, who had been consecrated his queen, and had her deprived of all that she owned in land, and in gold, and in silver, and of everything, and committed her to his sister at Wherwell.

Abbot Spearhafoc was then driven out from the bishopric

(*continued on p.* 177)

D 1052
[1051]
from
p. 175
had got ready for himself earlier and provisioned. The king sent Ealdred, the bishop of London, with a force to intercept him before he reached the ship, but they could not or would not. And Harold sailed out from the mouth of the Avon [Somerset], but met such severe weather that he barely survived, and many of them perished there. He sailed out to Ireland when he got a wind; and Godwine and those who accompanied him sailed from Thorney to Bruges to the land of Baldwin in one ship with as many treasures as they could possibly stow on board for each of them. If any Englishman had been told that events would take this turn he would have been very surprised, for Godwine had risen to such great eminence as if he ruled the king and all England: his sons were earls and favourites of the king, and his daughter was the king's wedded wife. She was brought to Wherwell and committed to the abbess.

Then soon came duke William from beyond the sea with a great retinue of Frenchmen, and the king received him and as many of his companions as it pleased him, and let him go again. In this same year William the priest was given the bishopric of London, which had been given to Spearhafoc.

1052.[2] In this year on 6 March passed away Ælfgifu, the Lady: she was the widow of king Æthelred and king Cnut.

In the same year Gruffydd, the Welsh king, harried in Herefordshire, so that he came very near to Leominster; and men gathered together against him, both the natives and the Frenchmen from the castle. And there were slain very many good Englishmen besides many from among the Frenchmen. This was the very same day on which thirteen years ago Eadwine was slain with his companions.

(*continued on p.* 179)

---

[1] *and this was denied him, and he was ordered to leave the country within five days, and he went oversea to Baldwin's land* F
[2] D repeats 1052 and so restores the chronology.

**E 1048
[1051]
from
p. 176**
of London, and William, the king's chaplain, was consecrated thereto.[2] And then Odda was appointed earl over Devon, and over Somerset, and over Dorset, and over Cornwall; and Ælfgar, earl Leofric's son, was given the earldom which Harold had had.

1052.[3] In this year passed away Ælfgifu Emma, the mother of king Edward and of king Harthacnut. In this same year the king and his council decided that ships should be sent out to Sandwich, and earl Ralph and earl Odda were put in command. Then earl Godwine sailed out from Bruges with his ships to the Yser, and put to sea the day before midsummer eve [23 June] so that he reached Dungeness, which is to the south of Romney. This then came to the knowledge of the earls out off Sandwich, and they sailed out to encounter the other ships, and the levies were called out against the ships. Meanwhile earl Godwine was warned and sailed in to Pevensey; the weather became so very stormy that the earls could not find out what had happened to earl Godwine. Earl Godwine sailed out to sea again until he came back to Bruges, and the other ships sailed back again to Sandwich. Then it was decided that these ships should sail back to London, and that other earls and other rowers were to be appointed to the ships, but it was so long delayed that the fleet did not move [4] [from Sandwich] and they all went home. Then earl Godwine learnt this and he and his household troops [5] hoisted sail and made their way west (*continued on p.* 178)

**F 1051
from
p. 153**
1051. In this year passed away Ælfgifu Emma, the mother of king Edward. And earl Godwine sailed out from Bruges with his ships to the Yser, and so to England, and landed at Dungeness to the south of Romney, and so on to the Isle of Wight, and there seized all the ships which were serviceable

(*continued on p.* 179)

[2] *capellano suo, nomine Willelmo, qui consecratus est a Rodberto archiepiscopo* F Lat
[3] E omits 1049, 1050, 1051 and so corrects the previous slips in dating.
[4] See BT Suppl. *belifan* I (i): E appears to have a more accurate version than C (p. 178), although F. M. Stenton, *op. cit.* 558, follows the latter.
[5] I have attempted to render *lið* in the next few pages (where it occurs ten times) by '(household) troops.'

on a direct course for the Isle of Wight, and landed there and
E 1052 harried until the inhabitants paid as much as they imposed
from upon them. Then they sailed westward until they came to
p. 177 Portland,[1] where they landed and did whatever damage they
could.

Meanwhile Harold was sailing from Ireland with nine ships, and
landed at Porlock, where many people were gathered to oppose him,
but he did not hesitate to provide himself with food. He went inland,
and slew a great part of the inhabitants and seized whatever he pleased
in cattle, captives, and property. Then he made his way east to his
father, and they both went eastward until they came to the Isle of
Wight, and took from there what they had left behind, and went thence
to Pevensey, taking along with them as many of the ships there as were
seaworthy, and *(continued on p. 179)*

1052. In this year earl Harold came from Ireland with ships
C 1052 into the mouth of the Severn near the borders of Somerset and
from Devonshire, and there did much plundering; and the inhabit-
p. 172 ants, both from Somerset and from Devonshire, gathered to
oppose him, and he put them to flight and slew there more than
thirty good thanes besides other men, and soon after this sailed round
Land's End. Then king Edward had forty small vessels fitted out
which lay at Sandwich for many weeks. They were to lie in wait for
earl Godwine, who was in Bruges that winter; however, he reached
this country first before they knew anything of it, and during the time
he was here in the land he won to his side all the men of Kent and all
the shipmen from the district of Hastings and everywhere there
along the sea coast, and all those in the east part of the country, the
people of Sussex and of Surrey and many places elsewhere besides.
Then they all declared that they would live and die with him. Then
the household troops which lay at Sandwich learnt about Godwine's
movements and set out in pursuit, but he escaped from them and took
evasive action wherever he could, and the troops went back to Sandwich and so homewards to London. Then when Godwine learnt that
the troops which lay at Sandwich had gone home, then he sailed back
towards the Isle of Wight, and lay thereabouts off the coast until earl
Harold, his son, joined forces with him. And they did no great harm
after they had joined forces, except to seize provisions, but they won over
to their side all the inhabitants along the sea coast as well as those up-
country. Then they went towards Sandwich, collecting to their side all
the shipmen they met as they went, and arrived then at Sandwich with
an overwhelming host. When king Edward learnt this,

(continued on p. 180)

---

[1] 'It is distinctly probable that this treatment was inflicted on the place
because it was a royal manor.' (F. E. Harmer, *Anglo-Saxon Writs* 526.)

E 1052
from
p. 178

so forth to Dungeness, taking possession of all the ships that were in Romney and in Hythe and in Folkestone. They then went east to Dover and landed, and seized as many ships and hostages there as they pleased, and so on to Sandwich where they did exactly the same; and everywhere hostages and provisions were given to them wherever they desired them. They made their way to the northern mouth of the [Kentish] Stour, and so towards London. Some ships (*continued on p.* 180)

D 1052
from
p. 176

And soon came earl Harold from Ireland with his ships to the mouth of the Severn near the borders of Somerset and Devonshire, and there did much plundering; and the inhabitants, both from Somerset and from Devonshire, gathered to oppose him, and he put them to flight and slew there more than thirty good thanes besides other men, and soon after this sailed round Land's End. Then king Edward had forty small vessels fitted out which lay at Sandwich. They were to lie in wait for earl Godwine, who was in Bruges that winter: however, he reached this country first before they knew anything of it, and during the time he was here in the land he won to his side all the men of Kent and all the shipmen from the district of Hastings and everywhere there along the sea coast, and all the people of Essex and of Surrey and many places elsewhere besides. Then they declared that they would live and die with him. Then the household troops which lay at Sandwich learnt about Godwine's movements and set out in pursuit, but he escaped from them, and the troops went back to Sandwich and so homewards to London. Then when Godwine learnt that the troops which lay at Sandwich had gone home, then he sailed back towards the Isle of Wight, and lay thereabouts off the coast until earl Harold, his son, joined forces with him. Thereafter they were reluctant to do any great harm, except to seize provisions. However, they won over to their side all the inhabitants along the sea coast as well as those up-country. Then they went towards Sandwich, collecting to their side all the shipmen they met as they went, and arrived then at Sandwich with an overwhelming host. When king Edward learnt this, then he sent (*continued on p.* 181)

F 1051
from
p. 177

and hostages, and so turned eastward. Harold had landed at Porlock with nine ships, and there slew many of the inhabitants, taking cattle, captives, and property; and made his way eastward to his father, and together they sailed to Romney, to Hythe, to Folkestone, to Dover, and to Sandwich, always seizing hostages and those ships which they found to be serviceable: thus did they proceed and came (*continued on p.* 181)

went within the Isle of Sheppey and did much damage there,
E 1052 and made their way to Milton Royal and burnt it to the ground,
from and went towards London after the earls. When they came to
p. 179 London the king and all the earls opposed them with fifty
ships. Then the earls sent to the king and desired that they
might legally possess all the things [1] of which they had been wrongfully
deprived. Then the king objected for a time, however, and for so long
that all the earl's supporters were greatly incensed against the king and
against his host, so that the earl himself had difficulty in restraining his
followers. Then bishop Stigand *(continued on p.* 181)

then he sent up-country for reinforcements, but they were very
C 1052 slow in coming, while Godwine kept moving on London with
from his troops until he came to Southwark, and there waited for a
p. 178 while until the tide came up, using the opportunity, as he had
done earlier, to come to an arrangement with the citizens that
they would fall in with his wishes in almost everything. When he had
arranged his course of action, then the tide came up and they immediately raised their anchors and held on their way through the bridge
near to the south bank; and his supporters on land came down and
arrayed themselves along the strand. Then they veered round with
the ships towards the north bank as if they were going to surround the
king's ships. The king also had great land levies on his side in addition
to his shipmen, but it was hateful to almost all of them to have to fight
against men of their own race, for there were few men else of any consequence except Englishmen on either side; and besides, they were unwilling
to increase the danger of leaving this land wide open to the invasion of
foreigners, were each side to destroy the other. It was decided that
wise men should act as intermediaries and arrange a truce between each
side; and Godwine landed with Harold his son and as many of their
troops as they considered sufficient, and a meeting of the council was
then held; and Godwine's earldom was restored to him without reservation, as fully and as completely as ever he possessed it,[1] and to his sons
likewise all that they had possessed, and to his wife and to his daughter
as fully and completely as they had ever possessed; [1] and the council
ratified complete friendship between them, and made a promise of good
laws for the whole nation; and they outlawed all the Frenchmen who
had *(continued on p.* 182)

[1] For the technical formulas see F. E. Harmer, *Anglo-Saxon Writs* 444
and 63–4.

intervened with God's help, and the wise men both inside and
E 1052 outside the city, and advised that hostages should be given as
from surety on either side, and so it was done.   When archbishop
p. 180 Robert and the Frenchmen learnt this, they took their horses,
and some went west to [Osbern] Pentecost's castle[2] [probably
Ewias Harold, Herefordshire], some north to Robert's castle, and archbishop Robert and bishop Ulf and their companions went out by the
East Gate [of London] and slew and otherwise injured many young
men, and made their way straight to the Naze, where he [Robert] took
(*continued on p.* 183)

up-country for reinforcements, but they were very slow in
D 1052 coming, while Godwine kept moving on London with his troops
from until he came to Southwark, and there waited for a while until
p. 179 the tide came up, using the opportunity, as he had done earlier,
to come to an arrangement with the citizens that they would
fall in with his wishes in almost everything.   Then when he had
arranged his course of action, the tide came up and they immediately
raised their anchors and held on their way through the bridge, always
near to the south bank; and his supporters on land came down and
arrayed themselves along the strand.   Then they veered round with the
ships as if they were going to surround the king's ships.   The king also
had great land levies on his side in addition to his shipmen, but it was
hateful to almost all to fight against men of their own race, for there
were few men else of any consequence except Englishmen on either
side; and besides, they were unwilling to increase the danger of leaving
this land wide open to the invasion of foreigners, were each side to
destroy the other.   It was decided that wise men should act as intermediaries and arrange a truce between each side; and Godwine landed
with Harold and as many of their troops as they considered sufficient,
and a meeting of the council was then held; and Godwine's earldom was
restored to him without reservation, as fully and as completely as ever
he possessed it, and to all his sons all that they had possessed, and to his
wife and to his daughter as fully and completely as they had possessed;
and the council ratified complete friendship between them, and made a
promise of effective laws for the whole nation; and they outlawed all
the Frenchmen who had (*continued on p.* 182)

then to London.   When they came to London, the king and
F 1051 all his earls opposed them with fifty ships.   Then the earls sent
from to the king and desired that they might legally possess all their
p. 179 things and property of which they had been wrongfully
deprived.   Then the king objected for a time, but Stigand (who
was the king's adviser and his chaplain) and the other wise men . . .
and they counselled that hostages should be given as surety on either
side (and that thus friendship should be established).   When archbishop Robert learnt this he took his horse and went to the Naze,
where he took an unseaworthy (*continued on p.* 183)

---

[2] See F. M. Stenton, *op. cit.* 554 note.

Ā 1053
from
p. 170

1053. In this year earl Godwine passed away.

(*continued on p.* 194)

C 1052
from
p. 180

promoted injustice and pronounced unjust judgments and counselled evil within this realm, with the exception of as many of those whom they decided that the king was pleased to have about him, who were loyal to him and to all his people. And bishop Robert and bishop William and bishop Ulf escaped with difficulty with the Frenchmen who were with them, and so arrived oversea. And earl Godwine and Harold and the queen were restored to their dignities. Swein had gone earlier from Bruges to Jerusalem [on a pilgrimage], and died while on his way home at Constantinople on St Michael's day [29 September]. It was the Monday after the Nativity of the Virgin [i.e. on 14 September] that Godwine arrived at Southwark with his ships, and the next morning on the Tuesday when they became reconciled, as it is described above. Godwine was taken ill soon after he landed and afterwards recovered, but he made far too few amends regarding the church property which he had taken from many holy places. In this same year came that high wind on St Thomas's eve [20 December] which did much damage everywhere. In this year too Rhys, the brother of the Welsh king, was put to death.

1053. In this year the king was at Winchester at Easter, and with him earl Godwine and earl Harold, his son, and Tostig. When on the second day of Easter he sat at table with the king, he suddenly sank down against the footstool, speechless and helpless: he was carried into the king's chamber and it was thought it would pass off, but it was not to be; yet he lingered on like this, unable to speak and helpless, until the Thursday, and then gave up his life. He is buried in the Old Minster [Winchester], and his son Harold succeeded to his earldom, and gave up the earldom he had had, which went to Ælfgar.

In this same year died Wulfsige, bishop of Lichfield, and Leofwine,

(*continued on p.* 184)

D 1052
from
p. 181

promoted injustice and pronounced unjust judgments and counselled evil within this realm, with the exception of as many of those whom they decided that the king was pleased to have about him, who were loyal to him and to all his people.

And archbishop Robert and bishop William and bishop Ulf escaped with difficulty with the Frenchmen who were with them, and so came oversea.

1053. In this year [1052] there was a high wind on St Thomas's eve [20 December], and the high wind lasted over Christmas. And Rhys, the brother of the Welsh king, was condemned to death for the crimes which he had committed, and his head was brought to Gloucester on the eve of the Epiphany. This same year, before All Saints' day [1 November], Wulfsige, bishop of Lichfield, passed away, and Godwine, abbot of Winchcombe, and Æthelweard, abbot of (*continued on p.* 185)

an unseaworthy ship and went immediately oversea, forsaking his pallium and all Christendom here in this land, which was from God's purpose since he had obtained that dignity against His will. Then a great council was summoned outside London, and all the earls and the most distinguished men in this land were present. There earl Godwine set forth his case, and cleared himself before king Edward, his lord, and before all the people of the country, that he was innocent of the charges brought against himself and against Harold, his son, and all his children. And the king took the earl and his children back into favour, and gave him back the whole of his earldom, and restored to him and all his supporters everything they had previously owned. Moreover the king restored to the Lady all her former possessions. Archbishop Robert was declared an outlaw unconditionally, together with all the Frenchmen, for they had been mainly responsible for the discord which had arisen between earl Godwine and the king. Bishop Stigand succeeded to the archbishopric of Canterbury. At this time Earnwig, abbot of Peterborough, resigned although still in good health, and gave the abbacy to Leofric the monk, with the king's permission and with the consent of the monks; and abbot Earnwig survived eight years. Abbot Leofric endowed the monastery thereafter so that it became known as 'Golden Borough': when it increased greatly in land, in gold, and in silver.[1]

1053. In this year, on 15 April, passed away earl Godwine. He is buried in Winchester in the Old Minster; earl Harold, his son, succeeded to the earldom and to all (*continued on p.* 184)

ship and went immediately oversea, forsaking his pallium. Then a great council was summoned outside London, and all the most distinguished men in the land were present. There Godwine set forth his case, and cleared himself before king Edward of all the charges brought against him and his children. Archbishop Robert was declared an outlaw, together with all the Frenchmen, for they were the cause of all the ill feeling which had arisen between him and the king. Bishop Stigand succeeded to the archbishopric of Canterbury. (*continued on p.* 188)

---

[1] Cf. pp. 198–9 and note.

**E 1053
from** his father's possessions. Earl Ælfgar succeeded to the earldom which Harold had had.

p. 183 1054. Bellum apud Mare mortuum. In this year

(continued on p. 185*)*

**C 1053
from** abbot of Coventry, succeeded to the bishopric. Also in this year died Æthelweard, abbot of Glastonbury, and Godwine, abbot of Winchcombe.

p. 182 Also in this year the Welsh slew a great number of the English frontier guards near Westbury.

In this year there was no [lawfully constituted] archbishop in this land, although bishop Stigand occupied the see of Canterbury in Christ Church: Cynesige of York and Leofwine and Wulfwig sought and received consecration oversea. Wulfwig succeeded to Ulf's bishopric during his lifetime and exile.

1054. In this year earl Siward marched with a great host into Scotland, and made great slaughter of Scots and put them to flight, but the king escaped. On his [Siward's] side fell many, both Danes and English, also his own son. This same year the church of Evesham was consecrated on 10 October. In this same year bishop Ealdred went south oversea to Germany, and was received there with great honour. In this same year Osgod Clapa died suddenly in his bed.

1055. In this year passed away earl Siward at York, and his body lies within the church at *Galmanho*,[1] which he himself had built to the glory of God and all His Saints. A short time after this there was a council in London, and earl Ælfgar, son of earl Leofric, was outlawed without having done anything to deserve his fate. Thereupon he went to Ireland, and added a force of eighteen ships to his own household troops,[2] and sailed to Wales to king Gruffydd with that host; and he took him under his protection. Then they raised great levies of Irish and Welsh, and earl Ralph gathered great levies *(continued on p.* 186*)*

---

[1] Galmanhowe, York, a lost place-name. (14 EPN 288)
[2] His *comites* evidently voluntarily went into exile with him. 'If the lord was driven into exile his men were expected to follow him' (H. M. Chadwick, *The Origin of the English Nation* 167). After Ælfgar's reinstatement (*v.* p. 186), these recruits to his personal following (*sciplið*) go to Chester to be paid for their services.

E 1054 from p. 184
passed away Leo, the holy pope in Rome. In this year there was a great pestilence among cattle, greater than anyone could remember for many years previous. Victor was elected pope. 1055. In this year earl Siward passed away; and a full council was summoned seven days before mid Lent [19 March], and earl Ælfgar was outlawed on the charge of being a traitor to the king and the whole nation. He admitted his guilt (*continued on p.* 186)

D 1053 from p. 182
Glastonbury, all within a month. Leofwine succeeded to the bishopric of Lichfield, and bishop Ealdred to the abbacy of Winchcombe, and Æthelnoth to the abbacy of Glastonbury. This same year passed away Ælfric, brother of Odda, at Deerhurst, and his body rests at Pershore. This same year earl Godwine passed away; he was taken ill while he was staying with the king at Winchester. Harold, his son, succeeded to his father's earldom, and earl Ælfgar to the earldom which Harold had had.

1054. In this year earl Siward invaded Scotland with a great host both by sea and land, and fought against Scots. He put to flight their king Macbeth, and slew the noblest in the land, carrying off much plunder such as none had previously gained; but his son,[3] Osbern, and his sister's son, Siward, and numbers of his housecarles as well as those of the king, were slain there on the festival of the Seven Sleepers [27 July]. This same year bishop Ealdred went oversea to Cologne on a mission for the king, and was there received with great ceremony by the emperor. He stayed there almost a year, and was entertained both by the bishop of Cologne and by the emperor, and he gave permission to bishop Leofwine to consecrate the monastery church at Evesham on 10 October. In this same year Osgod died suddenly in his bed. Pope St Leo passed away, and Victor was elected pope in his stead.

1055. In this year passed away earl Siward at York, and he was buried at *Galmaho*[1] in the church which he himself had had built and consecrated in the name of God and [St] Olaf,[4] and Tostig succeeded to his earldom. Archbishop Cynesige fetched his pallium from pope Victor.

Not long afterwards earl Ælfgar, son of earl Leofric, was outlawed almost without having done anything to deserve his fate; but he went to Ireland and to Wales and raised there a great force, and marched on Hereford; but earl Ralph came against him with a great host, and after a brief encounter (*continued on p.* 187)

---

[3] Cf. Shakespeare's *Macbeth* V. 3.
[4] Cf. Bruce Dickins, 12 *Saga-book of the Viking Society* 56.

E 1055
from
p. 185
before all the men there assembled, although the confession escaped him unawares.

To Tostig, son of earl Godwine, the king gave the earldom
(*continued on p.* 187)

C 1055
from
p. 184
to oppose them at Hereford, and they came together there: but before a spear was thrown, the English fled, because they had been made to fight on horseback. Many of them were slain, about four hundred or perhaps five, but none of their opponents, who went to the town and burned it to the ground. And the famous cathedral which the venerable bishop Athelstan had had built, that they plundered and despoiled of relics, vestments, and all its treasures: they slew the inhabitants and some they carried off. Then levies were called out from all the neighbouring districts of England; and they came to Gloucester and went a little way into Wales, and remained there for a time whilst Earl Harold had an earthwork built around the town [i.e. Hereford]. Meanwhile terms of peace were proposed: and earl Harold and those who were with him came to Billingsley, and established peace and friendship between them there. The sentence of outlawry against earl Ælfgar was revoked, and he was restored to all the possessions of which he had been deprived. The household troops in the ships went to Chester, and there waited for their pay which Ælfgar had promised them. That massacre had taken place on 24 October. In this same year, soon after the raid, Tremerig, the Welsh bishop, passed away; he was bishop Athelstan's deputy after he [Athelstan] became an invalid.

[1056.] In this year died the venerable bishop Athelstan on 10 February, and he was buried at Hereford. Leofgar, who was earl Harold's chaplain, was appointed to succeed him; he wore his moustaches during his priesthood until he became bishop. After his consecration he forsook his chrism and his cross, his spiritual weapons, and seized his spear and his sword, and thus armed joined the levies against Gruffydd, the Welsh king: and there he was slain and his priests who were with him, together with Ælfnoth the sheriff, and many good men with them, while the rest escaped. This took place eight days before midsummer. It is heart-breaking to tell of all the hardship, and of all the marching and campaigning, and of all the toil and loss of men and horses, which all the English host endured, until earl Leofric arrived with earl Harold and bishop Ealdred and made peace between them. In consequence, Gruffydd swore oaths that he would be a loyal and faithful under-king to king Edward. Bishop Ealdred succeeded to the bishopric which Leofgar had held for eleven weeks and four days. In this same year died the emperor Cona [Henry III, who succeeded Conrad II]. This same year died earl Odda, and he was buried at Pershore: he became a professed monk before his end. He died on 31 August. (*continued on p.* 190)

186

which had previously been earl Siward's. Earl Ælfgar sought
E 1055 Gruffydd's protection in Wales; and in this year Gruffydd and
from Ælfgar burnt to the ground St Æthelberht's [1] cathedral and all
p. 186 the borough of Hereford.

1056. Hic Henricus Romanorum imperator obiit, cui
successit filius eius Henricus.

1057. In this year came prince Edward, king Edmund's

(*continued on p.* 188)

they were put to flight, and many were slain in that rout.
D 1055 Then they entered Hereford and plundered it, burnt to the
from ground the famous cathedral which bishop Athelstan had
p. 185 built, killed the priests inside the cathedral and many others
besides, and seized all the treasures therein and carried them
off. And then when they had done most damage, it was decided to
revoke the sentence of outlawry against earl Ælfgar, and to restore him
to his earldom and all the possessions of which he had been deprived.
This raid took place on 24 October. In this same year, soon after the
raid, Tremerin, the Welsh bishop, passed away; he was bishop Athelstan's deputy, after he [Athelstan] became an invalid.

1056. In this year bishop Æthelric gave up his bishopric at Durham
and retired to Peterborough to St Peter's, and his brother Æthelwine
succeeded him. Also in this year bishop Athelstan passed away on
10 February, and he was buried at Hereford. Leofgar, who was earl
Harold's chaplain, was appointed to succeed him: he kept his moustaches during his priesthood until he became bishop. He forsook his
chrism and his cross and his spiritual weapons, seized his spear and his
sword, and thus armed joined the levies against Gruffydd, the Welsh
king: and there he was slain and his priests who were with him, together
with Ælfnoth the sheriff and many other good men. This took place
eight days before midsummer. Bishop Ealdred succeeded to the
bishopric which Leofgar had held for eleven weeks and four days.
This same year earl Odda passed away, and he was buried at Pershore:
he became a professed monk before his end. He was a good man, pure
and very noble: he died on 31 August. And the emperor Cona [Henry
III, who succeeded Conrad II] passed away.

1057.   Now came prince Edward to England,
           Son of the brother of king Edward,
           Son of king Edmund, known as Ironside
           For his valour.

(*continued on p.* 188)

---

[1] The East Anglian king slain by Offa (see annal 792).

son, hither to this land, but died soon after, and was buried in
E 1057 St Paul's cathedral in London. In this year pope Victor
from passed away and Stephen was elected pope: he had been abbot
p. 187 of Monte Cassino.[1] Earl Leofric passed away, and Ælfgar,
his son, succeeded to the earldom which his father had had.

1058. In this year pope Stephen passed away, and Benedict was consecrated pope, the same who sent the pallium to archbishop Stigand
hither to this land. And in this year Heca, *(continued on p.* 189)

	This prince king Cnut had banished
D 1057	Into Hungary to be put out of the way,
from	But he there grew up to be a good man
p. 187	As God granted and as became him well,

So that he won the emperor's kinswoman for wife
(And by her begat a noble family),
Whose name was Agatha.
We do not know for what reason
It was so arranged that he could not see
His kinsman, king Edward.
Alas! his was a cruel fate, and disastrous
To all this nation:
That he ended his life so soon
After he came to England,
To the misfortune of this wretched people.

In this same year, on 30 October, earl Leofric passed away. He was
very wise in all matters, both religious and secular, that benefited all
this nation. He was buried at Coventry, and his son Ælfgar succeeded
to his authority. In this year, on 21 December, earl Ralph passed away
and was buried at Peterborough. Also died Heca, bishop of Sussex,
and Æthelric was exalted to his see. In this year pope Victor passed
away, and Stephen was elected pope.

1058. In this year earl Ælfgar was driven out of the country, but he
soon returned with violence through the help of Gruffydd. In this year
came a pirate host from Norway; *(continued on p.* 189)

1058. . . . In this year pope Stephen passed away, and Bene-
F 1058 dict was consecrated in his place. This same year he sent the
from pallium to archbishop Stigand, hither to this land. Bishop
p. 183 Heca passed away, and archbishop Stigand consecrated
Æthelric from Christ Church as bishop of Sussex, and abbot
Siward as bishop of Rochester.

Here ends F

---

[1] With the Latin of these words (*s.a.* 1057) and the numeral 1058 ends
F Lat

bishop of Sussex, passed away; and archbishop Stigand conse-
E 1058 crated Æthelric, who was a monk at Christ Church [Canter-
from bury], as bishop of Sussex, and abbot Siward as bishop of
p. 188 Rochester.

1059. In this year Nicholas was elected pope: he had been bishop of the city of Florence. The previous pope, Benedict, was expelled.

1060. Hic Henricus rex Francorum obiit, cui successit Phylippus filius eius. In this year passed away Cynesige, archbishop of York, on 22 December, and bishop Ealdred succeeded him. Walter succeeded to the bishopric of Hereford.

1061. In this year Duduc, bishop of Somerset, passed away and Giso succeeded him. In this same year, on 9 March, Godwine, bishop at St Martin's [Canterbury], passed away. In this same

(*continued on p.* 190)

it is tedious to tell how it all happened. In this same year
D 1058 bishop Ealdred consecrated the church at Gloucester which he
from himself had restored to the glory of God and of St Peter: there-
p. 188 after he went to Jerusalem, with greater ceremony than any
before him, and there commended himself to God. He made
an offering of a splendid gift to our Lord's Sepulchre: it was a golden chalice of the value of five marks, and of most admirable workmanship. In this same year pope Stephen passed away, and Benedict was appointed pope. He sent the pallium to bishop Stigand. Æthelric was consecrated bishop of Sussex and abbot Siward bishop of Rochester.

1059. In this year Nicholas was elected pope: he had been bishop of the city of Florence. The previous pope, Benedict, was expelled. On 17 October this same year, the tower at Peterborough was consecrated.

1060. In this year, on the festival of the Translation of St Martin [4 July], there was a great earthquake. In France king Henry passed away. Archbishop Cynesige of York died on 22 December, and he lies at Peterborough, and was succeeded by bishop Ealdred. Walter succeeded to the bishopric of Herefordshire. Duduc, who was bishop of Somerset, also passed away; and Giso, the priest, was appointed to succeed him.

1061. In this year bishop Ealdred went to Rome for his pallium, and received it from pope Nicholas. Earl Tostig and his wife also went to Rome: and the bishop and the earl suffered great (*continued on p.* 191)

year Wulfric, abbot of St Augustine's [Canterbury], passed
E 1061 away on 18 April in Easter week. When word came to the
from king that abbot Wulfric had passed away, he appointed
p. 189 Æthelsige, a monk from the Old Minster [Winchester], in his
place, and complied with the wish of archbishop Stigand. He
was consecrated abbot at Windsor on St Augustine's day [26 May].

1062. Hoc anno subiuguta [*sic*] est Cynomannia comiti Normanniæ
Willelmo.

1063. In this year earl Harold and his brother earl Tostig invaded
Wales both with land and naval levies, and conquered that land: the
inhabitants gave hostages and submitted to them, and then turned
against Gruffydd, their king, and slew him, and brought his head to
Harold, who put another king in his place.

1064[1] [1063]. In this year the Northumbrians united to outlaw
Tostig, their earl. They slew all his retainers whom they could catch,
whether English or Dane, and took his stock of weapons to York, his
gold and silver and all his treasures which they came to hear of anywhere there. They sent for Morcar, sone of earl Ælfgar, and chose him
to be their earl. He marched south with all the men of the shire,
together with men from the shires of Nottingham, Derby, and Lincoln,
and until he came to Northampton, where he was joined by his brother
Edwin and men from his earldom, with whom were many Welshmen.
There came earl Harold to meet them, and they charged him with a
mission (*continued on p.* 191)

1065. In this year before Lammas [1 August] earl Harold
C 1065 had building started at Portskewet in Wales now he had
from conquered it; there he gathered together much property,
p. 186 thinking to invite king Edward there for the sake of the
hunting. When most of it had been assembled, Caradog,
Gruffydd's son, came up with as large a force as he could muster, slew
most of the workmen, and carried off the movables which had been got
together there. This slaughter took place on St Bartholomew's day
[24 August]. Then, after Michaelmas, all the thanes of Yorkshire met
at York, and there slew all the housecarles of earl Tostig whom they
could discover, and seized his treasures. (*continued on p.* 192)

---

[1] All the chronicles leave the year 1064 blank except E, who has written
the events of 1065 under that figure. He omits 1065, and so returns to the
correct dating with 1066.

E 1064
[1065] to king Edward, and sent messengers to accompany him
from   (*continued on p.* 192)
p. 190

hardship on their homeward journey.   In this year Godwine,
D 1061 bishop at St Martin's [Canterbury], passed away, also Wulfric,
from   abbot of St Augustine's [Canterbury], on 19 March [*sic*].
p. 189 Pope Nicholas passed away, and Alexander, bishop of Lucca,
was elected to succeed him.

1063. In this year [1062] after Christmas, earl Harold marched from
Gloucester to Rhuddlan, the seat of Gruffydd, and burnt his residence,
his ships and all their sails, and put him to flight.   Then, towards
Rogation days, Harold sailed with a fleet from Bristol, round Wales,
and the Welsh made peace with him and gave hostages.   Meanwhile
Tostig marched against them with land levies, and overran the country.
This same year, however, in autumn, on 5 August, king Gruffydd was
slain by his own men, on account of the struggle he was waging against
earl Harold.   He was king over the whole of Wales.   His head was
brought to earl Harold, who brought it to the king, together with the
figure-head of his ship and the adornments with it.   King Edward
entrusted that country to his two brothers, Bleddyn and Rhiwallon:
they gave hostages to the king and to the earl and swore oaths that they
would be loyal to him in all things, ready to serve him everywhere on
sea and land, and to render such tribute from that country as had
formerly been paid to their late king.

1065. In this year before Lammas [1 August], earl Harold had
building started at Portskewet in Wales now he had conquered it: there
he gathered together much property, thinking to invite king Edward
there for the sake of the hunting.   But when all was ready, then
Caradog, Gruffydd's son, came up with as large a force as he could
muster, slew most of the workmen, and carried off the movables which
had been got together there.   We do not know who first suggested
this mischief.   It happened on St Bartholomew's day [24 August].
Soon afterwards all the thanes of Yorkshire and Northumberland
came together and outlawed their earl Tostig, slew all his retainers
whom they could catch, whether English or Dane, and seized his
stock of weapons in York, his gold and silver and all his treasures which
they came to hear of anywhere there.   They sent for Morcar, son of
earl Ælfgar, and chose him to be their earl.   He marched south with all
the men of the shire, together with men from the shires of Nottingham,
Derby, and Lincoln (*continued on p.* 193)

E 1064 [1065] from p. 191   to request that they could have Morcar as their earl. This the king granted, and sent Harold back to them at Northampton, on the eve of the festival of St Simon and St Jude [27 October], to announce this same decision to them, giving them pledges, and re-enacted there the laws of Cnut. While he was away on their mission, the northerners did much damage around Northampton: not only did they slay men and burn houses and corn, but carried off all the livestock they could find, amounting to many thousands. They took many hundreds of captives, and carried them off north with them, so that that shire and the other neighbouring shires were for many years the poorer. Tostig, (*continued on p.* 193)

C 1065 from p. 190   Tostig was then at Britford with the king. Very soon thereafter a great council was held at Northampton, and another at Oxford, on the festival of St Simon and St Jude; and earl Harold was present and tried to do all he could to bring them to an agreement, but was unsuccessful. All the men of his [Tostig's] earldom were unanimous in repudiating him, and outlawed him and all those with him who had promoted injustice, because he robbed God first, and then despoiled of life and land all those over whom he could tyrannize. They took Morcar as their earl, and Tostig then went oversea with his wife to the land of Baldwin, and took winter-quarters at St Omer. King Edward came to Westminster towards Christmas, and there had the abbey church consecrated which he himself had built to the glory of God, St Peter, and all God's saints: the consecration of the church was on Holy Innocents' day [28 December]; and he passed away on the vigil of the Epiphany, and was buried on the Epiphany [6 January 1066] in this same abbey church as is told hereafter:

> Now did king Edward, lord of the English,
> Send his righteous soul to Christ,
> His holy spirit into God's keeping.
>   Here in the world he dwelt for a time
> In royal majesty, sagacious in counsel;
> A gracious ruler for twenty-four years
> And a half, he dispensed bounties.
> Ruler of warriors, son of Æthelred,
> Greatly distinguished, he ruled Welsh,
> Scots and also Britons too,
> Angles and Saxons and their champions.
>   So, surrounded by the cold sea wave,
> Lived those squires young and brave,
> Loyally obeying Edward their noble king.

(*continued on p.* 194)

E 1064
[1065] the earl, and his wife and all his supporters sailed south
from   (*continued on p.* 195)
p. 192

           until he came to Northampton, where he was joined by his
D 1065 brother Edwin and men from his earldom with whom were
from many Welshmen. There came earl Harold to meet them, and
p. 191 they charged him with a mission to king Edward, and sent
           messengers to accompany him to request that they might have
Morcar as their earl. This the king granted, and sent Harold back to
them at Northampton, on the eve of the festival of St Simon and St
Jude [27 October], to announce this same decision to them, giving them
pledges, and re-enacted there the laws of Cnut. While he was away on
their mission, the northerners[1] did much damage around Northampton:
not only did they slay men and burn houses and corn, but carried off all
the livestock they could find, amounting to many thousands. They
took many hundreds of captives, and carried them off north with them,
so that that shire and the other neighbouring shires were for many years
the poorer. Earl Tostig and his wife and all his supporters sailed south
oversea with him to count Baldwin, and he gave them all shelter, and
they were there the whole winter. King Edward came to Westminster
towards Christmas, and there had the abbey church consecrated which
he himself had built to the glory of God, St Peter, and all God's saints:
the consecration of the church was on Holy Innocents' day [28 December];
and he passed away on the vigil of the Epiphany, and was buried
on the Epiphany [6 January 1066] in this same abbey church as is told
hereafter:

           Now did king Edward, lord of the English,
           Send his righteous soul to Christ,
           His holy spirit into God's keeping.
              Here in the world he dwelt for a time
           In royal majesty, sagacious in counsel;
           A gracious ruler for twenty-four years
           He dispensed bounties and prosperous days.
           Ruler of warriors, son of Æthelred,
           Greatly distinguished, he ruled Welsh,
           Scots and also Britons too,
           Angles and Saxons and their champions.
              So, surrounded by the cold sea wave,
           Lived those squires young and brave,
           Loyally obeying Edward their noble king.

                                                    (*continued on p.* 195)

---

[1] MS. *þa ryðrenan*. Plummer considers this an error for *þa norðernan*.
If so, Prof. Dickins considers that the original form *nyrðrenan* suggests
Scandinavian influence (cf. ON *nyröri*, 'more northerly').

Ā **1066** 1066. In this year passed away king Edward, and earl Harold
from came to the throne and ruled for forty weeks and a day.
p. 182   *(continued on p.* 196)

    Ever full of cheer was the blameless king,
C 1065 Though for long in the past, deprived of his land,
from He had trodden an exile's path across the wide world,
p. 192 After Cnut had conquered the race of Æthelred,
    And Danes ruled over this dear land
    Of England for twenty-eight years
    All told, squandering its riches.
     In time he succeeded; noble in armour,
    A king of excellent virtues, pure and benign,
    Edward the noble protected his fatherland,
    His realm and people: until suddenly came
    That bitter death, which took so cruelly
    The prince from the earth. Angels bore his
    Righteous soul within Heaven's light.
     Yet did the wise king entrust his kingdom
    To a man of high rank, to Harold himself,
    The noble earl, who ever
    Faithfully obeyed his noble lord
    In words and deeds, neglecting nothing
    Whereof the national king stood in need.

In this year was Harold consecrated king, but was not to enjoy a
tranquil reign while he ruled the kingdom.

[1066.] In this year came king Harold from York to Westminster the
Easter following the Christmas of the king's death, Easter being on 16
April. At that time, throughout all England, a portent such as men
had never seen before was seen in the heavens. Some declared that the
star was a comet,[1] which some call 'the long-haired star': it first
appeared on the eve of the festival of *Letania maior*, that is on 24
April, and shone every night for a week. Soon thereafter came earl
Tostig from across the sea to the Isle of Wight, with as many household
troops as he could muster, and there he was given both money and provisions. He sailed thence, and did damage everywhere along the sea
coast where he could, until he came to Sandwich. When king Harold,
who was in London, learnt that his brother Tostig had come to Sandwich, he gathered together greater naval and land levies than any king
               (continued on p. 196)

---

[1] Pictured on the Bayeux Tapestry (cf. E. Maclagan, King Penguin Books,
1953, Plate 34)

oversea with him to count Baldwin, and he gave them all
E 1064 shelter, and they were there the whole winter.

[1065]   1066. In this year [1065] the abbey church at Westminster
from   was consecrated on Holy Innocents' day [28 December], and
p. 193   king Edward passed away (*continued on p.* 197)

Ever full of cheer was the blameless king,
D 1065   Though for long in the past, deprived of his land,
from   He had trodden an exile's path across the wide world,
p. 193   After Cnut had conquered the race of Æthelred,
And Danes ruled over this dear land
Of England for twenty-eight years
All told, squandering its riches.
    In time he succeeded; noble in armour,
A king of excellent virtues, pure and benign,
Edward the noble protected his fatherland,
His realm and people: until suddenly came
That bitter death, which took so cruelly
The prince from the earth.   Angels bore his
Righteous soul within Heaven's light.
    Yet did the wise king entrust his kingdom
To a man of high rank, to Harold himself,
The noble earl, who ever
Faithfully obeyed his noble lord
In words and deeds, neglecting nothing
Whereof the national king stood in need.

In this year was Harold consecrated king, but was not to enjoy a
tranquil reign while he ruled the kingdom.

1066. In this year came king Harold from York to Westminster, the
Easter following the Christmas of the king's death, Easter being on 16
April.   At that time, throughout all England, a portent such as men had
never seen before was seen in the heavens.   Some declared that the star
was a comet, which some call 'the long-haired star': it first appeared
on the eve of the festival of *Letania maior*, that is on 24 April, and
shone every night for a week.   Soon thereafter came earl Tostig to this
country from across the sea to the Isle of Wight, with as many household troops as he could muster, and there he was given both money and
provisions.   King Harold, his brother, gathered together greater naval
and land hosts than any king (*continued on p.* 197)

Ā 1066
from
p. 194
In this year came William and conquered England; and in this year Christ Church [Canterbury] was burned, and a comet appeared on 18 April. (*continued on p.* 204)

C 1066
from
p. 194
in this country had ever gathered before, for he was credibly informed that duke William of Normandy, kinsman of king Edward, was about to invade to conquer this land, just as it subsequently came to pass. When Tostig learnt that king Harold was on his way to Sandwich, he sailed away, taking with him shipmen from the port; some went willingly, but others unwillingly. He sailed north into [the Humber],[1] and there harried in Lindsey, slaying many good men there. When earl Edwin and earl Morcar perceived this, they marched thither and drove him out from the land. Thereupon he sailed to Scotland, where the king of Scots took him under his protection and helped him to obtain provisions, and there he stayed the whole summer. Then came king Harold to Sandwich, and waited there for his household troops to gather, because it took a long time for them to be mobilized. When they had assembled, he then sailed to the Isle of Wight, and lay there the whole summer and autumn, and the levies were stationed everywhere along the coast, although in the end it was all to no purpose. When the festival of the Nativity of St Mary came [8 September], the men's provisions had run out, and no one could keep them there any longer: they were therefore given permission to return home. Then the king rode up and the ships were sailed in to London, but many were lost before they arrived. Then while the ships were in port, king Harold from Norway came unexpectedly north into the Tyne with a great pirate host—it was anything but small, for it numbered about [three hundred ships] [1] or more—and earl Tostig joined him, as they had previously agreed, with all the host he had been able to muster. They sailed together with their combined troops along the Ouse up towards York. King Harold, to the south, was informed when he came ashore that king Harold of Norway and earl Tostig had landed near York. Thereupon he marched northward, day and night, as quickly as he could assemble his levies; but before king Harold could arrive, earl Edwin and earl Morcar had gathered as great a force as they could from their earldom, and fought that host and made great slaughter of them; but a great number of the English were either slain or drowned or driven in flight, and the Norwegians had possession of the place of slaughter. This battle took place on the vigil of St Matthew the Apostle [20 September] which was a Wednesday. After the battle (*continued on p.* 197)

[1] Space in MS.

on the vigil of, and was buried on, Epiphany [6 January] in the newly consecrated abbey church of Westminster. Earl Harold succeeded to the kingdom of England as the king granted it to him and as he was elected thereto. He was consecrated king on Epiphany. In the same year in which he became king, he sailed out against William with a naval force. Meanwhile earl Tostig came into the Humber with sixty ships, and earl Edwin came with land levies and drove him out, and the shipmen deserted him. He sailed to Scotland with twelve small vessels, where he was met by Harold, the Norwegian king, with three hundred ships, to whom Tostig gave allegiance. Together they sailed into the Humber until they came to York, where earl Morcar and earl Edwin fought against them, and the Norwegian king gained the victory. When king Harold was informed what had happened and come to pass, he came with a great host (*continued on p.* 198)

(left margin: E 1066 from p. 195)

had ever done in this country, because he was informed that William the Bastard was about to invade this land to conquer it, just as it subsequently came to pass. Meanwhile earl Tostig came into the Humber with sixty ships, and earl Edwin came with land levies and drove him out, and the shipmen deserted him. He sailed to Scotland with twelve small vessels, where he was met by king Harold from Norway with three hundred ships, to whom Tostig gave allegiance and became his man. Together they sailed into the Humber until they came to York, where earl Edwin and earl Morcar, his brother, fought against them, but the Norwegians had the victory. Then king Harold was informed how the fight had gone—it took place on the vigil of St Matthew's day [20 September]. Then Harold our king came unexpectedly upon the Norwegians, and met them beyond York at Stamford Bridge with a great host

(*continued on p.* 199)

(left margin: D 1066 from p. 195)

king Harold of Norway and earl Tostig entered York with as great a force as seemed to them necessary and received hostages from the borough, besides assistance in the way of provisions, and so retired thence to their ships. They offered to conclude an abiding peace with the citizens provided that they all marched southwards with them to conquer this realm. Then meanwhile came Harold, the king of the English, with all his levies on the Sunday to Tadcaster and there drew up his household troops in battle order;[1] and on the Monday he marched through York. Harold, king of Norway, and earl Tostig and their (*continued on p.* 198)

(left margin: C 1066 from p. 196)

---

[1] i.e. expecting an attack from York. For this interpretation of *lið fylcade* I am indebted to Prof. Dickins.

of Englishmen, and met him at Stamford Bridge, and slew him
E 1066 and earl Tostig and courageously defeated all that host.
from Meanwhile duke William landed at Hastings on St Michael's
p. 197 day [29 September], and Harold marched from the north,
and fought against him before all his host came up; and there
he fell with his two brothers, Gurth and Leofwine. William
conquered this land, and came to Westminster, and bishop Ealdred
consecrated him king. Men paid him tribute, and gave him hostages,
and then redeemed their lands from him.

[1] Leofric, abbot of Peterborough, took part in this campaign, and
there fell ill and returned home: he died soon afterwards on the eve of
All Saints [31 October]. God have mercy on his soul. In his day the
abbey of Peterborough enjoyed complete happiness and prosperity,
and he was beloved by everybody. So the king gave to him and St
Peter the abbacy of Burton-on-Trent, and the abbacy of Coventry,
which his uncle, earl Leofric, had founded, and those of Crowland and
Thorney. More than any man before or since he enriched the abbey of
Peterborough with gold and silver, with vestments and land.

(*continued on p.* 199)

force had gone from their ships beyond York to Stamford
C 1066 Bridge, for it had been expressly promised them that hostages
from would be brought to meet them there from the whole of the
p. 197 shire. Then Harold, king of the English, came upon them
unawares beyond the bridge. They joined battle and fierce
fighting went on until late in the day; and there Harold, king of Norway,
was slain and earl Tostig and countless numbers of men with them, both
English and Norwegians. The Norwegians *fled from the English, but
there was one Norwegian who stood firm against the English forces, so that
they could not cross the bridge nor clinch victory. An Englishman shot
with an arrow but to no avail, and another went under the bridge and stabbed
him through under the coat of mail. Then Harold, king of the English, crossed
the bridge and his levies went forward with him; and there made great slaughter
of both Norwegians and Flemings: and Harold let the king's son, who was
called Mundus* [the 'Elegant'],[2] *return to Norway with all the ships.*

Here ends C, the conclusion (from *fled*) having been added by a
twelfth-century scribe. (See Bruce Dickins, 5 *Proc. Leeds Philosophical
Society, Lit.-Hist.* 148–9.) The orthography of the conclusion is discussed by C. T. Onions, 4 *MLR* 505–7.

[1] On the resemblance of this and other entries to entries in the Latin
Chronicle of Hugo Candidus, a Peterborough monk writing about the
middle of the twelfth century, see W. T. Mellows, *The Chronicle of Hugh
Candidus* (Oxford 1949) xxiv ff.; this was translated by C. & W. T. Mellows
(Peterborough 1941). Leofric was the nephew of Earl Leofric of Coventry,
and Lady Godiva was his aunt. Hugh describes (Mellows 66) abbot Leofric's gifts to the monastery: Sed et magnam crucem que super altare est
mirabili opere de argento et auro fecit. Candelabra etiam aurea et argentea

Then 'Golden Borough' became 'Wretched Borough.' The
E 1066 monks chose Brand the provost as abbot, because he was a very
from good and wise man: they sent him to prince Edgar because the
p. 198 people of that district thought he ought to be king, and the
prince gladly consented to Brand's election. When king
William heard of it, he was very angry, and said that the abbot had
slighted him. By the intervention of good men, they were reconciled,
because the abbot was a virtuous man. He gave the king forty marks
of gold in reconciliation, and lived for but a short time thereafter, for
only three years. Thereafter all manner of calamities and evils befell
the monastery.[3] God have mercy upon it. (*continued on p.* 200)

of Englishmen, and that day a very stubborn battle was fought
D 1066 by both sides. There were slain Harold the Fairhaired [*recte*
from Hardrada] and earl Tostig, and the remaining Norwegians
p. 197 were put to flight, while the English fiercely assailed their rear
until some of them reached their ships: some were drowned,
others burnt to death, and thus perished in various ways so that there
were few survivors, and the English had possession of the place of
slaughter. The king then gave quarter to Olaf, the son of the king
of the Norwegians, to their bishop, to the jarl of Orkney, and to all
those who were left aboard the ships. They then went inland to our
king, and swore oaths that they would ever maintain peace and friendship with this land; and the king let them sail home with twenty-four
ships. These two pitched battles were fought within five days.
Then duke William sailed from Normandy into Pevensey, on the eve
of Michaelmas [28 September]. As soon as his men were fit for service,
they constructed a castle at Hastings. When king Harold was informed
of this, he gathered together a great host, and came to oppose him at the
grey apple-tree, and William came upon him unexpectedly before his
army was set in order. Nevertheless the king fought against him most
resolutely with those men who wished to stand by him, and there was
great slaughter on both sides. King Harold was slain, and Leofwine,
his brother, and earl Gurth, his brother, and many good men. The
French had possession of the place of slaughter, as God granted
them because of the nation's sins. Archbishop Ealdred and the
citizens of London wished to have prince Edgar for king, as was indeed
his right by birth, and Edwin and Morcar promised that they would
fight for him, but always when some initiative should have been shewn
(*continued on p.* 200)

---

et magnam tabulam ante altare totam auro et argento et preciosis gemmis, et
plurima feretra et texta euuangeliorum et multas alias res, similiter omnia
ex auro et argento fecit. . . . Ditatusque est locus ille in tempore eius in
terris et in auro et argento et uariis ornamentis incredibiliter, ita ut non iam
simpliciter Burch, set Gildineburch, hoc est aurea ciuitas, merito uocaretur.
[2] The original reading (partly erased) was *sunu þe het mundus*
[2] Cf. *The Chronicle of Hugh Candidus* (ed. Mellows), 76–7. Abbot Brand
was the uncle of Hereward the Wake.

1067. In this year the king went oversea, and took with him hostages and treasure. He returned the next year on St Nicholas's day [6 December]. That same day Christ Church in Canterbury was burned to the ground. When he returned he gave away every man's land. In the summer of the same year

E 1067
from
p. 199

(continued on p. 201)

there was delay from day to day until matters went from bad to worse, as everything did in the end. This battle took place on the day of pope Calixtus [14 October]. Duke William returned to Hastings, and waited there to see if there would be any surrender; but when he realized that none were willing to come to him, he marched inland with what was left of his host, together with reinforcements lately come from oversea, and harried that part of the country through which he advanced until he came to Berkhamsted. There he was met by bishop Ealdred, prince Edgar, earl Edwin, earl Morcar, and all the best men from London, who submitted from force of circumstances, but only when the depredation was complete. It was great folly that they had not done so sooner when God would not remedy matters because of our sins. They gave him hostages and swore oaths of fealty, and he promised to be a gracious lord to them. Nevertheless, in the meantime, they harried everywhere they came. Then on Christmas day archbishop Ealdred consecrated him king in Westminster; and William gave a pledge on the Gospels, and swore an oath besides, before Ealdred would place the crown on his head, that he would govern this nation according to the best practice of his predecessors if they would be loyal to him. Nevertheless he imposed a very heavy tax on the country, and went oversea to Normandy in the spring, taking with him archbishop Stigand, Æthelnoth, abbot of Glastonbury, prince Edgar, earl Edwin, earl Morcar, earl Waltheof, and many other good men from England. Bishop Odo and earl William were left behind here, and they built castles far and wide throughout the land, oppressing the unhappy people, and things went ever from bad to worse. When God wills may the end be good.

D 1066
from
p. 199

1067. In this year the king returned to England on St Nicholas's day [6 December]. That same day Christ Church in Canterbury was burnt down. Bishop Wulfwig passed away, and is buried in Dorchester, his episcopal see. Eadric 'the Wild'[1] and the Welsh rose in rebellion and attacked the garrison of the [Norman] castle at Hereford, and inflicted severe losses upon them. In this year the king imposed a heavy tax upon the unhappy people of the country,

(continued on p. 201)

---

[1] MS. *Eadric cild*. Plummer suggests *cild* is a mistake here for *se wilda* (i.e. Eadric 'the Wild'). See Ordericus Vitalis, *Ecclesiastical History*, trans. Forester II. 4, 26.

E 1067
from
p. 200 prince Edgar left the country, accompanied by Mærleswein and many others: they went to Scotland where king Malcolm received them all, and took Margaret, the young prince's sister, to wife. (*continued on p.* 202)

D 1067
from
p. 200 yet notwithstanding he allowed his men to harry wherever they came. He marched to Devonshire, and besieged the borough of Exeter for eighteen days. Although a great part of his host was destroyed there, he made favourable promises to the citizens which were badly kept: they surrendered the borough to him, because the thanes had deserted them.

In the summer of this year prince Edgar left the country, accompanied by Agatha, his mother, his two sisters, Margaret and Christina, and Mærleswein and many good men with them. They came to Scotland and took sanctuary with king Malcolm, who welcomed them all. King Malcolm was very anxious to marry Edgar's sister, Margaret, but both the prince and his men opposed it for a long time, and the lady herself was unwilling.

> She swore she would be no man's bride,
> Nor his, should the Celestial Mercy so ordain
> Her heart within the flesh to keep,
> In maidenhood and purest continence,
> In this brief life, her Mighty Lord to please.

The king eagerly pressed his suit with her brother, until he gave his consent: in fact he dared not do otherwise, for they had sought refuge in his kingdom. So it came to pass as directed by God's Providence: it could not be otherwise, just as He Himself says in His gospel that not even one sparrow can fall into a snare without His foreknowledge. The prescient Creator knew beforehand what His will was for her: for she was destined to increase the glory of God in that land, to turn the king aside from the path of error, to incline him together with his people towards a better way of life, and to abolish the vices which that nation had indulged in in the past—all of which she subsequently accomplished.

She was then [1] married to the king, although against her will: and her conduct pleased him. He thanked God, who in His omnipotence had given him such a wife, and reflected wisely, since he was an exceedingly prudent man, and turned toward God, and despised every kind of impurity. As Paul, the apostle, the teacher of all nations, said, *Saluabitur uir infidelis per mulierem fidelem.* (*continued on p.* 202)

[1] 1070.

E 1068
from
p. 201

1068. In this year king William gave earl Robert the earldom of Northumberland, but [1069] the inhabitants opposed and slew him and nine hundred of his men. Prince Edgar came to York with all the Northumbrians, and the citizens came to terms with him. King William marched from the south with all his levies and ravaged the borough, slaying many hundreds, and the prince returned to Scotland.

1069. In this year bishop Æthelric of Peterborough was accused, and he was sent to Westminster, and his brother, bishop Æthelwine, was outlawed. Then between the two festivals of St Mary [The Assumption, 15 August, and the Nativity, 8 September], the sons of Swein [1] and his brother, jarl Osbern, came from the east from Denmark with three hundred ships; (continued on p. 203)

D 1067
from
p. 201

Sic et mulier infidelis per virum fidelem, et r[e]l[iqua], which in our language means: 'Very often an unbeliever is sanctified and saved by a righteous woman; and in like manner, a woman by a devout husband, etc.' This aforesaid queen performed many useful works in that land to the glory of God, and proved of great advantage to the monarchy, as was to be expected from her ancestry. She was sprung from devout and noble kindred; her father was prince Edward, the son of king Edmund, the son of Æthelred, the son of Edgar, the son of Eadred [*sic*], and so forth in that royal line: on her mother's side she was descended from the emperor Henry who had dominion over Rome.[2]

In this year Gytha, mother of Harold, went out to the Isle of Flatholme and the wives of many good men accompanied her: she remained there for some time, and went thence oversea to St Omer.

In the Easter of this year the king came to Winchester. In that year [1068] Easter was on 23 March. Soon the Lady Matilda came hither to this land, and archbishop Ealdred consecrated her queen in Westminster on Whit Sunday [1068]. When the king was informed that the people in the north had gathered together, and would oppose him if he came, he marched to Nottingham and built a castle there, and so on to York, and there built two castles, and also in Lincoln, and in many other places in that part of the country. Earl Gospatric and the best men went into Scotland. (continued on p. 203)

---

[1] Swein Estrithson, king of Denmark.
[2] For a more realistic estimate of her character see A. L. Poole, *From Domesday Book to Magna Carta* (Oxford 1951), 267.

then earl Waltheof took the field, and with prince Edgar and many hundreds of men came and joined those troops [3] that were lying in the Humber, and set out for York. They landed and stormed the castles, slaying many hundreds. They carried off much treasure to their ships and made prisoners of the leading citizens, and lay between the Ouse and the Trent the whole winter. King William marched into that shire and completely devastated it. In the same year, on 27 November, passed away Brand, abbot of Peterborough. (*continued on p.* 205)

E 1069 from p. 202

In the meantime [1068] Harold's sons came [4] unexpectedly from Ireland into the mouth of the Avon with a pirate host, and straightway harried all that part of the country; then they sailed to Bristol to storm the borough, but the citizens stoutly resisted them; and when they were unable to gain anything from the borough, they retired to their ships with their plunder, and sailed to Somerset and landed there. Eadnoth, the staller, fought against them, and was slain there, together with many good men on each side; and the survivors sailed away thence.

D 1067 from p. 202

1068. In this year king William gave earl Robert the earldom of Northumberland, but [1069] the inhabitants surprised him inside the borough of Durham, and slew him and nine hundred of his men. Immediately thereafter came prince Edgar to York with all the Northumbrians, and the citizens came to terms with him. King William came unexpectedly upon them from the south with an overwhelming host, and routed them, and slew several hundreds of those who could not escape. He plundered the borough, and made St Peter's church an object of scorn, and also plundered and humiliated all the others. The prince returned again to Scotland.

After these events, towards midsummer of that year, the sons of Harold came from Ireland into the mouth of the Taw,[5] and there incautiously landed. Earl Brian surprised them with a considerable force, fought against them, and slew all the best men from the troops [3] while the few survivors escaped to their ships. The sons of Harold returned again to Ireland.

In this year passed away Ealdred, archbishop of York: he is buried there (*continued on p.* 204)

---

[3] Here *lið* is used of Swein's Danish forces (cf. also pp. 206–7), and also of those of the sons of Harold Godwineson from Ireland.

[4] Prof. Dickins suggests that the MS *com an* is a wrong division of *coman* (pret. pl.)

[5] Which runs into Bideford Bay, Devon.

1070. In this year Lanfranc, who was abbot of Caen, came to
Ã **1070** England, and after a few days became archbishop of Canter-
from bury. He was consecrated on 29 August in his own see by
p. 196 eight of his suffragans; the others who were not present gave
reasons for their absence, either by messengers or by letter.
In this year Thomas, who had been elected bishop of York, came to
Canterbury to be consecrated according to ancient custom. Then
when Lanfranc demanded a sworn profession of obedience,

(continued on p. 206*)*

D 1068 at his episcopal see. He died on the feast of Protus and St
[1069] Hyacinthus [11 September], having held the archiepiscopal see
from with great dignity for ten years all but fifteen weeks. Soon
p. 203 thereafter three sons of king Swein with two hundred and forty
ships came from Denmark into the Humber, and with them
jarl Osbern and jarl Thurkil. There they were met by prince Edgar,
earl Waltheof, Mærleswein, earl Gospatric with the Northumbrians,
and all the people of the country. Forming an immense host, riding
and marching in high spirits, they all resolutely advanced on York
and stormed and destroyed the castle, seizing innumerable treasures
therein, slaying many hundreds of Frenchmen and carrying off great
numbers to their ships. Before the shipmen had come thither, the
French had burnt the borough to the ground, and had completely laid
waste and burnt down the sacred church of St Peter. When the king
learnt this, he marched northward with all the levies he could muster,
and plundered and utterly laid waste that shire. The troops lay all
winter in the Humber, where the king could not reach them. The king
spent Christmas in York and remained in the north all the winter,
returning to Winchester for Easter of that [1070] year. In this year
bishop Æthelric, who was in Peterborough, was accused, and taken to
Westminster, and his brother, bishop Æthelwine, outlawed.

1071 [1070]. In this year earl Waltheof made his peace with the king.
In the spring of the same year the king had all the monasteries in England plundered, and in this same year there was a great famine. The
monastery at Peterborough was plundered by the same men whom
bishop Æthelric had excommunicated earlier, *(continued on p.* 206*)*

[1] Hereward was a tenant of the abbacy. Some phrases from the account
of these events given in *The Chronicle of Hugh Candidus* (ed. Mellows), 77–
80, are given below.
    [2] 'Whom William translated to Peterborough [from Malmesbury] with the
remark that, since Turold behaved like a soldier rather than a monk, he
would provide him with somebody to fight' (Dom David Knowles, *The
Monastic Order in England*, Cambridge 1950, 105).
    [3] *quidam secretarius in monasterio Yuuarus dictus.* He subsequently
attempted to recover the relics from Denmark.
    [4] *in textis euuangeliorum et casulis et capis et albis et talibus paruis*
    [5] *ad portam Bolhithe* near the East End of the Abbey (cf. the translation of
Hugh's chronicle by C. & W. T. Mellows, 39 note 3).
    [6] *scabellum sub pedibus.* In Hugh's account *duo feretra* [portable shrines
in which were kept the relics of saints] *aurea et nouem alia argento et auro et
gemmis bene parata* are taken before the tower is climbed.

1070. In this year earl Waltheof made his peace with the E 1070 king. In the spring of the same year, the king had all the from monasteries in England plundered. Then, in this same year, p. 203 king Swein came into the Humber from Denmark, and the people of the country met him and came to terms with him, thinking that he was sure to conquer the whole country. Christian, the Danish bishop, came to Ely with jarl Osbern and Danish house-carles with them. Englishmen from all the fenlands came to meet them, thinking that they were sure to conquer the whole land.[1] Then the monks of Peterborough heard it said that their own men, namely Hereward and his band, wished to plunder the monastery, because they had heard it said that the king had given the abbacy to a French abbot called Turold,[2] and that he was a very ferocious man and had arrived at Stamford with all his French followers. Now in the monastery there was a sacristan called Yware[3] who at night stole all he could: gospels, chasubles, copes, albs, and any similar things of little value he was able to take.[4] He went immediately before dawn to the abbot Turold, and said that he sought his protection, telling him how the outlaws meant to come to Peterborough. This he did entirely on the advice of the monks. Then, in the morning, without delay, all the outlaws came with many boats, determined to get into the monastery, but the monks resisted them so that they could not force an entrance. Then they set it on fire, and burnt down all the monastic buildings and the entire town, except for one house. By fire they forced an entrance at Bolhithe Gate.[5] The monks came to meet them and begged to be spared, but they took no heed and entered the monastery. They climbed up to the holy cross and took the diadem all of pure gold from our Lord's head, then took the foot-support made entirely of red gold which was underneath His feet.[6] They climbed up to the tower, and brought down the altar-frontal[7] made entirely of gold and silver that was hidden there. They seized there two golden and nine silver shrines, and fifteen great crosses made both of gold and of silver. It is impos-sible for anyone to estimate how much gold and silver they took from there and what riches, whether in money, vestments, or books. They said they had done this out of (*continued on p.* 207)

---

[7] *magnam tabulam quam ibi absconderant monachi totam ex auro et argento et gemmis preciosis que solent* [*v.l. solebat*] *esse ante altare.* The OE word is *hæcce*. It was given to the abbey by Abbot Leofric (*v.* p. 198 note). C. & W. T. Mellows (p. 39) translate 'the great table . . . which was wont to be in front of the altar.' Perhaps, however, the reference is to an altar-frontal (*antependium*), 'a movable covering for the front of the altar, generally of embroidered cloth, silk etc., but sometimes of metal' (*N.E.D.*). Edward Phillips (1696) defines it as 'a large silver-skreen that covers the Front of a Popish Altar . . . hung on with skrews upon a high day.' Why OE *hæcce* ('hatch,' dialect 'hetch,' 'heck,' 'hack') is used as its equivalent is not clear, unless in relation to the upper part of the altar it was thought to resemble 'a half-door, gate, or wicket with an open space above; the lower half of a divided door' (*N.E.D.* HATCH 1); or possibly because the frame supports sometimes used for the frontal may have reminded the fenmen of hanging 'a flood-gate or sluice' (HATCH 6).

Ā 1070
from
p. 204

he refused, saying he was under no obligation to give it. Then archbishop Lanfranc was very angry with him, and ordered the bishops and all the monks, who were in attendance at archbishop Lanfranc's command to say service, to unrobe themselves. This they did at his command. So Thomas on that occasion went back without consecration. Then soon after this it happened that archbishop Lanfranc went to Rome, and Thomas went with him. When they arrived thither, and had discussed the matters which they wished to raise, Thomas put forward his case and told how he had come to Canterbury, and how the archbishop had demanded his sworn profession of obedience and how he had refused to give it. Then archbishop Lanfranc proceeded to show by lucid and discriminating argument that what he had demanded he had demanded with justification, and in cogent phrases he established his case before pope Alexander and before the whole council there assembled; and so they returned to this country. After this came Thomas to Canterbury, and humbly fulfilled all the archbishop's demands, and thereafter received consecration.[1]

Here ends the English text of the Parker Chronicle (Ā): it is followed by an account in Latin of Lanfranc and his synods and canons, closing with the consecration of his successor Anselm.

D 1071
[1070]
from
p. 204

because they had carried off everything he possessed. In the same summer the [Danish] troops sailed into the Thames, and lay there two days, and set sail afterwards for Denmark. Count Baldwin passed away, and Arnulf, his son, succeeded him. The king of France and earl William [fitz Osbern] [2] were to be his guardians, but count Robert came there, and slew Arnulf, his nephew, and earl William, putting the king [3] to flight, and slaying many thousands of his men.

1072 [1071]. In this year earl Edwin and earl Morcar took to flight, and went different ways through woods and across open country, until Edwin was slain by his own men, and Morcar went by ship

(*continued on p.* 208)

---

[1] On the relationship between the archbishops of Canterbury and York, see F. M. Stenton, *op. cit.* 656–7.

[2] Earl of Hereford.

[3] Philip I, king of France. The battle of Cassel, Flanders (*dép* Nord), was in 1071.

loyalty to this monastery. Then they returned to their ships,
E 1070 and went to Ely, and there handed over all those treasures.
from Then the Danes, thinking they would get the better of the
p. 205 French, drove out all the monks, until none remained there,
except one monk called Leofwine the Tall,[4] who lay sick in
the infirmary. Then came abbot Turold and eight times twenty
Frenchmen with him, all fully armed. When he arrived he found
everything inside and out destroyed by fire: only the church was left
standing. By then, however, the outlaws, knowing he would come
thither, were all afloat. This happened on 2 June. When the two
kings, William and Swein, came to terms, the Danes left Ely with all the
afore-mentioned treasures which they took with them. When they
were well out at sea, a great storm arose, and scattered all the ships
which carried the treasure: some of them sailed to Norway, others to
Ireland, others to Denmark—thither came only the altar-frontal, some
shrines, some crosses, and many of the other treasures: they were taken
to a royal manor called   ,[5] and all of them were placed in the
church. Thereafter, through their carelessness and drunkenness, the
church and all it contained was destroyed in one night by fire. Thus
was the monastery of Peterborough burnt down and devastated.
God Almighty in His great compassion have mercy upon it! Thus did
the abbot Turold come to Peterborough and the monks returned to
it again, and performed the service of God in their church, which had
remained for a whole week without divine service of any kind being
said. When bishop Æthelric heard tell of this, he excommunicated all
those who had done that evil deed. This same year there was a great
famine, and then the same summer the [Danish] troops sailed south
from the Humber into the Thames, and lay there for two days, and set
sail afterwards for Denmark. Count Baldwin passed away, and
Arnulf, his son, succeeded him. Earl William [fitz Osbern] and the
king of France were to be his guardians, but count Robert came there
and slew Arnulf, his nephew, and the earl, putting the king to flight,
and slaying many thousands of his men.

1071. In this year earl Edwin and earl Morcar took to flight and
went different ways through woods and across open country. Then
came Morcar to Ely by ship, but earl Edwin was basely slain.

(continued on p. 208, and thenceforward without interruption)

---

[4] See F. E. Harmer, *Anglo-Saxon Writs* 254 note.
[5] A space left in the manuscript for the name.

by his own men. Bishop Æthelwine and Siward Barn and
E 1071 many hundreds of men with them entered Ely. When king
from William learnt of this, he ordered out naval and land levies, and
p. 207 surrounded the district, building a causeway as he advanced
deeper into the fens, while the naval force remained to seaward.
Then the outlaws surrendered to him, namely bishop Æthelwine and
earl Morcar and all their followers, except Hereward alone and all who
wished to follow him; and he courageously led their escape. The king
seized ships, weapons, and many treasures, and dealt with his prisoners
as he pleased: he sent bishop Æthelwine to Abingdon where very soon
he passed away in the winter of this year.

1072. In this year king William led naval and land levies against
Scotland, and blockaded that country to seaward with his ships. He
invaded the country with his land levies at the Ford [i.e. the Forth], but
gained no advantage from it. King Malcolm came and made his peace
with king William, gave hostages and became his vassal, and the king
returned home with all his levies. In this year passed away bishop
Æthelric: he had been consecrated bishop of York, but he was unjustly
deprived of that see and given the bishopric of Durham, which he held
as long as he wished (*continued on p.* 209)

D 1072 to Ely, and there came bishop Æthelwine and Siward Barn
[1071] with many hundreds of men with them. But when king
from William learnt of this, he ordered out naval and land levies,
p. 206 and entirely surrounded the district, built a causeway and made
naval patrols to seaward, so that they all surrendered to him,
namely bishop Æthelwine and earl Morcar and all their followers,
except Hereward alone and all who were able to escape with him; and
he courageously led their escape. The king seized their ships, weapons,
and many treasures, and captured them all and dealt with them as he
pleased; he sent bishop Æthelwine to Abingdon, and there he passed
away.

1073 [1072]. In this year king William led naval and land levies
against Scotland, and blockaded that country to seaward with his ships.
He himself with his land levies invaded the country over the Ford
[i.e. the Forth], but gained no advantage from it. King Malcolm came
and made his peace with king William, became his vassal, and gave him
hostages; and William returned home with all his levies. In this year
bishop Æthelric passed away: he had been consecrated bishop of York
but he was unjustly deprived of that see, and given the bishopric of
Durham, (*continued on p.* 209)

and later gave it up, and went to Peterborough to St Peter's
E 1072 church, where he lived as a monk for twelve years. When
from king William had conquered England, he took him from
p. 208 Peterborough and sent him to Westminster. He passed away
on 15 October, and is buried in the abbey church in the chapel
of St Nicholas.

1073. In this year king William led an English and French host oversea, and conquered the province of Maine, and the English laid it
completely waste; they destroyed the vineyards, burnt down the towns,
and completely devastated the countryside, and brought it all into
subjection to William. Thereafter they returned home to England.

1074. In this year king William went oversea to Normandy,
(*continued on p.* 210)

D 1073 which he held as long as he wished, and later gave it up, and
[1072] went to Peterborough to St Peter's church, where he lived as a
from monk for twelve years. When king William had conquered
p. 208 England, he had him taken from Peterborough and sent him to
Westminster, where he passed away on 15 October. He is
buried there in the chapel of St Nicholas.

1074 [1073]. In this year king William led English and French levies
oversea, and conquered the province of Maine, and the English laid it
completely waste; they destroyed the vineyards, burnt down the towns,
and completely devastated the countryside, and brought it into subjection to the king. Thereafter they returned home.

1075 [1074]. In this year king William went oversea to Normandy,
and on St Grimbald's day [8 July] prince Edgar came from Flanders to
Scotland, and king Malcolm and his sister Margaret received him with
great ceremony. At the same festival, Philip, the king of France, sent a
letter to him, bidding him to come to him, and he would give him the
castle of Montreuil so that thereafter he could daily work mischief upon
his enemies. Indeed king Malcolm and his sister Margaret then gave
him and all his men great gifts and many precious things: skins covered
with rich purple cloth, pelisses of marten-skin, miniver and ermine,
robes of costly purple, and golden and silver vessels. He conducted
him and all his sailors from his domain in great state. But disaster
overtook them on the voyage, when they were out at sea; very rough
weather overtook them, and the raging sea and the violent gale cast
them ashore on that land so that all their ships were dashed to pieces,
and they themselves got ashore with difficulty, and almost all their
treasures (*continued on p.* 210)

and prince Edgar came from Scotland to Normandy, and the
E 1074 king revoked the sentence of outlawry against him and all his
from men: he remained at the king's court and received such privi-
p. 209 leges as the king granted him.

1075. In this year king William gave the daughter of William
fitz Osbern in marriage to earl Ralph: this same Ralph was a Breton on
his mother's side, and Ralph his father was English, and was born in
Norfolk. The king gave his [Ralph's] son the earldoms of Norfolk and
Suffolk. He then brought his bride to Norwich.

There that bridale
Led men to bale.

Earl Roger was present at the wedding, together with earl Waltheof
and bishops and abbots; and they plotted to depose the king,

(*continued on p.* 211)

D 1075
[1074] were lost. Some of his men were also seized by the French,
from but he himself and those of his men best fit to make the journey
p. 209 returned again back to Scotland, some pitiably walking on
foot, others wretchedly mounted. Then king Malcolm advised
him to send to king William oversea, and make his peace:
and so indeed he did, and the king granted his request and sent for
him. King Malcolm and his sister again gave countless treasures to
him and to all his men, and sent him once more from their domain in
great state. The sheriff of York came to meet him at Durham, and
accompanied him the whole way, and arranged for food and fodder to
be obtained for him from each castle they came to, until they arrived
oversea to the king. King William then received him with great ceremony, and he then remained at the king's court there, and accepted
such privileges as he granted him.

1076 [1075]. In this year king William gave the daughter of William
fitz Osbern in marriage to earl Ralph: this same Ralph was a Breton on
his mother's side, and Ralph his father was English, and was born in
Norfolk. On this account the king gave his [Ralph's] son the earldom
there, and the earldom of Suffolk as well. He then brought his bride to
Norwich.

There that bridale
Led many to bale.

Earl Roger was present at the wedding, together with earl Waltheof
and bishop and abbots, (*continued on p.* 211)

from the realm of England. The details of the scheme were
E 1075 soon made known to the king in Normandy. Earl Roger and
from Earl Ralph were the principals in the foolish plot, and they won
p. 210 over the Bretons to their side, and sent east to Denmark for a
pirate host to support them. Roger went west to his earldom
and gathered his people together to the king's detriment, but he was
prevented. Ralph, too, in his earldom endeavoured to take the field
with his people, but the garrisons of the [Norman] castles which were in
England, together with the inhabitants of the country, opposed him,
with the result that he accomplished nothing, but had to take ship at
Norwich. His wife remained in the castle, which she held until she was
given safe conduct, whereupon she left England with all her followers
who wished to accompany her. The king returned thereafter to
England and seized his kinsman, earl Roger, and imprisoned him.
Earl Waltheof was also arrested.

Soon after this two hundred ships came from the east from Denmark,
with their two leaders Cnut, son of king Swein, and jarl Hakon on
board, but they durst not join battle with king William

(*continued on p.* 212)

D 1076 and there they plotted to drive their royal lord from his king-
[1075] dom. This was soon made known to the king in Normandy.
from Earl Ralph and earl Roger were the leaders of this plot, and
p. 210 they won over the Bretons to their side, and also sent to Denmark for a pirate host. Roger went west to his earldom,
and gathered his people together to the king's detriment as he thought,
whereas events turned out greatly to their own misfortune. Ralph,
too, endeavoured to take the field with people from his earldom, but
the garrisons of the [Norman] castles which were in England, together
with the inhabitants of the country, opposed them and did everything
to hinder them, so that nothing was accomplished and he was glad to
escape to his ships. His wife remained behind in the castle, which
she held until they made terms with her, whereupon she left England
with all her followers who wished to accompany her. The king
returned thereafter to England, and seized his kinsman, earl Roger,
and imprisoned him. Earl Waltheof went oversea, and confessed his
treachery: he asked for pardon and offered treasures, but the king made
light of his offence until he returned to England, and then had him
arrested.

Soon after this two hundred ships came from Denmark with their
leaders Cnut, son of king Swein, and jarl Hakon on board, but they
durst not join battle with king William, but (*continued on p.* 212)

but took their way across the sea to Flanders.

E 1075   Edith, the Lady-dowager, passed away at Winchester, seven
from days before Christmas, and the king had her body brought to
p. 211 Westminster with great ceremony, and buried her beside king
Edward, her lord.

The king spent Christmas at Westminster, and there all the Bretons
who attended that bridal at Norwich were ruined:

> Some of them were blinded,
> Some of them were banished.
> So all traitors to William
> Were laid low.

1076. In this year passed away Swein, king of Denmark; and Harold,
his son, succeeded to his kingdom.

And the king gave the abbacy of Westminster to abbot Vitalis, who
had been (*continued on p.* 213)

D 1076   went to York and broke into St Peter's church, carrying off
[1075] much property from the interior, and so went away: but all
from who took part in this exploit perished, namely the son of jarl
p. 211 Hakon, and many others with him.

Edith, the Lady-dowager, who had been the consort of king
Edward, passed away at Winchester seven days before Christmas, and
the king had her body brought to Westminster with great ceremony, and
buried her beside king Edward, her lord.

The king spent Christmas at Westminster, and there all the Bretons
who attended that bridal at Norwich were sentenced to punishment:

> Some of them were blinded,
> Some of them were banished,
> Some were brought to shame.
> So all traitors to the king
> Were laid low.

1077 [1076]. In this year passed away Swein, king of Denmark, and
Harold, his son, succeeded to his kingdom. In this year king William
gave the abbacy of Westminster to abbot Vitalis who had been a monk
[*v.l.* abbot] of Bernay. In this year earl Waltheof [1] was beheaded at
Winchester on St Petronella's day [31 May], and his body was conveyed
to Crowland, where he is buried. King William went oversea

(*continued on p.* 213)

[1] On the life and death of Earl Waltheof see the recently published paper
by Forrest S. Scott, 'Earl Waltheof of Northumbria' (iv/30 *Archaeologia
Aeliana* 149–213).

abbot of Bernay; earl Waltheof was beheaded at Winchester,
E 1076 and his body conveyed to Crowland.
from The king went oversea, and led his levies into Brittany, and
p. 212 there besieged the castle of Dôl, but the Bretons held it until
the king [of France] came from France; and William retreated thence and lost there both men and horses, and many of his
treasures.

1077. In this year the king of France and William, king of England,
came to an agreement, but it was of short duration.

In this year, the day before the Assumption of St Mary [14 August],
London suffered extensively from fire, more so than ever before since
its foundation.

In this year [1078] Æthelwig, abbot of Evesham, passed away on
16 February. Bishop Hereman also passed away on 20 February of
this year.

1079. In this year king Malcolm came from Scotland into England
between the two festivals of Mary [the Assumption, 15 August, and the
Nativity, 8 September] with great levies, which harried the land of the
Northumbrians as far as the Tyne, (*continued on p.* 214)

D 1077 and led his levies into Brittany, and besieged the castle at Dôl,
[1076] but the Bretons held it until the king [of France] came from
from France; and king William retreated thence, and lost there both
p. 212 men and horses, and countless treasures.
1078. In this year the moon was eclipsed three days before
Candlemas [30 January], and Æthelwig, the abbot of Evesham, who
was wise in secular affairs, passed away on 16 February; and Walter
was appointed abbot in his place. Bishop Hereman passed away.
He was bishop of Berkshire, Wiltshire, and Dorset. In this year king
Malcolm captured the mother of Maelslæhta . . . [2] and all his best men,
and all his treasures, and his live-stock, and he himself escaped with
difficulty. . . .[3] This year it was a dry summer, and wildfire spread into
many shires, burning down many villages, and many boroughs were
also destroyed by fire.

1079. In this year Robert, the son of king William, fled from his
father to his maternal uncle Robert in Flanders, because his father
(*continued on p.* 214)

---

[2] Nearly a line left blank in the manuscript. Maelsnechtai, son of Lulach,
king of Moray, died in 1085 (Annals of Ulster).
[3] Six lines left blank in the manuscript.

and slew many hundreds, taking home much money and
E 1079 treasure, and carrying off people into captivity.
from   The same year king William fought against his son Robert
p. 213 outside Normandy, near a castle called Gerberoy. King
    William was wounded there, and his horse killed under him.
His son William was also wounded, and many men slain.

1080. In this year Walcher, bishop of Durham, was slain at an
assembly, and a hundred men with him, French and Flemish. He
himself was born in Lorraine. This the Northumbrians did in the
month of May.

1081. In this year the king led levies into Wales, and there freed many
hundreds.

1082. In this year the king arrested Bishop Odo; and in this year
there was a great famine.

1083. In this year discord arose at Glastonbury between the abbot
Thurstan and his monks. Its origin was the abbot's folly in abusing
his monks about many matters.[1] The monks made an amicable
complaint to him about it, and asked him to rule them justly and have
regard for them, and in return they would be faithful and obedient to
him. The abbot, however, would have none of it, but treated them
badly, threatening them with worse. One day the abbot went into
chapter and spoke against (*continued on p.* 215)

would not let him govern his earldom in Normandy which he
D 1079 himself and also king Philip with his consent had given him:
from   and the leading men in the country had sworn him oaths and
p. 213 accepted him as lord. In this year Robert fought against his
    father, and wounded him in the hand; and his horse was killed
under him; and he who brought up another for him—that was Toki,
son of Wigod—was immediately killed by a bolt from a crossbow, and
many there were slain or taken prisoner; and Robert returned to
Flanders. We do not wish, however, to chronicle here more of the
harm which he [did to] his father. . . .

1080 [*recte* 1130]. In this year was Angus [earl of Moray] slain by
the army of Scots, and great was the slaughter there of his companions.
God's justice was vindicated in his death, because he was utterly forsworn.[2]

---

[1] 'The monks of Glastonbury, a stronghold of tradition, were probably
not a body of men easy to handle. . . . An *impasse* was finally reached over
a question of ceremonies and chant, the abbot insisting on the substitution
of the methods of the Dijon school for the Gregorian tradition of which
Glastonbury claimed to be inheritor.' (Dom David Knowles, *The Monastic
Order in England*, Cambridge 1950, 114–15.) Cf. the brief account in
Ordericus Vitalis (trans. Forester) II. 52.

[2] Here ends D, the last entry being much later in palæography and
spelling.

E 1083
from
p. 214
the monks, and threatened to maltreat them. He sent for
laymen, who entered the chapter fully armed against the monks.
Not knowing what they should do, the monks were terrified
of them and fled in all directions. Some ran into the church [3]
and locked the doors against them, but their pursuers went
after them into the monastic church,[3] determined to drag them out
since they were afraid to leave. Moreover a pitiful thing took place
there that day, when the Frenchmen broke into the choir and began
pelting the monks in the direction of the altar where they were. Some
of the men-at-arms climbed up to the gallery,[4] and shot arrows down
into the sanctuary, so that many arrows stuck in the cross which stood
above the altar. The wretched monks lay round about the altar and
some crept underneath, crying aloud to God, desperately imploring His
mercy when none was forthcoming from men. What more can we find
to say except to add that they showered arrows, and their companions
broke down the doors to force an entrance, and struck down and killed
some of the monks, wounding many therein, so that their blood ran
down from the altar on to the steps, and from the steps on to the floor.
Three of the monks were done to death and eighteen wounded.

In this same year passed away Matilda, king William's queen, on the
day following All Saints' day [2 November].

In this same year, after Christmas, the king levied a heavy and severe
tax upon the whole of England, which amounted to seventy-two pence
for every 'hide' of land.

1084. In this year passed away Wulfwold, abbot of Chertsey, on
19 April.

1085. In this year men reported and declared it to be true that Cnut,
king of Denmark, son of king Swein, was on his way hither, determined
to conquer this country with the help of count Robert of Flanders,
since Cnut had married Robert's daughter. When king William learnt
of this—he was then residing in Normandy because he owned both
England and Normandy—he returned to England with a vast host of
horse and foot from France and from Brittany which was greater than
any that had ever come to this country. It was so vast that men
wondered (*continued on p.* 216)

---

[3] Perhaps the use of *cyrice* and *mynster* denotes the difference between the
major ecclesia and the *vetusta ecclesia* at Glastonbury (Cf. A. W. Clapham,
op. cit 49); the men-at-arms sought to get into the former through the latter.

[4] Possibly a timber gallery at the west end of the nave such as once existed
at Deerhurst (Gl), or more probably a chamber above the side-aisle (A. W.
Clapham, *English Romanesque Architecture before the Conquest*, Oxford
1930, 91). On galleries over side-aisles in Saxon churches, see also Baldwin
Brown, *The Arts in Early England* II. 170; 147 (at York), 152 (at Hexham).

how this land could feed such a host. The king, however, had
E 1085 the host spread over the whole country, quartering them with
from each of his vassals according to the produce of his estate.
p. 215 Men suffered great hardship during this same year, for the king
gave orders for the coastal districts to be laid waste, so that if
his enemies landed they would find nothing which could be quickly
seized. When, however, the king learnt for a fact that his enemies had
been hindered and that it was impossible for them to carry out their
expedition, he allowed one part of his host to return to their own
country, but retained the rest in this country over the winter.

The king spent Christmas with his councillors at Gloucester, and
held his court there for five days, which was followed by a three-day
synod held by the archbishop and the clergy. At this synod Maurice
was elected bishop of London and William bishop of Norfolk and
Robert bishop of Cheshire: they were all chaplains of the king.

After this the king had important deliberations and exhaustive
discussions with his council about this land, how it was peopled, and
with what sort of men. Then he sent his men all over England into
every shire to ascertain how many hundreds of 'hides' of land there
were in each shire, and how much land and live-stock the king himself
owned in the country, and what annual dues were lawfully his from each
shire. He also had it recorded how much land his archbishops,
and his diocesan bishops, his abbots and his earls, and—though I may
be going into too great detail—and what or how much each man who
was a landholder here in England had in land or in live-stock, and how
much money it was worth. So very thoroughly did he have the inquiry
carried out that there was not a single 'hide,' not one virgate of land,
not even—it is shameful to record it, but it did not seem shameful to
him to do—not even one ox, nor one cow, nor one pig which escaped
notice in his survey. And all the surveys were subsequently brought
to him.

1085 [1] [1086]. In this year the king wore his crown and held his
court in Winchester at Easter; and journeyed so that by Whit Sunday
he was at Westminster, and there he dubbed his son

(*continued on p.* 217)

---

[1] So the manuscript. Owing to this mistake the annals up to 1089 are one
year behind the true date. The scribe ultimately rights matters by omitting
the number 1088 altogether.

E 1085 [1086] from p. 216 Henry knight. Thereafter he journeyed around the country so that he came to Salisbury by Lammas, where he was met by his council and all the landholders who were of any account [2] throughout England, no matter whose vassals they might be. All did him homage and became his men, and swore him oaths of allegiance that they would be faithful to him against all other men. From thence he journeyed to the Isle of Wight because he purposed to go to Normandy, and so he did thereafter. First, however, he did as he was wont, he levied very heavy taxes on his subjects, upon any pretext, whether justly or unjustly. He journeyed thereafter into Normandy. and prince Edgar, the kinsman of king Edward, then left his court because he had had little honour from him: but may the Almighty God give him honour in the future. Christina, the prince's sister, retired into the nunnery at Romsey and took the veil.

And this same year was very disastrous, and a very vexatious and anxious year throughout England, because of a pestilence among live-stock; and corn and fruits were at a standstill. It is difficult for anyone to realize what great misfortune was caused by the weather: so violent was the thunder and lightning that many were killed. Things steadily went from bad to worse for everybody. May God Almighty remedy it when it shall be His will!

1086 [1087]. One thousand and eighty-seven years after the nativity of our Lord Jesus Christ, in the twenty-first year of William's rule and reign over England, as God had granted to him, there was a very disastrous and pestilential year in this land. Such a malady fell upon men that very nearly every other person was in the sorriest plight and down with fever: it was so malignant that many died from the disease. There-after, in consequence of the great storms which came as we have already told, there came a great famine over all England, so that many hundreds died miserable deaths because of it. Alas! how wretched and how unhappy (*continued on p.* 218)

[2] See Sir Frank Stenton, *The First Century of English Feudalism*, pp. 111–112.

E 1086
[1087]
from
p. 217

the times were then! So fever-stricken lay the unhappy people in those days that they were never far from death's door, until the pangs of hunger finished them off.

Who can fail to be moved to compassion by days such as these? Or who is so hard-hearted that he cannot bewail such misfortune? But such things come to pass because of a nation's sins, because its people will not love God and righteousness. So was it then in those days, when little righteousness was to be found in this land in any man's heart, but only amongst the monks where they lived virtuously. The king and the leading men were fond, yea, too fond, of avarice: they coveted gold and silver, and did not care how sinfully it was obtained, as long as it came to them. The king granted his land on the hardest terms and at the highest possible price. If another buyer came and offered more than the first had given, the king would let it go to the man who offered him more. If a third came and offered still more, the king would make it over to the man who offered him most of all. He did not care at all how very wrongfully the reeves got possession of it from wretched men, nor how many illegal acts they did; but the louder the talk of law and justice, the greater the injustices committed. Unjust tolls were levied and many other unlawful acts were committed which are distressing to relate.

Also, in the same year, before autumn, the holy church of St Paul, the episcopal see of London, was burnt down, as well as many other churches and the largest and fairest part of the whole city. Likewise too, at the same time, almost every important town in the whole of England was burnt down. Alas! a miserable and lamentable time was it in that year, which brought forth so many misfortunes.

Also, in the same year, before the Assumption of St Mary [15 August], king William went from Normandy into France with levies, and made war against his own lord, Philip the king, and slew a great number of his men, and burnt down the town of Mantes and all the holy churches inside the town. Two holy men who served God living in an anchorite's cell were there burnt to death.

After these events, king William returned again to Normandy. A cruel deed he had done, but a crueller fate befell him. How crueller? He fell sick and suffered terribly. (*continued on p.* 219)

E 1086
[1087]
from
p. 218

What can I say? That bitter death that spares neither high nor low seized him. He died in Normandy on the day following the Nativity of St Mary [9 September], and was buried at Caen in the abbey of St Stephen, which he had formerly built and afterwards endowed in various ways.

Alas! how deceitful and transitory is the prosperity of this world. He who was once a mighty king, and lord of many a land, was left of all the land with nothing save seven feet of ground: and he who was once decked with gold and jewels, lay then covered over with earth.

He left behind him three sons. The eldest was called Robert, who became duke of Normandy after him. The second was called William, who wore the royal crown in England after him. The third was called Henry, to whom his father bequeathed treasures innumerable.

If anyone desires to know what kind of man he was or in what honour he was held or how many lands he was lord over, then shall we write of him as we have known him, who have ourselves seen him and at one time dwelt in his court. King William, of whom we speak, was a man of great wisdom and power, and surpassed in honour and in strength all those who had gone before him. Though stern beyond measure to those who opposed his will, he was kind to those good men who loved God. On the very spot where God granted him the conquest of England he caused a great abbey to be built; and settled monks in it and richly endowed it. During his reign was built the great cathedral at Canterbury, and many another throughout all England. This land too was filled with monks living their lives after the rule of St Benedict. Such was the state of religion in his time that every man who wished to, whatever considerations there might be with regard to his rank, could follow the profession of a monk.[1]

Moreover he kept a great state. He wore his royal crown three times a year as often as he was in England: at Easter at Winchester, at Whitsuntide at Westminster, at Christmas at Gloucester. On these occasions (*continued on p.* 220)

---

[1] Or, as Miss Pamela Gradon has suggested (25 *Medium Ævum* 100), 'Christendom was such in his day that every man who so desired followed what pertained to his order.'

all the great men of England were assembled about him: arch-bishops, bishops, abbots, earls, thanes, and knights. He was so stern and relentless a man that no one dared do aught against his will. Earls who resisted his will he held in bondage. Bishops he deprived of their sees and abbots of their abbacies, while rebellious thanes he cast into prison, and finally his own brother he did not spare. His name was Odo. He was a powerful bishop in Normandy, and Bayeux was his episcopal see; he was the foremost man after the king. He had an earldom in England, and was master of the land when the king was in Normandy. William put him in prison. Among other things we must not forget the good order he kept in the land, so that a man of any substance could travel unmolested through-out the country with his bosom full of gold. No man dared to slay another, no matter what evil the other might have done him. If a man lay with a woman against her will, he was forthwith condemned to forfeit those members with which he had disported himself.

He ruled over England, and by his foresight it was surveyed so care-fully that there was not a 'hide' of land in England of which he did not know who held it and how much it was worth; and these particulars he set down in his survey. Wales was in his domain, in which country he built castles and so kept its people in subjection. Scotland also he reduced to subjection by his great strength. Normandy was his by right of birth, while he also ruled over the county called Maine. If he had lived only two years more he would have conquered Ireland by his astuteness and without any display of force. Assuredly in his time men suffered grievous oppression and manifold injuries.

> He caused castles to be built
> Which were a sore burden to the poor.
> A hard man was the king
> And took from his subjects many marks
> In gold and many more hundreds of pounds in silver.

(*continued on p.* 221)

These sums he took by weight from his people,

Most unjustly and for little need.

He was sunk in greed

And utterly given up to avarice.

He set apart a vast deer preserve and imposed laws concerning it.

Whoever slew a hart or a hind

Was to be blinded.

He forbade the killing of boars

Even as the killing of harts.

For he loved the stags as dearly

As though he had been their father.

Hares, also, he decreed should go unmolested.

The rich complained and the poor lamented,

But he was too relentless to care though all might hate him,

And they were compelled, if they wanted

To keep their lives and their lands

And their goods and the favour of the king,

To submit themselves wholly to his will.

Alas! that any man should bear himself so proudly

And deem himself exalted above all other men!

May Almighty God shew mercy to his soul

And pardon him his sins.

We have set down these things about him, both the good and the evil, so that men may cherish the good and utterly eschew the evil, and follow the path that leads us to the Kingdom of Heaven.

Many things we can set down which happened in the same year. It happened in Denmark that the Danes, who were once regarded as the most loyal of all peoples, became guilty of the most faithless and treacherous conduct imaginable. They elected Cnut king, submitted to him, and swore him oaths of fealty, and then basely slew him inside a church. Also it happened in Spain that the heathen made war against the Christians, and brought much of the country under their sway: but the Christian king, whose name was Alfonso, (*continued on p.* 222)

**E 1086
[1087]
from
p. 221**
sent everywhere into each land, and begged for assistance; and support came to him from every Christian country. All the heathen were attacked, slain, and driven off, and the country reconquered, by God's help.

Moreover, in our own country, in this same year, passed away many great men: Stigand, bishop of Chichester, and the abbot of St Augustine's [Canterbury], and the abbot of Bath and the abbot of Pershore, and then the lord of them all, William, king of England, of whom we have spoken before. After his death, his son, who bore the same name as his father, came to the throne and was consecrated king at Westminster by archbishop Lanfranc, three days before Michaelmas [26 September]; and all the men in England submitted to him and swore him oaths. This done the king went to Winchester and inspected the treasury and the riches which his father had accumulated; untold wealth was gathered together there in gold, in silver, in vessels, in costly robes, and in jewels, and in many other precious things which are difficult to enumerate. The king then did as his father had commanded him before he died: he distributed these treasures to each monastery in England for his father's soul; to one monastery ten marks of gold, to another six, and to each country church sixty pence; and into every shire was sent a hundred pounds in money to be distributed to poor people for his soul. Before he passed away, he commanded that all those who were in his power in captivity should be set free. And the king spent Christmas in London.

1087 [1088]. In this year there was great commotion in this country and treason was everywhere, with the result that the most powerful Frenchmen in the land plotted to betray their lord the king, and make his brother Robert king, he who was duke of Normandy. The leaders in this conspiracy were bishop Odo, bishop Geoffrey, and William, bishop of Durham. So generously did the king behave to that bishop, that all England was governed on his advice and direction, and yet he planned to act towards him as Judas Iscariot did to our Lord. Earl Roger was also in that foolish conspiracy, (continued on p. 223)

E 1087
[1088]
from
p. 222

and very many others too, all Frenchmen: and this conspiracy [1] was formed during the spring. As soon as Easter came, then they set out to harry and burn, and laid waste the king's farms, and devastated the lands of all those men who owed allegiance to the king. Each of them went to his castle, and manned and provisioned it as best they could. Bishop Geoffrey and Robert of Mowbray went to Bristol, and harried, and brought the booty to the castle; thereafter they sallied forth from the castle and ravaged Bath and all the surrounding countryside, laying waste all the district of Berkeley Harness. The chief men of Hereford, together with all the men of that shire, with the men of Shropshire and a great force from Wales, came and harried and burnt in Worcestershire, and on until they came to the town itself. They planned to burn down the town, and despoil the cathedral, and bring about the surrender of the king's castle. Seeing these things, the venerable bishop Wulfstan was very troubled in his mind, for the castle had been entrusted to his keeping: nevertheless the men of his household sallied out from the castle with a few men, and by God's mercy and the merits of the bishop, slew and captured five hundred men, and put all the others to flight. The bishop of Durham did as much damage as he could everywhere in the north. One of them was called Roger, who scuttled away into the castle at Norwich; and yet in all the land no one behaved worse than he. Hugh was another who did nothing to improve matters, neither in Leicestershire nor in Northampton. Bishop Odo, who was the instigator of these troubles, went to his earldom in Kent and did great destruction. His men utterly laid waste the lands of the king and the archbishop, and all the spoil was taken into his castle at Rochester.

When the king perceived all these things, and what treason they did against him, then he was greatly troubled in mind, and summoned Englishmen and put his difficulties before them, and desired their assistance, promising them the best law there had ever been in this land; he prohibited every unjust tax, and granted men their woods and hunting rights; but his promises were short-lived. But the Englishmen, nevertheless, came to the assistance of their lord the king: they went towards (*continued on p.* 224)

---

[1] On the events of this annal see A. L. Poole, *From Domesday Book to Magna Carta* (Oxford 1951), 100 ff.

E 1087
[1088]
from
p. 223 Rochester, determined to seize bishop Odo, thinking that if they had him who was the prime mover in the plot, they could more easily seize the rest. They came then to the castle at Tonbridge; inside the castle were the knights of bishop Odo and many others determined to support him against the king. But the Englishmen attacked and stormed the castle, and its defenders made peace with the king. The king with his host went towards Rochester, thinking that the bishop was inside the town, but learnt that the bishop had gone to the castle at Pevensey; and the king with his host followed after, and besieged the castle on all sides with a very great host for fully six weeks.

In the meanwhile Robert, duke of Normandy, the king's brother, gathered a very great force, and thought to conquer England with the help of those men in this country who were in rebellion against the king; and he sent some of his men to this land, intending to come afterwards himself. But the Englishmen who guarded the sea captured some of these men and slew them, and drowned more than anyone could reckon.

Thereafter food ran short inside the castle; then they asked for a truce, and surrendered it to the king. The bishop swore on oath that he would leave England, and return no more to this country unless the king sent for him, and promised to surrender the castle at Rochester. So the bishop departed in order to surrender that castle [of Rochester] and the king's men went with him. Then the garrison of the castle arose, seized the bishop and the king's men and put them in chains. Within the castle were some very good knights: Eustace the young, and three sons of earl Roger, and all the best born men who were in this land or in Normandy.

When the king perceived these things, he went in pursuit with the host that he had there, and sent over all England, and called on every honest man, whether French or English, to rally to him, from town and from country. A great force came to his assistance, and he went to Rochester and besieged the castle, until the garrison within came to terms and surrendered the castle. This bishop Odo, with the men who had been within the castle, (*continued on p. 225*)

E 1087 [1088] from p. 224 went oversea, and the bishop thus relinquished the dignity which he had held in this land. The king thereafter sent a host to Durham and had the castle besieged; and the bishop asked for a truce and surrendered the castle. He relinquished his bishopric and went to Normandy. Many Frenchmen also surrendered their lands and went oversea; and the king gave their lands to the men who were faithful to him.

1089. In this year the venerable father and consolation of monks, archbishop Lanfranc, departed from this life, but we are confident that he has gone to the heavenly kingdom. Moreover there was a great earthquake over all England on 11 August; and it was a very backward year for corn and produce of every kind, so that many reaped their corn about Martinmas [11 November] and even later.

1090. INDICTION XIII. These events having taken place, even as we have described above, between the king and his brother and his men, the king was considering how he could take vengeance on his brother Robert, pay him out most effectively, and conquer Normandy from him. However, whether by reason of his astuteness, or by means of costly gifts, he took the castle and the harbour at St Valéry. Likewise too he won the castle of Aumale and garrisoned it with his knights; and they did damage in the land by harrying and burning. After these events he seized more castles within that land and garrisoned them with his knights.

After the duke of Normandy perceived that his sworn vassals had deceived him, and surrendered their castles to his disadvantage, he sent to his lord, Philip, king of the French, and he came to Normandy with a great host. With vast levies the king and the duke besieged the castle wherein were men of the king of England. King William of England sent to Philip, king of the French, and he for love of him, or on account of his great costly gifts, abandoned his vassal, duke Robert, and his land, and went back to France and let matters take their course. While these events were taking place, this country was utterly ruined by unjust taxation and by many other misfortunes.

1091. In this year [1090] [1] king William held his court at

(*continued on p.* 226)

---

[1] The chronicler begins his year at Christmas, as in most of the annals which follow.

Christmas in Westminster; and thereafter at Candlemas [2
E 1091 February] he went, to his brother's discomfiture, from England
from into Normandy. Their reconciliation came about while he
p. 225 was there, on condition that the duke surrendered Fécamp to
him, with the county of Eu, and Cherbourg. Furthermore
the king's men were to be left unmolested in the castles which they had
won from the duke against his will. In return the king promised him to
reduce Maine to submission, which their father had won, and which
was then in revolt against the duke; and promised him all that his father
had possessed there oversea, except what he had given to the king;
moreover, all those who in England had lost their lands earlier in the
duke's cause were to have them again as a result of this agreement;
and the duke was to get as much land in England as was laid down in
their treaty. If the duke should pass away without son by lawful wedlock, the king was to be heir of all Normandy: by this same treaty, if the
king should die, the duke was to be heir of all England. This treaty
was ratified by twelve of the noblest men on the king's behalf, and by
twelve on the duke's, and yet did not remain inviolate for long.

As a result of this treaty, prince Edgar was deprived of those lands
which the duke had previously assigned to him: he left Normandy and
went to Scotland to the king, his brother-in-law, and to his sister.

Whilst king William was out of England, king Malcolm invaded
England from Scotland and harried a great part of it, until the good men
who were governing this country sent levies against him and turned him
back. When king William in Normandy heard of this, he made ready
for his departure and came to England, his brother, the duke Robert,
accompanying him. The king straightway had his levies called out,
both the fleet and land levies; but before he could reach Scotland, four
days before Michaelmas, almost the entire fleet was disastrously lost.
The king and his brother marched with the land levies, but when king
Malcolm heard that levies were approaching, he left Scotland and went
into Lothian in England with his levies and there waited. Then when
king William approached with his levies, *(continued on p. 227)*

226

E 1091
from
p. 226

duke Robert and prince Edgar intervened, and succeeded in making peace between those kings, with the result that king Malcolm came to our king and became his man, rendering obedience to him in all respects as to his father before him, and confirmed it with oath. King William promised him, in land and in all things, all that he had formerly held under his father.

In this peace also prince Edgar was reconciled with the king. Then the kings parted in great friendship, but it was not to last long. Count Robert remained in this country with the king almost until Christmas, and discovered during that time that there was little good faith in their agreement: two days before that festival he took ship in the Isle of Wight and went to Normandy, and prince Edgar with him.

1092. In this year king William went north to Carlisle with great levies, and restored the town, and built the castle. He drove out Dolfin who had formerly ruled that district, and garrisoned the castle with his men. Thereafter he returned hither southwards, sending very many peasants thither with their wives and live-stock to settle there and till the soil.

1093. In this year, in Lent, king William was taken so seriously ill at Gloucester that he was everywhere reported dead. During his illness he made many vows to God: to lead his own life righteously, and to grant peace and protection to God's churches and never again to sell them for money, and to maintain all just laws amongst his people. The archbishopric of Canterbury, which he had retained in his own possession, he committed to Anselm, who had been abbot of Bec; to Robert, his chancellor, he gave the bishopric of Lincoln. To many monasteries he made grants of land, which he subsequently withdrew when he recovered, and did away with all the good laws which he had promised us earlier.

Then after these events, the king of Scotland sent and desired the fulfilment of the treaty which had been promised him: and king William summoned him to Gloucester, and sent hostages to him in Scotland, followed by prince Edgar, and then afterwards men to meet him who brought him to the king with great ceremony. When, however, he

(*continued on p.* 228)

227

came to the king he was not considered worthy of an audience **E 1093** of our king, nor of the assurances which had formerly been **from** promised him. Hence they parted in great enmity, and king **p. 227** Malcolm went back to Scotland. But quickly, after his arrival, he gathered together his levies, and invaded England, harrying with greater recklessness than was at all proper for him, when Robert, the earl of the Northumbrians with his men surprised and slew him. Morel of Bamburgh, who was the earl's steward and had spiritual affinity to king Malcolm struck him down. With him was also slain his son Edward, who should have been king after him had he survived. When the good queen Margaret heard that her dearest lord and son had been thus betrayed, she became fatally distressed in mind and went to church with her priests. She received her last offices and prayed to God that she might yield up her spirit. The Scots elected Donald, brother of Malcolm, king, and drove out all the English who had been with king Malcolm. Then when Duncan, king Malcolm's son, heard all that had taken place—he was in king William's court since his father had given him as a hostage to the father of our king and he had remained so ever after—he came to the king, and gave such pledges as the king demanded from him, and, with his consent, went to Scotland. With such English and French assistance as he could obtain, he deprived Donald, his kinsman, of the kingdom, and was received as king. But some of the Scots afterwards came together, and slew almost all his followers, and he himself with a few escaped. Thereafter they became reconciled, on condition that he never again introduced Englishmen or Frenchmen into that country.

1094. In this year [1093] king William held his court at Christmas at Gloucester, and thither came to him messengers from his brother, Robert of Normandy. They announced that his brother entirely renounced the covenant of peace which had previously been made, unless the king fulfilled all that had originally been laid down in the covenant; and furthermore called him forsworn and faithless, unless he maintained those covenants; or else went thither, and there exculpated himself where the covenant had been drawn up and ratified.

(*continued on p.* 229)

E 1094
from
p. 228
Then the king went to Hastings at Candlemas [2 February], and whilst he was there waiting for a breeze he had the abbey at Battle consecrated, and deprived Herbert Losanga, bishop of Thetford, of his pastoral staff. Thereafter, at mid Lent, he sailed oversea into Normandy. After he arrived thither, he and his brother duke Robert agreed to meet amicably; and so they did, yet could not be reconciled. Afterwards they met together with the same guarantors who had originally made the treaty and ratified it, who laid the entire responsibility for the breach of the treaty upon the king, but he would not accept their verdict, nor indeed keep the covenant; and for this reason they parted with great ill feeling.

Thereafter the king seized the castle at Bures, and took prisoner the duke's men therein, and sent some of them hither to this country. The duke, in retaliation, with the support of the king of France, took the castle at Argentan, and captured therein Roger of Poitou and seven hundred of the king's knights with him; and afterwards the castle at Le Houlme. Each of them frequently burned down the other's towns and took prisoners.

Then sent the king hither to this country, and ordered twenty thousand Englishmen to be called up to go to his assistance in Normandy, but when they came to the sea, they were ordered to turn back and, to help the king in his need, to surrender the ten shillings each man had taken with him for the campaign: and this they did.

Thereafter in Normandy the duke, with the king of France and with all the men they could muster, went towards Eu where king William was in residence, meaning to besiege him therein. They proceeded thus until they came to Longueville where intrigue compelled the king of France to retire and in consequence the entire campaign petered out. Meanwhile king William sent for his brother Henry, who was in the castle at Domfront, but since he could not pass through Normandy in safety, he sent ships for him and Hugh, earl of Chester; but instead of making for Eu where the king was, they sailed to England, and landed at Southampton on All Saints' eve [31 October]. They stayed there afterwards, and by Christmas were in London. (*continued on p.* 230)

Also in this same year the Welsh joined forces and stirred up
E 1094 hostilities against the French, in Wales or in the neighbourhood,
from who had deprived them of their lands. They destroyed many
p. 229 fortresses and castles and slew the garrisons, and split up into
several detachments as their numbers increased. One of
these was defeated by Hugh, earl of Shropshire, and put to flight:
nevertheless during all the year the others did not rest from doing all the
evil of which they were capable.

Also in this year the Scots entrapped and slew Duncan, their king,
and thereafter for a second time took Donald, his paternal uncle, to be
their king, by whose counsel and instigation he was betrayed to his
death.

1095. In this year [1094] king William was at Wissant for the first
four days of Christmas; and after the fourth day returned to this
country and landed at Dover. Henry, the king's brother, stayed in
this country until Lent, and then sailed oversea to Normandy with great
treasures as the king's deputy against their brother, duke Robert. He
frequently warred against the duke, and inflicted severe losses both
on his land and on his men. Then at Easter the king held his court at
Winchester. When Robert, earl of Northumbria, refused to attend,
the king was greatly incensed against him, and sent and sternly commanded him to come to his Whitsuntide court if he wished to be entitled
to the king's protection. In this year Easter was on 25 March. Then
after Easter on the eve of St Ambrose, which is on 4 April [*recte* 3 April],
almost everywhere in this country and almost the whole night, stars in
very large numbers were seen to fall from heaven, not by ones or twos,
but in such quick succession that they could not be counted. Later in
the year on Whit Sunday the king was at Windsor with all his councillors except the earl of Northumbria, because the king would neither
give him hostages nor pledge his word that he would be allowed to come
and go in safety.

The king therefore summoned his levies and went to Northumbria
against the earl, (*continued on p. 231*)

E 1095
from
p. 230
and as soon as he came thither he captured many prisoners in a fortress, including almost all the best men of the earl's retinue, and imprisoned them. He besieged the castle at Tynemouth until he took it, taking prisoner therein the earl's brother and all who were with him. Thereafter he proceeded to Bamburgh, and besieged the earl therein. But when the king saw that he could not storm it, he ordered a castle to be built in front of Bamburgh, and called it in his language 'Malueisin,' which in English means 'Evil Neighbour.' He garrisoned it strongly with his men, and thereafter went south. Soon after the king had gone south, the earl sallied forth one night from Bamburgh towards Tynemouth; but those in the new castle became aware of it and went after him. They attacked and wounded him, and afterwards took him prisoner: some of his followers were slain and others taken alive.

Meanwhile the king learnt that the Welsh had destroyed a castle in Wales called Montgomery, and had slain earl Hugh's men who were there to garrison it. He therefore ordered other levies to be quickly called out, and after Michaelmas invaded Wales. The levies were divided into detachments to make deep penetrations into the country, finally converging on Snowdon on All Saints' day [1 November]; but the Welsh kept continuously out of reach, moving into the mountains and moors where they could not be got at. The king then turned homewards, because he saw nothing more could be done there that winter.

When the king returned, he had Robert, earl of Northumbria, taken and brought to Bamburgh, and ordered both of his eyes to be put out unless the garrison would surrender the castle, which was held by his wife and Morel, who was both his steward and nephew. In consequence the castle was surrendered, and Morel joined the king's retinue and was the means of exposing many, both ecclesiastics and laymen, who in their conspiracy had been disloyal to the king. Some of these men had already been arrested by the king, who subsequently issued a peremptory proclamation throughout the whole of the country that all those who held land from the king in so far as (*continued on p.* 232)

they wished to be entitled to his protection must attend his
E 1095 court at the appointed time. The king had earl Robert taken
from to Windsor, and kept him prisoner there within the castle.
p. 231 Also in this same year, towards Easter, the pope's legate
came hither to this country: this was bishop Walter, a man of
very good life from the city of Albano. On Whit Sunday, on behalf of
pope Urban, he gave archbishop Anselm his pallium, who received it at
his archiepiscopal see at Canterbury. Bishop Walter remained in this
country for a good part of the year, and thereafter Peter's pence was
sent along with him to Rome as had not been done for many years
previous.

In this same year also the weather was very unseasonable; consequently all the crops were poor throughout the whole country.

1096. In this year [1095] king William held his court at Christmas at
Windsor, and William, bishop of Durham, passed away there on New
Year's day. On the octave of the Epiphany [13 January], the king and
all his councillors were at Salisbury. There Geoffrey Bainard accused
William of Eu, the king's kinsman, of treason against the king, and
maintained it against him in combat, overcoming him in a trial by
battle. After he was defeated, the king ordered his eyes to be put out,
and then had him castrated. His steward, William by name, the son of
his mother's sister, he ordered to be hanged. There too Odo, count of
Champagne, the king's son-in-law [*recte* uncle], and many others, were
deprived of their lands: others were taken to London and there
mutilated.

In this year also, at Easter, there was a very great stir throughout all
this nation, and in many other nations too, because of Urban who was
called Pope, although he was not in possession of the see in Rome.
A countless number of people with their wives and children set out
wishing to fight against the heathen. As a result of this crusade, the
king and his brother, duke Robert, came to terms so that the king went
oversea and released the whole of Normandy from him for a sum of
money, and this brought about their reconciliation. The duke set out
on the crusade and with him went the counts of Flanders and Boulogne,
together with many other persons of high rank. Duke Robert and
those who set out with him spent the winter in Apulia; but many
thousands of those who went by Hungary perished miserably there and
on the way; (continued on p. 233)

and many of them, miserable and hunger-bitten, made their

E 1096 from p. 232

way back at the approach of winter. This was a very disastrous year throughout all England, both on account of numerous taxes and because of a very serious famine which this year greatly afflicted this country. Moreover, in this year, the chief men who ruled this land frequently sent levies into Wales, greatly oppressing many in this way: but nothing came of it there, save loss of men and waste of money.

1097. In this year [1096] king William spent Christmas in Normandy, and towards Easter was to return to this country, for he purposed to hold his court at Winchester; but he was detained by bad weather until Easter eve, so that he landed first at Arundel, and therefore held his court at Windsor.

Thereafter he proceeded into Wales with a great host. Assisted by some of the Welsh, who joined him and acted as guides, he made deep penetrations into the heart of the country where he remained from midsummer almost until August; and whilst he was there he suffered great losses of men and horses, and of many other things besides.

Thereafter the Welsh revolted against their king, and chose for themselves many rulers from their number, one of whom was Cadwgan who was the noblest of them; he was the son of king Gruffydd's brother. But when the king saw that he could in no way achieve his purpose there, he returned to this country, and quickly thereafter had castles built along the marches.

Then after Michaelmas, on 4 October, a strange star appeared, shining in the evening and setting early. It was seen in the south-west, and the trail of light that shone out from it towards the south-east appeared to be very long, and was visible like this for almost a whole week. Many men said it was a comet.

Soon after this Anselm, archbishop of Canterbury, had the king's permission to go oversea, although it was realized that this was displeasing to the king. He left the country because, in his opinion, little was done lawfully in this land or as he directed. Thereafter, at Martinmas, the king went oversea into Normandy; but, while he waited for a breeze, his retinue did much greater harm within the shires where they were (*continued on p.* 234)

than a retinue or host ever ought to do in friendly country.
E 1097 In all respects this was a very severe year, and particularly
from disastrous on account of the bad weather, both when the land
p. 233 was to be tilled and again when the crops were to be harvested;
and there was no relief from excessive taxation. Moreover
men from many shires, in fulfilling their labour service to the city of
London, were sorely oppressed in building the wall around the Tower,
and in repairing the bridge nearly all of which had been carried away,
and while engaged on the construction of the king's hall at Westminster:
many were oppressed in consequence.

Also in this same year, soon after Michaelmas, prince Edgar with the
king's support invaded Scotland with levies, and in a fierce battle
conquered the country; he drove out king Donald, and established his
kinsman Edgar, son of king Malcolm and queen Margaret, as king and
vassal to king William. He then returned to England.

1098. In this year [1097], at Christmas, king William was in Normandy. Walchelin, bishop of Winchester, and Baldwin, abbot of
Bury St Edmunds, both passed away during this festival. In this year
also Turold, abbot of Peterborough, passed away. Moreover, in the
summer of this year, in Berkshire at Finchampstead, a pool bubbled up
blood, as many faithful witnesses reported who were said to have seen it.

Earl Hugh was slain in Anglesey by pirates[1] from oversea, and his
brother Robert became his heir, with the consent of the king.

Before Michaelmas the sky appeared almost the whole night as if it
were on fire. This was a very disastrous year because of excessive
taxation, and on account of the heavy rains which did not leave off
throughout the whole year: nearly all the cultivated land in low-lying
districts was ruined.

1099. In this year [1098] king William spent Christmas in Normandy,
and returned hither at Easter, and on Whit Sunday held his court for the
first time in his new residence at Westminster; and there gave to Rannulf,
his chaplain, the bishopric of Durham, (*continued on p.* 235)

---

[1] 'Their leader was none other than Magnus Bareleg, king of Norway,
the son of Harold Hardrada. He had with him Harold the son of Harold,
son of Godwine. This union of the sons of the victor and the vanquished
of Stamford Bridge is an interesting fact' (Plummer II. 286).

he who formerly had directed and superintended all the king's
E 1099 councils throughout all England. Soon thereafter the king
from went oversea, and drove count Helias [de la Flèche] out of
p. 234 Maine, and brought it into subjection to him; and so at
Michaelmas returned to this country.

In this year also, at Martinmas, the incoming tide rushed up so
strongly and did so much damage that no one remembered anything
like it before; and on the same day there was a new moon.

In this year, too, Osmund, bishop of Salisbury, passed away during
Advent.

1100. In this year [1099] king William held his court at Christmas in
Gloucester, and at Easter in Winchester, and at Whitsun in Westminster.

On Whit Sunday of this year at a village in Berkshire blood was seen
bubbling forth from the ground, as many reported who were said to
have seen it. And thereafter, on the morning after Lammas, king
William was killed with an arrow while hunting [1] by one of his men.
He was afterwards brought to Winchester, and buried in the diocese in
the thirteenth year of his reign.

He was very harsh and fierce in his rule over his realm, and towards
his followers and to all his neighbours, and very terrifying. Influenced
by the advice of evil councillors, who were always agreeable to him,
and by his own covetousness, he was continually exasperating this
nation with depredations and unjust taxes. In his days, therefore,
righteousness declined, and evil of every kind towards God and man
put up its head. He oppressed the Church of God; and in his days
when the head of a bishopric or an abbacy died, he either sold them all
for money, or kept them within his grasp and let them for rent, for he
claimed to be the heir of every man, cleric or lay. On the day that he
fell, therefore, he had in his possession the archbishopric of Canterbury
and the bishoprics of Winchester and Salisbury and eleven abbacies,
from all of which he was drawing revenues. I may be delaying too long
over all these matters, but everything that was hateful to God and to
righteous men was the daily practice in this land during his reign.
Therefore he was hated by almost all his people and abhorrent to God.
This his end testified, for (*continued on p.* 236)

---

[1] *In nova foresta quæ lingua Anglorum Ytene nuncupatur* (Florence of
Worcester, *Chronicon ex Chronicis*, II. 44–5).

he died in the midst of his sins without repentance or any atone-
E 1100 ment for his evil deeds.
from He was slain on the Thursday and buried the next morning.
p. 235 After he was buried, those councillors who were near at hand
elected his brother Henry to be king. He straightway gave the
bishopric of Winchester to William Gifford and then went to London.
On the following Sunday, before the altar at Westminster, he vowed to
God and all the people to abolish all the injustices which were prevalent
during his brother's reign, and to maintain the best laws which had
stood in the time of any of his predecessors. Thereafter Maurice, the
bishop of London, consecrated him king, and all the people in this land
submitted to him and swore him oaths of allegiance, and became his
men.

And soon after this, following the counsel of his advisors, he had
Rannulf, bishop of Durham, arrested and brought to the Tower of
London and held there. Then before Michaelmas, Anselm, archbishop of Canterbury, returned to this country, since king Henry had
sent for him, following the advice of his councillors, for he had left the
country on account of the great injustice which king William had done
to him.

And then soon hereafter the king took to wife Matilda, daughter of
Malcolm, king of Scotland, and the good queen Margaret, king
Edward's kinswoman, of the rightful royal house of England. At
Martinmas she was given to him in marriage at Westminster with great
ceremony, and archbishop Anselm wedded her to him and afterwards
consecrated her queen. Soon afterwards passed away Thomas, archbishop of York.

Also in this same year, in autumn, duke Robert returned to Normandy, and count Robert of Flanders and Eustace, count of Boulogne,
from Jerusalem. As soon as duke Robert came into Normandy, he
was joyfully received by all the people, except the garrisons of king
Henry's men occupying the castles, against whom he had many
encounters and battles.

1101. In this year [1100], at Christmas, the king held his court at
Westminster, and at Easter in Winchester. (*continued on p. 237*)

Soon thereafter the chief men in the country became hostile
E 1101 towards the king, both on account of their own great disloyalty
from and because duke Robert of Normandy was planning a hostile
p. 236 invasion. The king then sent his ships to sea to inflict losses
upon his brother and to delay him, but some of them afterwards failed at need, deserting the king and submitting to duke Robert.
Then, at midsummer, the king went out to Pevensey with all his levies
to oppose his brother, and waited for him there. Meanwhile, however, duke Robert landed at Portsmouth, twelve days before Lammas;
and the king came against him with all his levies. But persons of high
rank went between them, and the brothers were reconciled on the
condition that the king should relinquish all that he held within Normandy by force of arms in defiance of the duke; and that all those
in England who had lost their lands in the duke's cause should have
them restored; moreover count Eustace [of Boulogne] should recover
all the land his father had owned in this country; and that duke Robert
should receive each year three thousand marks of silver from this
country; and whichever of the brothers survived the other should be
the heir to the whole of England and Normandy, provided that the
deceased had no heir in lawful wedlock. This agreement was ratified
by oath by twelve men of high rank from each side. Thereafter, the
duke remained in this country until after Michaelmas; and his men
did much damage wherever they went during the duke's stay in this
country.

In this year also at Candlemas bishop Rannulf escaped by night out
of the Tower of London where he had been imprisoned, and went to
Normandy: it was largely due to his scheming and instigation that duke
Robert had this year come to this country with hostile intent.

1102. In this year [1101] king Henry spent the Nativity at Westminster, and Easter at Winchester.

And soon afterwards discord arose between the king and the earl
Robert of Bellême, who held the earldom of Shrewsbury in this country,
which his father Roger had previously held, and a vast territory
besides, both here in this country and oversea. The king went and
besieged the castle at Arundel, but when he could not take it quickly
he had castles built before it and garrisoned them with his men; and
thereafter proceeded with all his levies to Bridgnorth

(*continued on p.* 238)

and remained there until he took that castle, and deprived earl Robert of his lands, and confiscated everything he possessed in England. The earl in consequence went oversea, and the levies thereafter turned homewards.[1]

Then, after these events, at Michaelmas, the king was at Westminster, together with all the chief men in the land, both ecclesiastics and laymen. Archbishop Anselm held a synod of the clergy, and they there laid down many canons relating to Christianity; and many, both French and English, were deprived there of their pastoral staffs and offices, which they had acquired unjustly or had occupied in perversity of life.

In this same year in Whit week came thieves, some from Auvergne, others from France and Flanders, and broke into the monastery of Peterborough, and stole much of value in gold and silver, namely crosses, chalices, and candlesticks.

1103. In this year [1102] king Henry spent Christmas at Westminster. Soon afterwards bishop William Gifford left the country, because he refused to act uncanonically and accept consecration from the archbishop Gerard of York. In the Easter of this same year the king held his court at Winchester; and thereafter Anselm, archbishop of Canterbury, went to Rome as he and the king had agreed.

In this year too duke Robert of Normandy came to this country to speak with the king; and before he went hence he remitted the three thousand marks which king Henry, according to agreement, had promised to give him each year.

In this year too, at Finchampstead in Berkshire, blood was seen coming from the ground. It was a very disastrous year here in this country by reason of numerous taxes and also as a result of murrain and the ruin of the harvest, both of the corn and of the fruit on all the trees. Further, on the morning of St Lawrence's day [10 August], the wind did such great damage here in the land to all the crops that nobody remembered anything like it before.

In this same year passed away Mathias, abbot of Peterborough, who lived no longer than one year after he had been made abbot. After Michaelmas, on 21 October, he was with solemn procession received as abbot, and on the same day next year he died in Gloucester and was buried there. (continued on p. 239)

---

[1] Cf. A. L. Poole, op. cit. 117–18, who draws attention to a fragment of a popular ballad, preserved in the Latin of Ordericus Vitalis, Ecclesiastical History (trans. Forester III. 337), reflecting the sentiment of joy and relief at Robert's capture and banishment: 'Gaude, rex Henrice, Dominoque Deo gratias age, quia tu libere coepisti regnare, ex quo Rodbertum de Belismo vicisti et de finibus regni tui expulisti.'

E 1104
from
p. 238

1104. In this year [1103] at Christmas the king held his court at Westminster, and at Easter at Winchester, and at Whitsun again at Westminster.

In this year the first day of Whitsuntide was on 5 June, and on the following Tuesday at noon there appeared four intersecting halos around the sun, white in colour, and looking as if they had been painted. All who saw it were astonished, for they did not remember seeing anything like it before.[2]

Hereafter duke Robert of Normandy was reconciled to Robert of Bellême, whom king Henry had deprived of his lands and driven out of England. As a result of their agreement the king of England and the duke of Normandy were set at variance. The king sent his officers oversea into Normandy, and the leading men there in the land received them, and acting treacherously to their lord the duke, admitted them into their castles, whence they harassed the duke with many vexations by harrying and burning. In this year also William, count of Mortain, fled hence from this country to Normandy; but after his departure he worked against the king, for which the king deprived him of all the possessions and lands which he owned here in this country.

It is not easy to describe the miseries which this country was suffering in these days through various and manifold injustices and taxes which never either ceased or became less. Moreover wherever the king went his wretched subjects suffered from the wholesale depredations of his retinue, very often including arson and manslaughter.

> All this was greatly God to provoke
> And also to harass poor wretched folk.

1105. In this year [1104] at the Nativity king Henry held his court at Windsor; thereafter, in the spring, he went oversea to Normandy against his brother, duke Robert. Whilst he remained there he won from his brother Caen and Bayeux and almost all the castles, and the leading men there in the land had to submit to him. Later, in the autumn, he returned again to this country. The territory which he had conquered in Normandy remained peaceful and submissive to him thereafter, except those who lived anywhere near to William, count of Mortain, whom *(continued on p. 240)*

---

[2] Earle pointed out that this was a description of a parhelion.

E 1105

from

p. 239 he [William] frequently harassed to the utmost of his power because of the loss of his lands here in this country. Then, before Christmas, Robert of Bellême came to this country to the king.

This was a very disastrous year here in this country on account of the destruction of the crops, and because of the numerous taxes from which there was no relief, either before the king went oversea, or while he was abroad, or after his return.

1106. In this year the king spent the Nativity at Westminster, and held his court there; and at that same festival Robert of Bellême, unable to come to terms with the king, left the country and went to Normandy.

Hereafter, before Lent, the king was at Northampton, whither came to him duke Robert, his brother, from Normandy; and, because the king would not restore to him what he had taken from him in Normandy, they parted in enmity, and the duke went straightway back oversea.

In the first week of Lent, on the Friday, 16 February, a strange star appeared in the evening, and for a long time afterwards was seen shining for a while each evening. The star made its appearance in the south-west, and seemed to be small and dark, but the light that shone from it was very bright, and appeared like an enormous beam of light shining north-east; and one evening it seemed as if the beam were flashing in the opposite direction towards the star.[1] Some said that they had seen other unknown stars about this time, but we cannot speak about these without reservation, because we did not ourselves see them. On the eve of Cena Domini, the Thursday before Easter, two moons were seen in the sky before day, one to the east and the other to the west, and both at the full, and that same day the moon was a fortnight old.

At Easter the king was at Bath, and at Whitsuntide at Salisbury, because he did not wish to hold a court on his departure oversea. Thereafter, before August, the king went oversea into Normandy, and almost all who were there in the land submitted themselves to his will, with the exception of Robert of Bellême and the count of Mortain, and a few other leading men who still supported the duke of Normandy. Therefore the king afterwards went with levies and besieged a castle belonging to the count of Mortain, which was called Tinchebrai.

(*continued on p.* 241)

---

[1] i.e. the light of the tail of the comet seemed to be streaming towards, instead of from, the nucleus (cf. BT Suppl. s.v. *ongeanweardes*).

E 1106
from
p. 240

While the king was besieging the castle, duke Robert of Normandy came against the king with his levies, on the eve of Michaelmas, and with him Robert of Bellême, William, count of Mortain, and all their supporters; but the strength and the victory were the king's.   There the duke of Normandy was taken prisoner, and the count of Mortain and Robert of Estouteville, and they were afterwards sent to England and placed in captivity. Robert of Bellême was put to flight there, and William Crispin taken prisoner and many besides.   Prince Edgar, who a short time previously had gone over from the king to the duke, was also taken prisoner, but the king afterwards let him go unmolested.   Thereafter the king conquered the whole of Normandy, and made it subject to his will and sway.   This year also there was very serious and unending strife between the emperor of Germany and his son; during these conflicts the father passed away, and the son succeeded to the empire.

1107. In this year [1106] at Christmas king Henry was in Normandy, and brought that land under his control and administration.   Thereafter he returned hither to this country in Lent, and at Easter held his court at Windsor, and at Whitsuntide at Westminster.   Afterwards, at the beginning of August, he was again at Westminster, and there made appointments to those bishoprics and abbacies which in England or in Normandy were without head or shepherd.   There were so many of them that there was nobody who remembered so many being given together.

At this same time, among others who received abbacies, Ernulf, who had been prior at Canterbury, succeeded to the abbacy of Peterborough. This was exactly seven years since the accession of king Henry, and the forty-first year of French rule in this country.   Many declared that they saw various portents in the moon during the year, and its light waxing and waning contrary to nature.

In this year passed away Maurice, bishop of London, and Robert, abbot of Bury St Edmunds, and Richard, abbot of Ely.   In this year also passed away Edgar, king of Scotland, on 13 January, and Alexander, his brother, succeeded to the kingdom, as king Henry granted him. (*continued on p.* 242)

1108. In this year [1107] king Henry spent the Nativity at Westminster, and Easter at Winchester, and returned to Westminster for Whitsuntide. Thereafter, before August, he went to Normandy. Philip, the king of France, passed away on 5 August, and his son Louis succeeded to the throne, and thereafter there arose many struggles between the kings of France and England while the latter remained in Normandy.

In this year too passed away archbishop Gerard of York before Whitsuntide, and Thomas was afterwards appointed to succeed him there.

1109. In this year [1108] king Henry was in Normandy at Christmas and at Easter, and before Whitsuntide returned hither to this country, and held his court at Westminster. There the contracts were completed and the oaths sworn for the marriage of his daughter to the emperor.

In this year there were very many thunderstorms, and those very terrifying. Anselm, archbishop of Canterbury, passed away on 22 March; and the first day of Easter was on *Letania maior* [25 April].

1110. In this year [1109] king Henry held his court at Christmas at Westminster; and at Easter he was at Marlborough. At Whitsuntide he held his court for the first time in New Windsor.

In this year, before Lent, the king sent his daughter oversea with innumerable treasures, and gave her in marriage to the emperor. On the fifth day of May, the moon appeared in the evening shining brightly, and afterwards little by little its light waned, so that as soon as it was night it was so completely extinguished that neither light, nor circle, nor anything at all could be seen of it: and so it remained until almost daybreak when it appeared at the full and shining brightly. On this same day it was a fortnight old. All night the sky was very clear, and the stars over all the heaven were shining brightly. That night the fruit on the trees was badly damaged by frost. Later, in the month of June, a star appeared in the north-east, its rays shining before it to the south-west: it was observed like this for many nights; later on in the night, when it rose higher, it was seen moving away in a north-westerly direction. (*continued on p.* 243)

In this year Philip de Braose, William Malet, and William
E 1110 Bainart were deprived of their lands. Also in this same year
from passed away count Helias [de la Flèche] who had held Maine
p. 242 from king Henry and acknowledged his overlordship; after
his decease the count of Anjou succeeded to the province and
held it against the king.

This was a very disastrous year here in this country on account of the
Aid which the king levied for the marriage of his daughter, and also
because of bad weather as a result of which the crops were badly
damaged: everywhere in the land the fruit harvest was very nearly all
ruined.

In this year work was first started on the new abbey church at
Chertsey.

1111. In this year [1110–11] king Henry did not wear his crown at
Christmas, nor at Easter, nor at Whitsuntide; and in August he went
oversea to Normandy on account of the hostility which some on the
borders of France were showing towards him, particularly the count of
Anjou who held Maine against him. After his arrival thither, they
carried out many cruel raids [1] against each other, burning and harrying.

In this year passed away count Robert of Flanders, and his son
Baldwin succeeded him.

The winter this year was very long, the weather bitter and severe; in
consequence the crops were badly damaged, and there was the worst
murrain in living memory.

1112. King Henry remained in Normandy all this year, on account
of hostilities against France and the count of Anjou who held Maine
against him.

While he was there he deprived the count of Evreux and William
Crispin of their lands, and drove them out of Normandy; and restored
to Philip de Braose his confiscated lands. He had Robert of Bellême
seized and put into prison.

This was a very good year and very productive in woods and open
country; but it was a very sad and anxious time on account of a fearful
pestilence.

1113. In this year [1112–13] king Henry spent Christmas, Easter,
and Whitsuntide in Normandy, and thereafter, (*continued on p.* 244)

A COTTONIAN FRAGMENT (H) 1113

H 1113 1113. . . . so that they could hardly speak. Thereafter died
(*continued on p.* 244)

---

[1] *unrada*, so also in 1116 E (p. 246); possibly an example of the intensive
prefix *un-*.

in summer, he sent hither to this country Robert of Bellême to
E 1113 the castle at Wareham, and soon thereafter returned himself
from to this country.
p. 243 1114. In this year [1113] king Henry held his court at the
Nativity at Windsor, and did not hold his court again this year.

At midsummer he went with levies into Wales, and the Welsh came
and made peace with the king; and he had castles built in that country.
Thereafter, in September, he went oversea into Normandy.

In this year, towards the end of May, a strange star was seen, shining
with a long trail of light for many nights.

Also one day in this same year there was an ebb-tide which was
everywhere lower than any man remembered before; so people went
riding and walking across the Thames to the east of London Bridge.
In this year there were very strong winds in the month of October,
but exceptionally violent on the night of 18 November, and left a trail of
damage everywhere in woods and villages.

Also in this year the king gave the archbishopric of Canterbury to
Ralph who had been bishop of Rochester; and Thomas,

(*continued on p.* 245)

Peter, abbot of Gloucester, on 17 July, and the king appointed
H 1113 William, who was a monk in the same monastery, to succeed
from him on 5 October.
p. 243 [1114]. In this year [1113] king Henry was in Windsor at
Christmas, and wore his crown there. There he gave the
bishopric of Worcester to Theobald, his chaplain. He also gave the
abbacy of Ramsey to Rainald, a monk of Caen, and the abbacy of York
to Richard, who was a monk in the same monastery. He also gave the
abbacy at Thorney to Robert, who was a monk at St Evroul. He also
gave the earldom of Northamptonshire to David, who was the queen's
brother. Thereafter Thomas, archbishop of York, died on 17 February; and thereafter he gave the abbacy of Cerne Abbas to William,
who was a monk at Caen. (*continued on p.* 245)

the archbishop of York, passed away, and Thurstan succeeded
E 1114 him; he had formerly been the king's chaplain.
from At this same time the king went towards the sea meaning to
p. 244 cross, but the weather delayed him. In the meantime he sent
his writ to Ernulf, abbot of Peterborough, and commanded
him to come to him with the utmost haste, since he wished to speak with
him privately. When he came to him, he urged him to accept the
bishopric of Rochester, and the archbishops, bishops, and the nobility
of England supported the king. Although he resisted for a long time,
yet it was of no avail; and the king ordered the archbishop to lead him
to Canterbury and consecrate him bishop willy nilly. This was done in
the village called Westbourne [1] on 15 September. When the monks of
Peterborough heard the news, they had never been so overcome with
grief, for he was a very good and kind man, and did much good both
inside *(continued on p. 246)*

The king spent Easter at Kingsthorpe [1] near Northampton.
H 1114 Thereafter he gave the archbishopric of Canterbury to Ralph,
from who was bishop of Rochester, and he took office on 24 Feb-
p. 244 ruary. Thereafter, on 3 May, died Nigel, abbot of Burton-on-
Trent. Thereafter, on 5 May, Chichester was burnt down, and
the cathedral church there as well.
The king spent Whit Sunday at St Albans. Thereafter, at midsummer, he went with his levies into Wales, and built castles in that
land; and the Welsh kings came to him and became his men and swore
him oaths of allegiance.
Thereafter he came to Winchester and while he was there gave the
archbishopric of York to Thurstan, his chaplain; the abbacy at Bury St
Edmunds he gave to Albold, who had been a monk of Bec, on 16
August. Thereafter, on the feast of the Exaltation of the Holy Cross
[14 September], he gave the abbacy of Muchelney to Ealdwulf, who was
a monk in the same monastery. He also gave the abbacy of Burton-on-
Trent to Geoffrey, who was a monk at the Old Minster [Winchester]. At
the same time, archbishop Ralph gave the bishopric of Rochester . . .

[1] For these identifications I am indebted to Professor Bruce Dickins.
Henry was awaiting a favourable breeze at Westbourne (Sussex) to sail
from Portsmouth near by. Cf. *The Chronicle of Hugo Candidus* (ed. Mellows), 96, *cum rex mare transfretatus esset et uentum attendisset ad uillam
que dicitur Burne*. Cf. 34 *EHR* 373–4. The reference is not to the *consecration* of Ernulf.

Kingsthorpe, a N.W. suburb of Northampton, was a royal manor in
Domesday Book (10 EPN 133–4). Neither *Burne* nor *þorp* is cited in
DEPN.

and outside the monastery whilst he was there. May God
Almighty ever dwell with him.

Soon thereafter the king, at the desire of the archbishop of
Canterbury, gave the abbacy to a monk of Séez who was called
John; and soon afterwards the king and the archbishop of
Canterbury sent him to Rome for the archbishop's pallium: [1] with him
went a monk,[1] who was [1] called Warner, and archdeacon John, the
archbishop's nephew; and they had a successful mission there. This
took place on 21 September in the village called Rowner [Ha]; and the
same day the king took ship at Portsmouth.

1115. In this year [1114] king Henry spent the Nativity in Normandy;
and while he was there he made all the leading men in Normandy do
homage and swear allegiance to William, his son by his queen. Thereafter he returned to this country in the month of July.

This year the winter was so severe with snow and frost that no man
living remembered a severer: because of it there was fearful pestilence
among cattle.

In this year pope Paschal sent the pallium hither to this country to
Ralph, archbishop of Canterbury, and he received it with great ceremony at his see of Canterbury. It was brought from Rome by abbot
Anselm, nephew of archbishop Anselm, and by abbot John of Peterborough.[2]

1116. In this year [1115] king Henry spent the Nativity at St Albans,
and had the abbey church there consecrated. He spent Easter at
Odiham.[3] Winter again this year was very long, the weather bitter and
severe for the cattle and for everything. The king went oversea to
Normandy immediately after Easter, and in the numerous cruel raids
and forays between France and Normandy many castles were taken.
The main cause of this strife was the support which king Henry gave to
his nephew, count Theobald of Blois, who was then at war with his lord,
Louis, king of France.

This was a very hard year and disastrous for the crops, because of the
very heavy rains that came just before August and which proved very
vexatious and troublesome until Candlemas came. This year, too,

(*continued on p.* 247

---

[1] These words (*for the archbishop's pallium, monk, was*) were added later at
Peterborough.

[2] The phrase is a later Peterborough addition.

[3] Ha; another royal manor.

there was such a shortage of mast, that neither in the whole of
E 1116 this land, nor in Wales too, was any to be heard of. This land
from and our people frequently suffered grievous oppression during
p. 246 this year from the taxes which the king levied within boroughs
and without.[4]

In this same year the monastery of Peterborough was completely
destroyed by fire, and all the buildings, except the chapter-house and the
dormitory; in addition, most of the town was also completely burned
down. All this happened on 4 August, which was a Friday.[5]

1117. King Henry spent the whole of this year in Normandy, on
account of the hostility of the king of France and his other neighbours.
Towards summer of this year, the king of France and the count of
Flanders with him invaded Normandy with levies, and remained therein
for one night, but retired in the morning without a battle. Normandy
suffered grievous oppression both from taxation and from the levies
which king Henry had gathered to defend it. This nation too in this
same year suffered severe oppression from numerous taxes.

In this year also, on the night of 1 December, there were violent
storms, with thunder, lightning, rain, and hail. And for a great part of
the night of 11 December, the moon appeared to turn all bloody and
afterwards was eclipsed. Also on the night of 16 December the heaven
was seen very red, as if there were a conflagration in the sky. On the
octave of St John the Evangelist [3 January] occurred the great earthquake in Lombardy, as a result of which many churches, towers, and
houses collapsed, and wrought great havoc upon the people. This was
a very disastrous year for grain, because of the rains which hardly
stopped all the year.

Abbot Gilbert of Westminster passed away on 6 December; and
abbot Faricius of Abingdon on 23 February. In this same year . . .[6]

1118. King Henry spent the whole of this year in Normandy, on
account of the war with the king of France, the count of Anjou, and the
count of Flanders. The count of Flanders was wounded when he was
in Normandy, and retired to Flanders with his wound. As a result of
the hostility of these men, the king was put to infinite trouble, suffering
great loss (*continued on p.* 248)

---

[4] For the formula see F. E. Harmer, *op. cit.* 428–9.

[5] *per incuriam combustum est totum monasterium preter capitulum, et
dormitorium et necessarium et refectorium nouum, nisi solummodo per tres
dies manducauerant, refectis prius pauperibus. Set et tota uilla combusta est*
(*The Chronicle of Hugh Candidus*, ed. Mellows, 97).

[6] More than a line and a half is left blank in the manuscript.

both in property and in land: but his greatest difficulties arose
E 1118 from the frequent revolts of his own men who betrayed him and
from deserted to his enemies, surrendering their castles to them to
p. 247 compass the king's discomfiture and betrayal. England dearly
paid for all this in numerous taxes from which there was no
relief all the year.

In this year, one evening, in the week of the Epiphany, there was severe
lightning followed by terrible claps of thunder.

On 1 May queen Matilda passed away at Westminster, and was
buried there. In this year also count Robert of Meulan passed away.

Also in this year, on St Thomas's day [21 December], there was an
exceptionally high wind, more violent than any in living memory and
its effect on houses and trees was everywhere to be seen.

In this year also passed away pope Paschal; and John of Gaeta, also
called Gelasius, succeeded him in the papacy.

1119. King Henry spent the whole of this year in Normandy, on
account of the war with the king of France and strife with his own
subjects, who treacherously deserted him to submit to the enemy, causing
him frequent embarrassment. Finally the two kings joined battle with
their armies in Normandy; and the king of France was put to flight and
all his best men taken prisoner. Thereafter many of king Henry's own
subjects who had opposed him in their castles submitted to him and
came to terms; some of the castles, however, he took by force.

In this year William, son of king Henry and queen Matilda, went into
Normandy to his father, and there he was married to the daughter of
the count of Anjou, who became his wedded wife.

On the eve of Michaelmas [28 September] a great earthquake was felt
in some places here in this country, but it was most severe in Gloucestershire and in Worcestershire.

In this year pope Gelasius passed away on this side of the Alps and
was buried at Cluny. To succeed him the archbishop of Vienne was
elected pope; his name was Calixtus. On the feast of St Luke the
Evangelist [18 October] he came to Rheims in France, and there held a
council. Archbishop Thurstan (*continued on p.* 249)

of York went to it; and because he had received his office from the pope uncanonically and in opposition to the see of Canterbury and contrary to the king's wishes, the king forbade him any return to England; and thus he lost his archbishopric and went with the pope towards Rome.

Also in this year passed away count Baldwin of Flanders from the wounds which he had received in Normandy; and Charles, his father's sister's son, succeeded him: he was a son of St Cnut, king of Denmark.

1120. In this year the kings of England and France were reconciled; and after their reconciliation king Henry's own subjects inside Normandy came to complete agreement with him, as did also the counts of Flanders and Ponthieu. Thereafter king Henry made the arrangements he considered necessary for the administration of his castles and his land in Normandy, and so returned hither to this country before Advent.

On the passage two of the king's sons, William and Richard, were drowned, together with Richard, earl of Chester, and Ottuel, his brother, and a great many of the king's household, stewards, chamberlains, cupbearers, and officials of different kinds, besides a countless number of very outstanding men. To their friends the death of these men was a double tragedy; not only because they departed this life so suddenly, but also because few of their bodies were recovered afterwards.[1]

Twice in this year came that light to the Sepulchre of the Lord in Jerusalem; once at Easter, and a second time on the Assumption of St Mary [15 August], as the faithful told who had come from thence. Through the intervention of the pope, archbishop Thurstan of York became reconciled with the king and returned to this country: he recovered his bishopric, although the archbishop of Canterbury was very much displeased.

1121. In this year [1120] king Henry spent Christmas at Brampton.[2] Afterwards before Candlemas [2 February] he was married at Windsor to Adeliza, daughter of the duke of Louvain, who was thereafter consecrated queen.

The moon was eclipsed on the eve of 5 April [i.e. 4 April] when it was fourteen days old. (*continued on p.* 250)

---

[1] There are detailed accounts of the loss of the White Ship on the night of 25 November by Ordericus (trans. Forester IV. 32–42) and William of Malmesbury and others.

[2] Hu (3 EPN 233–5). See W. Farrer, *An Outline Itinerary of Henry the First* (reprinted from 34 *EHR*).

The king spent Easter at Berkeley, and thereafter on Whit Sunday he held a great court at Westminster; and later in the summer of the same year went into Wales with levies. The Welsh came to meet him, and agreed to the king's terms.

In this same year the count of Anjou returned to his land from Jerusalem, and afterwards sent hither to this country to have his daughter brought back: she had been the wife of William, the king's son.

On the eve of the Nativity there was a very violent wind over all the country, and the effects were very noticeable.

1122. In this year [1121] king Henry spent Christmas at Norwich and Easter in Northampton.

In the preceding Lent the borough of Gloucester was burnt down while the monks were singing their mass, and the deacon had begun the gospel *Preteriens Jesus*.[1] Then the fire caught the upper part of the tower, and the monastery was completely burnt out, with all the treasures it contained, except for a few books and three chasubles: this happened on 8 March.

Thereafter, on the Tuesday after Palm Sunday, 22 March [*recte* 21 March], there was a very violent wind; after which numerous portents appeared far and wide in England, and many illusions were seen and heard. On the night of 25 July there was a very great earthquake over the whole of Somerset and Gloucestershire. Afterwards, on 8 September, on the feast [of the Nativity] of St Mary, a violent wind blew from morning until pitch dark.

In this same year, on 20 October, Ralph, archbishop of Canterbury, passed away. Thereafter there were many sailors on sea and on inland water who said that they had seen a great and extensive fire near the ground in the north-east which continuously increased in width as it mounted to the sky. And the heavens opened into four parts and fought against it as if determined to put it out, and the fire stopped rising upwards. They saw that fire at the first streak of dawn, and it [2] lasted until full daylight: this happened on 7 December. (*continued on p.* 251)

---

[1] i.e. the gospel for the Wednesday after the fourth Sunday in Lent. Easter Sunday was 26 March.

[2] Presumably an aurora borealis; cf. annal 1131.

E 1123
from
p. 250

1123. In this year [1122] the king spent Christmas at Dunstable, and messengers from the count of Anjou visited him there. Thence he went to Woodstock, his bishops and all his court in attendance. On Wednesday, 10 January, it happened that the king was riding in his deer park, with the bishop of Salisbury on one side of him and Robert Bloet, bishop of Lincoln, on the other; and they were talking as they rode. Then the bishop of Lincoln sank down in the saddle, and said to the king: 'Lord king, I am dying.' The king sprang down from his horse, and caught him in his arms, and had him carried home to his lodging, but he died immediately. He was conveyed to Lincoln with great ceremony, and buried in front of St Mary's altar by Robert Pecceth, bishop of Chester.

Immediately afterwards the king sent his writs over all England, summoning all his bishops, his abbots, and his thanes to come to a meeting of his council at Gloucester at Candlemas, and meet him there; and so they did. When they were all assembled, the king asked them to choose for themselves an archbishop of Canterbury, whomsoever they wished, and he would give his consent to the election. Then the bishops discussed this amongst themselves and declared that they would never again agree to the appointment of a man from one of the monastic orders to be archbishop over them, but all went in a body to the king and desired that they might have permission to elect as their archbishop a man from the secular clergy, whomsoever they wished; and this the king granted them. The bishop of Salisbury and the bishop of Lincoln before his death were originally responsible for this, for they had never had any love for the monastic rule, but were ever in opposition to monks and their rule. The prior and the monks of Canterbury, and all the others there who belonged to a monastic order, held out against it for two whole days to no effect, since the bishop of Salisbury was powerful and ruled all England, and opposed it with all his strength and for all he knew. Then they chose a cleric [3] called William of Curbeil: he was (*continued on p.* 252)

---

[3] i.e. one of the (secular) clergy

a canon from a monastery called St Osyth's. They presented
him to the king, and the king gave him the archbishopric, and
although all the bishops accepted him, the monks, earls, and
almost all the thanes who were present opposed him.

At this same time the messengers of the count [of Anjou]
departed without coming to any agreement with the king, and cared
nothing for his favours.[1]

At the same time came a certain legate from Rome, who was called
Henry. He was abbot of the abbey of St Jean d'Angély, and came
about the payment of Peter's pence. He told the king that it was
unlawful that one of the secular clergy should be set over monks;
moreover they had already canonically chosen an archbishop in their
chapter; but the king would not revoke his decision because of the love
he bore the bishop of Salisbury. Soon thereafter the archbishop went
to Canterbury, and was there admitted, although it was against their
will. He was immediately consecrated bishop by the bishop of
London, and Ernulf, bishop of Rochester, and William Gifford, bishop
of Winchester, and Bernard, a bishop from Wales,[2] and Roger, bishop of
Salisbury. Soon afterwards, in the spring, the archbishop went to
Rome for his pallium; and with him went Bernard, a bishop from
Wales, and Sigefrith, abbot of Glastonbury, and Anselm, abbot of
Bury St Edmunds, and John, archdeacon of Canterbury, and Gifford,
the king's court chaplain.

At the same time went Thurstan, archbishop of York, to Rome at the
pope's command, and arrived thither three days before the archbishop
of Canterbury, and was there received with great ceremony. After
the arrival of the archbishop of Canterbury, it was a whole week
before he could obtain an audience of the pope; this was because
the pope was given to understand that he had accepted the primacy
in opposition to the monks of the monastery, and uncanonically.
Yet Rome, like the rest of the world, was won over by gold and
silver. The pope relented, and gave him his pallium; and the archbishop swore by the head of St Peter and of St Paul to be obedient
to him in all those things which the pope enjoined him, and was sent
home with his blessing.

While the archbishop was abroad, the king gave the bishopric of
Bath to the queen's chancellor, who was called Godfrey and born at
Louvain. The appointment was made on the day of the Annunciation
of St Mary [25 March] at Woodstock. Soon thereafter the king went
to Winchester, (continued on p. 253)

---

[1] As Henry refused to return the dowry of his son's widow to her father,
count Fulk of Anjou, it would seem more natural for *gyfe* to have its
meaning 'dowry' (*fædrenfeoh*) in this context. If so perhaps the scribe has
written the preterite of one of the *reccan* verbs for the other. If so, render
(cf. BT *reccan* vi) 'and got no satisfaction about his (Fulk's) dowry.'
[2] Bishop of St David's.

E 1123
from
p. 252

and was there all Eastertide, and while he was there he gave the bishopric of Lincoln to a cleric called Alexander. He was the 'nephew' of the bishop of Salisbury, and this he did all for love of this bishop.

Thence the king went to Portsmouth and lay there all through Whit week. Then as soon as he had a wind, he sailed across to Normandy, and entrusted all England into the care and rule of Roger, bishop of Salisbury. The king remained in Normandy for the rest of this year, and great hostility arose between him and his thanes, with the result that Waleran, count of Meulan, and Almaric, and Hugh of Montfort, and William of Roumare, and many others turned aside from their allegiance and held their castles against him. The king held out boldly against them, and this same year won from Waleran his castle of Pont Audemer, and Montfort from Hugh; and afterwards, the longer he went on, the better he succeeded.

In this same year, before the bishop of Lincoln arrived in his bishopric, almost the whole borough of Lincoln was destroyed by fire and a countless number of people, both men and women, were burnt to death. It was impossible to describe the great damage that was done there. It happened on 19 May.

1124. King Henry spent the whole of this year in Normandy, on account of the hostilities he was engaged in against King Louis of France and the count of Anjou, but most of all against his own subjects.

Then on the feast of the Annunciation of St Mary [25 March], it happened that Waleran, count of Meulan, went from one of his castles, called Beaumont-le-Roger, to another of his castles, called Vatteville. With him went Almaric, the seneschal of the king of France, Hugh Fitz Gervase, Hugh of Montfort, and many other brave knights. Then the king's knights from all the castles round about came against them and fought with them and put them to flight, taking prisoner count Waleran, Hugh Fitz Gervase, Hugh of Montfort, and twenty-five other knights, and brought them to the king. The king had count Waleran and Hugh Fitz Gervase imprisoned in the castle at Rouen, but sent Hugh of Montfort to England (*continued on p.* 254) and had him placed in durance vile [1] in the castle at Gloucester, and sent as many of the others at his discretion north or south to imprisonment in his castles. Then thereafter the king went and won all the castles belonging to count Waleran in Normandy, and all the others which his enemies held against him.

E 1124 from p. 253

All this strife was on account of the son of duke Robert of Normandy, named William. This same William had taken to wife the younger daughter of Fulk, count of Anjou; and for this reason the king of France, all the counts, and all the powerful men supported him, and said that it was wrong for the king to hold his brother Robert in captivity and unjustly to banish his son William from Normandy.

In this same year in England there were many failures in grain and in crops of every kind, so that between Christmas and Candlemas the two seed-lips of seed required to sow an acre of wheat cost six shillings, and the three seed-lips for an acre of barley cost six shillings, while the four seed-lips for an acre of oats cost four shillings. The reason for this was the shortage of grain, and the coinage was so debased that if anyone took a pound to market he found it impossible to buy twelve penn'orth with it.

In this same year passed away the blessed bishop Ernulf of Rochester, who had earlier been abbot of Peterborough: this happened on 15 March. Thereafter, on 23 April, king Alexander of Scotland passed away, and David, his brother, who was earl of Northamptonshire, succeeded to the kingdom, and held them both together, the kingdom of Scotland and the earldom in England. On 14 December, in Rome, passed away the pope whose name was Calixtus; and Honorius succeeded to the papacy.

In this same year, after St Andrew's day before Christmas [30 November], Ralph Basset held a court of the king's thanes at *Hundehoh* in Leicestershire, and hanged there more thieves than ever before: forty-four of them in all were dispatched in no time, and six had their eyes put out and were castrated. Many honest men said that a great injustice had been done in executing many of them; but our Lord God Almighty, from whom (*continued on p.* 255)

---

[1] *on ifele bendas* an early rendering of the French expression.

no secrets are hid, He sees the poor oppressed by every kind
E 1124 of injustice: first they are bereft of their property, and then
from they are slain. A very distressful year this was! He who
p. 254 had any money was deprived of it by violent extortions and
by oppressive courts; he who had none died of hunger.

1125. In this year [1124] before Christmas king Henry sent from
Normandy to England and gave instructions that all the moneyers who
were in England should be deprived of their members, namely the right
hand of each and their testicles below: the reason for this was that
anyone who had a pound found it would not buy a penn'orth in a
market. Bishop Roger of Salisbury sent over all England, and commanded them all to assemble at Winchester by Christmas. When they
came thither they were then taken one by one, and each deprived of the
right hand and the testicles below. All this was done in the twelve
days between Christmas and Epiphany, and was entirely justified
because they had ruined the whole country by the magnitude of their
fraud [2] which they paid for to the full.

In this year the pope sent a cardinal from Rome to this country;
his name was John of Crema. He first visited the king in Normandy,
and the king received him with great ceremony, and commended him
afterwards to the archbishop, William of Canterbury, and he conducted
him to Canterbury, where he was received with great honour and
solemn procession. He sang high mass on Easter day at Christ's altar.
Afterwards he went over all England to all the bishoprics and abbacies
in this country, and everywhere he was received with ceremony, and all
gave him great and splendid gifts. Thereafter, on the Nativity of St
Mary in September [8 September], he held his council in London for
three whole days, with the archbishops, the diocesan bishops, the
abbots, the clergy, and laity; and there enjoined those same canons
which archbishop Anselm had previously laid down and many more,
though little came of it. Thence he went oversea soon after Michaelmas, and so to Rome, accompanied by William, archbishop of Canterbury, and Thurstan, archbishop of York, and Alexander, bishop of
Lincoln, and John, bishop of Lothian [i.e. of Glasgow], and Geoffrey,
abbot of St Albans. They were received there by pope Honorius with
great ceremony, and remained there all that winter.

On St Lawrence's day [10 August] in this same year there was so
great a flood (*continued on p.* 256)

---

[2] *mid here micele fals.* In II Canute § 8 (ed. A. J. Robertson, *The Laws of
the Kings of England from Edward to Henry I* 178), the word *fals* is used with
the meaning 'bad money' or 'adulteration.' In IV Æthelred § 5 (Robertson
74), coiners of bad money are called *falsarii.* For Henry I's decree concerning the coinage, see Robertson p. 284 f.

that many villages were inundated and men were drowned;
E 1125 bridges were broken down, and the corn and the meadows
from were completely laid waste, bringing hunger and death to men
p. 255 and live-stock; and there was more unseasonableness in crops
of every kind than for many years past.

In this same year, on 14 October, abbot John of Peterborough passed
away.

1126. King Henry was in Normandy all the year until after autumn,
and returned to this country between the Nativity of St Mary [8 September] and Michaelmas. With him came the queen and his daughter
whom he had formerly given in marriage to the emperor Henry of
Lorraine. He brought with him count Waleran and Hugh Fitz
Gervase: he sent the count into captivity to Bridgnorth, and later sent
him thence to Wallingford, and Hugh to Windsor, and had him kept in
strict confinement.

Then after Michaelmas came David, the king of Scots, from Scotland
to this country: and king Henry received him with great ceremony, and
he remained the whole year in this country.

In this same year the king had his brother Robert taken out of the
custody of Roger, bishop of Salisbury, and committed him to his son
Robert, earl of Gloucester: he had him taken to Bristol and there
imprisoned in the castle. This was done entirely on the advice of his
daughter and of her maternal uncle, David the king of Scots.

1127. This year [1126] king Henry held his court at Christmas in
Windsor. David, the king of Scots, was present, and all the most
important men in England, ecclesiastics and laymen; and there he
obtained an oath from archbishops, bishops, abbots, earls, and all those
thanes present, that England and Normandy should pass after his death
into the possession of his daughter Æthelic,[1] wife of the late emperor of
Germany. He then sent her to Normandy, and with her went her
brother Robert, earl of Gloucester, and Brian, son of count Alan
Fergant, and married her to Geoffrey Martel, son of the count of
Anjou. This marriage, however, gave as much offence, or more,[2] to
the French as to the English, but the king arranged it in order to secure
the friendship of the (*continued on p.* 257)

---

[1] i.e. Adeliza, later known as Matilda.

[2] *napema* is used twice in this annal in unusual constructions, probably
because of ellipsis. Most translators read *napeles* here ['it displeased all
the French and the English'] and render the passage on p. 257 (l. 21) 'But
that did not make it any truer—he simply wanted to have possession of
both' (*s.a.* Rositzke).

count of Anjou, and to secure assistance against William, his nephew.

In the spring of this same year, count Charles of Flanders was slain [3] by his own men in a church as he lay and prayed to God before the altar during mass. The king of France put forward William, the son of the duke of Normandy, and gave him the county, where he was accepted by the people as their lord. This same William had been married to the daughter of the count of Anjou, but, entirely through the efforts of Henry, king of England, the marriage had been dissolved on the grounds of consanguinity. Afterwards he married the [half-] sister of the queen of France, and on that account the king gave him the county of Flanders.

In this same year he gave the abbacy of Peterborough to an abbot named Henry of Poitou,[4] who already held the abbacy of St Jean d'Angély. The archbishop and all the bishops said this was uncanonical, and that he could not have charge of two abbacies; but the same Henry gave the king to understand that he had left his abbacy on account of the great strife in that country, and that he had done so on the advice and with the permission of the pope of Rome and the abbot of Cluny, and also because he was the legate sent from Rome to collect Peter's pence.[5] This was true enough, but the reason was rather that he wished to have charge of both abbacies—which, in fact, he did succeed in doing as long as it was God's will. As a secular clerk he had been bishop of Soissons; afterwards he became a monk of Cluny, and later became prior in the same monastery, and then prior of Savigny-le-Vieux. Thereafter, since he was a relation of the king of England and of the count of Poitou, the count gave him the abbacy of St Jean d'Angély. Afterwards by great intrigue he managed to get possession of the archbishopric of Besançon, but only for three days, for it was only fitting that he should forfeit what he had come by uncanonically. Thereupon he got possession of the bishopric of Saintes, which was five miles from his abbacy, and held it for almost a week, but the abbot of Cluny got him out, just as he had done before from Besançon. Then it occurred to him that if he could get firmly rooted in England, he could

(*continued on p.* 258)

[3] Cf. the account by Ordericus Vitalis, *Ecclesiastical History* (trans. Forester IV. 87–8).
[4] *The Chronicle of Hugh Candidus* (ed. Mellows 99–104) gives an account of Abbot Henry and the incident of the Wild Hunt. The Latin phrases below are quoted therefrom.
[5] *Et quia numquam quietus esse uoluit, adquisiuit legacionem colligendorum denariorum Rome in Anglia, ut per hoc abbaciam adquireret.*

get all his own way, so he besought the king, and said to him
E 1127 that he was a broken-down old man, who could not endure the
from great injustices and disturbances which were prevalent in their
p. 257 land; and begged to be given the abbacy of Peterborough
through his agency and that of all his friends whom he mentioned by name. And the king granted it to him because he was his
kinsman, and because he had been the chief witness to swear oath and
testify when the marriage of the son of the duke of Normandy and the
daughter of the count of Anjou was dissolved on the ground of consanguinity. Thus despicably was the abbacy bestowed between Christmas and Candlemas in London; and so he accompanied the king to
Winchester, and from there he came to Peterborough, where he took up
his abode just as drones do in a hive. Everything bees gather, drones
devour and carry off, and so too did he. Everything that he could take,
from within the monastery or outside it, from ecclesiastics and laymen,
he sent oversea. He did nothing for the monastery's welfare and left
nothing of value untouched. Let no one be surprised at the truth of
what we are about to relate, for it was general knowledge throughout
the whole country that immediately after his arrival—it was the Sunday [1] when they sing *Exurge Quare o[bdormis]*, *D[omine]*? [2]—many men
both saw and heard a great number of huntsmen hunting. The huntsmen were black, huge, and hideous, and rode on black horses and on
black he-goats, and their hounds were jet black, with eyes like saucers,
and horrible. [3] This was seen in the very deer park of the town of
Peterborough, and in all the woods that stretch from that same town to
Stamford, and in the night the monks heard them sounding and winding
their horns. Reliable witnesses who kept watch in the night declared
that there might well have been as many as twenty or thirty of them
winding their horns as near as they could tell. This was seen and heard
from the time of his arrival all through Lent and right up to Easter.
Such was his entrance: of his exit we cannot yet say. Let it be as God
ordains!

1128. King Henry spent the whole year in Normandy on account of
the strife that existed between himself and his nephew, the count of
Flanders. However, the count was wounded [4] in a certain battle by a
foot soldier, and retired with his wound into the monastery of St
Bertin, [5] and straightway became a monk there, but lived for only five
days before he died and was buried there. God have mercy on his
soul! This happened on 27 July. (*continued on p.* 259)

---

[1] i.e. 6 February 1127. Lent began on 16 February.

[2] Introit (Ps. xliii, 23 ff.) on Sexagesima (as Professor Dickins has pointed
out to me).

[3] *Nam uisi sunt quasi uenatores cum cornibus et canibus, set omnes nigerimi
erant et equi eorum et canes, et aliqui quasi edos [= haedos] equitabant, et
oculos grandes habebant, et erant quasi uiginti aut triginta simul. Hoc non
est falsum, quia plurimi ueracissimi homines uiderunt et audierunt cornua.*

In this same year passed away bishop Rannulf Flambard of Durham: he was buried there on 5 September.

In this same year the fore-mentioned abbot Henry went back to his own monastery in Poitou, by permission of the king.

He gave the king to understand that he would entirely relinquish that monastery and leave that country to dwell with him there in England in the monastery of Peterborough, but it was far from being so. He acted thus because he wished, by means of his great cunning, to stay there for perhaps twelve months or more, and then return. God Almighty have pity on that unhappy foundation!

In this year Hugh of the Knights Templars came from Jerusalem to the king in Normandy; and the king received him with great ceremony, and gave him great treasures of gold and silver, and sent him thereafter to England, where he was welcomed by all good men. He was given treasures by all, and in Scotland too; and by him much wealth, entirely in gold and silver, was sent to Jerusalem. He called for people to go out to Jerusalem. As a result more people went, either with him or after him, than ever before since the time of the first crusade, which was in the day of pope Urban: yet little was achieved by it. He declared that a decisive battle was imminent between the Christians and the heathen, but, when all those multitudes got there, they were pitiably duped to find it was nothing but lies.

1129. In this year the king sent to England for count Waleran and Hugo Fitz Gervase and hostages were given for them. Hugh went home to his own lands in France, but Waleran remained with the king, who restored to him all his lands, with the exception of his castle. Afterwards, in the autumn, the king returned to England, and the count came with him, and they then became as good friends as they had previously been foes.

Soon thereafter, at the king's suggestion and by his leave, William, archbishop of Canterbury, sent over all England, and summoned the bishops, abbots, archdeacons, and all the priors, monks, and canons that were in all the cells in England, and all those whose duty it was to look after and care for Christendom, fo assemble in London at Michaelmas where they should discuss all the rights of the church.[6] When they were assembled thither, then began (*continued on p.* 260)

I am indebted to Professor Dickins for a reference to A. H. Krappe, *The Science of Folk-lore* (Methuen 1929) which explains (p. 259) why he-goats were regarded as sinister beasts—'Then after the coming of Monotheism the theriomorphic divinities were rudely identified with the Christian Devil, it was a natural consequence that quite a number of animals formerly sacred to the inhabitants of Olympus and Walhal should now be devoted to the service of His Satanic Majesty. This is particularly true of the goat, very closely associated with the devil.'

[4] Cf. Ordericus Vitalis, *op. cit.* IV 92–3.

[5] At St Omer (dép. Pas de Calais).

[6] Cf. F. E. Harmer, *Anglo-Saxon Writs* 487 for a note on *Godes gerichte*.

the council on a Monday, and continued right on till the Friday.
E 1129 When it all came out, it was found that it had concerned itself
from solely with ordering archdeacons and priests to put away their
p. 259 wives by St Andrew's day [30 November]: anyone refusing to
do so was to lose his church, his house, and his glebe, and have
no further claim to them. This was decreed by William, archbishop of
Canterbury, and by all the diocesan bishops then in England; and the
king gave them all permission to disperse, which they did. All the
decrees were of no avail, for they all kept their wives by the king's
permission, as they had formerly done.

In the same year passed away William Gifford, bishop of Winchester,
and was buried there on 25 January. After Michaelmas the king gave
the bishopric to his nephew, abbot Henry of Glastonbury, and he was
consecrated bishop by William, archbishop of Canterbury, on 17
November.

In this same year passed away pope Honorius. He was barely dead
before two popes were elected. One was called Peter; he was a monk
of Cluny and came of the richest families in Rome; he was supported
by Rome and the duke of Sicily. The other was called Gregory; he
was a secular clerk and was driven out of Rome by the other pope and
his kinsmen; he was supported by the emperor of Germany, and the
king of France, and Henry, king of England, and by all this side of the
Alps. Now more heresies were rife in Christendom than ever before.
Christ give counsel to His wretched people!

In this same year, on the eve of St Nicholas's day, there was a great
earthquake shortly before dawn.

1130. In this year, on 4 May, the cathedral church of Canterbury
was consecrated by archbishop William, who was attended by bishops
John of Rochester, Gilbert Universal of London, Henry of Winchester,
Alexander of Lincoln, Roger of Salisbury, Simon of Worcester, Roger
of Coventry, Godfrey of Bath, Everard of Norwich, Sigefrith of
Chichester, Bernard of St David's, Audoenus of Evreux from Normandy, John of Séez. (*continued on p.* 261)

On the fourth day thereafter king Henry was in Rochester when the borough was almost burnt down, and archbishop William, attended by the fore-mentioned bishops, consecrated St Andrew's cathedral. In the autumn king Henry went oversea to Normandy.

This same year abbot Henry of Angély came to Peterborough after Easter, and said he had entirely relinquished the monastery [of Angély]. After him, with the king's permission, the abbot of Cluny, named Peter, came to this country, and he was welcomed with great ceremony everywhere wherever he went. He came to Peterborough, and there abbot Henry promised him that he would secure the monastery of Peterborough for him, so that it would be subject to Cluny. However, there is a proverb which says, 'Hedge abides that fields divides.'[1] May God Almighty frustrate evil counsels! Shortly afterwards the abbot of Cluny went back to his own country.

1131. In this year [1130] after Christmas, on Sunday evening,[2] just after bedtime, all the northern sky appeared like a blazing fire, so that all who saw it were more terrified than ever before; this happened on 11 January. In this same year, over the whole of England, murrain among cattle and pigs was worse than any within living memory; so that in a village where ten or twelve ploughs were in use, not a single one was left working; and a man who had owned two or three hundred pigs found himself with none. After that the hens died, and then meat and cheese and butter were in short supply. May God improve matters when it is His will!

King Henry came to England after the earlier St Peter's day [29 June], and before autumn.

In this same year, before Easter, abbot Henry went oversea to Normandy from Peterborough, and there spoke with the king. He told him that the abbot of Cluny had ordered him to report and hand over the abbey of Angély; after he had done that he said he would return to England if the king gave permission. So he went to his own monastery [of Angély], and remained there right up to midsummer day; but the day following St John's day [i.e. 25 June], the monks chose an abbot from their own number, and brought him into church in solemn procession; they sang the Te Deum, and rang the bells, and placed him in the abbot's seat, and proffered him the unqualified obedience

(*continued on p.* 262)

---

[1] Or, as Dom David Knowles, *The Monastic Order in England* (Cambridge 1950) 283, puts it: 'National sentiment and love of independence would have proved an insurmountable obstacle.'

[2] 11 January was a Sunday in 1131.

which monks owe to their abbot: and the duke [of Aquitaine]
E 1131 and all the leading men and the monks drove Henry, the other
from abbot, out of the monastery. The necessity to do this was
p. 261 forced upon them, for in five and twenty years they had not
enjoyed one single happy day. Here all his boasted ingenuity
failed him: now he had good cause to creep into his capacious bag of
tricks, and explore it in every corner, to see if by chance there might be
at least one shifty dodge left there by which he could yet again deceive
Christ and all Christian folk.[1] Then he went into the monastery
at Cluny, where he was held so that he was unable to go either east or
west. The abbot of Cluny said that they had lost the monastery of St
Jean d'Angély through him, and because of his utter stupidity. Then
he knew no better way out of his predicament than to promise them,
upon oaths sworn on holy relics, that he would secure for them the
monastery of Peterborough, if he might reach England; and would
install a prior from Cluny there, as well as a sacristan, a treasurer, and a
keeper of the wardrobe, to ensure that they got complete control of
both the internal and external affairs of the monastery. Thus he went
into France[2] and there abode all the year. May Christ provide for the
wretched monks of Peterborough and for that unhappy foundation!
Now they stand in need of the help of Christ and of all Christian people.

1132. In this year king Henry returned to this country. Then came
abbot Henry, and accused the monks of Peterborough to the king
because he wanted to subject the monastery to Cluny, so that the king
was wellnigh deceived, and sent for the monks. Through God's compassion and the help of the bishop of Salisbury, the bishop of Lincoln,
and the other leading men who were present, the king learnt that he was
acting treacherously. When he could get no further, he planned to
make his nephew abbot of Peterborough, but Christ did not wish it.
It was not long thereafter that the king sent for him, and made him give
up the abbacy of Peterborough and leave the country; and the king gave
the abbacy to a prior of St Neot's named Martin. He came to the
monastery on St Peter's day [20 June] and was received with great
ceremony.

1135. At Lammas [1 August] of this year king Henry went oversea;
and on the following day, while he lay asleep on board, the light of
day was eclipsed (*continued on p.* 263)

---

[1] Hugh Candidus, who follows the OE closely in his account, has, however, a poor substitute for this sentence (*Nec potuit ingredi uel egredi donec
iterum arte sua et astucia eos fefellit*).
[2] Cluny being in Burgundy.

over all lands, and the sun looked like a moon three nights old,
E 1135 and there were stars around it at midday.

from Then men were greatly astonished and terrified, and said
p. 262 that some important event should follow upon this; and so it
did, for in that very year the king died in Normandy the day
after St Andrew's day [30 Novemver]. Then at once this country was
in eclipse,[3] for every man who could was quick to rob his neighbour.
Then his son and his friends took his body and brought it to England,
and they buried him at Reading. He was a good man, and was held in
great awe. In his days no man dared to wrong another. He made
peace for man and beast. Whoever bore a burden of gold and silver,
no man dared say to him aught but good.

Meanwhile his nephew, Stephen of Blois, landed in England, and
came to London, and the people of London received him, and sent for
the archbishop William of Curbeil, who consecrated him king on
Christmas day. In the days of this king there was nothing but strife,
evil, and robbery, for quickly the great men who were traitors rose
against him [1136]. First of all Baldwin de Redvers held Exeter
against him: the king besieged it, and Baldwin came to terms. Then
the others manned and held [4] their castles against him; and David, king
of Scotland, began to make war upon him; then, notwithstanding, their
ambassadors went between them, and they met and were reconciled,
but it was to little purpose.

1137. In this year king Stephen went oversea to Normandy, and was
welcomed there because they imagined he would be all his maternal
uncle was, and because he was still in possession of the royal treasury;
but he gave it away and squandered it foolishly. Much gold and
silver had king Henry amassed, but it was not used to good purpose for
the salvation of his soul.

When king Stephen landed in England he held his council at Oxford,
and there he arrested Roger, bishop of Salisbury, and his 'nephews,'
Alexander, bishop of Lincoln, and the chancellor Roger. He put them
all in prison until they surrendered their castles. When the traitors saw
that Stephen was a good-humoured, kindly, and easy-going man who
inflicted no punishment, then they committed all manner of horrible
crimes. They had done him homage and sworn oaths of fealty to him,
but not one of their oaths was kept. (continued on p. 264)

---

[3] For the reading cf. N. R. Ker, 3 *Medium Ævum* 136–7.
[4] *manned and held*: more correctly 'proceeded to hold' (cf. Celia Sisam,
52 *RES* 385).

They were all forsworn and their oaths broken. For every
E 1137 great man built him castles and held them against the king;
from and they filled the whole land with these castles. They sorely
p. 263 burdened the unhappy people of the country with forced labour
on the castles; and when the castles were built, they filled them
with devils and wicked men. By night and by day they seized those
whom they believed to have any wealth, whether they were men or
women; and in order to get their gold and silver, they put them into
prison and tortured them with unspeakable tortures,[1] for never were
martyrs tortured as they were. They hung them up by the feet and
smoked them with foul smoke. They strung them up by the thumbs,
or by the head, and hung coats of mail on their feet. They tied knotted
cords round their heads and twisted it till it entered the brain. They
put them in dungeons wherein were adders and snakes and toads,
and so destroyed them. Some they put into a 'crucethus'; that is to
say, into a short, narrow, shallow chest into which they put sharp
stones; and they crushed the man in it until they had broken every bone
in his body. In many of the castles were certain instruments of
torture [2] so heavy that two or three men had enough to do to carry one.
It was made in this way: a weight was fastened to a beam which was
attached to a sharp iron put round the man's throat and neck so that
he could move in no direction, and could neither sit, nor lie, nor sleep,
but had to bear the whole weight of the iron. Many thousands they
starved to death.

I know not how to, nor am I able to tell of, all the atrocities nor all
the cruelties which they wrought upon the unhappy people of this
country. It lasted throughout the nineteen years that Stephen was
king,[3] and always grew worse and worse. At regular intervals they
levied a tax, known as 'tenserie' [protection money] upon the villages.
When the wretched people had no more to give, they plundered and
burned all the villages, so that you could easily go a day's journey
without ever finding a village inhabited or a field cultivated. Then
was corn dear and flesh and cheese and butter, for there was none in
the land. The wretched people perished with hunger; some, who had
been great men, were driven to beggary, while others fled from the
country.

Never did a country endure greater misery, and never did the
heathen act more vilely than they did. Contrary to custom,[3a] they
spared neither church nor churchyard, but seized everything of value
that (*continued on p. 265*)

[1] See N. R. Ker, *loc. cit.* 137–8.
[2] *lof and grin:* On these unusual terms for instruments of torture, see
Bruce Dickins, 'The Peterborough Annal for 1137' (2 *RES* 341–3). F. P.
Magoun, Jr (40 *MLN* 411–12), suggests as a translation: 'In many of the
castles were "head-band and noose" which were of chains.'
[3] These words indicate thet the annal was not written before Stephen's
death in 1154. [3a] *contrary to custom:* C. Sisam, *op. cit.*, prefers 'often.'
[4] A similar account of Martin's abbacy is given in *The Chronicle of Hugh
Candidus* (ed. Mellows, 105, 122).
[5] The two documents are given in full by Hugh (ed. Mellows, 109–19).
On their nature and purpose, see Bruce Dickins and R. M. Wilson, *Early*

was in it, and afterwards burned the church and all it contained.
E 1137 They spared not the lands of bishops, nor of abbots, nor of
from priests, but plundered the monks and the clergy; and every
p. 264 man who could robbed his neighbour. If two or three men
came riding towards a village, all the villagers fled for fear of
them, believing that they were robbers. The bishops and the clergy
were for ever cursing them, but that was nothing to them, for they were
all excommunicated and forsworn and lost.

Wherever the ground was tilled the earth bore no corn, for the land
was ruined by such doings; and men said openly that Christ and His
saints slept. Such things and others more than we know how to relate
we suffered nineteen years for our sins.

During all these evil days, abbot Martin [4] governed his abbacy with
great energy for twenty and a half years and eight days. He provided
everything necessary for the monks and the visitors and was liberal
in alms-giving; he was careful to see that the monks got their commons, and punctilious in holding commemoration feasts. Nevertheless he extended the church and set apart the income from various
estates and also other moneys for the building costs, and greatly
adorned it and had it roofed. He brought the monks with great
ceremony into the new church on St Peter's day [29 June]: that was
anno ab incarnatione domini mcxl, a combustione loci xxiii. He
went to Rome and was well received there by pope Eugenius, and there
obtained a grant [5] of special rights and immunities, one concerning all
the lands of the abbacy, and another concerning the lands that apper-
tain to the office of sacrist; and, had he lived longer, he intended to do
the same for the office of chamberlain.[6] He recovered monastery
property in the shape of lands which great men held by force. From
William Malduit, who held the castle of Rockingham, he recovered
Cottingham and Easton Maudit; and from Hugh of Waterville he
recovered Irthlingborough and Stanwick, and a yearly rent of sixty
shillings from Aldwinkle. He admitted many monks and planted vineyards, and built many domestic buildings, and changed the site of the
town to a better position than formerly. He was a good monk and a
good man, and therefore he was loved by God and by good men.

Now we wish to say something of the events of king Stephen's reign.
In his days the Jews of Norwich bought a Christian child before Easter,
and tortured him with all the same torments with which our Lord was
tortured. On Good Friday they hanged him on a cross because of his
love for our Lord, and afterwards buried him. They thought that his
death would be concealed, but our Lord showed that he was a holy
martyr: and the monks took his body and buried him with great ceremony in the monastery church, and (*continued on p.* 266)

Middle English Texts 157. The two manors assigned for the provision of
clothes are mentioned in an addition to Hugh's chronicle made by Walter of
Whittlesey (ed. Mellows, 173): [*Adhuc de abbate Martino*] *Maneria quoque
de Colingham et de Fisckartona cum suis pertinenciis ad uestitum monachorum
illis omnino libere concessit habere*.

[6] The officer in charge of the stores of clothing and bedding for the
monastery.

wonderfully, and in various ways, he performs miracles
E 1137 through our Lord.   He is called St William.

from   1138. In this year David, king of Scotland, invaded this
p. 265 country with immense levies, determined to conquer it.   He
was met by William, earl of Aumale, to whom the king had
entrusted York, and by the other trustworthy men with a few followers:
they fought against them, and put the king to flight at [the battle of] the
Standard, and slew a great number of his host.

1140 [1137]. In this year king Stephen attempted to seize Robert,
earl of Gloucester, the son of king Henry, but was unable to do so, for
he became aware of it.

[1140]. Afterwards in Lent, the sun and the light of day was eclipsed
about noon when men were eating, and candles had to be lit for them to
eat by.   This happened on 20 March, and men marvelled greatly.

[1136]. Thereafter William, archbishop of Canterbury, passed away,
and [1139] the king made Theobald, abbot of Bec, archbishop.

[1140]. Thereafter very great strife arose between the king and
Rannulf, earl of Chester; not because he was less generous to him than
to all others (whose requests he could never deny), but ever the more
he gave them, the worse they behaved towards him.   The earl held
Lincoln against the king, and deprived him of all that he ought to
have.   The king went thither, and besieged him and his brother
William de Roumare in the castle: and the earl stole out and went to get
the assistance of Robert of Gloucester, and brought him thither with
great levies.   [1141] They fought hard against their lord on Candlemas
day [2 February], and took him prisoner, for his men betrayed him and
fled.   They led him to Bristol, and put him in prison there and in
fetters.   Then was all England disturbed more than ever before, and
evil reigned in the land.

[1139]. Thereafter landed the daughter of king Henry, who had been
the empress of Germany and was now countess of Anjou, and came to
London; [1141] and the people of London wished to take her prisoner,
but she fled and suffered there great loss.

[1141]. Thereafter Henry, the bishop of Winchester, who was the
brother of king Stephen, spoke with earl Robert and with the empress,
and swore them oaths that never more would he side with the king,
his brother, and cursed all those men who supported him.   He
promised them that he would deliver up Winchester to them, and made
them come thither.   When they were inside the city, then came the
king's queen with all her forces (*continued on p.* 267)

E 1140 [1141] from p.266 and besieged them, so that there was great famine within the city. When they could endure it no longer, they stole out and fled, but the besiegers got to know and followed them and captured Robert, earl of Gloucester, and took him to Rochester and put him in prison there. The empress fled into a monastery. Then wise men went between the friends of the king and the friends of the earl, and in consequence an agreement was reached to release the king from prison in exchange for the earl, and the earl for the king, and this was done.

[1142]. After this the king and earl Rannulf were subsequently reconciled at Stamford, and swore oaths and plighted their troths that neither of them should deceive the other. [1146] But it availed nothing, for the king, acting on bad advice, subsequently arrested him in Northampton [1] and put him in prison, and soon after, on worse advice, let him out, on condition that he gave hostages and swore on holy relics to yield up all his castles. Some he did yield up, but others he did not; and then did worse here than he should.[2]

Then was England much divided: some supported the king and some the empress. For when the king was in prison, the earls and the great men were of the opinion that he should never again be allowed his freedom, and came to terms with the empress, and brought her [1141] to Oxford and gave her the city. When the king got out of prison he heard tell of it and took his levies and [1142] besieged her in the tower. At night she was let down from the tower by ropes and escaped. She fled away and went on foot to Wallingford.

[1147]. Thereafter she went oversea, and [1141–4] all the people of Normandy turned from the king and gave fealty to the count of Anjou, some of them willingly, others unwillingly, for he besieged them in their castles until they surrendered them, and they had no help from the king.

[1140]. Then Eustace, the king's son, went to France and took to wife the sister of the king of France and thought to acquire Normandy thereby, but he had little success, and with just cause, for he was an evil man. Wheresoever he went he did more evil than good: he robbed the lands and laid heavy taxes upon them. He brought his wife to England, and put her in the castle at Canterbury. (*continued on p.* 268)

---

[1] or perhaps 'Southampton'.

[2] More correctly, 'and then did worse than anything reported of him before' (Cf. Celia Sisam, *op. cit.*, 386).

She was a good woman, but enjoyed little happiness with him.
E 1140 Christ would not permit him to tyrannize long, and both he
from [1153] and his mother [1152] met their deaths.
p.267 [1151]. When the count of Anjou was dead, his son Henry
succeeded to the county. [1152] The queen of France was
divorced from the king, and she came to the young count Henry, and
he took her to wife, and all Poitou with her. [1153] Then he landed in
England with great levies, and took castles, and the king went against
him with a much greater force: nevertheless they did not fight, but the
archbishop and the wise men went between them and came to terms
that the king should be lord and king while he lived, and after his day
Henry should be king. He was to regard the king as father, and the
king him as son, and peace and concord should exist between them and
throughout all England. The king, the count, the bishops, the earls,
and all the great men swore to keep this and the other agreements
which they made. Then was the count received with great ceremony in
Winchester and in London. All did him homage and swore to keep
the peace. Soon there was a good and lasting peace such as had never
been here before, and the king was stronger than he had ever been.
The count went oversea, and all the people loved him, for he adminis-
tered justice fairly and made peace.

1154. In this year king Stephen died, and was buried with his wife
and son in the monastery of Faversham which they had founded. The
count was oversea when the king died, yet no man dared do other than
good, for he was held in great awe. When he landed in England, he
was received with great ceremony, and was consecrated king in London
on the Sunday before Christmas day.[1] He held there a great court.

The very day that Martin, the abbot of Peterborough, should have
gone thither [to court] he sickened, and died on 2 January. The monks
within the day chose his successor from their number. His name is
William de Waterville. A learned man and good, he is well loved
by the king and by all good men. The abbot was buried with great
ceremony in church; and forthwith the abbot elect, accompanied by
the monks, went to Oxford to the king, and he gave him the abbacy.
He made his way forthwith to Lincoln, and was there consecrated
abbot before he returned home. He was subsequently received with
great (*continued on p.* 269)

---

[1] 19 December in 1154.

ceremony at Peterborough and with solemn procession. He
E 1154 was received likewise at Ramsey, and at Thorney, and at Crow-
from land [2] and Spalding, and at St Albans, and [?] [3], and is now
p. 268 abbot, and has made a good beginning. Christ grant that he
may end as well! [4]

[2] For fresh light on this damaged passage I am indebted to Miss Cecily
Clark and to Mr Peter Clemoes. Miss Clark has most generously allowed
me to make use of her important new readings, some of which are discussed
in 23 *Medium Ævum* 71–5.

[3] Miss Clark tells me that the sequence of letters best fitting the fragments
which can be made out in this gap is *Ferstan*. Unfortunately, however, as
she admits, the early forms of Freiston (S. Lincs.), where there was a Benedictine priory dependent on Crowland, usually have *tūn*, not *stān*, as the
second element, and this throws some doubt on the validity of this reading.
Another possibility she allows (though this is more difficult to harmonize
with the visible remains) is some form of Eynsham, likewise the site of a
considerable Benedictine house. It has been suggested that the gap may
not have contained a place-name, but some phrase such as *For ham* or *Ferd
ham* (i.e. 'went home').

[4] Abbot William was deposed in 1175. Cf. *The Chronicle of Hugh
Candidus* (ed. Mellows), 131–2.

APPENDIX A

THE EASTER TABLE CHRONICLE (I)

(Note: The Old English of the first few annals is given below so that a comparison may be made with the plate on pages xxiv and xxv.)

925. In this year was St Dunstan born, and he lived for sixty-three years, and in the sixty-fourth year he passed away on 19 May.

988. In this year archbishop St Dunstan passed away.
990. In this year bishop Siric [i.e. Sigeric] went to Rome [cf. p. 125 note].
996. In this year archbishop Siric passed away.
997. In this year bishop Ælfric went to Rome.
1005. In this year bishop Ælfric passed away.
1006. In this year bishop Ælfeh [i.e. Ælfheah] went to Rome.
1011. In this year Canterbury was taken [i.e. by the Danes, see p. 141].
1012. In this year was St Ælfeh [i.e. Ælfheah] martyred.
1016. In this year king Ægelred [i.e. Æthelred the Unready] passed away [see 1016 F, p. 148].
1017. In this year Cnut was chosen as king.
1020. In this year archbishop Lyfing passed away, and dean Ægelnoð [i.e. Æthelnoth] succeeded to the bishopric.

925. On þison geare wæs sancte Dunstan geboren. *and* he leofode lxiii geare *and* on þam lxiiii geare he forðferde xiiii *kalendas* Iun*i*i.

988. Her forðferde sancte Dunstan arcebiscop.
990. Her Siric biscop for to Rome.
996. Her Siric arcebiscop forðferde.
997. Her Ælfric biscop for to Rome.
1005. Her forðferde Ælfric biscop.
1006. Her Ælfeh biscop for to Rome.
1011. Her wæs Cantwarabyrig gewunnan.
1012. Her wæs sancte Ælfeh gemartyrod.
1016. Her forðferde Ægelred kyng.
1017. Her wæs Cnut gecoran to kynge.
1020. Her forðferde Lyfing arcebiscop *and* Ægelnoð decanus feng to þan biscoprice.

270

1022. In this year bishop Æthelnoth went to Rome.
1023. In this year [the body of] St Ælfheah was translated from London to Christ Church [Canterbury].
1028. In this year passed away dean Æthelwine.
1035. In this year passed away king Cnut.
1038. In this year passed away archbishop Æthelnoth, and bishop Eadsige succeeded to the bishopric.
1040. In this year bishop Eadsige went to Rome, and king Harold [i.e. Harold Harefoot] passed away.
1042. In this year passed away king Harthacnut.
1043. In this year Edward was consecrated king.
1050. In this year passed away archbishop Eadsige, and Robert succeeded to the bishopric.
1053. In this year passed away earl Godwine.
1058. In this year pope Benedict sent Stigand the pallium.
1061. In this year passed away bishop Godwine and abbot Wulfric.
1066. In this year passed away king Edward, and William came.
1067. In this year burnt Christ Church.
1070. In this year came abbot Lanfranc and he was consecrated to the see of Christ Church [Canterbury].
1073 [1072]. In this year archbishop Lanfranc established [the primacy of] Christ Church [Canterbury] on 9 April.
1076. In this year Waltheof was executed on 31 May.
1085. In this year archbishop Lanfranc had the body of St Eadburh [died c. 750] at Lyminge translated to St Gregory's priory [Canterbury—founded by Lanfranc 1070–89].
1087. In this year passed away king William, and his son William succeeded to the kingdom.
1089. In this year passed away archbishop Lanfranc.
1094. In this year Anselm was consecrated [arch]bishop on 4 December [1093], and in the same year king Malcolm was slain.
1096. In this year went the Christians in order to fight the heathen.
1097. In this year went Anselm to Rome on 25 October.
1100. In this year was king William slain on 2 August; and Henry, his brother, succeeded. Anselm returned from his pilgrimage to Rome.
1105. In this year St Ælfheah's remains were examined, and his body was found uncorrupted, and was seen by both cleric and [lay].
1109. In this year archbishop Anselm passed away.
1110. Hoc anno Henricus rex Anglorum dedit filiam suam Henrico imperatori in conjugem.
1114. Hic Radulfus Rofensis episcopus suscepit archiepiscopatum Cantuariæ. vi kal. Mai.
1115. Pascalis papa, susceptis legatis Radulfi, misit ei pallium per legatum suum.
1122. Hic Radulfus archiepiscopus obiit 13 kl. Nov.
[1123]. Willelmus suscepit; et consecratus est 12 kl. Mar. et Romam vadit 3 Id. Mar.
1123. Willelmus archiepiscopus rediit a Roma cum pallio.
1130. In this year [the cathedral church of] Christ Church was consecrated on 4 May.

1133. 4 N. Aug. sol fere defecit meridie.
1135. Hic obiit Henricus rex Anglorum k. Decemb. Cui successit Stephanus nepos ejus et unctus est in regem 10 kal. Januarii.
1136. Hic obiit Willelmus archiepiscopus 11 k. Decemb.
1138. Hic Theodbaldus suscepit archiepiscopatum Cantuariensem et sacratus est 6 idus Jan. ab Alberico Ostiensi episcopo apostolicæ sedis legato.
1139. Hoc anno venit filia Henrici regis, que fuit imperatrix in Anglia[m] et Robertus frater ejus. Eodem anno facta est eclipsis solis 13 kal. Aprilis hora nona.
1140. Hoc anno factum est prelium inter Stephanum regem et Robertum comitem et captus est rex [1141] 4 No. Feb.
1141. Aug. combusta est civitas Wintonie et pene omnes ecclesie infra et extra civitatem, et magna et famosa crux Sancti Petri de Hida combusta est, in cujus ruina tonitruum auditum est, et combusta est ecclesia Werwellensis ab exercitu episcopi. Et Stephanus rex, qui tenebatur a comite Rodberto, liberatus est alter pro altero in festivitate Omnium Sanctorum.
1144. Hoc anno kal. Oct. horrida tempestas, et e vestigio subsecuta terribilis aquarum inundatio e[o]tenus inaudita habitantes in terra conturbavit et eodem anno ventus seculis inau[ditus] f[uit].
1147. Hoc anno imperator Alemannie et rex Francie duxerunt innumerabilem exercitum Jerosol[i]mis contra paganos. Obiit Rodbertus comes Gloecestrie.
1154. Hic obiit Stephanus rex. Cui continuo successit Henricus II Matildis imperatricis filius.

ETC

272

APPENDIX B

DEFINITIONS OF SOME TECHNICAL TERMS

[Old English terms are in *italics*, the equivalents used in the translation are in CAPITALS.

The reader will find convenient descriptions of early English social life and institutions in Volumes II and III of the Pelican History of England.]

burh FORTIFIED PLACE, fortified either with stockade, earthwork, or stone wall; FORT, FORTRESS, or strongpoint fortified and manned for the defence of a district; a county, or other important, TOWN BOROUGH, or CITY, which was a trading centre and place of defence.
THE FIVE BOROUGHS: Lincoln, Stamford, Leicester, Nottingham, Derby.
THE SEVEN BOROUGHS: see note to p. 146.

ealdorman EALDORMAN, an important official of the royal household, sometimes of the blood royal, the king's deputy; a nobleman who rules a shire or shires under the king, and a leader of the levies.
From the time of Cnut (earlier in Northumbria) the term is superseded by *eorl*, EARL.
In annal 495 the term may mean 'prince'.

eorl JARL, nobleman next in dignity to a Scandinavian king, sometimes holding royal power but never assuming the kingly title. EARL, from the time of Cnut (earlier in Northumbria) a nobleman appointed by the king to rule a shire or shires (see *ealdorman*).
WARRIOR (in verse).

fyrd LEVIES, able-bodied thanes and freemen whom a king had the right to call up for the defence of his realm.

gerefa, wicgerefa REEVE, an official of the king responsible for the supervision of trade, collection of tolls, etc., within a town.

gyld TAX, TAXES, TRIBUTE; PAY for a *liðsman*; AID, a money grant in aid to the king (e.g. for his daughter's marriage).

gyrd VIRGATE, 'yardland,' a tenement held from a lord varying in size but notionally about 30 acres (a quarter of a 'hide').

heahgerefa HIGH-REEVE, an official responsible for the administration (especially in Northumbria) of a royal estate or large district, probably not very different in status from the ealdorman; the reeve of a large borough-district.

here HOST, a large band of marauders, usually the forces of the Scandinavian invaders, but also for invading Romans and Scots.

hid HIDE, a measure of land varying in size at different times and in different parts of the country, the amount of land an eight-ox plough could keep under cultivation, the normal peasant holding, notionally about 120 acres.

273

hold BARON, a Scandinavian officer of rank in the Danelaw with the same wergild as a king's 'high-reeve.'
ON *hǫldr*, in Norway a hereditary landowner, but with only half the wergild of the OE *hold*.

hundred HUNDRED, a sub-division of the shire for administrative purposes, notionally of one hundred 'hides.'

huscarlas HOUSECARLES, picked fighting men forming the bodyguard of a Scandinavian king or jarl or the nucleus of his host. Adapted from ON *húskarl*.

lið, liðsmen, litsmen HOUSEHOLD TROOPS, TROOPS, the personal following or retainers of a king or earl (cf. Byrhtnoth's *heorðwerod*), soldiers or sailors in the pay of king, earl, or jarl. Adapted from ON *lið, liðsmaðr*, and properly used of the pirate host of the sons of Swein Estrithson [*s.a.* 1069 E].

port TOWN, a trading centre or market-town, usually fortified in some way.

sciphere PIRATE HOST, see *here*. NAVAL FORCE (when English).

scirgerefa SHERIFF, an official of the king in the late Anglo-Saxon period, responsible to him for the administration of a shire.

stallere STALLER (ON *stallari*), a term probably not much earlier than 1045, 'which could be applied to anyone with a permanent and recognized position in the king's company' (Stenton).

tun HOMESTEAD, farmstead and its buildings; VILLAGE, enclosed land with dwellings upon it; TOWN, cluster of houses usually with no fortification around. *cyninges tun* ROYAL MANOR.

ðegn THANE, a retainer, usually of noble birth.

INDEX OF PERSONS

abp archbishop; abt abbot; B bishop; b brother; ct count; d daughter; E earl; emp emperor; f father; K king; s son; w wife. The references are to pages.

INDEX OF PLACES

*The county abbreviations are those used by the English Place-Name Society
dép département; r river*

289